RIVER OF BLOOD

River of BLOOD

*The Genesis
of a Martyr Cult in
Southern Malawi,
c. A.D. 1600*

J. Matthew Schoffeleers

The University of Wisconsin Press

The University of Wisconsin Press
114 North Murray Street
Madison, Wisconsin 53715

3 Henrietta Street
London WC2E 8LU, England

Library of Congress Cataloging-in-Publication Data
Schoffeleers, J. M.
    River of blood: the genesis of a martyr cult in southern Malawi,
 c. A.D. 1600 / J. Matthew Schoffeleers.
    340 pp.   cm.
    Includes texts and translations of seven Mbona myths.
    Includes bibliographical references and index.
    ISBN 0-299-13320-6   ISBN 0-299-13324-9 (pbk.)
    1. Mbona cult—Malawi—History.   2. Malawi—Religion.   I. Title.
 BL2470.M34S364   1992
 299'.67—dc20   92-50258

When Mbona was killed, blood flowed in profusion and, splashing to the ground, it turned into a dark stream, a river of blood.

—Headman Mphamba

Wherever violence threatens, ritual impurity is present. When men are enjoying peace and security, blood is a rare sight. When violence is unloosed, however, blood appears everywhere — on the ground, underfoot, forming great pools. Its very fluidity gives form to the contagious nature of violence. Its presence proclaims murder and announces new upheavals to come. Blood stains everything it touches the color of violence and death. Its very appearance seems, as the saying goes, to "cry out for vengeance."

—René Girard, *Violence and the Sacred*

Myth, then, is a dramatic shorthand record of such matter as invasions, migrations, dynastic changes, admission of foreign cults, and social reforms. . . . A proper study of myths demands a great store of abstruse geographical, historical and anthropological knowledge; also familiarity with the properties of plants and trees and the habits of wild birds and beasts.

—Robert Graves, *New Larousse Encyclopedia of Mythology*

To a much greater extent than many historians realize, oral traditions provide indirect evidence of the nature of historical events; they are "witnesses in spite of themselves."

—Steve Feierman, *The Shambaa Kingdom*

CONTENTS

ILLUSTRATIONS

MAPS AND CHARTS

MAPS

CHARTS

ACKNOWLEDGMENTS

MY FIRST INTERVIEW with the "Mbona people" took place in August 1964, my last in January 1982. The pilgrimages to the shrine thus cover a period of over seventeen years. It goes without saying that I have been helped along by numerous individuals and institutions. I am indebted to the Nuffield Foundation, London; the University of Malawi; and the Free University of Amsterdam for financing part of the research. I am greatly indebted also to my field assistants, notably Stephen Mbande, my "brother" in the *nyau* mask society, and Elias Mandala, a great friend and fine scholar. Besides these, I am indebted to hundreds of people who patiently answered my questions or who provided me with food and shelter on one occasion or another. Mention must be made also of my fellow missionaries who gave me every help possible; first and foremost among them were the late Fathers Gerard Hochstenbach and Jan Dirkx, whose hospitality was limitless and whose kindness will never be forgotten. Finally, I wish to thank those who have given me the benefit of their comments, among them Rodney Needham, Terence Ranger, Dick Werbner, Kings Phiri, Jocelyn Murray, Roy Willis, Joe Chakanza, Christopher Wrigley, and Steve Chimombo. I am greatly indebted also to Paula Duivenvoorde, Petra Nesselaar, and Anja Stoevenbeld for helping with much of the material work. I dedicate this study to the memory of Tom Price, coauthor of *Independent African*, linguist and historian, friend and critic, who meticulously checked and rechecked the translations of the texts in Part 2.

RIVER OF BLOOD

INTRODUCTION

THE PERIOD between the middle of the sixteenth and the middle of the seventeenth centuries was a particularly dramatic one in the history of northern Zambesia. It all began with the murder of the Jesuit missionary Gonçalo da Silveira at the Monomotapa's court in March 1561, an event which provided the Portuguese with a pretext to dispatch a large armed force to Zambesia. Due to funding problems and political chicaneries, the army arrived there only eleven years later, but from the very beginning it was incapacitated by illness and famine. By the end of the year 1572 only a handful of soldiers were still alive, and the venture had to be called off. But despite the fact that the expedition itself was an outright failure, it heralded the beginning of a new policy in regard to the white settlements in the interior. The latter, instead of continuing to place themselves under the protection of local rulers, as had been the custom, now began to transform into independent Portuguese enclaves. Forts were built, and before long the captains of these forts became powerful local rulers.

In this situation slavery also took on a new significance. Due to the growing number of settlers and the expansion of their holdings, the slave population kept steadily growing. As a result the number of fugitive slaves also increased, one of their favorite hideouts being the Shire Valley on the north bank of the Zambezi.[1] Some of these slave groups built fortified settlements from which they raided the countryside. It is within this context that one has to understand the origin of the much-discussed Zimba army, which twice defeated a Portuguese force and which wrought havoc in much of northern Zambesia in the closing decade of the sixteenth century.

It is probably true to say that prior to 1590 one cannot speak of sizable centralized states immediately north of the Zambezi. The impression created is rather one of a collectivity of relatively small chiefdoms, bound together by regional trade and shifting alliances. Statelets which controlled trade routes were at an advantage, however, and could, given the right conditions, grow in size and importance. One such was the Lundu kingdom in the Shire Valley, which from 1590 onward managed to extend its

3

influence from Tete on the middle Zambezi to the east coast.[2] This feat was achieved with the help of the Zimba, who for a decade operated as a mercenary army in the service of the incumbents. Not only did they help subject neighboring peoples, but they were also instrumental in keeping the population of the kingdom itself in subjection. This involved the eradication of the principal sources of resistance, among which were the secret mask societies and an influential rain shrine. Like similar shrines elsewhere, the rain shrine functioned as a rallying point of popular resistance against the increasing power of the political elite. Local oral traditions suggest that many inhabitants lost their lives on account of this campaign, while others took refuge elsewhere. The shrine was restored some time after Lundu's defeat in 1622, but with a different organizational structure and a different theology. Instead of its being dedicated to Chiuta, the High God under his python manifestation, as were the other regional rain shrines, its patronal deity became a human martyr, Mbona, who above all symbolized the suffering of the commonalty. The story of Mbona's life and death has been transmitted in a number of versions, and the present study shows that despite their legendary character they constitute an important source of information about the religious and political transformations which took place at the time of the Zimba campaigns.

The first time I heard about the Mbona cult was in 1959, the year I began work as a missionary in the Shire Valley. When paying a visit to the Nsanje station in the southern part of the valley, I was told by a senior colleague that there was a shrine a few kilometers away, dedicated to a rain god bearing the name Mbona. The same person also told me that a woman, said to be Mbona's wife, lived at the shrine and that she, like a cloistered nun, was not allowed to leave the premises. The missionary who gave me this information had never been there himself, and neither had his predecessors. He thought that such a visit would not be appreciated by his congregation. But this apart, he did not think the cult had much influence, and one might as well ignore it. True enough, in the station's journal, which went back to the early 1920s, I came across Mbona's name only once, in connection with some exceptionally heavy rains in December 1945. The journal contained no indication that the missionaries had taken a more than superficial interest in the cult.

Since it would be pointless to seek contact with the cult organization without at least some knowledge of the Mbona traditions, I began recording such bits of information as came my way, when making the rounds of the wattle-and-daub village chapels and "bush schools" which in those days were my responsibility. From time to time I even asked school children to put in writing what they knew about Mbona. Although I did not learn overly much that way, the occasional gem made the effort worthwhile. One of the children described Mbona as "a huge white hippo with blazing eyes, who made his way up the Chikwawa escarpment to build the city of Blantyre." The boy said he had this information from his grandmother. I have often thought about the meaning of this remarkable piece of imagery, which continues to intrigue me. A few details seem easy enough to explain. The hippo as a water animal would be an obvious symbol of a rain god. As an aquatic mammal he could also be seen as a mediating figure between water and land, or between the dry and the wet seasons, keeping the two in balance. White is the color of the spirit world of which Mbona forms a part. But what of the blazing eyes and the building of what the old grandmother thought of as the largest city imaginable, though she had probably never seen it? I decided in the end that the blazing eyes suggest power and determination, and that Mbona as the builder of a city with its glittering shops and imposing buildings is the modern equivalent of the culture hero of old, who brought fire and introduced various crafts.

From the more knowledgeable, however, I learned that Mbona had been a rainmaker of great renown, who many generations ago had taken refuge in the valley from some enemies from the north who sought his life. Although he had been able for some time to elude his pursuers, he was in the end nonetheless tracked down and killed. After they had killed him, his murderers cut his head off, tossing it in a forest patch, while leaving the body behind at the place of the crime. Miraculously, however, blood kept gushing from the body in such quantities that it formed a small lake and finally a river. A few days later, according to one line of traditions, Mbona manifested himself in a storm wind and made it known through the mouth of a medium that he wanted a shrine dedicated to his name. The local villagers obeyed his command, buried his head, and built a shrine over the place. In time that shrine became known over a large area, and people from far and wide came to worship there.

It was clear that people saw Mbona as a counterpart of the biblical Christ, referring to him as their Black Jesus. As some explained it, God had two sons, the one white, the other black. The white one was to look after the Europeans, the black one after the Africans. According to the more radical section of the community, this meant that Christianity had no business in Africa. Although both sons were at first equally powerful, Christ had become the more prominent because the whites were more cunning than the Africans. Despite the antiwhite sentiments which transpired from some of these folk theologies, most people had little problem participating in both cults. As I was to find out later, some of the Mbona officers were practicing Christians as well. In time I even made the acquaintance of a prominent teacher and church elder who used to make the rounds of the local shops to collect contributions for the annual rain ceremony.

The older generations of missionaries also noted intersections with Christianity. A hundred years before my investigations Anglican missionaries had made a dramatic but unsuccessful attempt to establish contact with the cult. The account of that event and its aftermath, which was published in the United Kingdom a few years later, stimulated the interest of later generations of missionaries. One such was Joseph Booth, who was to make a name for himself as a critic of the colonial government and as the mentor of John Chilembwe, the nationalist and revolutionary.

My direct contacts with the cult organization date from August 24, 1964, when I was granted a lengthy interview with two of the shrine guardians.[3] At their insistence our meeting took place at the Nsanje mission station and not in or near the shrine grounds, where they lived. The official reason was that, as a white person, I was not allowed to come near the shrine, at least not without first having made a formal application to the cult's principals. As it turned out, however, there was a lot more to it. I realized this only two years later, in October 1966, when I had a chance to interview some of the other officials as well.[4] To my surprise the latter made it a point to contradict virtually everything I had been told by their colleagues, maintaining that I had been lied to by these people who were only "after their personal interests" and who, "being of foreign extraction," had no right to be part of the cult organization. It was thus that I became aware of a rift which ran through the entire organization and which made it difficult to contact one section without arousing suspicion among the others. Apparently, this conflict had led my earlier informants to insist that the interview be held at the mission, since at that place they would not be disturbed by their rivals.

My next discovery was that, however much these cult officers may have been divided among themselves, they were nonetheless united in their opposition to Mbona's medium, who lived a few kilometers from the shrine. Despite his position, he was not allowed to set foot there. They hinted among other things that his possession bouts were sometimes simulated and that he caused unnecessary unrest among the villagers by speaking out on politically sensitive issues. Yet virtually no one dared tell him this to his face for fear of being held responsible should something untoward happen. Whatever the cult establishment might hold against him, the population at large regarded him as Mbona's personal representative, even if most people knew of him only from hearsay. The medium, for his part, in all the years that I knew him (he died in May 1978 and had not yet been succeeded when I was in the area last in January 1982), never ceased criticizing the officialdom for neglecting the upkeep of the shrine and making a racket of the cult.[5] Gradually I came to understand that these conflicts were a structural feature of the cult and not just something incidental. As far as the medium and the officers were concerned, they stemmed from different perceptions of social reality, and as far as the officers themselves were concerned, they stemmed from claims and counterclaims about rights and privileges which sometimes dated back many generations but which continued to be revived each time a major ritual was to be organized or an important decision had to be taken.

Apart from the officials and the medium, I or my field assistants also interviewed a great many people who had no direct dealings with the cult. We were thus able to get some indication of people's familiarity with the Mbona story. Our findings — much like those of the author of Text IV in the second part of this book — were that, whilst everybody was able to mention a few generalities about the cult, relatively few were capable of giving a coherent account, however brief, of Mbona's life. Gradually it became clear that those who were capable of providing a coherent account were usually people who had a political interest in the story, either because they were close to the ruling elite or because they were critical of it.

The Mbona traditions in their totality present the familiar three-tiered structure of so many bodies of oral tradition in Africa.[6] Thus they have much to say about the more recent period, extending in our case from the middle of the nineteenth century to the present. A great deal is said also about the beginnings of the cult, which in our case refers to the period before the middle of the seventeenth century. But there is rather less information about the middle period, from the middle of the seventeenth century to the middle of the nineteenth.[7] The main emphasis of the present study will be on the early period. More specifically, an attempt has been made to reconstruct some of the processes which led to the emergence of the only martyr cult in premodern Malawi. Before elaborating this point, however, it will be necessary to take a look at the Mbona cult from a sociological perspective.

TERRITORIAL CULTS

There are many cults like Mbona's in sub-Saharan Africa. One need but think of the Earth Cult of the Tallensi in Ghana, the Rain Queen of the Lovedu in South Africa, and the Mwari, Chaminuka, Karuva, and Dzivaguru cults in Zimbabwe, to mention but a few.[8] They have variously been called earth cults, rain cults, or rain and fertility cults, but I prefer the term *territorial cults*, since they are centrally concerned with the political life of a specific land area and since their constituency is a group identified by their common occupation of and rights in that land area.[9]

One of the first to identify and describe these cults as a sociologically distinct category was the anthropologist Clyde Mitchell, who in a brief but perceptive analysis of the founding myth of the Chidzere shrine in the Zambezi Valley sketched some of the central issues prominent in these cults, among which is the concept of ownership of the land. In his formulation, "the 'owners of the land' are usually the earliest known occupiers of the region — the autochthons who transformed the forest suitable only for animal habitation into fields suitable for human beings. Under a very general principle this transformation gives them special rights over it so that their ancestors exercise control over the natural forces that operate on it."[10]

Mitchell also observed that in many cases such land shrines are controlled by the local chief, especially when he is held to be a descendant of the original lineage which came to work the land. He added, however, that when invaders conquer an autochthonous people, the political and ritual aspects of land may be separated. In that case the autochthons often continue to exercise ritual control over the land and its products even after they have been conquered. Having cited a number of cases from different parts of Africa illustrating that principle, Mitchell comes to his central statement: "Given the belief in the power of the spirits of the ancestors to influence natural events related to the land, it follows that conquest must set up an ambiguous relationship between the victors and the vanquished since the victors have no direct communication with the spirits of the ancestors of the autochthons. The very weakness of the vanquished in a sense becomes their strength. The consequence of this is that these beliefs provide the mechanism through which the formerly hostile groups may be linked together in a common society. There is a division of labour between the conquerors and the conquered so that the stability and continuity of society depend on the exercise of secular authority through the usual media of law and authority on one hand, and on the equally essential spiritual authority through land rituals on the other."[11]

It appears that this type of arrangement is typical of a number of societies in south central Africa and elsewhere. Yet Mitchell does recognize that there are exceptions to this rule. One such are the Ngoni, who established conquest states in several parts of Malawi, Zambia, and Tanzania but apparently ignored the ritual "ownership" of the land by the original inhabitants.[12] Another is Shaka, who, upon rising to power among the Zulu, expelled all rainmakers from his kingdom, saying that only he could control the heavens.[13] By way of contrast, the Ndebele, of common origin with the Ngoni, recognized the Mwari cult of the conquered Kalanga people, and even the Ngoni were in the end forced to recognize the autochthonous cult.[14] The case is therefore not as clear-cut or as simple as it seems at first sight. Whether or not an existing territorial cult is recognized from the beginning by the new rulers and whether or not it will gain some degree of recognition at a later stage depend on a multiplicity of factors, which have been discussed elsewhere and need not concern us here.[15] The point to be retained is that African territorial cults constitute an arena in which people claiming to be "owners of the land" regularly confront others who are considered "invaders" and that these confrontations may lead to changes in the allocation of ritual positions. A further point to be made is that the term *invaders* need not always be taken literally, since it may also refer to an elite which rose to power from within a society. Shaka's following is one example.

On the whole, Mitchell's sociology of territorial cults contains quite useful insights, but it has to be supplemented on a number of points. As we have just seen, the organizational arrangements of territorial cults are not static but have often been subject to considerable change in the period following confrontation with invaders. For instance, cults which were initially suppressed may later have reasserted themselves, and control over them may in the end have come to be shared between autochthons and invaders. Actually, this seems to have occurred so frequently that, rather than accepting a clear-cut division of ritual and secular power as the norm, which Mitchell's article hints at, one ought to see it as an exception.

The next observation to be made is that the opposition between autochthons and conquerors may be neither the only one nor necessarily the most relevant one in the politics of a community. In the case of the Mbona cult, and no doubt in other cases as well, that opposition has in the course of time been overlaid by a number of others, such as the opposition between chiefs (including "autochthonous" chiefs) and commoners, between descendants of free men and descendants of former slaves, or between cattle holders and subsistence farmers, to name but a few. In sum, territorial cults are not just institutions which, after an initial confrontation, withdraw from the political arena. Instead, they themselves function as political arenas where different interest groups confront each other over issues of communal importance. This brings us to a third comment on Mitchell's concept of territorial cults, which is that they may possess several competing and conflicting versions of how they originated, instead of just one. It is this aspect in particular which will occupy us a great deal in this book.

Another anthropologist who has made a significant contribution to our understanding of territorial cults is Victor Turner. That contribution consists among other things in his distinction between two types of cults in sub-Saharan Africa, which he refers to as "earth and fertility cults" (our territorial cults) and "ancestral and political cults." In his view, each of these types tends to be focused on "different types of shrines situated in different localities," resulting in "overlapping and interpenetrating fields of ritual relations." He summarizes the crucial difference between them:

> Ancestral and political cults and their local embodiments tend to represent crucial power divisions and classificatory distinctions within and among politically discrete groups, while earth and fertility cults represent ritual bonds between those groups and even, as in the case of the Tallensi, tendencies toward still wider bonding. The first type stresses exclusiveness, the second inclusiveness. The first emphasizes sectional interests and conflict over them; the second disinterestedness and shared values. In studies of African cults of the first type, we find frequent reference to such topics as lineage segmentation, local history, factional conflict, and witchcraft. In cults of the second type, the accent is laid on common ideals and values, and, where there has been misfortune, on the guilt and responsibility of all rather than the culpability of individuals or factions.[16]

Whilst both Mitchell and Turner emphasize the integrative potential of territorial cults, they differ insofar as Mitchell attributes that potential to the complementary nature of the relationship between cult and state, whereas Turner appears to ascribe it directly to the inclusivist ideology of these cults. Whatever the case, acknowledgment of the integrative potential of territorial cults does not imply that they stand above social conflict. On the contrary, as stated earlier, they are to be viewed as arenas where conflicts of communal importance can be brought into the open, and more often than not cult officers appear to be party to such conflicts.

Turner himself rightly cautions his readers that the contrast between political cults and earth cults, as sketched by him, is a simplification of what may be a much more complex situation. Thus, functions that he associates with mutually exclusive cults may actually be exercised by one and the same cult complex. This is the case in the Mbona cult, where communal and sectional interests are polarized within a single organization, each alternative being emphasized by different protagonists. The champion of the communal interests is the medium, whereas sectional interests, as we shall see, are particularly represented by the cult principals. Within the Mbona cult there is a persistent struggle between the representatives of political hierarchy — the cult principals as chiefs — who assert the legitimacy of social differentiation, and the representative of their people — the medium — who puts forward the conception of a nondifferentiated society.[17]

In line with this, the principals put much emphasis on local history as a means of legitimating their position and status, whereas the medium tends to emphasize shared values. But alongside the oral traditions of the aristocracy, there also exists a body of commoner traditions. What we have, then, is two sets of oral traditions commenting on the same issues, processes, and events from opposing angles. The traditions of the commonalty do not constitute an egalitarian history in the sense of challenging the institution of chiefship as such. Rather, they challenge absolutist tendencies inherent in the political system as well as instances of abuse of power on the part of the chiefs.

If Turner's description of territorial cults as inclusivist of "democratic" is essentially correct and if Mitchell's view that, historically, they stand in opposition to "invaders" or a political elite is equally correct, then the conclusion suggests itself that, where we find an influential territorial cult, there is a chance that we may find a dual body of oral traditions: the one aristocratic, the other populist. The fact that such dual histories have largely remained unnoticed is to be attributed to the continuing neglect of the historical study of African religion despite occasional attempts to correct that situation.[18] More specifically, the precolonial history of territorial cults has received little or no attention.[19]

INTERPRETATIONS OF ORAL TRADITIONS

In regard to the historiographical potential of mythical tales or legendary chronicles such as the Mbona narratives, we may distinguish five major positions. First, the well-known Malinowskian viewpoint asserts that such narratives are to be interpreted as "charters" explaining why a particular personage or interest group claims the right to control a particular institution.[20] Second, there is the idea that oral traditions of the mythical or legendary type are to be regarded as symbolic interpretations of values held by contemporary society.[21] Third, the structuralist theory defines them as essentially cosmological representations, which should be interpreted along structuralist lines and from which it is virtually impossible to extract historical information.[22] Fourth, the viewpoint in much of Vansina's work implies that it is necessary to make a distinction between mythical and nonmythical elements in these chronicles and that only the latter can possibly convey historical information.[23] Finally, there is the suggestion that even so-called mythical events may contain historical information, albeit in symbolic form.[24]

Most of these perspectives are directly applicable to the Mbona narratives. Thus they clearly function as charters, legitimating particular claims. They can also be validly interpreted as statements about central values or ideas held by the community, one of those ideas being that chiefly authority is to be exercised with consideration and restraint. The Mbona narratives may also be read as cosmologies. Indeed, some insist that the Mbona biographies be read as nature myths pure and simple.[25] Finally, the Mbona narratives may contain instructive instances of historical information packed in symbolic language. One of the leading ideas of the present study is that in the Mbona myths the beheaded snake of Central African mythology has transformed into a human martyr whose biography is anchored in identifiable historical events.[26] True, we do not know whether there ever lived a rain priest called Mbona who was persecuted and murdered. On the other hand, it is perfectly imaginable that members of the Mbona priesthood were persecuted and killed at one time and that these priests, together with other victims, have become symbolized by that name. Few readers will object to the possibility of such a process having taken place. What they want to know, though, is whether and when such a thing took place in reality and what evidence we think we can produce to make our point.

There are in the history of the Shire Valley two periods which may be regarded as possible sources for the emergence of this martyrdom theology. The first is the period between the late 1580s and the early 1620s, which is marked by the Zimba wars and the rise of the first powerful kingdom. The second is the period which commenced around the time of David Livingstone's arrival in the valley in 1859 and ended with the proclamation of the Nyasaland Protectorate in 1892. The latter period was marked by an exceptionally severe famine in 1862–63, continuous slave raids between 1863 and 1874, and armed attempts by the Kololo invaders to extend their domination over the entire valley, including the southern part where the main shrine is situated.[27] Both periods witnessed the emergence of a strongly centralized state system; in both cases this process was accompanied by much bloodshed, and we have reason to believe that in both cases the shrine was physically destroyed and the cult temporarily suspended. Theoretically, the martyr theology could have originated on either occasion. The viewpoint to be forwarded in this book, however, is that it emerged on the earlier occasion, that is to say, around 1600, and that the nineteenth-century events only reaffirmed a theology which had already been in existence for more than two centuries. I intend to show that the Mbona myths contain identifiable indications for dating the origin of the martyrdom cult in the late sixteenth and early seventeenth centuries. I also hope to show that the Zimba were more than the product of Portuguese imagination, as is sometimes maintained.[28] In addition, I shall adduce evidence that the Zimba were deployed not only against surrounding chiefdoms and Portuguese settlements but also against the population of the Shire Valley itself. It is this latter element in particular which is going to add to our understanding of the Zimba episode, because it allows us to tap an extensive corpus of oral traditions. If evidence about the external wars of the Zimba has reached us exclusively through Portuguese documents, evidence about their operations inside the Shire Valley has reached us exclusively through the Mbona cult.

But, as noted earlier on, there is more to the Mbona stories than reminiscences of the past. Dual traditions such as we find in the Mbona cult are to be viewed also from a political angle as part of an ongoing discussion about mutual rights between opposing sections of a community.[29] The main question which the participants in that discussion are trying to answer is what those rights are and how they are validated. In our case that discussion primarily focuses on the legitimacy and the rights of the aristocracy, and it examines these in the light of the circumstances under which the Mbona cult originated.[30] If it is a discussion in the real sense of the word, the participants will have to follow certain rules about what may and what may not be omitted from or changed in the fund of objective history which forms the basic material of that discussion. If that supposition is correct, then a systematic comparison of elitist and populist traditions should make it possible, at least in theory, to identify these rules and thereby to answer some basic questions about the limits of manipulation. The present study demonstrates how that possibility may be realized and how thereby a new line of historical research may be opened up.

STRUCTURE OF THE ARGUMENT

This book consists of two parts, the first of which contains background information on the peoples of the Shire Valley, a historical reconstruction of the cult's early and later history, and a discussion of the structure and content of the Mbona narratives. Part 2 contains seven Mbona texts with an extensive critical apparatus.

Part 1 has seven chapters. The opening chapter familiarizes the reader with the geography of the Shire Valley, its present population, and earlier residential groups, insofar as these have a bearing on the Mbona narratives and the history of the cult. Chapter 2 concerns the cult's regional topography, its main organizational features, and its ritual cycle. Chapter 3 emphasizes the conflicting relationships between the cult principals, both of whom belong to the aristocracy, and the medium, who is a commoner and who represents the interests of the community at large. These conflicts replicate the discussion that is going on in the myths. In Chapter 4 we turn to the more recent history of the cult, covering the period from the middle of the nineteenth century to the early 1980s. This is a necessary preliminary to Chapter 5, where we examine the formative period of the cult, between the final quarter of the sixteenth century and the second quarter of the seventeenth. Chapter 6 contains an overview of the corpus of Mbona traditions, which appears to consist of three "streams," each of which seems to reflect a particular form (or phase) of political organization and to be associated with a particular interest group. From these streams we can derive a developmental history of the Mbona myth as a continuing social construction and deconstruction. Chapter 7 identifies the two contrapuntal worldviews that constitute the myth and at the same time preserve historical information by cross-checking and counterbalancing each other. The confrontation of the two key texts further allows us to formulate some of the rules underlying the manipulation of objective history.

Five chapters were published at an earlier stage. A large part of Chapter 3 appeared in R. P. Werbner, ed., *Regional Cults.* Half of Chapter 4 appeared in T. O. Ranger and J. Weller, eds., *Themes in the Christian History of Central Africa.* The other half of that chapter was published in W. Beinart et al., *Malawi: An Alternative Pattern of Development.* Chapter 5 on the Zimba wars and their relation to the cult, appeared in the *Journal of African History.* Chapter 6 was first published in W. Van Binsbergen and M. Schoffeleers, eds., *Theoretical Explorations in African Religion.* An earlier version of Chapter 7 appeared in *History in Africa: A Journal of Method.* Finally, Text III/B in Part 2 was first published in R. Schefold et al., eds. *Man, Meaning and History.*[31]

PART ONE

*The Mbona Cult
in the Shire Valley*

CHAPTER 1

The Shire Valley and Its Population

TRAVELING FROM the Shire highlands to the Shire Valley via the Chikwawa escarpment with its countless bends and hairpins, many a visitor feels compelled to halt for a while to take in the savage beauty of the landscape. All around in the arid foothills is the shrieking metallic noise of the cicadas. Down below, the valley lies shimmering in the hot tropical sun. The river meanders lazily through the lush vegetation on its banks. At the side of the Chikwawa Boma, a high perpendicular bank of red clay towers above the waters, and beyond it the valley floor stretches for countless kilometers until it is lost in the hazy blues of the horizon. At the bottom of the escarpment the oppressive heat, the parched soil, and the baobabs bring home, better than words can, the difference between this part of the country and the one just left behind in the hills. The difference in altitude is less than a thousand meters, the distance a bare fifty kilometers, but their physical environments seem to belong to entirely different worlds.

NATURAL ENVIRONMENT AND ECONOMICS

Most of the valley floor consists of alluvial and colluvial deposits with outcrops of sandstone along the western border.[1] It is traversed from north to south by the Shire, which flows into the Zambezi south of the border between Malawi and Mozambique. On its northeastern side it is bounded by a scarp which culminates in Mount Thyolo (1200 m), and on its southwestern side by the Matundu Hills, the highest

17

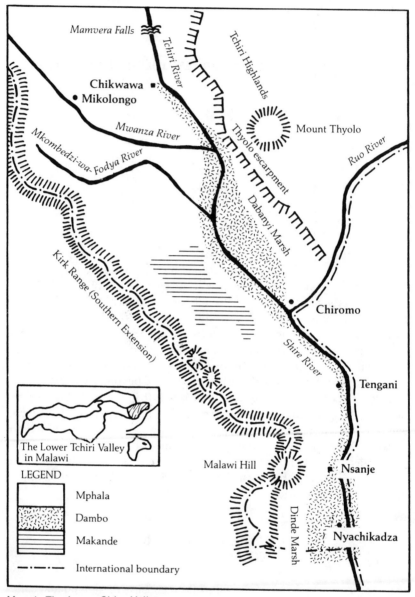

Map 1. The Lower Shire Valley
     Source: Mandala 1990:4.

Legend labels within map:

Mamvera Falls
Tchiri River
Tchiri Highlands
Chikwawa
Mikolongo
Mwanza River
Thyolo escarpment
Mount Thyolo
Mkombedzi-wa-Fodya River
Ruo River
Dabanyi Marsh
Kirk Range (Southern Extension)
Chiromo
Shire River
Tengani
The Lower Tchiri Valley in Malawi
Nsanje
Malawi Hill
LEGEND
Mphala
Dambo
Makande
International boundary
Dinde Marsh
Nyachikadza

18

of which is Malawi Hill (970 m). The main economic pursuit in the valley is agriculture. The staple crops are, in descending order of hardiness, finger millet, bulrush millet, sorghum, and maize. In Nsanje, the southernmost of the valley's two administrative districts, finger millet and bulrush millet form the staple food. The rainfall in this area — with the significant exception of the tract of land between Nsanje township and the Mbona shrine — is not great enough for maize, which, however, is successfully grown in the Matundu Hills and in the northern part of the Chikwawa District.[2] Besides these staple crops, people cultivate several varieties of beans, pulses, and groundnuts, as well as vegetables, cassava, and sweet potatoes. Rice is considered a cash crop rather than a domestic one. The main cash crop in the valley, however, is cotton, which at one time made up about 80 percent of the national output. Several of these crops, notably millet, rice, sorghum, and cotton, have a local history of at least four centuries.[3]

The average rainfall is 640 to 800 millimeters, but rain is erratic in its temporal and spatial incidence. On the hills the fall is greater, and in any one year variations occur in different parts of the plain as most of the rain falls in sharply localized electrical storms, for which the southern part is especially noted. Droughts are rather common. Minor ones, leading to partial but still serious crop failure, average out at about one in every five to seven years.[4] Major droughts, leading to total crop failure, are more widely spaced, four or five having occurred so far this century.

The valley comprises two extensive marsh areas, which partially compensate for these vicissitudes. The northernmost of these, known as the Dabanyi or Elephant Marsh, is the larger of the two, with a surface of about 425 square kilometers. South of Nsanje township lies the smaller Dinde Marsh, which spills over into Mozambique. At both places perennial water is available, and high water table land, periodically replenished with silt, provides rich soils. Along these marshes people practice, wherever possible, a dual system of agriculture, concentrating partly on rain-fed (*phala*) crops and partly on river-fed (*dimba*) crops.[5] the *phala* system used to be basically one of rotational bush-fallow, by which soil deterioration could be avoided. Several crops were interplanted on mounds, which were fertilized with the ashes of burnt tree branches and plant vegetation.[6]

In the past, the effects of drought could to a considerable extent be neutralized by making more extensive use of the *dimba* land, and this particular feature sets the Shire Valley apart from most of the Zambezi Valley. People from the Zambezi Valley used to take refuge in the Shire Valley at times of severe drought, seeking admission by placing themselves under the protection of established families, a practice known as *kutama*.[7] Droughts were fatal only when they coincided with war or civil unrest — in these cases the valley population had to take refuge in the hills — or when a drought was followed by floods and wetland gardens were washed away. In more recent times, however, the effects of drought have become more acutely felt, due to serious overcultivation and the ravages wrought by the numerous cattle herds. From the 1890s onward the population began to increase steadily, due mainly to continuous migrations from Mozambique. In 1907 the total population of the valley was estimated at about fifty thousand. A census conducted in 1923 in the central valley area revealed that of the adult population no less than 48 percent were immigrants. Part of this immigration had occurred in 1917 following the Barwe rebellion.[8] In 1931 the population stood at 117,302; in 1966, at 258,879; in 1977, at 319,206. By now it may be nearing the 500,000 mark.[9]

The effect of this rapid population increase on the natural environment is all too visible. Over most of the valley, cultivation has destroyed the original vegetation, leaving only a few of the larger trees, such as baobab (*Adamsonia digitata*), *njale* (*Sterculia appendiculata*), and *mgoza* (*Sterculia africana*). Game, too, has become scarce, but three game reserves preserve something of the rich fauna which not very long ago covered the whole area.

Although in precolonial times the basic economic activities – agricul-

Illus. 1. District headquarters, Nsanje, 1965

Illus. 2. Nsanje market, 1966

ture, hunting, and fishing — were the same throughout the valley, the north specialized in the manufacturing of iron and salt, while the emphasis in the south was on the cultivation of rice and cotton and the manufacturing of a coarse cloth (*machira*), which as early as the sixteenth century was exported on a large scale to the chiefdoms south of the Zambezi.[10] Iron and salt manufacturing were traditionally affected by numerous restrictions: among other things, they were only engaged in by specific categories of people who possessed the ritual qualifications for that kind of work.[11] They could therefore not become popular economic pursuits, as were rice growing and cotton weaving, both of which were free of such restrictions.

One wonders how much this economic differentiation has influenced the division of power between north and south. Earlier on we quoted Victor Turner's assertion that cults such as Mbona's are inclusivist in character, stressing similarities between social groups rather than differences. That kind of attitude may have found support in the open character of the rice and cotton economies, which could be engaged in by locals and immigrants alike. That this actually was the case we know from Livingstone, who conducted regular business in the neighborhood of the shrine with immigrant rice growers on behalf of his Portuguese acquaintances on the Zambezi.[12]

By way of contrast, we can see political capitals as exclusivist in character, stressing differences and inequality rather than common rights. That kind of attitude in its turn may have found support in the pronounced social regimentation inherent in the iron and salt industries. It is arguable that this was one of the reasons why political centralization took root in the northern rather than the southern half of the valley. Had the founders of the Lundu kingdom opted to establish their capital in the south, they might have been far less successful, due to the south's inclusivist and poly-ethnic tradition. It is worth noting that something similar occurred in the late nineteenth century, when the Kololo as the successors to the Lundu throne managed to establish themselves firmly in the northern ecosystem but failed to extend their power effectively over the south despite sustained efforts in that direction.

ETHNIC GROUPS: MANG'ANJA AND SENA

Nowadays, the main ethnic division in the Lower Shire Valley is that between the Mang'anja, who claim to be the owners of the land, and a congeries of immigrant groups, mostly from south of the Zambezi, which were formerly called Chikunda but are now collectively referred to as Sena, since Chikunda is felt to have derogatory overtones. Historically, the term Chikunda referred to armed slave squads in the service of Portuguese landholders (*prazeiros*) in the Zambezi Valley. These Chikunda formed a powerful military class, whose principal function was to police the local populations. They were deployed on the frontiers of the estates to prevent individuals or entire populations from fleeing, and they also carried out slave-raiding activities on behalf of their masters.[13] In later days the term was used as an ethnic designation and came to be applied to the entire *prazo* population, while in the Shire Valley it became for a while a blanket term for any immigrant from the Zambezi Valley.

In the first quarter of the present century the two largest groups within the Sena congeries identified themselves respectively as Sena proper and Tonga. The Sena proper were those who had moved in from the hinterland of the township of Sena. The name Tonga was more specifically applied to immigrants from the chiefdom of Makombe. To complicate matters further, sections of these Tonga also referred to themselves as Zimba, a name which as we know plays an important role in the Mbona traditions and which for that reason merits special attention.

Ethnic groups known as Zimba are found in the Zairian province of Shaba (Katanga), where they belong to the Luba cluster, and in Zambia and northwestern Mozambique, where they are regarded as a branch of the Chewa.[14] The Zimba of the Nsanje District, however, come from south of the Zambezi, and they have no historical ties or cultural affinity with the Zimba branch of the Chewa.

In the various dialects of the local peoples, *mzimba* (pl., *azimba* or *mazimba*) denotes both "hunter" and "warrior."[15] Among the Mang'anja the term referred also to the young men whose task it was to guard the chief's compound and to check visitors seeking an audience with the ruler. Tonga immigrants, for their part, use it among themselves as a praise name when recounting their military past.[16] One of the annual district reports describes the *azimba* as expert hunters of elephant and other big game, who originally worked their way up from Zimbabwe.[17] All this points to the fact that in the Lower Zambezi Valley the name Zimba, like the name Chikunda, was originally a professional designation, which in time came to function as an ethnic label. But like the term Chikunda, the term Zimba is also used as a term of abuse. Unpopular Mang'anja chiefs are referred to as Zimba, suggesting not only that they are of foreign descent but also that they behave like robbers and pillagers.

The Mang'anja form part of the Maravi; in early Portuguese documents the term covered an agglomeration of peoples living north of the Zambezi, to the south and west of Lake Malawi.[18] Like the other branches of the Maravi, the Mang'anja are traditionally matrilineal and uxorilocal, whereas the majority of the immigrants are patrilineal and virilocal.[19] Due to inter-marriage, however, the traditional Mang'anja system of kinship and mar-riage has begun to show a great deal of variation. Despite these changes, people prefer to identify themselves as Mang'anja, as the name still de-notes rights to traditional political and ritual offices.

Since the Mbona narratives contain numerous references to the Mang'anja kinship organization, it will be helpful to familiarize ourselves with its chief characteristics. One of its basic components is the matrilineal de-scent group called *mbumba*, a term rendered by Mitchell as "sorority group."[20] This consists of a group of sisters and their children under the leadership of their brothers, who are known as their *nkhoswe* (guardians). One of these men is regarded as the leader of the *mbumba* (*mwini mbumba*; lit., "owner of the *mbumba*"). When such a man refers to his *mbumba*, he includes not only his sisters and their descendants but also his younger brothers. Thus, in that case the term is used in a broader sense. A woman normally belongs to more than one *mbumba*, namely, that of her brother, that of her mother's brother (*malume*), and possibly also that of her mater-nal grandmother's brother. The directly effective one, however, is that of her mother's brother, who will be assisted by her elder brother, if the latter is an adult.

The head of the *mbumbu* is responsible for the behavior of those under his charge. He has to see to their general well-being, conduct their mar-riage negotiations, appear for them in court, and pay fines on their behalf. After a court case the matter will be settled within the *mbumba*, and its head will decide on the action to be taken against his convicted ward. He may request restitution in cash or in kind, or occasionally he may even decline further responsibility. Under the heading of general well-being come especially his duties to consult a diviner and procure the necessary treatment in cases of illness and to preside over funerals in his *mbumba*. He also has a special responsibility toward the upbringing of his sisters' children, particularly in connection with his nieces' initiation. At her first menstruation, a girl is given private instructions (*chinamwali chaching'ono*), while some time later, in the slack period preceding the next hoeing season, all those who received their first instructions gather for communal instructions (*chinamwali chachikulu*). These are given in a special camp outside the village, and the instructors are elderly women, who were assigned by the headman.[21] Goods and traditional offices are normally inherited through the female line by the younger brothers and sisters' sons.

Marriage is uxorilocal, and a man goes to live in the village of his wife's matrilineage after a period of bride service. If a man is called to the headmanship of his village of origin, he will return to it with his wife and children. The village headmanship is thus a coveted position, not only because of the status attached to it but also because it allows a man to settle

Illus. 3. Borehole, Nsanje District, 1967. Photograph by C. Zonneveld.

Illus. 4. Bridge over the Shire at Chiromo, 1966

among his own kin. Theoretically, the eldest brother is elected headman, but in practice there is considerable freedom of choice, and other factors such as the candidate's popularity with his kinsmen are also taken into account. Potential sources of conflict in the *mbumba* system are the relationships between a man and his brothers and between a man and his mother's brother. The cause of the conflict is usually competition for effective control over the *mbumba* and positions of authority which follow from it.

THE EARLIEST REMEMBERED INHABITANTS

Although the Mang'anja pride themselves on being owners of the land, their oral traditions mention two other groups as having lived in the valley before them. One of these is called Kafula (or, more popularly, Batwa), the other Chipeta. The Chipeta in particular play an important role in the Mbona mythology, which makes it necessary to discuss them in some detail. But the Kafula too deserve attention as supposedly the earliest inhabitants of the valley.

Oral traditions describe the Kafula as small, bearded people who lived by hunting and gathering. North of the Shire Valley they are remembered as thievish and treacherous, qualities which reportedly led to regular clashes with the Maravi.[22] They are commonly associated with mountainous areas, and more especially with the locations of important rain shrines. The Kafula traditions accord with archaeological records of a small-statured Negroid population, characteristic of the Later Stone Age, which in Malawi ranged from about 8000 B.C. to about A.D. 200, but sections of the Kafula population may have survived well into the Iron Age.[23] the Kafula reminiscences thus function as an important channel through which present-day society retains its links with its preagricultural past.

The earliest cultivators and metal workers appeared about the middle of the second century. According to the archaeologist Desmond Clark, movement by these Iron Age cultivators and stock owners is likely to have been a steady but gradual process by small groups. Only much later, possibly from the sixteenth century onward, did competition for land and other resources lead to major conflict among the populations of Malawi.[24] Widespread oral traditions about armed clashes between Kafula and Maravi—an instance of which is provided in our Text II/A—suggest that a significant element of the hunting and gathering population actually resisted being incorporated into the agricultural community.[25] Sightings of Kafula continue to be reported even in our days with a certain regularity. Consequently, they are alternatively referred to as spirits and as human beings.[26]

In the Shire Valley the Kafula are particularly associated with Malawi Hill. Unlike Kafula traditions elsewhere, in the Shire Valley nothing is said about clashes ever having taken place with peoples coming in after the Kafula. Senior Headman Nkhuche, whose village is situated in the neighborhood of Malawi Hill, confirms this:

> The Mang'anja came face to face with them here, on Malawi Hill, but they [the Mang'anja] did not do them any harm, because they are spirits. They dwell in the neighborhood of the rock Mwala-Ndebvu ["Rock of the Beard"], which is one of the spirit places on that hill. I remember well how I went to Nsanje one day, when one of these small people [i.e., Kafula] had also gone there. He went to the market, where women gathered around him and people made him presents of fish and sweet potatoes. He was quite short, wearing his hair long. From the marketplace he proceeded to [Chief] Chiphwembwe's burial grove [msitu]. It was when he was on his way there that we heard about him, all of us rushing up to have a look at him. He was very shy, and he was still carrying what he had been given at the market. He spoke a language which no one understood. From the msitu he returned to Malawi Hill.[27]

One of the reasons why clashes between Kafula and Maravi groups did not take place in the Shire Valley may have been that the agriculturalist population was concentrated along the Shire and one or two smaller streams, leaving the dry, heavily forested area on its western flank to the descendants of the original inhabitants.

The Chipeta are also said to have occupied the Shire Valley at a very early stage. Nowadays, people called Chipeta are found mainly in the Dowa, Dedza, and Ntcheu districts in the Central Region of Malawi and in adjoining areas of northwestern Mozambique and eastern Zambia.[28] S. J. Ntara, an authority on Chewa history, avers that they came with the Ngoni from Sukumaland.[29] But the more common tradition holds that the name Chipeta was invented by the Ngoni as a nickname to mock the Chewa they had conquered because of the latter's habit of hiding in the high grass (*chipeta*) whenever the Ngoni raided their villages.[30] The general belief then appears to be that the Chipeta are a branch of the Chewa, which developed their distinctive identity only in the second half of the nineteenth century under Ngoni influence. An exception is found in the *Handbook of Nyasaland* (1910), which summarizes a corpus of traditions collected by colonial administrators around the beginning of the century, according to which the Chipeta were already established long before the arrival of

Illus. 5. Mang'anja homestead, Chikwawa District, 1967. Photograph by C. Zonneveld.

Illus. 6. Woman returning from marsh garden (Sena folk art), 1960s. Artist unknown. Formerly in the collection of the Museum of Malawi. Photograph by C. Zonneveld.

the Ngoni.[31] As will presently be shown, there is convincing evidence in favor of that viewpoint, which suggests that the Ngoni traditions are *post factum* elaborations on a preexisting name, designed to illustrate and inculcate the superior power of the invader and the supposed cowardly disposition of the conquered population.

Chipeta, as a noun, however, refers not only to tall grass but also to a distinct ecosystem consisting of tall grass (*tsekere*) and sparse tree growth (mainly *Acacia*), which is characteristic of areas with a long tradition of annual burns.[32] The ethnic designation Chipeta may therefore be taken as originally referring to communities inhabiting that type of ecosystem. That interpretation is confirmed by the Portuguese traveler A. C. P. Gamitto, who in the year 1831 — more than thirty years before the Ngoni incursions into Malawi and eastern Zambia — came across Chipeta communities in what is now the border area between eastern Zambia and northwestern Mozambique.

According to Gamitto, these Chipeta ("Chupeta") occupied an enclave in the middle of "Marave land." Their district was flat, with few trees, and those that existed were very small. They kept many cattle, the dung of which was used as fuel in the absence of firewood. The Chipeta had the same habits as the Maravi, but they were much more warlike, fiercely independent, and "much given to lying and stealing." Most important, they were an acephalous society. Each village was governed by the head of the lineage composing it. Such a headman recognized no political superior. According to Gamitto, they preferred annihilation or destruction to obeying another. In case of a dispute or outbreak of war between two headmen, which seems to have been a frequent event, the members of their villages fought one another. The battle never finished with the first fight: "He who weakens retreats and gets another one to help him, and thus the two factions grow incessantly to the point where often all the chiefs [i.e., headmen] are involved in the contest. On each occasion the quarrel is brought to an end by the appointment of arbitrators to judge the matter, which may be nothing more than the purloining of a millet stalk."[33]

There are important parallels between Gamitto's description and the fragments of Chipeta lore cited earlier on. In both cases the Chipeta are associated with a grassland economy. Also, Gamitto's Chipeta, like those in present-day Malawi, were culturally indistinguishable from their neighbors. What made them different was their acephalous organization and their custom of intervillage warfare, which regularly resulted in a temporary splitting up of the entire populace.[34] If Chipeta communities elsewhere resembled those described by Gamitto, it is understandable that manifestations of independence such as those he described must have led to serious conflicts with the Ngoni, who were better equipped than the Maravi to deal with recalcitrant village communities. This in its turn would explain why the name Chipeta is so consistently and emphatically linked with the Ngoni conquests.[35]

The importance of Gamitto's account of the Chipeta should not be underestimated, as it suggests a rather different conception of the precolonial political situation than the one with which we have long been familiar.[36] Instead of the entire Maravi area having been divided up among kingdoms and chiefdoms, we must now also entertain the possibility that the Maravi area was interspersed with stateless enclaves. This raises important questions which cannot be pursued here.[37] The relevant question at this point is whether the Chipeta presence ever extended into the Lower Shire Valley. To answer that question we may begin by pointing to a body of oral traditions which maintain that Mbona himself was a muChipeta.

The traditions represented in this study by Texts I/A and I/B are considered to refer to the earliest phase in the cult history. They describe Mbona as someone who either was forced to flee from some place in Chipeta country or who led a Chipeta migration from the Central Region to the Shire Valley, where he became a famous rainmaker and the object of cultic veneration.[38] This layer of traditions has become part of local topographical lore: a much-weathered rock boulder known as Nnembo-za-Chipeta ("Chipeta Tattoos") lies on the eastern slopes of Malawi Hill, and on its surface

Illus. 7. Nnembo-za-Chipeta rock boulder, Malemia village, Nsanje

Mbona or his fellow Chipeta are said to have carved their facial tattoos.[39] Engraving one's emblem on a rock in a strategic place is tantamount to claiming ownership of that place, which no doubt is what the episode symbolizes. In view of the consistency of these traditions and topographical mnemonics, it seems reasonable to assume the presence of an early Chipeta population in the valley.

To broaden our discussion of the Chipeta and the prestate population somewhat, we must pay attention also to traditions about the clan system. All Maravi groups hold that originally they had only two clans. Banda and Phiri, which were exogamous and which had come into existence at the time when the Maravi were entering their new country. S. J. Ntara describes the genesis of this dual clan system:

> One day two groups went about in search of arrowroots and some edible roots. They did not return home but slept in the bush. One group slept on a hill-top and the other at the foot of the hill. When morning came, those who slept on the hill-top were nicknamed Phiri ("of the hill") and those who slept at the foot of the hill and had to level or lay out the grass were called Banda ("those who tread the grass under their feet"). So it came to pass that the two clans were created in this way. The advantage was that the creation of these clans made it possible for anyone from the Banda clan to marry into the Phiri clan and vice versa.[40]

In the Shire Valley, Phiri and Banda have remained the two most important clan names, even if the Phiri nowadays far outnumber the Banda. I personally recorded a number of traditions to the effect that the ancestral Mang'anja, when migrating to the Lower Shire Valley, divided into two sections, one of which, called Phiri, kept to the hills, while the other, called Banda, kept to the valley floor. In order that they would not lose sight of each other, the Phiri section used to set the hills alight.[41]

R. A. Hamilton, who has undertaken research in various parts of Malawi, including the Shire Valley, has suggested that these stories may actually refer to the arrival of chiefly immigrants, symbolized by the name Phiri, who gained control over long-established autochthons, symbolized by the name Banda.[42] M. G. Marwick, an authority on the Chewa of eastern Zambia, has provided substantial support for Hamilton's hypothesis by establishing that it accords with the traditional division of functions between the two clans. The Phiri, to whom most of the traditional chiefs belong, appear to specialize in political power, whilst the Banda have a close relationship with the land and are credited with the power of making rain.[43] This, as we saw in the Introduction, is not an isolated case but accords with traditions of dual authority structures elsewhere. Further confirmation is provided by the observation that until the late nineteenth century the name Phiri overlapped to a great extent with the name Maravi, suggesting once again more than just a superficial identification between the two.[44]

Some of the properties ascribed to the Chipeta apply equally to the Banda population. Both are referred to as plains people, both are associated with tall grass (remember Ntara's story about the Banda flattening the grass on which they slept), and both are described as somehow standing in contrast with the Phiri/Maravi. This suggests that both names are equally to be associated with a pre-Maravi population. It is possible that the names stood for different sections of that population, but it is equally possible that they function as a kind of shorthand for two crucial properties of the pre-Maravi communities, namely their acephalous organization — symbolized by the name Chipeta — and the presence among them of important territorial shrines — symbolized by the name Banda.

Our next step will be to examine two institutions which were typical of the Banda/Chipeta culture and which have a bearing on our understanding of the functioning of the Maravi states, namely the territorial shrines and the *nyau* societies.

THE TERRITORIAL SHRINES

It is a common theme in the oral traditions of the Mang'anja and related peoples that they once lived in a place called Kaphirintiwa on the border between present-day Zambia and Malawi.[45] Kaphirintiwa (lit. "little flat-topped hill") is also believed to be the place where the first men and animals descended from heaven and where life on earth began. Finally, Kaphirintiwa is the name of the territorial shrine from which all other territorial shrines are thought to be descended.[46] According to the Kaphirintiwa myth, one day Chiuta-God sent a man and a woman down from the sky with a hoe, a grain mortar, and a winnowing basket. With them came pairs of animals as well as Chiuta ("Great Bow") himself, who was accompanied by the first rains. They all alighted on a flat-topped hill by the name of Kaphirintiwa. Because of the rain, the earth, which until then had lain barren, sprang to life, and man began to cultivate his gardens. During this initial period Chiuta, men, and animals lived together in peace. That situation, however, was changed when man invented fire by rubbing two sticks, one soft, the other hard. This set the grass ablaze and made the animals flee, full of rage against man. Chiuta, being too old to run, was rescued by Spider, who spun a thread along which Chiuta climbed back to the sky, whence he had come. Thus driven away by the wickedness of man, God proclaimed that man would die and join him in the sky, where he would have to make rain clouds in order to quench the fires he had invented.[47]

The myth, which is definitely of pre-Maravi origin, is a reflection on the seasonal and occupational cycle of the country, which is marked by a wet and a dry season and by agriculture and hunting respectively. It also provides, as we shall see below, the scenario for the performances of the *nyau* secret societies, which take place at the female initiation ceremonies and the commemorative ceremonies for the dead.[48] Emphasis on a common descent from Kaphirintiwa, which is also a feature of the Mbona traditions,[49] functioned as a unifying device linking the major shrines between the lower Zambezi and Lake Malawi into a regional network.

Prestate shrines were located on narrow plateaus in mountainous areas that were rather difficult of access.[50] The choice of such places is explained by declaring them to have been former Kafula settlements. Thus the sacred drum of Kaphirintiwa, which is the central emblem of the Chewa rain cult, is said to have been taken from the local Kafula.[51] The original location of the Mbona shrine also was said to have been at the Kafula place Mwala Ndebvu on Malawi Hill.[52] The original location was confirmed by Headman Mwanda, who said that there were already Mang'anja in the valley before Mbona's arrival. Those ancient Mang'anja called themselves Chipeta, and their principal place of worship was on Malawi Hill.[53] A more practical reason for maintaining territorial shrines in such places, however, was that they could be more easily defended against invaders and other hostile groups. Ntara's account of a series of unsuccessful Maravi attacks on the Kaphirintiwa shrine supports that theory, as does a report by the first Anglican missionaries in the 1860s, who at the time of the great slave hunts found the shrine on Mount Thyolo heavily defended.[54] It is further to be noted that the territorial shrines functioned as places of refuge for the population in times of war.[55] At a later stage, probably after the rise of the Maravi states, when conditions were more secure, some of these shrines were transferred to the plains below. Kaphirintiwa thus moved to Msinja,[56] and the Mbona shrine moved from Malawi Hill to Khulubvi on the valley floor.

A common feature were the "spirit wives," women living in permanent celibacy and set apart for the cult of the godhead. One of their tasks was to transmit to those concerned messages of communal interest which they received in dreams. There are no longer any spirit wives among the Chewa and Mang'anja, at least not in the sense just described, but from the available literature it appears that, when they were still functioning — that is, until the second half of the nineteenth century — they were held in high esteem, their office being considered the highest in the cult hierarchy. They acted as overseers of the female initiation rites, and they are said to have been influential also in the field of secular politics, as confidantes of local rulers.[57] The spirit wives were members of the Banda clan and thus were associated with the prestate period in Malawi. This is emphasized in oral traditions cited by Ntara, according to which the Chewa at first had no chiefs but spirit wives, suggesting that they embodied a form of regional jural authority before the emergence of centralized state systems.[58]

A final feature to be considered is the apparent universality of a priesthood at the great shrines, which consisted of members of the Mbewe clan.[59] These Mbewe were also of pre-Maravi stock, and their presence at the great shrines functioned as an additional factor which bound these shrines together into some form of common organization. The central cult object was conceived of as a snake, called *tunga*, which was associated both with the shrine hut and with the sacred pool, another invariable feature of each cult complex. The snake spirit was visibly represented by the senior Mbewe official, who was himself known as *tunga* and who acted as the spirit wife's ritual consort.[60]

THE *NYAU* SOCIETIES

Another important institution typical of the Banda/ Chipeta culture is that of the *nyau* societies, which are found in Malawi, Zambia, and Mozambique.[61] These societies of masked dancers perform mainly at final mourning rites, which take place from a few months to a year after a person's death, and at communal initiation ceremonies for girls. Nowadays they also perform at national celebrations and cultural demonstrations.

The duration and lavishness of such performances vary a great deal. A *nyau* dance may last from one to five days, depending on the availability of beer and food and the expense that a family is prepared to undertake.[62] Most of the performances take place in the slack period between harvest and the next hoeing — the country's ritual season — when young people are initiated and lineages commemorate their dead.[63] This is how Gamitto described it in the 1830s: "When the harvest begins to ripen in June, there begin the Batukes; this is a name given to singing, dancing and drumming in general, but each entertainment has its own style and special name such as Kateko, Gondo, Pembera, etc. which can be told only by practice. These Batukes which last till October, the month in which cultivation starts afresh, keep the Maravi entertained all this time, and meanwhile they lead no other life than drinking Badwa [beer], dancing and singing, and remaining in a state of continual intoxication."[64]

Within the Republic of Malawi, *nyau* lodges are found over most of

Illus. 8. Instruction of a *nyau* novice, Chikwawa, 1967. Photograph by C. Zonneveld.

the Central Region and in parts of the Southern Region, including the northeastern part of the Shire Valley. In the valley and adjoining areas of the Shire highlands, however, there are two varieties of *nyau*, one being called "*nyau* of the Chipeta," the other "*nyau* of the Mang'anja."[65] The Mang'anja *nyau* are always fully dressed, leaving only their hands and feet uncovered. The Chipeta variant has a number of dancers, called *kapoli*, who wear nothing but a small piece of cloth. Their women also play a more active role by responding to the songs of the male dancers. More important, though, the Chipeta variant is considered more independent vis-à-vis the chiefs and more aggressive toward noninitiates.[66] The Mang'anja variety is the more recent of the two, dating back to the final quarter of the nineteenth century. There is evidence that it was introduced at the initiative of the Kololo chiefs, who seized power in that period.[67]

The *nyau* characters are of great variety, but there are certain structural divisions among them. Some represent human beings, others animals. An animal may be represented by a dancer wearing a face mask in the likeness of that animal or by an elaborate zoomorphic structure made of wickerwork, knotted maize leaves, and pieces of cloth, carried by several men hidden inside. These zoomorphic structures perform at night or at

Illus. 9. Eland structure of the *nyau*, Chipeta version, 1960s. Photograph by Montfort Press, Limbe, Malawi.

early dawn, and they are surrounded by more stringent restrictions than the characters appearing in the daytime.[68] Zoomorphic structures are normally burned after the performance, but those requiring a great deal of labor are stored in hidden caves for future occasions. *Nyau* masks and structures are considered sacred despite the rather comic or frivolous impression that some of them make. They are manufactured and stored in places which are sealed off from the intrusion of noninitiates by means of flags and other warning signals. Trespassers are made to pay heavy fines and are forcibly initiated.

Of the anthropomorphic masks in common use, some are said to represent ancestral figures, but there are also masks in the likeness of a British district commissioner, the movie actor Charlie Chaplin, and a European lady. Even structures in the shape of motorcars, motorcycles, and lake steamers have made their appearance.[69] These new masks and structures form a running commentary on developments in the region. To appreciate this, we need only look at the district commissioner and Charlie Chaplin, whose performances are hilarious caricatures of members of the colonial administration and the American Peace Corps respectively. On the other hand, many of the masks still in use nowadays are copies of older models. It is conceivable that some of them have a history of several centuries and that they depict personalities who, much like the colonial district commis-

Illus. 10. Eland structure of the *nyau*, Mang'anja version, 1967. Photograph by C. Zonneveld.

Illus. 11. *Nyau* motorcar structure, 1960s. From Makumbi 1964:60.

sioners and postcolonial Peace Corps workers, played a role in the history of the local communities.[70]

The *nyau* are in every respect men's societies. The carving of the masks, the manufacturing of the zoomorphic structures, as well as the dancing and the drumming are the work of the men. Women fulfill a supporting role, by brewing beer and cooking food for the dancers and drummers and by helping with the singing and clapping when a performance is on. Membership was traditionally obligatory, and initiation into the *nyau* constituted a young man's initiation into adulthood. Initiation into the *nyau* involves an elaborate procedure, part of which consists in the learning of a secret vocabulary and a set of passwords by which members communicate with each other without danger of being understood by outsiders.[71] Nowadays, particularly under mission influence, a large proportion of the population consists of noninitiates, and in some heavily Islamized areas the societies have disappeared altogether. Despite this, the *nyau* are still a vigorous institution: more than a hundred branches exist in the Lower Shire Valley alone, with an estimated membership of several thousand.[72]

Gule wamkulu (the great dance) is also called *pemphero lalikulu* (the great prayer), and the *nyau* societies are often likened by their members to the Christian churches or Islamic congregations. Yet on the surface, there is little that can be readily identified as religious.[73] If prayers and libations are made, they take place outside the *nyau* context, and neither the *nyau* instructions nor their songs seem to have religious content. A

Illus. 12. *Nyau* character, Chileka, Mang'anja version, Chikwawa, 1967. Photograph by C. Zonneveld.

most helpful insight concerning the religious meaning of the *nyau*, however, was suggested by the French traveler Edouard Foà, who in 1894 witnessed a Chipeta performance at Chief Chapananga's headquarters in the Chikwawa District. In Foà's view, *nyau* performances dramatize a temporary reconciliation between spirits, men, and animals, followed again by their separation.[74] Although that is by no means all there is to be said about the religious meaning of the *nyau*, it is an important insight, because it establishes a link with the institution of the sacred forests and with the Kaphirintiwa myth, which follows a similar scenario.

In the sacred forests, such as Mbona's, which will be described in the next chapter, men, animals, and spirits are said to live together without harming each other, there being no hunting or burning allowed. In that way they dramatize the condition as it was before man invented fire. *Nyau* does the same, when masks representing spirits and animals move from the forest to the village to associate with men. There, all three categories are united around the vessels of beer — an essential feature of a *nyau* performance — as they were once united around the waters with which they descended from the sky. But reconciliation in this case is only temporary, because when the performance is over, the zoomorphic structures are burned. By this act man repeats what happened at the time of the great cataclysm. The *nyau* performance may thus be seen as a mystery play, which relates the story of the beginnings of the world and which thereby symbolizes the movement of the seasons, with the intention of ushering in the rains. It is not without reason that the founding myths emphasize that the *nyau* originated during a famine, for the way to counteract a famine is to hunt and kill animals or to cause rain to fall. Both elements are symbolically represented in the *nyau* liturgy.[75]

Several authors regard the *nyau* societies as a social institution providing men living in a matrilineal and uxorilocal environment with a possibility of reacting against pressures exercised by their in-laws and the local lineages.[76] The *nyau* are able to exercise influence indirectly through their membership in the village councils. More directly, however, they may express their dislike and discontent during their performances, when they stand in principle above the law, for *nyau* members maintain that chiefs and headmen have no right to adjudge cases in connection with their societies.[77] In the Chikwawa District it is averred that this jural immunity was established by a Kololo chief, a *nyau* member himself, who told a complainant, "You cannot arrest and punish a wild animal (*chirombo*) which hurt you, because what it did was purely accidental (*ngozi*). There is no case (*mlandu*) because there is no accused (*mwini wache*)."[78] In view of what has been said so far, it is not difficult to understand that the *nyau* carry a considerable social and political load, which has made them important custodians of traditional culture and vehicles of opposition in situations of conquest.

THE COMING OF THE MARAVI

It is commonly accepted that the name Maravi (or its modern equivalent, Malawi) denotes "fire flames." As we have seen, the Phiri immigrants are said to have been called thus because they introduced the use of fire, or because they set the countryside afire at the time of their arrival.[79] Claims on the part of a particular group of people that they introduced the use of fire are common ways of asserting that they were the bringers of civilization.[80] That very idea is implied in a tradition from the shores of Lake Malawi according to which the Maravi offered the autochthons fried fish to eat, something they were not used to, as they were still in the habit of eating their food raw.[81]

Fire also functioned as a symbol of royal power and authority. Thus when a chief died all fires had to be doused. Undi, one of the three of four most important Maravi kings, is said to have lived in a hive-shaped structure, where he kept a perpetual fire which he fed day and night with pieces of mat cut by himself. These mats were the ones on which girls had been anointed at the conclusion of their pubertal ceremonies and which were clearly fertility symbols.[82] In myth and ritual, lighting a fire often also marks the end of a state of liminality and vulnerability, as, for instance, when the temporary shelters of initiates and huts of deceased persons are burned at the ends of the puberty rites and the mourning periods.[83] The fire symbolism thus conveys the idea that the Phiri ushered in a new order, which was both politically and culturally superior to the old order. One of the recurrent themes in the oral traditions of the Maravi peoples is that their ancestors came from Uluwa, a place which is commonly identified with the Luba area in the Shaba (Katanga) province of Zaire.[84] This may not be entirely without foundation, as there is archaeological evidence that the Luba area knew centralized states from the twelfth century.[85]

It is not yet possible to state with any degree of accuracy when the Maravi states came into being, since that process left no distinctive archaeological record. There can be no doubt, though, that by the second half of the sixteenth century Maravi states had come into existence on the lakeshore, in eastern Zambia and the Shire Valley.[86] Assuming that it took time for the emergent political culture of the Maravi to make its influence felt over a large area, it does not seem extravagant to postulate the beginnings of these states somewhere in the fifteenth century. The Maravi culture's predecessor, the Banda/Chipeta culture, may have developed from the late eleventh century, coinciding with the Luangwa pottery tradition of the archaeological record.[87] There is general consensus that the oldest Maravi state system was the one associated with the Karonga (or Kalonga) title on the southeastern shore of Lake Malawi. In the course of time this was followed by Undi's, straddling the border between northwestern Mozambique and eastern Zambia; Kaphwiti's, in the western part of the Shire highlands; and Lundu's, in the Shire Valley.[88]

The political history of the valley between the first half of the sixteenth century and the middle of the nineteenth shows six distinct phases. The first was an early states phase, associated in oral traditions with the name Kaphwiti, as illustrated by Text II/A. We may assume that these early states shared the valley with acephalous Chipeta communities, with which they exchanged goods and services, including ritual services. The second phase was characterized by the rise of the Lundu kingdom, which remained dominant from the closing decades of the sixteenth century to 1622. Thereafter the valley became for three or four decades part of the Muzura kingdom, which in its turn was absorbed by the Kalonga kingdom in the second half of the 1600s.[89] In the eighteenth century the valley became part of the Undi kingdom, a situation which may have lasted until 1800.[90] Thereafter a process of fragmentation set in, which by the time of Livingstone's arrival had resulted in a sizable number of smaller states, some of which were still governed by traditional chiefs, while others were ruled by enterprising commoners.[91]

THE MARAVI STATE SYSTEM

H. W. Langworthy notes that the judicial services provided by the new rulers were one of the more important reasons for the establishment of kingdoms in areas where people were already living. Before the coming of a state organization, there was no effective institution for the settling of disputes between lineages and villages short of warfare, as we have seen in Gamitto's description of the Chipeta communities. Text III/A makes this point quite forcefully when it describes the acephalous community into which Mbona was supposedly born as riven by conflict and as in dire need of a chiefly arbitrator.[92] The importance of the chief or king as a judge and arbitrator is indirectly emphasized also by the period of lawlessness which customarily followed upon a chief's death. During that period people might rob and steal "because there was nobody to take them to court as there was no chief."[93] That dispensing justice may have been not only an important but also a time-consuming task is suggested by a passage about a Maravi king (probably Kalonga) by a mid-seventeenth century Jesuit missionary: "That King continuously receives his people in audience and adjudges civil and criminal cases with incredible brevity. Even when he is ill he is still expected to judge cases. If he has been absent for two or three days, they go to his successor."[94]

Another factor which according to Langworthy contributed to the establishment and expansion of the Chewa kingdoms was the ability of the king to distribute gifts of cloth and beads to headmen who previously had little opportunity to benefit from external trade.[95] The continuing pattern of distribution by the king to chiefs and tributary kings of items collected in tribute as well as imported trade goods helped to ensure loyalty and obedience. In addition, this process of redistribution made the subordinate rulers to a certain extent economically dependent on the king. The king apparently also kept large storehouses of grain which could be drawn upon in times of famine.

Apart from exceptional cases such as Lundu's in the 1590s and Muzura's in the 1620s, the military power of the Maravi rulers seems to have been relatively unimportant.[96] What Pedro Barreto de Rezende observed in the early seventeenth century could still be confirmed two centuries later by A. C. P. Gamitto: the Maravi polities had no standing army and no formal recruitment system. If and when armed men were needed, a chiefdom's war drum would be sounded to call them up, and in case of a more general alarm, the surrounding chiefdoms would do the same. There was no need for lengthy preparations, as Barreto de Rezende explained:

> It is very extraordinary what a little each of these Kaffir soldiers carries with him, and more is not necessary, for his clothing is nothing, and when he wears a great deal it is never more than a piece of cloth which he girds around him, or a strip of some animal's skin, which covers no more. Each one carries his own arms, which are bows, arrows and assagais, which he never lays aside. Some carry shields, with which they often make a barrier when they defend a camp to prevent arrows and assagais from passing. Their food is anything they kill, from the smallest animal to the largest.[97]

The bow and arrow were the principal offensive weapons. The arrows were poisoned, and wounds caused by them were lethal in two hours. Spears were used only to finish off the wounded, and the axe and knife only to cut heads off the dead bodies.[98] The strength of these ad hoc armies consisted in their numbers. There was little military planning. Barreto de Rezende pointed out in 1635 what he considered to be the major shortcomings of African warfare in Zambesia:

> First: they neither storm nor make trenches, and when they find that they are being killed and cannot see by whom, they abandon the attack. Secondly: They are a people who will not endure the want of anything, but go in search of

the remedy wherever it may be and whatever they abandon by so doing. Thirdly: they will not persevere in a siege or war unless they are victorious at once, but, rather, no one can restrain them from dispersing and going in search of a living. And even if they are victorious in battle, it needs much to induce them to fight another, for they say they have finished the war for which they came, and if in the meanwhile the time for their harvests arrives, they care for nothing but to go and attend to them.[99]

We shall see in the chapter on the Zimba wars that this picture is not entirely correct. Occasionally local armies have made use of trenches and fortifications and have followed a well-planned strategy. This was the case especially when such armies had to confront a combined African/Portuguese force. On the other hand, Barreto de Rezende's and Gamitto's observations may have held good for small-scale warfare, which appears to have been endemic within or between chiefdoms. The eastern Maravi, with whom Gamitto was familiar, were continually engaged in small civil wars, and Barreto de Rezende's description evokes a similar situation for the seventeenth century. All this suggests that small-scale warfare was a structural device by which the internal political balance was constantly corrected and maintained.

Langworthy is of the opinion that one of the chief obstacles to the centralizing process was the succession system.[100] Inheritance of traditional positions was matrilineal. The selection process was basically a local affair which concerned members of the matrilineage, councillors, and subordinate headmen. The fact that a king did not appoint his subordinate rulers meant that it was more difficult to control them, to maintain their loyalty, and to ensure the collection of tribute. Apart from the succession system, however, there were two further agencies which militated against the centralizing process: the *nyau* and the territorial shrines. As the *nyau* have already been discussed, we will here confine ourselves to a brief examination of the tensions between state and territorial cult in the Maravi polities.

The Maravi religious organization was in several important respects different from that of the Banda/Chipeta. The cultic places of the Maravi were the royal graves, and the main religious function was exercised by a member of the local chiefly lineage who acted as a medium and rain caller.[101] Deceased chiefs were (and are) thought to manifest themselves in the form of a lion and to possess their mediums in that form. Spirit wives did not feature in their cults, nor did python manifestations or python rituals, and shrine complexes consequently contain no sacred pools. The unifying factor in their religious organization was not the veneration of an ahistorical zoomorphic spirit, but the veneration of a hierarchy of historical personages in the form of deceased rulers and other notable members of the ruling lineages. This spiritual hierarchy culminated in the apical

Illus. 13. Lawrence Makewana, chief ritualist of the Msinja shrine, with badge of office, Lilongwe District, 1969

Illus. 14. Nyangu's shrine, Chapananga chiefdom, Chikwawa, 1967. Photograph by C. Zonneveld.

ancestress Nyangu and was reduplicated in the ranking of living chiefs
and mediums.

There can be no doubt that the Maravi rulers saw the existing territorial shrines as a hindrance to their ambitions, and those who controlled
the shrines viewed the state cults as a threat to their position: the lion
and the python were pitted against each other.[102] Taking comparative eth-
nography for our guide, we may notice that several ways were open to
the Maravi: they could have destroyed the existing cult organization, they
could have accepted it as it was, they might have adapted it to some degree, or they could have set up a rival system. Destruction of the old system or the continued maintenance of a rival system seems to have been
problematic in view of the political situation, which made Maravi power
largely dependent on their capability of securing the support of the Banda/
Chipeta population. Accepting the existing system unaltered might have
placed the Maravi in a situation of undesirable dependency. Hence, the
only workable solution may have been some adaptation of the autochthonous religion in combination with their own cult. This would actually
happen in time, although with uneven success. A simplified but essentially
correct picture of the later situation would be that of the three principal
Maravi dynasties, the Kalongas were perhaps the least successful in ob-
taining direct and complete control.[103] The Lundus are considered to have
been the most successful, whereas the Undis should be assigned a position in between these two.[104] The main issue in the adaptation process
was the reallocation of prophetic and secular functions at the great rain
shrines. The varying results were due partly to the political capabilities
of the reformers and partly to the type of opposition they had to face.
It seems clear from traditions collected in several parts of Maravi country that the Mbewe clan put up a most vigorous resistance, which is understandable in view of their central role in the cult system. On several
occasions the Maravi resorted to the use of arms to bring about the de-
sired innovations. At a very early stage one of the Kalongas sent war
parties up to Kaphirintiwa, but these were successfully repulsed by the
Mbewe.[105]

The next stage may have been a Maravi attempt to set up a rival system. This is suggested by a body of tradition which is found among both
the northern and southern Maravi and which in our case is represented
by the biographies in the Mbona II and III traditions. In Texts II/A and
II/B the rulers of the early states try to establish their own rain-calling
agencies. In Text III/B Lundu himself attempts this. The tenor of that text
is that Lundu, unlike the other Maravi rulers, has for a while been successful in replacing the Mbona cult and that even after its restoration he
retained a great deal of authority over it by becoming the official wife-

giver, and thus "father-in-law" to the godhead. There is another significant difference with the other Maravi states: there were no *nyau* groups in the Lundu kindgom. Together, this suggests that there was a period of repression in which these typical pre-Maravi institutions were destroyed. That repression and its consequences form the subject of this book.

CHAPTER 2

The Ritual Cycle of the Mbona Cult

THE SACRED GROUNDS

KHULUBVI THICKET, which contains Mbona's shrine, is situated about four kilometers south of Nsanje township on a narrow strip of land between the district's main road and the railway line that links Malawi with the port of Beira in Mozambique. Directly to the west rise the Matundu Hills, dominated by Malawi Hill. To the east, between the shrine and the Shire River, lies the Dinde Marsh. The description of the shrine grounds which follows is based on observations made on October 12, 1966, the only occasion on which I was given the opportunity to inspect the premises in detail. The account is interspersed with fragments from an interview on features of the shrine and the sacred pool conducted two years earlier with two of the shrine guardians.[1]

Khulubvi consists of the sanctuary proper, an open space where meetings are held, and a settlement of seven modest huts.[2] The entire area comprises some four hectares in which it is forbidden to cut firewood, plant crops, or graze cattle. The shrine complex lies on an east-west axis, the poles of which are formed by Malawi Hill in the west and Ndione Pool in the east. In Mang'anja thought, the west is associated with maleness and the east with femaleness, for "it is from the east that the good rains come."

The sanctuary proper is a clearing in the shape of an ellipse, the western side of which is occupied by Mbona's hut, while on the eastern side we find the hut of the spirit wife, called Salima, and adjacent to it the hut of her maidservant. These two huts are separated from Mbona's by a distance of about sixty meters. The grounds are bordered all around by thick forest growth, with the exception of the part nearest the huts of the guard-

49

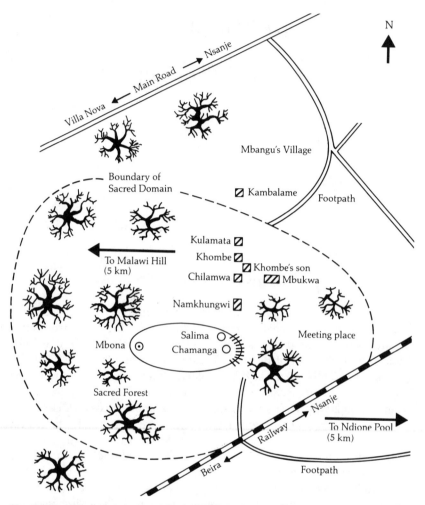

Map 2. The Mbona shrine and its immediate surroundings

ians. That section is screened off by a reed fence with an opening in the middle that serves as the official entrance.

The most conspicuous trees in and around Khulubvi thicket are the tall *mnjale* (*Sterculia appendiculata*), with their smooth whitish bark, which are visible from afar, and the wild fig trees with their contrasting dark green foliage. No special importance was attached to these species by my guides, but they figure prominently in rain songs and rain rituals.[3]

A stone's throw to the east of the entrance is an open space where the congregation assembles before and after the rituals. The huts which border the meeting ground belong to the woman Namkhungwi, keeper of Salima's hut; Chilamwa, the usher; Khombe, the cleaner; Mbukwa, headman and keeper of the sacred drum Kamango; and Kulamata, Salima's cook.

Mbona's hut is a circular structure some three meters in diameter, built on a clay platform about thirty centimeters high. It is made of poles implanted in the earth, with the intervals between the poles filled with reeds. The poles are cut on Malawi Hill.[4] It is said that Mbona's head lies buried under the floor of this hut and that after its burial a tall termite hill grew up above it where the center pole now stands.[5]

The shrine must always be made of perishable materials, and its inside is never cleaned or swept. As it begins to rot and collapse from the actions of termites and natural decay, the roof and sides fall in, and it has to be rebuilt. This is not as unproblematic as it sounds, since rebuilding requires the consent of a cult establishment riven by conflict. The two guardians with whom I had my first interview about the cult related a story about European sympathizers who apparently offered to build a permanent shrine, which would do away with the cumbersome practice of having to rebuild it every so often: "When the British came to this country, they said, 'Wouldn't it be wiser to build a brick house for Mbona, since the one that you have now collapses every two or three years, causing you a lot of trouble? Let us burn bricks for you people to free you from that burden!' We refused, however, saying, 'Putting up a brick house? No, we cannot accept that, for Mbona's spirit would refuse our offerings and turn away from us. Doing what you propose would mean accepting foreign customs. That is not what he commanded us to do, and it would be a mistake!'"[6] This story reveals an abhorrence of European borrowings, which is a recurrent theme in the cult. The rules that no repairs be carried out and that a type of wood be used which is an easy prey for termites, however, create the conditions also for Mbona's displeasure and the subsequent rites of reconciliation. The refusal to use permanent materials seems therefore based on more than just a conservative or antiwhite attitude.[7]

The roof of Mbona's hut is a structure of bamboo sticks and reeds. The frame is made on the ground and, when finished, is lifted onto the circular wall and thatched with grass. The reeds come from the nearby village of Mbenje, where they may apparently be cut without anybody's permission. The roof is supported by a single central pole. Formerly the roof's frame used to be built upon the head of Tengani, the senior Mang'anja chief, whose headquarters lies about twenty-three kilometers north of the shrine. It was explained to me that two thick rings (*nkhasa*) of tightly woven grass were placed on the head of the chief, who would be standing in an upright position. The sharpened ends of the bamboo rafters were stuck into those rings, and then the skeleton of the roof was made. The grass thatch followed only when the roof had been lifted onto the circular wall of the new hut.[8]

The doors of the three huts are all made of reeds and bamboo, and they are fastened with string and not with traditional wooden doorstoppers. A tradition says that in the past the doorstopper was an elephant's tusk, which disappeared at some stage. W. H. J. Rangeley suggests that this may have happened when the shrine was razed by the notorious slave raider Paul Mariano II (Matekenya), who was active in the 1860s.[9] When I questioned the officials about this, they strongly denied it, being reluctant to admit or accept that the shrine was ever destroyed by an invader. Instead, they offered the unlikely explanation that the ivory was eaten by white ants.

Inside Mbona's hut, to the right of the center pole, is Mbona's "bed," a structure about one meter high covered with black cloth. It consists of four forked poles implanted in the floor. These hold two sticks, about sixty centimeters long, across which a number of shorter sticks are laid, the whole resembling a drying rack.[10] The cloth is renewed whenever the shrine is rebuilt, and fresh pieces are laid on top of the old ones whenever an offering is made by a devotee. It is said that in deference to Mbona the inhabitants of Khulubvi village do not use beds or other nontraditional furniture.[11]

Mbona's hut contains two spears, both rusted to decay and their crudely made shafts badly damaged by ants. At the time of my visit they were lying on the earthen floor at the back of the hut.[12] I was also shown three cups. One, made of white china and with its ear missing, was said to be Salima's. Another, somewhat larger and of black wood, made by one of the wood turners in the district, belonged to no one in particular. The third one, of the same material and manufactured in the same way as the second, had the shape of an eggcup and stood on a matching saucer. I was told that this was Mbona's, although it was the smallest. The cups are used to make libations of *nipa*, a strong local liquor.[13]

Salima's hut and that of her maidservant are the same shape as Mbona's, but they are smaller. Salima's is also built on a platform lower than Mbona's and that of her maid is level with the surrounding area. In contrast with Mbona's, these two huts may be repaired whenever the need arises. in Salima's hut I saw two earthen vessels of the sort used to keep drinking water. In one of them was kept a piece of cloth, which belonged to Salima and which she had to wear on ceremonial occasions. The guardians said that it was stored thus to keep it from being eaten by termites. There is a tradition which says that in the beginning Mbona locked up all misfortunes with the injunction that no one was ever to lift their covers. In those days, so the story goes, the post of Salima was filled not by a mature or elderly woman as in more recent times, but by a young girl. One of these, a curious person, lifted the lids, and the country came to be plagued by droughts and the like. After that incident it was decided that the post should be filled by mature women only. Outside Salima's hut, half a dozen large pots are kept in readiness for the annual rain ceremony, when they are filled with beer, which plays a major role on that occasion.

A little to the left of the entrance of the sanctuary is a meeting place, half of it hedged in by trees. Here the participants assemble to make themselves ready before the rituals. The drum Kamango, which is used to call the worshipers together at daybreak, is kept in Mbukwa's hut. It is made of *mtondo* wood (*Cordyla africana*), the usual material for larger drums, and its tympanum is made of cowhide. Although the drum I saw did not look particularly old, the guardians nevertheless maintained that this was the very drum which Mbona had brought with him from Kaphirintiwa and to which he used to dance.[14]

THE SACRED POOL

The Ndione Pool lies about an hour's walk east of Khulubvi. A narrow footpath leads to it through five kilometers of *dimba* gardens full of fine maize patches and lush dark green *mbatata* (sweet potato) vines. When I went there in October 1966, at the height of the dry season, these *dimba* gardens formed a marked contrast with the barren landscape west of the shrine.

Ndione is a narrow forest patch on the edge of the Dinde Marsh, visible from afar by its tall trees. The pool forms part of a series of small lakes which are separated from the Shire River by a bank ranging from .8 to 3.2 kilometers in width and intersected by natural ditches, which drain the marsh into the Shire when the river falls. This is the place where according to all traditions Mbona was killed and where his truncated body was buried in a lake formed by his own blood. As mentioned before, my visit was made in the middle of the dry season, when the water level was at its lowest and the pool was nearly choked with vegetation. There was nothing unusual about the place, apart from four huge monitor lizards, which sat in one of the trees and which, upon seeing our party, plunged one by one into the pool with a crashing sound.[15] The place did not seem to inspire extraordinary respect. My guides chattered freely, did not clap their hands — which would have been the normal sign of respect upon approaching a holy place — and freely cut bamboo poles to take home. They pointed out a number of trees which they said were normally found only in the hills and on higher ground, but which had been planted there by Mbona in person.[16]

I was also told that until recently the trees and plants at Ndione had great medicinal value. According to my informants, this had something to do with the fact that the waters of the pool in those days were still red. But the color of the pool changed to normal, and the surrounding flora consequently lost its curative powers in 1936, when the cult began to decline under the influence of Chief Molin Tengani, who in that year acceded to the chieftaincy.[17] There is some substance in this story, though, since the reddish color of the pool is caused by iron oxide, which becomes more concentrated and its color more pronounced when the water level recedes. Conversely, the pool loses much of its reddishness when the water level rises. This is precisely what happened in the late 1930s, around the time of Tengani's enthronement, when the level of the Shire rose dramatically, permanently inundating a large part of the Dinde area.

There are countless stories about the Ndione Pool containing quantities of large and tasty fish, which people are not allowed to catch except at times of famine. Even then they are allowed only one or two. Those disregarding this injunction would, instead of fish, hook a human head, a dead goat, or, worse, a couple of cudgels with which they were clobbered senseless.[18] Ndione was also a place for human sacrifices:

> In the olden days we used to sacrifice a person, whom we captured in secret, taking him to the Ndione Pool, where Mbona's body lies buried. When the victim's blood mixed with the waters of the pool, we presented him to Mbona, pretending it was no more than a goat, and we would say, "Mbona, we have killed a goat for you today. Maybe you had already been grumbling to yourself, 'What of me? Must I live here uncared for?' If so, you can now say that you were given a real sacrifice." This done, we left the body where it was. Such a person had to be of our own kind, for we were not allowed to kill a stranger as a sacrifice to Mbona. Since the coming of the Europeans, however, we no longer kill human beings, but we take a goat instead. We cannot give up making sacrifices, as this would mean neglecting our father, who in his turn would withdraw from us.[19]

Similar stories are told about Khulubvi. There, as in other sacred forests, it is not permitted to kill animals because they are said to be Mbona's children. Let us once again listen to the guardians Chapirira and Kumbiwanyati describing the shrine grounds to me two years before I set foot there myself:

> If you are to visit Khulubvi, where we live, and enter the thicket, you will see a great many baboons and monkeys, the latter so tame that they will sit on your shoulders. Francolins, too, come up to you without a trace of fear, but you on your part have to leave them in peace, and you are not allowed to hurt or kill them. You will also see different kinds of snakes, such as puff-

adders, pythons, and cobras. They look quite frightening, when they move in your direction — enough to make you shiver all over — but they are not dangerous. The baboons and monkeys even come to our huts, when the women put their freshly pounded maize on mats to dry. We allow them to eat their fill without chasing them away, for they are Mbona's children. To a stranger all this looks rather frightening, but the animals in Mbona's thicket are quite harmless.[20]

The only animals I observed there myself were vervet monkeys (*pusi*, pl. *apusi; Cercopithecus aethiops*), which were roaming between the huts of Mbona's village and which upon my arrival quickly took to the trees. Whenever Mbona wishes to send a message to a chief or some other important person, the monkeys function as messengers.[21] They go with him wherever he goes, and when they temporarily disappear from the sacred thicket, which seems to happen from time to time, it is believed that Mbona has gone elsewhere because he is angry.

THE GEOGRAPHY OF THE CULT'S REGION

The region in which the Mbona cult is active may be represented as consisting of a core area surrounded by three concentric circles (map 3). The core, some four hectares in area, comprises the sacred grove and the adjacent village of the guardians (map 2). These grounds are considered to be outside the jurisdiction of any secular authority and thus not subject to rules and regulations concerning land use and taxes.[22]

The circle directly surrounding the core area is about thirty-two square kilometers in area and is demarcated by topographical features associated with Mbona's martyrdom. Prominent among these are Malawi Hill on the western side, where he was arrested; the Ndione Pool on the eastern side, where he was killed and decapitated; the Nyamadzere Stream on the northern side, along which he made his ascent into the hills; and the Nyachipere Stream on the southern side, along which he made his descent. There are many indications that in precolonial days this area too enjoyed extraterritoriality. Within this territory reside Ngabu and Malemia, the two principals of the cult, as well as Mbona's medium and a number of other officials, among them Senior Headman Mbango, whose house stands guard over the entrance to the shrine grounds. All of these persons hold their positions by virtue of their residence within this area.[23] Even the medium, whose position, unlike that of the others, is not hereditary and not related to residence in a specific village, must hail from within

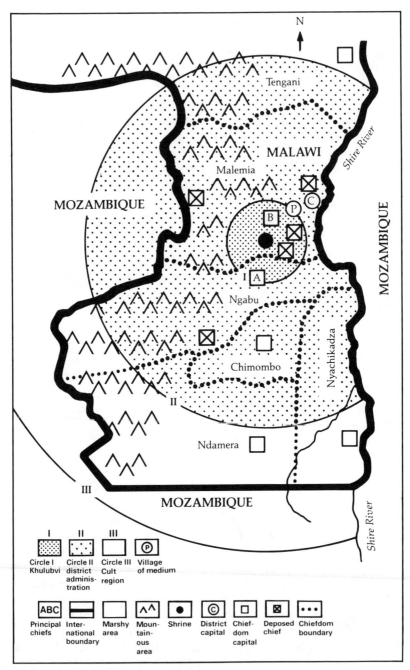

Map 3. The shrine and surrounding chiefdoms
Source: Adapted from Werbner 1977.

Illus. 15. Malawi Hill, Nsanje District, 1965

this territory. This circle is activated annually at the time of the communal rain ceremony.

The second circle corresponds with the Nsanje District. This is where the various cult officers who hold chiefships or headmanships confront the modern state system. Although this second circle in its present form is a result of relatively recent developments, it existed in a different form well before the creation of the modern district.[24] The central person here is Tengani, and this circle is activated when the shrine has to be rebuilt, an event which takes place every three to five years on average.

The third circle encompasses the entire area over which the Mbona organization is influential. Until recently this included not only the Nsanje District but also adjacent areas in Malawi and Mozambique, while further back in history it included areas even farther afield, such as the Ntcheu District in the Central Region of Malawi, the Zambezi estuary, and Maganja da Costa on the east coast.[25] The central person in this circle is Lundu, and it is activated in particular when a new spirit wife has to be provided, an event which no longer takes place but which may have occurred about once in a generation, usually on the occasion of a major drought. Immigrants are not supposed to hold major hereditary positions in the cult. The only posts open to them, apart from the mediumship, which is non-hereditary, are of secondary importance.

OCCASIONAL RITUALS AT THE SHRINE

Among the rituals performed at the Mbona shrine, a distinction is made between occasional rituals and rituals which form part of the cult cycle proper. Occasional rituals are performed on behalf of villages suffering from crop-ravaging birds or some other localized misfortune, and on behalf of chiefdoms plagued by a more general form of misfortune such as drought. On such occasions the chief send his representatives to the shrine, but he does not go there in person. He waits until they return and, together with them, performs the final rites at his own shrine. The following is an account by an elderly headman whose family holds a hereditary office in the cult organization. His account is in the past tense, since due to a variety of reasons, political and otherwise, this type of communication between distant chiefdoms and the shrine has virtually become a thing of the past.

> When people from outlying areas came to worship, they brought with them black cloth or a black goat as an offering to Mbona. Upon their arrival, chiefs and headmen from the neighborhood would join them and take them to Mbona's and Salima's huts, while softly clapping hands. After they had prayed for rain the leader of the visiting party was handed a quantity of white flour in a gourd. He and his companions were then told to take special care of the gourd when they had to spend the night en route and not to wash their hands when they were offered food. Upon returning to their village, they were to hand the gourd to the chief or headman. After having made a libation of the flour brought to him the latter would fill it [i.e., the gourd] with water and let those who had been to Khulubvi wash their hands. No sooner had they done this than copious rains would fall on just that village or chiefdom. Because of this the custom spread, and people from many areas came to pray for rain.[26]

The chief ritualist, Ngabu, mentions some of the areas worshipers used to come from:

> Supplicants used to come to Khulubvi from Marromeu, Phodzoland, and Bororo. They were sent by the chiefs of those parts, most of whom were non-Mang'anja. They would first see Ngabu, who would then send for Tsangalambe [Malemia's delegate], who in his turn would inform the shrine guardians as well as chiefs Malemia, Chiphwembwe, and Chapirira. On that appointed day, all would assemble in the shrine's meeting ground, where the visitors would explain the purpose of their visit, which might be a drought or some other misfortune back home. Following this, they would produce their gifts, which always included black cloth. These would be taken to Salima's place. Ngabu then made an offering of flour inside Mbona's hut. Next day he would take some of that flour and put it in a gourd, which was given to the supplicants with the injunction that, while en route, they were not to wash their hands before or

Illus. 16. The guardians of the Mbona shrine, 1965. Photograph by C. Zonneveld.

after meals. At the conclusion of the journey the gourd was handed over to their chief, who would mix the flour with other ingredients to make an offering at the shrine of his own ancestors, calling upon them as well as Mbona.[27]

The handing over of the gourd and a quantity of blessed flour as well as the taboo on washing one's hands before and after meals were more or less universal customs. It should be understood, though, that the taboo on washing involved the whole of the body, as in the case of mourners. It was also mentioned that pilgrims on their way to the shrine might help themselves to green maize, cucumbers, and watermelons from gardens by the roadside without asking the owners' permission and without the latter taking offense: "On big occasions we always have worshipers coming in from distant places such as Tengani's, where Mbona lived for a while during his lifetime. While traveling, these people may help themselves to watermelons and cucumbers or anything else growing in gardens by the roadside. They may take these things, cut them up, eat them, or even throw them away in the presence of the owner without the latter being allowed to interfere, for on such occasions this is not considered an offense."[28]

The missionary-anthropologist Paul Schebesta, who lived at Sena from 1912 to 1917, mentions that people from the south bank traveled to the shrine and more particularly to Mbona's wife, Salima, "to have their fortunes told."[29] Although this sounds as though people consulted Salima on private matters, it is doubtful whether this ever was the case. Among the Maravi peoples spirit wives and mediums attached to territorial shrines made predictions about the weather, the likelihood of drought and famine, or political affairs, but there is no evidence of private fortune-telling. It is therefore likely that the consultations mentioned by Schebesta formed part of the occasional rituals on behalf of villages and chiefdoms.

Worshipers from afar were expected to bring news from their parts of the world. On the eve of the ritual they met with the cult officials to state why they had come. Even the overseer of the Massingire *prazo* across the Shire, a person of considerable influence and importance, is said to have occasionally turned to the shrine for advice and ritual assistance:

> Whenever he was in trouble he came to us. We would ask him, "How is your land?" And he would say, "Well, here everything seems to be well, but that is not so in our case." That is how he always began. Although he had sent us news beforehand, he still expected us to ask him everything. Afterward, he would make us lavish gifts. Depending on what he could find, he would send us large pieces of cloth and bottles of wine. He would then say [to his deputies], "Go to our mother [Salima] and give her this. I want to help this neighbor of ours." [Upon arrival] his deputies would call out, "Strangers have come!" We would then reply, "Why have they come?" And they would say, "Our country is deeply in trouble!" But when the British came, that practice was stopped for good.[30]

From this and other pieces of evidence we may infer that at one time the shrine served as a center where information of political importance was received and pooled, somewhat like the Wirirani shrine of the High God Mwari in the Matopo Hills of Zimbabwe.[31]

THE COMMUNAL RAIN PRAYERS

The ritual cycle consists of three parts: the communal rain prayers, the rebuilding of the shrine, and the induction of a new spirit wife. The annual rain prayers are usually held in October–November, at the close of the dry season, but they may be repeated when the rains are late. Depending on the seriousness of the drought, the rituals shift from village shrines to chiefdom shrines, Christian churches, and regional shrines. Since communal rain prayers have for centuries been among the most important rituals of the Maravi peoples, we have at our disposal a fair number of descriptions of these rituals, although actual eyewitness accounts of communal rain prayers are relatively rare. The oldest known account, little more than a page, stems from the Universities' Mission to Central Africa (U.M.C.A.) missionary H. Rowley, who described a rain ceremony which he witnessed in December 1861 near Magomero in the Shire highlands.[32] In 1907 S. S. Rattray, who began his distinguished career in what

Illus. 17. The sacred grounds, 1965. Photograph by G. Hochstenbach.

Illus. 18. Worshipers at Mbona's shrine, 1967. Photograph by C. Zonneveld.

was then the Nyasaland Protectorate, published a brief description of a rain ceremony as related to him by an informant.[33] In the 1950s, J. P. Bruwer published an account of a rain ceremony among the Chewa of Chirenje in the Central Region of Malawi, and around the same time W. H. J. Rangeley published his fairly extensive articles on the Makewana cult and the Mbona cult, in which he gives some information on the rain prayers as well.[34] In the 1970s the Malawian author J. W. Ngwengwe published a brief chapter on rain rituals, which contains a collection of rain songs.[35] J. W. M. van Breugel's doctoral thesis also contains a small collection of rain songs alongside informants' accounts of rain prayers at the Bunda, Tsang'oma, and Chinteche shrines.[36] Finally, J. N. Amanze's doctoral thesis on the Bimbi cult of the Upper Shire Valley contains a detailed eyewitness account of a rain ceremony at that shrine.[37]

Prior to a rain ceremony held at the Mbona shrine on December 18, 1967, beer had been brewed, and the shrine grounds had been swept. It was said that the millet necessary for the libational beer had been contributed by the villages of the district "the way this was done in the past." Whether or not this was the case is difficult to know without making separate investigations. The Mbona officials like to create the impression that things are still being done according to some age-old pattern. Grain needed for the libational beer had to be collected from all villages, none excluded, and no family was supposed to contribute more than one cob of maize or one ear of millet. This was supposed not only to give every family a chance to take part in the ritual but also to demonstrate the unity of the entire cult region. Stole Chimbuto, an acknowledged oral historian in the Lower Shire Valley, relates:

> Whenever there were dangerous diseases or epidemics about and people went through a lot of suffering, that person at Mbona's shrine — the medium we just mentioned — became possessed and began to make utterances, saying, "I want everybody in the land to contribute some grain — no more than a head of millet or Guinea corn or some other food — and I want those gifts brought here." Gifts were collected at Michiru near Blantyre, Changata's in Thyolo, Ngabu's and Chapananga's in Chikwawa, and thence taken to Nsanje, where all the offerings came together. The medium would thereupon say, "Prepare an offering!" and the inhabitants would make an offering so that their sufferings might come to an end.
>
> Whenever the rains were late, it would no longer be a problem. They would act in the same way, saying, "We must make a libation." This they would do in their own villages. Orders were given to each village to build its own shrine in the form of a small hut. These [little shrines] may be compared with the village schools built by the Europeans. Every village would build its own hut as a place of worship, where the inhabitants would take their maize, or the beer they might have brewed, as an offering. Rain would already begin to fall when they were still performing the rain dance and singing their rain songs, and all would rejoice. If sometimes they were less fortunate and rain did not fall, they still kept to this custom, trusting that another time they would have better luck.[38]

Another piece of information unfailingly provided by informants is that those engaged in the brewing of the ceremonial beer and those participating in the rain ceremony have to abstain from sex, which is said to have the effect of making people "hot." This would work against the "coolness" of the ritual and make it ineffective. The same idea is emphasized by the facts that no one is allowed to wear red clothes and that the ritual is performed at daybreak.

On December 18, 1967, everybody had already assembled by 6:30 A.M. in front of the hut of Mbukwa, the headman of the shrine settlement. The men were all wearing loincloths, "to remind us that we are his slaves and that we must approach him with great reverence as our well-being depends on him."[39] The women were dressed in larger pieces of cloth which left their breasts uncovered. When all had assembled, Mbukwa told the women to carry the large jars of beer to the sanctuary. When they were loading the pots onto their heads, the drum Kamango was beaten by Chief Malemia. The participants then moved in procession to Mbona's hut. Chief

Ngabu and some assistants went inside to say prayers and make a libation. Their voices were so low that it was impossible for those outside to hear what was being said. To give an idea of what those prayers may have been, I reproduce here the text of a prayer volunteered by Ngabu's delegate Chapirira in the course of our 1964 interview: "Before the beer is poured we pray as follows: 'Please, great spirit of ours, look. We beseech you to look upon us! We are unhappy with what is happening to us these days. We want our crops to flourish, and we are asking you to make us prosper in our country the way our ancestors prospered in their days!' When the beer is poured out, we say, 'Lord, have mercy on us and bless us as we make this offering of beer to you!'"[40]

After the prayers, Ngabu and his assistants reappeared and washed their hands, the guardian Chilamwa pouring water. Following this, the shrine's messenger Kambalame ("Little Bird") posted himself in front of the shrine, followed by the other participants, the women at his right and the men at his left. Kambalame was the only person wearing a shirt and shoes. These were said to form part of his "uniform," as he was the "policeman" of the shrine. While the women sang, the entire group began to dance. This dance consisted of short shuffling movements backward, the dancers all the while facing the shrine. The impression given was one of people reluctant to move away from the shrine. After the dance, during which the congregation had moved to the eastern side of the enclosure, the presiding chiefs and other dignitaries handed some of the beer to the women. Having tasted it, they took one jar to the trees around the open space. At the foot of each tree they made an offering to deceased members of the Mang'anja dynasties. Starting from the eastern end, they moved to the western part of the enclosure, and they concluded that part of the ceremony at the foot of a tree between the huts of Mbona and Salima.

This done, the congregation went to the backyard of Salima's house, which was screened off by a reed fence. There, beer was offered to the chiefs, the headmen, and other functionaries. Following this, the participants left the sacred enclosure for the meeting ground outside, carrying the remainder of the beer. This was divided among those who had no ceremonial function. While this was going on, the old lady (*namkhungwi*) gave pounded malt (*ufa wa chimera*) to a group of small children. Next, the women started the rain dance (*mgwetsa*). The songs included "Kamtambo ndi aka ndi aka" (Little cloud here, little cloud there), which may be the most widespread rain song of the Maravi, and the hymn of the *mnjale* tree, which refers to the sacredness of the place and the sexual taboos to be respected by the participants.[41]

The ceremony followed the outline of the Maravi rain ceremonies reported from elsewhere. The one important difference was that after the libation in the shrine hut, the participants did not continue their prayers lying on their backs, which is a common feature elsewhere and which is not unknown at the Mbona shrine.[42] Rowley, who witnessed a rain ceremony near Magomero in 1861, reports that the chief officiant, who happened to be the sister of the village headman, after coming out of the shrine hut after the libation, sat on the ground and threw herself on her back. All the people followed her example, and while in this position, they clapped their hands and repeated their supplication for several minutes.[43] Amanze also reports having participated in that ritual at the time of his research in the 1980s.[44] The reason why this part of the standard ritual was not followed at the ceremony in December 1967 is not clear. The medium, who is not allowed to attend the ceremony himself but who had received reports about it, complained afterward that the cult officers had been greedy and disrespectful.[45]

THE REBUILDING OF THE SHRINE

Although the shrine is made of highly perishable materials, it is never to be repaired, but always fully rebuilt. This is not a simple matter, since it requires the permission and cooperation of the higher echelons of the cult hierarchy, who may not always be willing to grant a request of that nature without demanding that their own grievances be attended to first. Officers wanting to obstruct the rebuilding can always do so by insisting that the ritual be executed in full detail, something which is virtually impossible. Thus the rebuilding of the shrine becomes a political event in which those involved test each other's strength and try to improve their positions in the cult constellation. One of the consequences of this state of affairs is that negotiations for the rebuilding of the shrine can only be successfully initiated when there is considerable pressure on the part of the general public. In the next chapter we shall see how this builds up.

A central role in the ritual of rebuilding was played by Tengani. Two things are invariably mentioned about his person: first, that the roof of the shrine had to be built "upon his head" and, second, that any Tengani who had subjected himself to this ritual would die within a year or so after the first or second occasion.[46] It is said that some of the incumbents in the past took flight rather than participate. The following is an account of the rebuilding by the officials Chapirira and Kumbiwanyati. After explaining that they had been summoned by the medium to undertake the rebuilding of the shrine, they continued:

Back in our village, we set to work without delay. We dare not disregard Mbona's orders as this would mean getting ourselves into trouble. We therefore call a meeting next morning to which people come from the entire area, including the villages in the [Matundu] hills and the [Dinde] marsh. Everyone comes, no matter what there is to be discussed, whether it is repairs to Salima's hut, which has a badly leaking roof and may be on the point of collapsing, or whether it is the rebuilding of Mbona's own hut. After [the meeting] one of our number goes to see Chief Tengani, with the message "We as Mang'anja and as persons responsible for Mbona's worship have decided to appoint you, Tengani, to take charge of the work we have been ordered to do. Or have you not heard what has been going on?" Tengani then says that he has and, as soon as the necessary arrangements have been made, gives orders for the work to proceed. On the appointed day everybody comes, including of course Tengani. As soon as he arrives, work on the hut commences, starting with the circular roof, which is always made on the ground. As soon as the measurements have been taken, he positions himself in the middle and the entire roof is then built upon his head. In the meantime, others are busy putting up the circular wall on which the roof is to rest. One really has to work fast if the job is to be finished before sunset, but this is not too difficult with so many people around. Spurred on by the sound of the great drum, Kamango, they move busily to and fro. While we are building the hut, it is impossible to distinguish chief from commoner, for on that occasion we are all equals. All of us, including our little children, are Mbona's slaves. When the hut is finished and the place has been cleaned, we elders begin rolling about in the dust, first Ngabu, then Tengani, and finally the others. Meanwhile the great drum is beaten and all of us pray, "We have now built a hut for you. Have mercy on us and do not carry out your threats, for it can no longer be said that we disobeyed you! Do not reject us, your slaves, for we have given you the honor you deserve!" Afterward we disperse until the day of libation. This usually follows soon after the rebuilding of Mbona's hut and is to be regarded as its concluding part.[47]

A passage from Text IV complements the foregoing:

While going about one's task, one had to take off one's clothes and remain naked [apart from a small loincloth]. When the walls of the hut were finished, they began building the roof upon the head of Chief Tengani. Some say that every Tengani who had taken part would die soon after, which is also why some incumbents absconded to Mozambique when being bidden to the rebuilding.

After finishing the roof, they would spread a blue cloth over the grass thatching. But before lifting it onto the walls, they invited the rains by swaying it in the direction of the four points of the compass, beginning with the east in the direction of Ndione. The moment they had finished their work, peals of thunder would be heard, lightning would flash, and a storm would break accompanied by heavy downpours, so that on their way home people would be drenched to the bone.[48]

A number of informants also mention that at the end of the rebuilding ceremony a black goat is slaughtered on the reed door of Mbona's hut. I found clear traces of blood and stomach contents on the door when I was allowed to inspect the shrine in October 1966.

I have never witnessed the rebuilding of the shrine myself, and I cannot therefore say how much what happens nowadays accords with any of these descriptions. One point on which we have certainty is that from the mid-1930s onward the Tengani incumbents have refused to take part in the ritual. Molin Tengani, the first openly to refuse, invoked the fact that he was a Christian and for that reason could not participate. Stonkin Tengani, who succeeded Molin in the early 1960s, at first said that he would cooperate but later on revoked this because he said that the shrine officials neglected the cult.[49]

THE INDUCTION OF A NEW SPIRIT WIFE

Mbona's spirit wife is called Salima, a name which may be translated as "she does not hoe," referring to the fact that she was not supposed to engage in manual work.[50] According to one group of traditions, the first Salima was installed at Mbona's own request, for after the murder he seized a person, who became possessed and in that condition told the population that Mbona wanted a wife and that a hut should be built for her. The spirit wife had to be provided by Lundu, but when this was impossible the shrine officers could turn to Lundu's senior kinsman Mankhokwe. This they did, as evidenced by the only eyewitness report in existence, dated August 1862.[51] The person elected on that particular occasion was a woman who still had small children to look after. The usual accounts one hears, however, maintain that the spirit wife had to be an elderly person:

> When [after Mbona's death] the hut had been [built and] covered with dark blue cloth according to his own instructions, Mbona also ordered the elders to find him a wife. "Since I do not want to live alone like a man shunned by women, I want Lundu to provide me with a wife, the way he did when I was still among the living. You shall not take one of Lundu's slaves to be my wife, for I am not going to allow that. Nor shall you take a young maiden or a woman still capable of childbearing. Instead, bring an elderly person, who no longer lies with men, and who is born free besides."
>
> Upon their arrival at Mbewe from the "Kaphirintiwa of the south," they went to Lundu with the message, "Hail, Lundu, our father! Mbona's house at Khulubvi is finished, and he now wants a wife." They then went on to explain everything Mbona had said. Lundu thereupon fetched one of his sisters and said, "Take this one here and depart with her!"[52]

Lundu was thus regarded as Mbona's classificatory father-in-law, a position which in normal life requires avoidance behavior. This accords with the rule that Lundu has to avoid the shrine and that contacts between the shrine and the court are only made through intermediaries. A number of traditions state that although Lundu appointed the woman to be Mbona's wife, she and her family would not know about this until she was taken away by force. This, too, is borne out by the eyewitness report just quoted. Finally, all the accounts maintain that her appointment was for life. It is quite imaginable that this was so in principle, but it is equally possible that a person might be released or dismissed from her position before her death. Once again, here is an account by Chapirira and Kumbiwanyati:

> When Salima, his wife, is dead, we say, "Whom are we waiting for? Our leader is Lundu! Some woman must come from his country, because he is our great father." We then go to Ngabu: "Let us go and visit Lundu." Ngabu answers, "Indeed, let us go and see him." So, we go from there, dressed in loincloths: "We, we, we, we!" until we arrive at Lundu's: "We have come, as you see. Since the woman we had has died, we need a new one from the country from which Mbona himself came. We have come to you, our leader. All of us are Mang'anja, are we not? We would be pleased if somebody could be found here to take Salima's name. It should not be left to die; it should continue to live. Therefore give us another woman. We want a mother to live with us, a wife for our father, for Mbona."
>
> Now, when Lundu has given us a woman, we take her to our place. She will stay in her own hut. If Mbona's hut is on the far side, hers will be at the near side [from the entrance]. That is the position of both huts. Up until now we do it that way. Salima is still with us, and she never leaves. She is not married; she is not allowed a husband. If a man should seduce her, it would be terrible. We would decide to kill him on the spot, for that is a great mischief.[53]

After her election and capture, Salima was taken to the shrine, some ninety kilometers to the south, in a solemn procession. This was not done in 1862, for on that occasion there was war on every side, and there was thus no opportunity to organize a protracted ceremony of this kind. Instead, she was taken downstream by canoe, and her journey may then not have taken more than a day or two. Normally, however, her journey from the northern to the southern part of the valley, a journey from the court to the shrine, is said to have been an elaborate occasion, Rangeley describes:

> A large party would then set out for Mbewe-wa-Mitengo [Lundu's capital] via Ngabu Banda at Makande, beating the little kassa drums, large drums, blowing on whistles and trumpets, and led by Kambalame [the messenger] with the two spears [of Mbona]. They would wait at Mbewe-wa-Mitengo until a Salima was supplied to them, and they would then escort her to Nkhulubvi.

When she was settled in at Nkhulubvi, Matumbo [Lundu's servant] would then be sent from Mbewe-wa-Mitengo with many people, and carrying baskets of maize, to visit Salima, to ensure that she was properly installed, and to carry the usual wedding gifts.[54]

The following account is also from Lundu's area:

Mbona's wife made the journey on a litter screened off from public view. Whenever the bearers saw a tree that had fallen across the track, they had to go around it, for if they tried to jump over it, Mbona's wife might be exposed to view. Should such a thing happen, Mbona would take possession of someone at Khulubvi, saying, "Let that woman return to her home, for she has been exposed!"

Hence, whenever they came across a branch or even a stalk, they avoided it and went around it. At nightfall they looked for a place where the woman could be bedded down decently. On the day of her arrival, when she was approaching Khulubvi, Mbona, knowing that this would be the day, took possession of a person, who then exclaimed, "This is a fine woman indeed. I want her to live at Khulubvi!"

When she had arrived at Khulubvi, people paid her much respect, for anyone who failed to show respect to Mbona's wife would be in great trouble. Nor did Mbona allow people to speak evil of her. After they had come with her, a goat was killed to provide special relish for her; and when they took her to her hut, there was ululating and dancing. Women strewed handfuls of flour on the heads of their companions, and she was installed amid great rejoicing.[55]

At the shrine, Salima would only be visited by elderly women and small children. From time to time she was allowed to visit neighboring villages in the chiefdom of Malemia. According to the traditions, these were days of great rejoicing. Salima would be offered gifts of all kinds, and she would be honored by all:

Salima's place is in the middle of a big forest. She just stays there, doing no work and talking to nobody. We are not allowed to see her very often. That would be wrong, for she is our great mother. Her only companion is her maidservant. Still, she sometimes decides to visit us, her children, and on those occasions she goes on her way dressed like an Indian woman in lengths of blue and black cloth we gave her. The day this happens the whole countryside resounds with songs in her honor, and people cry out, "Our mother is coming to the village of Chapirira!" and Chapirira himself cries, "Our mother is on her way to visit us!" When the visit is over and she is about to leave, people come forward with a great many gifts.[56]

It was believed also that during the night she was visited by Mbona in the form of a python and that he would tell her things pertaining to the future of the country.[57] "Whenever Mbona wants to visit Salima, he comes to her after dark. He comes to her in the form of a snake larger than a python. When this happens, the woman does not back away or cry out in fear, for she knows it is her husband, the spirit."[58] Thus Salima would indicate what to plant and what not in the next hoeing season:

> When she fell down [became entranced], she made a fist with her hands. All the nyakwawas [headmen] would go to see her. When she fell, with her fists clenched, she didn't know anything . . . it was if she were dreaming. What she uttered, she did not know either. Then she said, "This year the food to be pro-duced will be maize and bulrush millet. . . . That is what it will have to be." If she said there would be hunger, then there would be hunger. The plants that she mentioned would be in her hands when she got up. Those were the seeds that were to be planted. The ones that were not there should not be planted, for they would not grow.[59]

According to Rangeley, there were permanent Salimas until about 1900.[60] These Salimas, however, were of a different kind, as we shall see in Chapter 4. The restoration of the classic Salimaship became an impor-tant political issue in the 1930s, when it was coupled with an upsurge of Mang'anja nationalism, and in the 1960s, when preparations were being made to restore the Lundu paramountcy.

To conclude this chapter we may return briefly to the correspondence between the three geographic circles and the three components of the ritual cycle noted earlier. In connection with that correspondence, two additional observations have to be made. The first is that the main figure in each of the three circles, with his corresponding rituals, represents a different type of authority: a rain priest (Ngabu), a chief (Tengani), and a king (Lundu). Together these three types represented ever more intense forms of political centralization as they made their appearance over successive periods of history. Second, the ritual cycle reenacts that history theoretically within the span of one generation, involving ever-wider circles until the whole kingdom becomes involved. The geographic circles and the liturgical cycle thus constitute a way of retaining the past, which in its turn corresponds with the streams to be distinguished later on in the oral traditions of the Mbona cult.

CHAPTER 3

The Principals and the Medium

OUTSIDE THE CONTEXT of the Mbona cult, people belong to different countries, to different administrative units within these countries, to different churches, and to several other groups and sets which pursue their own, sometimes conflicting interests. Only in the Mbona cult do they have a conceptual basis for concerted action which transcends these boundaries. The occasion which demonstrates this best is the rebuilding of the shrine.

Rebuilding requires protracted consultations between the formal leadership of the cult and the rulers of the various chiefdoms of the region. On these occasions old animosities are habitually revived and fresh ones created. Often the ritual has to be postponed because the parties involved are unable to reach unanimity. They may, however, be forced into action by the cult medium, who, while in a state of possession, personifies the deity and compels the various factions to make peace so that the act of rebuilding may proceed. One also observes on this occasion a general resurgence of people's faith in Mbona. The ancient myths are retold, rumors about strange omens circulate, and when the shrine is finally rebuilt, contributions are made in the form of food and labor.

What characterizes the cult region in the first place is the shared belief that only the cult and its staff has the means to counteract such calamities as droughts, floods, locusts, and epidemics and that it is therefore in the interest of all to support it. Yet the authority of the cult and its staff reaches beyond these pragmatic considerations. On the basis of the equally common belief that natural disasters do not happen independently but are caused by an angry deity in punishment of sins, the cult's staff also pronounces on the nature of these sins and thereby on social behavior in general. In consequence of its acceptance of this authority, the cult region is more than a collection of pragmatically motivated people; it also presents itself as a moral community with its own axioms and values and its own standards of conduct.

To understand how people conceptualize their region in the context of the cult, two conceptions and the dialectical relations between them need to be analyzed. These contrasting conceptions are respectively hierarchical and egalitarian in orientation. The first is embedded in the activities and mythical representations of the leadership of the cult, and it underscores the legitimacy of the traditional (or quasitraditional) political organization. The second underlies the activities and myths of the population and the medium, and it emphasizes values and concerns which transcend all forms of political and economic inequality, including that between chief and subject. The hierarchical conception asserts itself in the day-to-day operation of the cult. The egalitarian conception, on the other hand, although continuously present as an undercurrent, asserts itself only intermittently, when the medium is possessed and during the processes which generate such possession. During the possession sequence, the authority of the medium takes precedence over that of the formal leaders of the cult, all of whom are government-acknowledged chiefs. Indeed, the medium may request that the chiefs act for the cult and their people in ways which they might otherwise have been unwilling to undertake. The cult leaders, on their part, may refuse to attend or accept the medium's demands: they may declare that his possession is simulated. The possession event thus assumes the character of a contest between a formal and informal type of leadership within the cult organization. Furthermore, such an event constitutes a moment in time when the two conceptions of the region are brought into direct confrontation by their respective protagonists.

Clearly, critical factors influence the decision of the cult leadership whether or not to attend the mediumistic séance. The most critical of these factors is the degree of support that the medium receives from the people. It is not accidental that this support finds its expression in the outbursts of rumor which precede possession. The evidence suggests that such outbursts provide the contents of the communication transmitted by the medium. Consequently, the possession sequence has to be regarded both as the summation and the climax of a wider process which, in principle, involves all the people.

In this chapter we will first examine the formal leadership in relation to the cult organization and its political setting. Next the medium's position has to be considered in relation to the formal leadership of the cult and to the entire population. Finally, the actions of the two kinds of cult leader — the formal leadership and the medium — must be related to the two opposing conceptions of a region.

THE FORMAL ORGANIZATION OF THE CULT

All Mang'anja territorial chiefs are agents of the cult by virtue of their offices. They have the right to be consulted about the performance of major rituals; they receive requests for and organize the collection of contributions to the central shrine; and they have the right to attend on major ritual occasions. Moreover, as we saw in the preceding chapter, when a particular area suffers from drought or some other calamity, petitions to the shrine organization for ritual assistance are made through its chief. Theoretically, therefore, the Mang'anja chiefs, whilst divided by different administrative systems, appear as one body in the Mbona cult. They can be said to share a common estate, that is, the cult organization; to hold common jural responsibilities in respect of that estate; and to be capable of concerted action for the maintenance of that estate.

As agents of the cult, the chiefs are differentiated according to their geographic location in relation to the inner concentric circle, the area delineated by events in the myth of Mbona's death. The two principals of the cult, both of whom are government-appointed chiefs, reside in this area.[1] Like the other chiefs, they have independent jurisdiction over cult matters in their own constituencies. In addition, they also exercise authority over the shrine grounds, its personnel, and the performance of rituals at the shrine. They have authority to grant permission for the performance of rituals on behalf of the other chiefdoms, to appoint or dismiss personnel, to judge cases of violation of the shrine grounds, and to preside over any deliberation which concerns the conduct of the cult. For most of the colonial period there were three principals, due to the splitting up of one chiefdom, but in 1968 one of the three was divested of his office. The relationship between the principals is characterized by perpetual conflict due to continuous attempts on the part of each of them to achieve ascendancy over his peers, which in turn leads to frequent accusations of abuse of authority.

The two remaining principals are Ngabu and Malemia. Ngabu is the chief ritualist. Malemia, on the other hand, is best described as the chief jural and administrative officer. He is responsible for receiving requests for ritual services and for hearing cases in relation to the cult. Each of these two men has a kind of double: Ngabu's is Chapirira, and Malemia's is Ntsangalambe. These positions used to alternate, in the sense that incumbents were drawn from two lineages, which alternately provided a candidate for one or the other title. Thus, if the ruling Ngabu belonged to lineage A, the next one would be drawn from lineage B. Conversely, if the serving Chapirira were a member of lineage B, the next one would come from lineage A. The same was true of the Malemias and Ntsangalambes.[2] This system of alternating positions, which was discontinued in the first quarter of the twentieth century, had for one of its consequences that none of the four lineages was able to gain permanent control over either principalship. The system had to be discontinued when the land area of the inner concentric circle came to be divided into chiefdoms, whereas originally it was administered in its entirety by the four lineages concerned. As a senior informant remarked, "Fixed boundaries in this area [the inner concentric circle] are a colonial invention. The struggle about the precise boundaries between Ngabu and Malemia began only when they were summoned to Zomba [the colonial capital] to receive a chief's ceremonial gown [mkanjo]."[3]

It is said that on that occasion Malemia had sent his underling Chiphwembwe, together with his sister's son and successor-designate, to receive the gown on his behalf, but the colonial government decided to give the title to Chiphwembwe instead. The truth behind it was that Chiphwembwe was one of the first converts of the South Africa General Mission. It was partly due to mission protection that he was officially recognized chief in 1913 and given precedence over Malemia. This situation continued until 1968, when the nationalist government restored Malemia to the chiefship and reduced Chiphwembwe to the status of senior headman. In 1972 he was even divested of that position, following charges of slander and sorcery against Malemia. After the Malemias had been reinstated, the Ntsangalambes once again became their deputies.

The two principals are continuously engaged in a quest for primacy, which is expressed in their origin myths. Thus the Malemia family claims the right to primacy because its founding ancestor was reputedly granted exclusive jurisdiction over the shrine grounds and the martyrdom area. The same founding father had then delegated the priestly functions inherent in that jurisdiction to Ngabu's ancestor, but without granting him any secular power. This, the Malemia family maintains, was the situation until the introduction of the colonial government, when Ngabu obtained his chiefly title from the government under false pretenses, saying that all his forebears had been chiefs.[4] Ngabu's version is that the first Ngabu was made a priest by Mbona himself, who also granted him secular jurisdiction over the martyrdom area. The Malemias came in at some later date when the Ngabus asked for their assistance with the administration of the territory.[5]

The permanent condition of conflict between the two principals reaches its climax in two different settings, which are in many ways related. One of these settings is the ritual cycle; the other presents itself whenever the district administration contemplates changes in the boundaries of chiefdoms or in the positions of individual chiefs. Until a few years ago the Nsanje District administration had for one of its constituent bodies a chiefs' council, whose chairman is the district commissioner, now known as the government agent. The chiefs' council, in its turn, is responsible to the district council, on which it is represented and to which it may make recommendations. A perennial problem of the Nsanje District administration has been the relative smallness of the chiefdoms in the southern part of the district, a state of affairs historically attributable to the presence of the Mbona shrine and the "secularization" of ritual positions. Consequently, there have been a number of attempts, partly for the sake of administrative efficiency, partly for the sake of more intensive political control, to arrange them into larger units. Between 1913, when chiefdoms for the first time became officially recognized administrative units, and 1972, when Chiphwembwe was stripped of the last remnant of his former power, there have been eight alterations of boundaries, five of which involved the martyrdom area. In each case this led to severe competitive struggles and to the creation of a powerful undercurrent of hostility in the relationships between individual chiefs.[6]

Competition for chiefships in the district as a whole affects the cult in a number of ways. Such competition is inextricably enmeshed with the competition between the principals, since their standing with the district administration is a major factor in their quest for primacy. It also affects the relationships between these two men and neighboring chiefs, to the extent that the latter frequently refuse to support the shrine organization. Even a catastrophic drought may not be sufficient to rally all the local chiefs around the shrine. A case in point was the 1948–49 drought, which led to a revival of rain cults all over Malawi, but which in Nsanje coincided with one of these periodic power struggles and made some of the chiefs decide to withhold their cooperation.[7] Finally, the competition emphasizes the ambiguous position of chiefs operating within a system of modern government. A chief's position under such a system is more directly dependent on the support of the government in power than on the support of the population. Capable individuals may be able to steer a cautious course between the demands of one party and those of the other, but the conflict is never far from the surface. In the Nsanje District, where the most sensitive issues have traditionally been those relating to taxation, cotton prices, and agricultural regulations, this situation has at times led to situations in which the chiefs, including Ngabu and Malemia, were expected to implement a particular governmental policy, whereas the cult medium encouraged disobedience and resistance to the same policy.

Against this background of conflict and ambiguity, one may ask how the principals are able to exercise effective authority. Part of the answer is that their position is similar to that of the other chiefs in that their authority largely depends on the support which the central government is willing and able to provide. The truth of this observation appears clearest in the history of Chiphwembwe, who was ultimately deposed but who, while his favor with the government lasted, was able to maintain his authority in the cult. In addition to this, the two principal officers, like all Mang'anja chiefs, are credited with the power to withhold rains or to cause some other calamity. In their case, however, this power, much like their cultic jurisdiction, is believed to operate also beyond the boundaries of their chiefdoms. To illustrate briefly, in November 1967 Ngabu had requested his people to repair the grass roof of his house, but without success. At the same time there was the threat of a drought, the rains already having been a few weeks late. It was decided to hold a rain ceremony, but Ngabu, normally the most important person, refused to be present. No rain fell afterward, and since it was the general opinion that this was due to Ngabu's sorcery, apologies were offered and the roof repaired. A second ceremony was held on December 18.[8]

The religious influence and secular authority of the principals, although protected by the same sanctions, are in part challenged by different agencies. In their role of secular rulers the principals are subject to challenges by the central government represented by the district commissioner; as religious authorities they are particularly open to challenges by the population at large, represented by the medium.

THE SPIRIT MEDIUM AND THE INFORMAL ORGANIZATION OF THE CULT

Within the cultural idiom of the Mang'anja, a medium is a person who is able and authorized to receive and transmit messages thought to emanate directly from supernatural beings. The word *directly* serves to distinguish mediums from diviners, whose contact with the supernatural, insofar as it is thought to exist, is mediated through an oracular instrument. The distinction between mediums and common diviners is socially important, among other reasons, because divination is sometimes resorted to by chiefs wishing to circumvent the services of spirit mediums.

Contact with the supernatural is commonly established through trance during possession. The medium is said to be seized (-*gwidwa*) by a spirit (*mzimu*), and while in a condition of dissociation (-*gwa*), he babbles and raves (-*bwebweta*). His utterings are often unintelligible to outsiders unless translated by the medium's acolyte or interpreter.

In the course of their history the Mang'anja have developed or adopted a variety of mediumistic institutions.[9] Broadly, Mang'anja distinguish between mediums who operate on behalf of private interests and those whose concern is with public interests. The former specialize in the diagnosis and treatment of diseases, whilst the latter, whom we shall designate *territorial mediums*, predict and explain disturbances in the natural environment.

Territorial mediumships show significant variations according to differences in sex, means of contact with the divine, relationships with chiefly lineages, and the spatial extent of their jurisdiction. Thus some mediumships are held exclusively by women, others by men and women. A few receive their revelations in dreams, while the majority receive and transmit them through possession. Some are members of the local chief's lineage; others operate independently. Finally, some have local significance, whereas others such as the Mbona mediums have regional significance. Politically, the most crucial variable is that of the relationship between medium and chief. It is considered that, where a medium is a member of the ruling lineage, he will be close to the interests of that lineage and that, where he is not so related, there is a definite potential for opposition to the ruling lineage's interests.

Much of the same can be maintained of the post-1900 history of the Mbona mediums (see chart 1). The leading mediums during this period were members of an immigrant lineage whose ancestress was granted asylum at the shrine. Josef Thom, the medium of that line at the time of my fieldwork, like his predecessors, was quite definitely independent of the principals, with whom he was in almost continuous conflict. Other mediums, however, have belonged to the lineage of one of the principals. One of them, Edward Harrison, enjoyed considerable renown between the mid-1930s and 1943. It will be remembered that this was a critical period in the history of the Nsanje District, due to the permanent flooding of the Dinde Marsh, which caused an acute problem of overpopulation, and to the coming to power of Molin Tengani, who became the main agent of colonial penetration. Harrison's was a case in which attachment to a chiefly lineage could be successfully combined with the confidence of the population. His success was due to the convergence of several favorable factors, including his personality, the popularity of the principal whose kinsman he was, and the political circumstances of the time. After his death, however, the credibility of the chiefs came increasingly to be questioned, during opposition to unwanted agricultural reforms and the imposition in

Name of Medium	Sex	Period	Biography
1. Mbote	Male	c. 1900–14	Immigrant lineage, independent, divested
2. Mbandera	Female	c. 1920–30	Full sister of 1, independent, died in office
3. Onsewa	Female	c. 1930–33	Relative of Malemia, died in office
4. Edward Harrison	Male	c. 1933–43	Relative of Ngabu, died in office
5. Jailos Thom	Male	1946–51	Son of younger brother of 1 and 2, independent, died in office
6. Thapuleni Mybeck	Male	1952	Claimed to be relative of Malemia, rejected
7. Josef Thom	Male	1954–78	Younger brother of 5, independent, baptized R.C., died in office
8. Kingy Butao	Male	1977	Member Ancestor Church, rejected

Chart 1. Mbona mediums in the twentieth century

September 1953 of the Federation of Rhodesia and Nyasaland. It would have been difficult in such a climate for any medium closely related to a chief to maintain himself. Although at least one aspirant did try, he was unsuccessful, and the Mbona mediumship has from 1946 onward remained in the hands of independents.

THE MEDIUM'S ENTOURAGE

One particular facet which needs to be made explicit is that the Mbona mediumship, at least in its present form, is not used as an oracular office: the medium cannot be called upon to provide divinely inspired solutions to such problems as succession disputes. In the context of the Mbona cult, possession is conceived of as an event which is entirely dependent on the initiative of the divinity, and solutions to specific problems, insofar as they are provided, are not given at the request of one party but only in response to a general feeling of crisis. Thus, the medium need not be in any way better informed than the average inhabitant of the region. All he needs is to keep in tune with the general sentiment of the population. In accordance with this principle, the medium does not travel widely, nor does he maintain a network of informants. What information he needs he can, in principle, pick up from village or market talk. There is one exception to this: he must be better informed than the average person about what goes on at the shrine. Since he lives only a few kilometers away and since little remains secret on account of the conflicts between the principals, this constitutes no particular problem.

Still, the medium has a small entourage of kinsmen and sympathizers who in various ways assist and support him. Within this entourage the important roles are those of the medium's guardian and of his acolyte-interpreter. The former is the head of the lineage section to which the medium belongs and is always male. The latter may be any adult member of the lineage, but preference is given to a woman of mature age. The guardian as the head of the lineage is co-responsible for the actions of its members, including the medium, unless their relationship is severed on account of some conflict. He is further entitled to act on behalf of a lineage member who is permanently or temporarily incapable of acting on his or her own behalf. When the medium is possessed, for instance, the guardian takes command by sending messages to the principals and by formally receiving them, if they decide to come.

The task of the interpreter is to render the ravings and mumblings of the medium intelligible and understandable to those to whom they are directed and to convey the replies of the latter back to the medium. Her role is a critical one, since the outcome of the séance partly depends on her ability to formulate. She must therefore be a person of proven ability. The choice of an interpreter is the exclusive affair of the lineage to which the medium belongs. Should one medium die and another emerge from the same lineage, as was the case with Jailos Thom and Josef Thom, then the interpreter will also serve the next medium. If the next medium comes from a different lineage, however, she will cease to function as an interpreter. Medium, guardian, and interpreter cooperate in the interest of their own lineage, which stands to benefit from its association with the mediumship. In the past, successful mediumship could, given the right conditions, be converted into some form of hereditary secular authority.[10] This no longer is the case, but Josef Thom and his kinsmen seemed to think that he or his successor might possibly become the sole head of the cult. This at least is the interpretation which the principals gave of the fact that he and his kinsmen built a separate possession hut, which at the same time was used as a rival shrine.[11] It appears, therefore, that the hostility between the medium and the principals, which was so much a feature of the situation as I knew it in the 1960s, was not merely incidental. Rather, it is to be viewed as a logical consequence of the fact that the medium is a potential rival of the principals, in their roles as secular rulers and as heads of the cult organization.

THE MBONA MEDIUM AND THE CHIEFS

The Mbona medium becomes possessed rather infrequently, sometimes at intervals of several years. Such possession may be provoked by three different types of events, namely, environmental calamities, offenses against the social order, and offenses against the cult. In fact, it may be difficult to establish in any particular case which of the three is to be regarded as the activating factor, since from the perspective of the actors nature, society, and cult appear to form an indivisible triad. Environmental and climatic disturbances are routinely explained in terms of social disturbances and vice versa, while both again are connected with the cult as the censor of public mores and as the possessor of the means of expiation. Whatever the immediate cause of possession, it invariably involves a pronouncement on the social and moral condition of the community. Moreover, the message transmitted by the medium is always centrally concerned with the chiefs and with the relationships between the chiefs and the population. Characteristically, the chiefs have to bear the brunt of the medium's criticism, because they are accused either of siding with the central government against the population or of failing to put an end to social abuses within their territories.

The antagonism between medium and chiefs, which manifests itself in possession, is equally apparent outside it. Josef Thom continuously criticized the actions of chiefs, particularly the Khulubvi chiefs. In their turn, they criticized the medium for trying to enhance his status by unlawful means. The chiefs were particularly critical of the fact that he had built his own shrine. They regarded this as a departure from tradition and as a sign that he wanted to make himself independent of the cult organization.[12] It was striking, however, that despite these allegedly unlawful acts, they left Josef in peace. One of the principals whom I questioned on this point replied that, notwithstanding such obvious irregularities, one still ought to respect the medium, since he spoke with the voice of Mbona.[13] Nevertheless, mediums in the past were sometimes discredited by the chiefs, and one may ask why the principals did not try to get rid of Josef. The answer is that he enjoyed renown among the people, a reputation which only grew when he was arrested as one of the suspected nationalist leaders during the political riots of March 1959.[14]

The principals may also express their disagreement with the medium by refusing to attend a possession séance. They themselves state that this depends on whether possession is real or feigned, and they claim that they are able to judge this by the medium's behavior. Thus one of Chief Ngabu's councillors said of Thapuleni Mybeck, a candidate medium who presented himself in the early 1950s, "I went to listen to his ravings, but

Illus. 19. The medium Josef Thom (Chamboto), 1967. Photograph by C. Zonneveld.

when I heard what he had to say, I turned away in disgust. The man was a drunkard."[15]

Nevertheless, the fact that they may decide to stay away from the séance before they have actually observed the medium suggests that their judgment may be based on an entirely different criterion. My suggestion would be that the criterion actually applied is the degree of political pressure by which a séance is generated. If this pressure is considered insufficient, chances are that the possession will be declared false and that none of the principals will attend. Lest this suggestion be taken to imply that those involved do not actually believe in the reality of spirit possession, I must stress that all my evidence indicates that they do. My suggestion does point to the fact that they may be using conscious and unconscious criteria simultaneously. Much the same can be said of the medium. Although, from the political viewpoint, the art of mediumship consists in choosing the right moment for possession, the medium himself may be under the impression that it occurs spontaneously.

THE ENCOUNTER BETWEEN MEDIUM AND PRINCIPALS

Formal encounters between medium and principals take place in the context of the possession sequence, which is always precipitated by a combination of social, environmental, and cultic factors. A closer look at the rebuilding of the shrine will clarify some of the factors in the cult itself which trigger such a possession sequence.

The shrine, it will be remembered, may not be repaired, even if it is on the verge of collapsing, and must remain untouched till the next rebuilding. The act of rebuilding is always combined with the reinstallation of the spirit wife and an animal sacrifice. In the past the spirit wife lived permanently at the shrine, but nowadays a woman is chosen who stays there only for the duration of the ceremony. Ideally, these actions require the cooperation of the paramount chief, Lundu, and of a number of senior chiefs, all of whom are supposed to perform certain parts of the ritual. The lesser chiefs are mainly involved through the collection of grain and other victuals for the sacrifice and the feeding of those who participate. Many refuse to cooperate because of their conflicts with the principals. The principals may make attempts at reconciliation, or they may try to bring pressure to bear on the unwilling through the offices of friendly chiefs, but the outcome is always the same: the rebuilding is performed with the help of substitutes and in what is considered to be a simplified and adapted form. The traditional ritual, as preserved in oral accounts, has in its entirety probably never been performed since the 1860s, and one may even ask whether it ever was. At any rate, the way the rebuilding is to be carried out nowadays is the source of endless altercation between those who may be conveniently labeled purists and pragmatists. One party demands that tradition be followed to the letter; the other allows for adaptation and simplification. The dispute is really a political one. No chief or headman will ever admit that he refuses cooperation because he has been outdone politically. Rather, he will maintain that his reason is a conservative one: he is opposed to one or more of his colleagues because they no longer care for the cult or perform its rituals according to the way of the past. The political losers thus tend to become the ritual purists. The usual result of these altercations, however, is that negotiations drag on without a decision being taken.

The negotiations about the rebuilding of the shrine are a major source of rumor among the people. While on the whole uninformed about the details, the people, even those living at a great distance from the shrine, are aware of the essentials, which they interpret in their own fashion. The medium, on the other hand, living close by the shrine, is fully informed about what goes on, although he does not directly participate in the negotiations himself. In the case of Josef Thom, possession announced itself days beforehand through severe aches in the back and the head. The decisive sign, according to his own information, always came when he saw a small cloud moving at great speed through an otherwise bright sky.[16] If he was away visiting or working his gardens, he would return home and tell his wife. Throughout the rest of the day he would shiver and mumble, and toward evening he was secluded in his hut, where he wrapped himself in a black cloth. Messages were then sent by his guardian and relatives to the principals and their assistants.

This summoning is a critical point in the possession sequence, for those called may or may not come, depending on their reading of the situation. If possession occurs in the midst of a drought or some other calamity, the decision will be easier to take. Failure to come might be interpreted as a sign of evil intentions, and the principal would then pit himself against the medium and the population, which involves considerable risk. The less pronounced the element of environmental and climatic crisis, therefore, the greater will be the chance of a clash of wills between medium and principals. If indeed the majority do not show up, the medium's career is in jeopardy and may be irreparably damaged. If, on the other hand, a majority has assembled, the medium begins to stir, and his acolyte-interpreter holds a roll call from behind the reed door of the hut. While this is being done, the medium makes what was described to me as the growling sound of a lion.[17] This is followed by the message proper, which is in three parts.

First, the nature of the crisis is stated. Then an explanation is given in terms of some delict committed. Finally, the means to avert disaster are indicated, and a promise is solicited.

The next critical moment arrives when it is time for the spokesman of the principals to reply. If everything goes well, he makes a formal act of submission by addressing the medium as his senior, by confessing to neglect of the shrine and such other offenses as may have been mentioned by the medium, and by promising that things will be done as requested. In that case the medium gives a parting admonition in a conciliatory tone, and all disperse. If, however, the principals find it impossible to accept the terms posed by the medium or if they feel offended by the medium's denunciations, the session may break up, and the medium's future is once again in jeopardy.

The specific and immediate effect of intervention by the medium is the rebuilding of the shrine, which ideally signals the end of a period of contestation and the beginning of a new era of unity and cooperation. The traditional accounts of the ritual lay particular stress on this aspect. Thus, no household was to give more than one cob of maize or head of millet, so that the gifts of all would form part of the libational beer. Nobody was allowed to carry more than one shaft of reed or a bundle of grass thicker than one's own arm, so that the labors of all would be required to rebuild the shrine.[18] This injunction is no longer followed, if it

Illus. 20. Ceremonial drum at Chief Tengani's court, 1967. Photograph by C. Zonneveld.

ever was, but contributions in the form of food and labor are still made by the public.

INTERMEZZO:
AN ACCOUNT OF A SÉANCE

I have never witnessed one of the medium's séances myself. Instead of a factual report, I reproduce therefore a somewhat idealized account by shrine guardians Chapirira and Kumbiwanyati:

As we have told you earlier on, Mbona's spirit may take possession also of a person other than Salima, and one such is still among us.[19] When the spirit comes, that person starts raving, *bwe, bwe, bwe!*[20] . . . , and soon word reaches us that Mbona has come to one of his children and that he wants us to inquire after the reasons for his coming. We in turn hurry on our way with the young men that brought the message to find out what is happening. When Mbona visits us, there is no time to tarry, and we run, our feet beating the road, *pha, pha, pha!* . . .

The first signs of possession are already noticeable when the sun is still in the sky. As soon as it begins, the man lies down on the floor of his hut, and his wives close the door, keeping watch outside. None of them dares go inside. They just keep waiting until all of us have arrived, which is always after sunset in view of the distances involved.

When all of us have gathered, we first clap hands, *kwa, kwa, kwa!* . . . Following this, one of us says, "Lord, we have come. Tell us here outside what you came to see us for. Speak to us!" Mbona then calls each one of us by name, "Have all of you come? Is Ngabu there and Mkanjawe? Is Mbangu present? Has Malemia come? And what of Mbukwa?"[21]

When everyone has answered the roll call, our spokesman continues, "Since you want to see us here outside your hut, what is it that worries you? Did we perhaps neglect your hut? We know it is in bad repair, and that it is time to rebuild it, but we were just thinking of calling a meeting to make the necessary arrangements." But Mbona hardly gives us time to state our case and immediately begins rebuking us: "Indeed, what about my hut? You are in no haste at all to rebuild it. Please, do it now without wasting any more time. Or should I perhaps sleep under the sky? My sons, why do you behave this way? Don't say the job is a difficult one, because it isn't. You yourselves have a decent place to sleep, but what do I have? Nothing but a dilapidated hut! Is that the way you act?"

We outside feel uneasy, when hearing this, but Mbona continues, "Look, when you are negligent about such an important duty, do not be surprised if unpleasant things happen to you. What if I send pests to destroy your crops? Is that perhaps what you want?"[22] We naturally hasten to reply, "Oh no, don't let that happen. We certainly don't want that!" But Mbona once again continues, "As you already seem to have understood the lesson that I came to teach you, this year will be a good one, provided you give me a good hut. If you do your duty, there will be no hardship, but peace and plentiful rain. Still, there is work to do, and if you do it without delay, I shall be with you and grant you what you are crying for . . . !" [silence follows]

"We are still listening!"

"I beg you, my sons, do as I told you, for should you decide not to, you will be calling disaster upon yourselves. There is one other thing: should you find that the hut of your mother Salima is in bad repair, see to it that something be done as soon as possible so that she, too, will be decently housed. Only when you have finished both jobs can you come to me with your offerings. Do you understand?"

"Yes, we out here have understood!"

"This is what I called you for. I have nothing else to say."

"We are still listening, though!"

"No, there is nothing else!"

We remain squatting in our places in silence. When conversing with him we do not use many words. Our duty is to listen and obey.

"So be it! I have said what I had to say. Set to work immediately. If you tarry, you will find yourselves in trouble, my sons. I have finished for today."[23]

RUMOR AND POSSESSION

The three types of events which may provoke spirit possession may also provoke spates of fantastic rumor. Many rumors circulated in the late 1960s, a time when particularly vigorous efforts were made to rebuild the shrine and to revive certain features of the organization.

According to one of these rumors, Mbona had sent a monkey from the sacred forest to Lundu with the message that Mbona wanted a wife from the paramount as had been customary in the past. Lundu, however, not only declined to grant the request, but he also had the monkey put to death. Because of this atrocious behavior all monkeys were said to have left Khulubvi, which in turn was interpreted as a sign that Mbona himself had withdrawn from the shrine and that some serious calamity would follow.[24]

Another rumor had it that fishermen on the Shire had dragged up a small iron box from which emerged a little man with a pronounced limp. When asked how he got his limp, he said he had broken his leg walking through gardens which had been contour-ridged and that he was now on his way to the district commissioner to tell him that this practice must be discontinued.[25] In another version of the same rumor Mbona was supposed to have declared (presumably through the medium) that he would no longer bless the gardens, because he might break his leg due to the ridges. According to yet another rumor, the waters of the sacred pool had turned red. This was taken as an omen of worse things to follow.[26] Finally, rumors circulated to the effect that the medium had already become possessed and that he had spoken out on issues concerning the cult and the region.

The body of rumor of which these particular instances formed part had at least four distinctive effects. They undoubtedly contributed to a revival of people's awareness of the cult on a regional level. Moreover, some of the rumors seemed to represent a collective effort by the people to establish unanimity on issues of general concern such as the obligatory ridging of the gardens. Furthermore, they appeared to provide much of the pressure which finally generated the possession séance. Finally, they also determined the contents of the message which the medium was to communicate.

Only a general estimate about the spatial distribution of these rumors can be given. I made no effort to establish with any degree of accuracy how widely they had spread, but the fact that they were repeated to me in locations some 150 kilometers apart may serve as a general indication of their appeal. Nor was it difficult to establish that the rumors were part of, and in their own way contributed to, a revival of people's interest in the cult. Indeed, for several weeks there was talk of little else. Regarding the causal connection between the outbursts of rumor and the possession event, particular attention needs to be paid to the rumors concerning the medium, since these provide the most explicit indication of such a connection. The very fact that it was widely rumored that possession had already taken place meant that it was part of people's expectation in this situation. In addition, those rumors purported to broadcast what the medium had said and thus made clear what people expected him to say. I was not able at the time to establish whether information about his own alleged prophecies did in fact filter back to the medium. If it did, as I suppose was the case, he never mentioned it. On the other hand, it became clear in the course of several interviews with him that he very much shared the concerns which the prophecies expressed. His complaint, however, was the quite telling one that the people remained too divided and too indifferent for him to force the principals and their fellow chiefs into action. He said this primarily in connection with the failed reinstatement of Mbona's wife, but he obviously meant it to apply to other issues as well. The significance of this complaint is that it suggested, at the very least, that the medium himself was conscious of the fact that he could not operate without the support of the people.

Peter Lienhardt has argued that "rumours of the more fantastic sort represent or may represent complexities of public feeling that cannot be made articulate at a more thoughtful level" and, furthermore, that "they join people's sympathies in a consensus of an unthinking or at least uncritical kind."[27] Whilst agreeing that in the case described here rumor very much seemed to have the effect of establishing and expressing widespread consensus on certain issues, I do not agree that this consensus was of an unthinking or uncritical kind. Nor would I agree that these issues could not be made articulate at a more thoughtful level. Indeed, it is not difficult to show that at least some of the issues had been the subjects of articulate discussion. This was not only so with regard to the reinstatement of Mbona's wife, which had been endlessly discussed by the shrine officials, but also with regard to the ridging of the gardens, the pros and cons of which were continuously being assessed by villagers and agricultural instructors. What the rumors did, though, was to establish an alternative level of discussion, where quite different nonrational arguments were brought into play and where the emphasis shifted from technical to social considerations. It is possible and indeed most likely that a number of people whose attitude toward agricultural innovations was not altogether unfavorable were thereby swayed in the other direction, but even so, one hesitates to apply such epithets as "uncritical" and "unthinking." It would be more helpful to view rumor in this case as part of an ongoing process of self-assessment in which the people of the region tried to come to terms with change and division within its boundaries.

THE CONCEPTUALIZATION OF A REGIONAL COMMUNITY

In the foregoing description, an explicit distinction has been made between the formal and informal operations of the Mbona cult. Formally, it has been suggested that the cult operates through a leadership which, although divided by participation in different state systems and administrations, is regarded in the cult as one elite group. From this viewpoint, then, the cult may be said to support a system of social differentiation in which a relatively small aristocratic group sees itself as possessing an unquestionable right to political rule. Our discussion of the informal operation of the cult has, in a sense, reversed this picture, by showing that in certain situations and under certain conditions the interests of the people can be made to prevail over those of the principals and the chiefs. The key figure in this process is the medium, who has recourse to possession and who could use it, given sufficient popular support, to effectively confront the traditional political establishment.

We can now consider further aspects of the contrast between these modes of operation. First, its pronounced ideological content has to be made explicit here. Second, the social antagonism enacted through it has to be viewed more broadly. This antagonism is not confined to the chief-subject relationship: it extends to antagonism of every kind which affects the population as a whole. To pursue the first point, it is useful to start with the ideological differences in the bodies of cultic myth which characterize the principals and chiefs, on the one hand, and the medium and the people, on the other.

The myths of the principals and chiefs are fundamentally concerned with history, the legitimation of their positions, and, in a more general way, the legitimacy of social inequality by discrimination between aristocrats and commoners and between autochthons and immigrants. The mythology of the medium and the population, by comparison, has, generally speaking, a less historical character. This is pointedly illustrated by the medium Josef Thom, who, for all his influence and importance, had almost no knowledge of or interest in the history of the cult. His interest was entirely in the present, notably in the deeds of principals and chiefs and the manifestations of public discontent. It would have been fairly easy for the medium to acquaint himself with the details of history, as easy as it would have been for any inhabitant of the district. The fact that he did not avail himself of this opportunity and felt no need to do so reflects a deep-seated aversion. This was readily understandable, given his identity: he belonged to a poor immigrant family and gained no legitimacy from cult history. Being, as it were, Mbona himself, he could afford to radiate timelessness.

What has been said of the medium also applies to the people. Exceptions such as Text III/B apart, their myths reveal a similar lack of concern with history and a similar emphasis on Mbona's relevance to the present condition of society. They differ further from the myths of the chiefs in that they project an image of a region which is unified on the basis of common concerns and a common morality. Distinctions between chiefs and commoners or between autochthons and immigrants are left unmentioned and are implicitly denied. Whereas the myths of principals and chiefs are cast in a purely traditional cultic idiom, those of the medium and the people have increasingly come to be expressed in biblical language. The Bible has thus provided an overarching idiom to which neither Mang'anja nor immigrant can lay exclusive claim and on the basis of which both may act in unison.

The concept of a nondifferentiated society is put forward as the ideology of a region through the informal organization of the cult, headed by the medium. That ideology is activated, as we have seen, by a concurrent awareness of social and environmental threats. In the light of this observation, climatic and environmental calamities or the fear of such calamities are to be viewed not only as causes of cultic revival but also as activators of an alternative mode of conceptualizing its constituency. A particular quality of this process of conceptualization is that, in principle, it concerns itself with all instances of social inequality which affect the population as a whole, but it subsumes them all under the chief-subject relationship. The same suggestion was made earlier in different terms: the communication transmitted by the medium in the possession sequence is always centrally concerned with the behavior of the chiefs and with the relations between chiefs and people. The chiefs are held accountable for the existence or persistence of almost every kind of social grievance, whether this springs from central government policy or from the actions of the chiefs themselves or of a section of the people. That this should be so is partly due to the extensiveness of the chiefs' jurisdiction and partly to the ambiguousness of their authority, which makes them both the representatives of the central administration vis-à-vis the people and the representatives of the people vis-à-vis the central administration. In situations of social discontent they thus become, from the viewpoint of the population, either the ones who have been instrumental in causing the discontent or the ones who are in a position to eliminate the cause of discontent, or both. It is this viewpoint which finds its dramatic expression in the encounter between the medium and the principals.

It would be gratifying at this point to conclude the analysis, were it not for one unresolved question: What explains the situation in which the medium is close to the interests of the principals, as apparently was the case in the 1930s and early 1940s, when Edward Harrison, one of Ngabu's relatives, was a medium, and a successful medium at that? In a wider context this raises questions about the structural position of the medium.

Given the chief-subject relationship as a constant factor in the region's organization, how is it that at one time the mediumship appears to support the social differentiation which this relationship implies, whereas at another time it manifests itself as decidedly antagonistic to the same differentiation? My explanation would be that this depends primarily on the degree to which the functioning of chieftainship is problematic in the perception of the people. Such was the case, for instance, after World War II, when the credibility of the chiefs had increasingly come to be questioned in connection with the Federation of Rhodesia and Nyasaland and the introduction of unwanted agricultural reform. This made it difficult, if not impossible, for any medium to maintain close ties with the principals and, through them, with the chiefs. The structural position of the medium, then, is changeable, not fixed. It would, however, be incorrect to view it as oscillating between the interests of the traditional political establishment and those of the people, for it has to remain within the orbit of the latter. Only insofar as public sentiment gives assent to the chiefs' performance of their office can the medium support them and the chieftainship. Whenever this is the case, one may expect also that the contrast between the two conceptions of a region will become submerged. The structural position of the medium would thus be an indicator of the degree to which tensions within the region have become acute.

Essentially, the Mbona cult functions as a mechanism by means of which the inhabitants of a particular geographic area perceive themselves as constituting a region. This perception springs from two different sources, each of which endows it with an entirely different character. One of these sources is the formal organization of the cult, which projects the image of a hierarchically structured region and which thereby underscores the legitimacy of social differentiation. The other source is constituted by widespread feelings of anxiety and discontent with issues that cannot be effectively dealt with by isolated groups. These feelings are characteristically focused on the chiefs, and they are cast in a symbolic idiom which in various ways denies the legitimacy of social differentiation. The situation which ultimately emerges is that of a coexistence of two opposing conceptions of a region and of an alternating movement by which now one and then the other conception is given emphasis.

CHAPTER 4

The Quest for a Spirit Wife and the Struggle for Mang'anja Political Supremacy, 1859–1983

DUE TO THE slave trade, the Mang'anja states were by the middle of the nineteenth century on the verge of collapse, but the arrival of British traders and missionaries prevented this. By siding with the British against the Portuguese, the Mang'anja chiefs were able to make a comeback and in the end to regain control over the larger part of the valley. For a while Chimang'anja even became the colony's official "native language." When Malawi gained its political independence from Great Britain, the Lundu paramountcy was officially restored and its historical importance publicly recognized. The cult and the paramountcy formed the twin focus of modern Mang'anja nationalism. These two institutions were wedded to each other through the spirit wife; the paramountcy as wife-giver, the cult as wife-receiver. Following the vicissitudes of her office will give us a chance to gain a more adequate understanding of the relationship between cult and state.

LIVINGSTONE'S TRAVELS AND THE SLAVE WARS

By 1860 Lundu had dwindled to such insignificance that the members of the Livingstone expedition and the first Universities' Mission to Central Africa (U.M.C.A.) missionaries were hardly aware of his existence. His place had been taken by Mankhokwe, who, though related to Lundu, had traditionally been his underling.[1] Due to Mankhokwe's rise in status, the Thyolo rain shrine, which was under his jurisdiction, had gained in importance to the extent even that one of the early missionaries compared the prevailing arrangement to a theocracy:

> Their form of government was something like a theocracy, for though the Rundo [i.e., Mankhokwe] was the supreme chief, he was not the supreme authority; there was a higher than he recognised in the affairs of the country. A certain spirit—whether of some great departed chief or not did not clearly appear—whom they called Bona, was supposed to have an abode on the top of a mountain called Choro [Thyolo], and to him the Rundo resorted for council in times of difficulty and danger, so that the Rundo's position was something like that of the Judges of Israel; if he was applied to by his people, he asked guidance of Bona. Bona was supposed to be eminently benevolent: when his power predominated war did not desolate the land; drought was unknown; he blessed the seed, and the fruits of the earth abounded; he was, in fact, a dispenser of peace and plenty as well as of wise counsel.[2]

Mankhokwe, however, could not get around the fact that Khulubvi had built up a much wider influence than Thyolo, and that, if he aimed at supplanting the Lundu paramounts, the Khulubvi shrine also had to be brought under his jurisdiction. The political situation of the 1860s brought him close to the realization of that ambition.

At the time of Livingstone's arrival Mankhokwe formed one power block with Tengani. Together they controlled both sides of the Shire below Chikwawa, which formed the core area of the traditional Lundu state. To the northwest there existed a second power block in what used to be Kaphwiti's chiefdom. Here, much the same situation prevailed as in Lundu's territory, Kaphwiti having become a mere shadow of his name. Instead, two strongmen ruled his country in the persons of Chibisa and Kabvina.[3] Both men controlled strategic points on the Tete trade route. The attitudes of the two blocks toward the Portuguese could not have been more different. Whereas Tengani and Mankhokwe did their utmost to keep traders and slavers out, both Chibisa and Kabvina allowed trading and slaving parties through their territories against payment.[4] It was into this situation that Livingstone marched in January 1859.[5]

From the beginning he made it a habit to call on "Mboma's village" at Khulubvi, not because it harbored a cult center (which he did not seem to have been particularly interested in) but because it was the only place where rice could be bought in great quantities and at very low prices. Upriver he had problems being allowed through Tengani's barricade, which he managed only after threatening to force his way through with the help of firearms. Nor was there much love lost between the Livingstone expedition and Mankhokwe.[6] Their hostile relationships were only aggravated when Livingstone struck up a friendship with Chibisa, who, under the guise of providing the expedition with guides and porters, was in fact making use of them to extend his influence into the Shire highlands.

To make matters worse, this particular instance of disregard for Mankhokwe's position coincided with another case of white intrusion into his territory, namely the founding of the U.M.C.A. highlands station at Magomero in 1861. The missionaries' stay at Magomero did not last long, however; they were forced to leave the following year on account of the Yao wars then going on. Upon returning to Chikwawa, where they became Chibisa's neighbors, they decided to see Mankhokwe about a more suitable site on Mount Thyolo. Stewart and Waller, two members of their party, were dispatched to see the chief but were not immediately admitted, as Mankhokwe had visitors from Khulubvi who were there requesting a new wife for Mbona. Mankhokwe was not unwilling to oblige the visitors, since their request implied that he was being recognized by the Khulubvi organization as the valley's senior ruler. The matter was urgent, as the valley was experiencing a severe drought, which in the months to come would claim thousands of victims. This is Stewart's account of the event:

> 6th August 1862
> On arriving within ¼ of a mile of Mankoque's village we dismissed the canoes, sent a message to Mankoque to say we should be glad to see him, and we sat down on the grass to await his answer. In a short time he came and we had our *menando* [palaver].
>
> We had come, however, at a bad time. From the hills at Kulubve, near the Rice Village, where Bona, the spirit of some departed chief (or some myth) is supposed to reside, there had come a party of men to Mankoque's village. They brought with them pumpkins and corn which Bona had blessed and to which he had promised rain so that there would be no more hunger. They also brought Bona's (sacred) spear. In accordance with established and time-honoured custom, a wife was to be provided for him. The lot of supplying this wife fell this time to Mankoque's village. This woman is taken, confined in a sacred hut; some say for a year, others for life. she is fed and cared for and supposed to act the oracle; to be, in fact, a sort of pytheness. That this was a new thing to us, but not a rare thing in the country, we were fated soon to discover to our cost. Mankoque was therefore busy.[7]

After the missionaries had stated their case, they retired for the night. Stewart continues,

> About three hours after I had fallen asleep I was awaked by a tremendous hubbub in the village. I thought it was morning. But it was only the excitement caused by the seizure of the wife of a man (a chief man) named Chimwale as the victim to be offered to Bona as a spouse in his solitary mountains. The robbed man set up a cry nearly as mournful as the death-wail, *M'kazi angu! M'kazi angu!* —My wife, my wife! According to all accounts, great sympathy

was expressed for the man thus bereaved by the Spirit of Kulubve. This puerile and debasing superstition is one of the many by which their soul is held in bondage more degraded by far than that of their bodies.[8]

Mankhokwe now found time to listen to his missionary visitors, who, after having stated their case, were given permission to look for a site on Mount Thyolo. In view of Mankhokwe's earlier distrust of Europeans and his appeal to Chibisa to expel them, his permission to let them settle on Thyolo was something of an about-face.[9] Two reasons may have accounted for this.

Livingstone's Kololo servants had been left behind at Chibisa's because of insubordination and had begun opening new gardens and raiding the surrounding areas for wives and laborers. Their raids led to innumerable complaints from the neighboring headmen, and there was a general feeling that on the first available occasion the Kololo would try to seize power. Although the missionaries tried to keep aloof from these conflicts, they were generally accused of siding with the Kololo, a rumor which the Kololo did nothing to contradict. The move to Thyolo was therefore seen by the missionaries as a way of publicly dissociating themselves from this band of robbers. As this would isolate the Kololo, Mankhokwe may have welcomed the move.

Also, Mankhokwe may have deliberately wanted the missionaries to get into difficulties that he knew would arise, difficulties which might hasten their departure from the country. If that was his intention, he got what he wanted, for when the missionary reconnaissance party moved up the slopes of Thyolo, they met with such fierce resistance from the inhabitants, most of them refugees from the valley, that they were forced to drop their plans. In Rowley's words, "The people seemed almost mad with superstitious apprehension; they seemed as though they were living in the actual but invisible presence of a mighty spirit to whom we were antagonistic, and whose wrath could be visited on them. We might have killed them before they would have consented to our coming."[10]

Dispirited, the missionaries returned to Chibisa's, where two of their number died after showing signs of dementia, an illness ascribed by the population to Mbona's vengeance.[11] The famine, aggravated by incessant slave hunts, continued well into the following year, and by February 1863 it was estimated that about 90 percent of the population was dead.[12] This was undoubtedly one of the most catastrophic events in the entire history of the valley:

> Large masses of people had fled down to the Shire, only anxious to get the river between them and their enemies. Most of the food had been left behind; and famine and starvation had cut off so many, that the remainder were too few to bury the dead. The corpses we saw floating down the river were only

a remnant of those that had perished, whom their friends, from weakness, could not bury, nor over-gorged crocodiles devour. It is true that famine caused a great portion of this waste of human life: but the slave-trade must be deemed the chief agent in the ruin, because, as we were informed, in former droughts all the people flocked from the hills down to the marshes, which are capable of yielding crops of maize in less than three months, at any time of the year, and now they were afraid to do so.[13]

Early in 1863, the *prazo* owner and notorious slaver Paul Mariano II (alias Matekenya, "the one who causes trembling"), who for years had been held at bay by Tengani's warriors, was finally able to push into the country. One of his aims was Mbona's village at Khulubvi, which had been hit less hard by the famine on account of its marsh gardens. The village and the shrine were destroyed by Mariano's men.[14] Mariano died in September 1863, an event which no doubt was attributed also to Mbona's vengeance, and was succeeded by his eight-year-old son, Paul Mariano III.[15] During the long minority of the new chief, Chagunda, one of the *capitaes*, became the de facto head of the *prazo* Massingire, which now included the southern part of the valley and the Khulubvi shrine. Chagunda made peace with the Mbona organization, offering gifts to the shrine and generally occupying Lundu's former position.[16] After his death he became a major territorial spirit and the object of cultic veneration. He holds the title of brother-in-law to Mbona, having provided him with a spirit wife.[17] She was probably the last of the permanent celibate spirit wives, as there is no record of another one's having been appointed in later years.

Her tenure, though, may have been of short duration. In 1868 Henry Faulkner, an elephant hunter, reported renewed unrest.[18] From 1870 onward Massingire came under repeated attack from Chiputula, the southernmost Kololo chief. In 1874 Chagunda was defeated by Chiputula, and in 1877 the latter swept down the right bank, destroyed the shrine once again, and put Sena in a state of alert.[19] In the memory of some of the cult officers, the persons of Matekenya and Chiputula have merged, and what had been a most traumatic experience, comparable only with the Zimba episode, came to be transformed into a clear victory for Mbona:

> When Mbona came to live with us here, he had a quarrel with a white man, a Portuguese by the name of Chiputula. In those days the country was under Portuguese rule, and Chiputula was the person in charge of these parts. He was a warlike man, who had taken to raiding the Mang'anja and who had already killed many of our people.
>
> Now, when this man Chiputula heard of the great things Mbona was doing among us, he was not pleased and decided to get rid of him, but he failed utterly. When he [Chiputula] realized this, Mbona told him, "You thought I would be no match for you, but you know now that you made a mistake,

for not only was I strong enough to hold out against you, I even beat you!"

This is what happened: Chiputula had a powerful band of fighting men under his command. Never doubting that he would crush Mbona at Khulubvi, he set out with his men, creating havoc on the way. Before he had gone very far, however, Mbona intervened, saying, "I am now going to give Chiputula something to regret. Let us see what he will do, when he and his men run out of food!" Then he caused a drought.

The sun beat down so fiercely that Chiputula, unable to find food and too weak to attempt crossing the Shire River, finally said, "I am in trouble, and it looks as if I shall have to admit defeat. Let me find some spears, a hoe, and a length of black cloth." These he took to Khulubvi with the words, "I am beaten; never again shall I go to war against that man. Accept this hoe and work your fields in peace." To this Mbona replied, "It is not difficult to see why you lost, for by thinking you could beat me you wanted to do the impossible, and you were beaten instead!"

Still he accepted the spears, the hoe, and the cloth. Once again, rain poured down, and there has been no drought since. The wars were over, and we could stay in our country. By offering those spears Chiputula meant to say that he no longer wanted war. We still have them. They lie on the floor in Mbona's hut, there being a rule that they are never to be in a standing position. If, for instance, we were to lean them against the wall, trouble would follow without fail. We also keep some very old cups, given us by the same Chiputula. We use them for pouring Mbona's beer.[20]

Matekenya's raids have gone down in popular memory as *nkhondo ya chiwalawala*, the "war of the great dispersal," because people went to many places to escape from Matekenya's warriors.[21] In the north of the valley the Mang'anja establishment fared even worse. Kaphwiti was killed by the Kololo, Lundu and Mankhokwe lost their chiefdoms, and the Thyolo shrine was destroyed by Chiputula, never to be revived.[22]

In 1879 the Portuguese reached an agreement with Paul Mariano III. There followed a period of relative peace, during which the shrine was once more rebuilt. In May 1881 Khulubvi was visited by the French traveler Paul Guyot, who reported that the post of Salima was then held by the wife of Khombe, a shrine guardian, who was old and blind.[23] She was the first of a long line of interim Salimas who served only on the occasion of major rituals, notably the rebuilding of the shrine.

Unrest, however, continued, culminating in the Massingire rising of 1884–85, which drove many of the *prazo*'s inhabitants to the right bank of the Shire. The uprising was caused by fears that the Portuguese, who at long last had gained a measure of influence in the *prazo*, were going to impose a system of taxation.[24] The upshot was once again disastrous. The British traveler W. M. Kerr, who visited the valley in 1885, wrote: "It would be impossible to exaggerate the untold wretchedness which has made the Shire valley a vale of blood and tears. Sad indeed has been the fate of its persecuted people. The ruthless work of fire and sword has driven them hither and thither. Slavery and war found here a congenial soil."[25]

These disturbances on the Shire finally caused the British government to accede to a suggestion made by the Scots missionaries, who had in the meantime established themselves in the country, that a consular officer be appointed. The Portuguese in their turn tried to reassert their rights over southern Malawi, albeit without success. The crisis ended with the signing of the Anglo-Portuguese Treaty of 1891, in which the present boundaries between Malawi and Mozambique were defined. It meant the end of three decades of uncertainty and bloodshed. The return to normality was celebrated in a popular song, which alludes to the fact that for much of the time people had been hiding in the Matundu Hills:

> *Mwana nyani*
> *Tsika maphiri*
> *Dziko labwera*

> Child of the baboon
> Come down the hills
> The country is on its feet again.[26]

THE BEGINNINGS OF COLONIALISM

Not until 1894 did the second face-to-face encounter between a Christian missionary and the Mbona organization take place. That missionary was Joseph Booth, who was a very different sort of man from Livingstone or the U.M.C.A. missionaries. More important, though, his visit in 1894 took place in a transformed political situation. Kololo rule in the northern part of the valley was ruthless, and when the first Scottish missionaries entered the area in 1875, some of them were highly critical of what they called the "Kololo slave government."[27] Despite such criticisms, the Kololo became valuable allies of the British. The early British officials tended to regard them as protectors of the Mang'anja rather than oppressors,[28] and the Kololo for their part loved to regard themselves as black Englishmen (except, it was remarked, in the matter of monogamy). They helped the British defend the Shire Valley against the Portuguese, and while the conflict lasted, they continued to extend their area of influence.[29]

Little of this gave the Mang'anja chiefs pleasure. They hated the Kololo, and British support for them merely confirmed their suspicions of British missionary intentions. But toward the end of the 1880s things changed. British relations with the Kololo became strained, and Tengani, who had now become the senior Mang'anja ruler, was able to enter into negotiations with the British for the recognition of his chiefdom. On July 21, 1891, Tengani, Ngabu, and others who exercised authority at the Khulubvi shrine signed a treaty in which they ceded sovereign rights and agreed to be taxed, while for their part the British recognized Tengani as chief.[30] Thus in 1894 the Mang'anja had reason to look more kindly on British power and intentions. Nevertheless, when Joseph Booth and John Chilembwe, later a nationalist revolutionary, came to Khulubvi, they did not at first have an easy time.[31] They presented themselves first to Chief Chataika and his headman Mkhuche.[32] But the two officials denied them a hearing and ordered all the people into their huts, taking their dogs and fowls with them. Booth was determined to communicate, and he and Chilembwe began to sing hymns as loudly as they could. After a while the people emerged from their huts, but again showed their contempt by drumming, dancing, and singing around the two men, drowning their hymns. Yet after a while this musical confrontation gave way to dialogue, and Booth was allowed to give a sermon on God and Christ.

According to Booth, Chataika's first response to Booth's sermon was that it was all nonsense: they knew for certain that God had spoken to them through Mbona, and they had no means of knowing whether God had spoken to Booth. In reply to this, Booth produced his Bible and read the Ten Commandments, which were carefully translated by Chilembwe. The discussion which followed focused on the issues of killing and stealing. Mbona's people argued that Mbona had also forbidden killing and the spilling of blood.[33] On the other hand, the whites did not seem to pay much attention to the biblical commandment, since Livingstone had brought guns and left them with the Kololo, who, in turn, had used their guns to make war and steal women. Possibly with an eye on Chilembwe, they added that his countrymen, the Yao, had done much the same thing with guns obtained from the Arabs. Finally, they pointed out that even the colonial government made use of guns to enforce its tax rules. Booth was able to stem the reiterated allegation that the missionaries were inseparably connected with violence. A convinced pacifist himself, he managed to convince them of the sincerity of his Christian nonviolence. Moreover, he offered to mediate on their behalf with the government and to present a petition against the tax rules and their enforcement. Dialogue had begun. The Khulubvi elders returned Booth's visit to discuss the petition and even went so far as to offer him a place in their village near the shrine. Nothing came of it, however, but the Kololo remained an issue.

In 1895 the missionary news sheet *Central Africa* carried the news that Mbona had sent locusts because not enough attention had been paid him in the matter of offerings:

> The cry at the River, as elsewhere (*e.g.*, Domasi), is one of the locusts and the coming hunger. An old native prophet, who dwells on a mountain named Khulubvi in the direction of the Machinjili Hills, has given forth that of late not enough attention has been paid him in the matter of offerings, and that it is he who has consequently sent the locusts to remind the people of their neglect. If, however, the Makololo chiefs and others who may have an interest in the matter, make some amends for the past neglect, he will reconsider his action, and take steps for the removal of the plague. The parties appealed to have sent liberal gifts of calico, and other goods to appease the offended seer.[34]

The fact that the Kololo were being singled out by the cult medium as the cause of the locust plague suggests that the antipathy against them was by no means confined to the old Mang'anja aristocracy. If the medium is to speak out authoritatively, he can do so only when the message to be transmitted is prompted by pressure from the public. Such pressure must therefore have been exercised, which is not difficult to understand in view of the Kololo reputation for cruelty.

The next important issue was that of taxation. The level of the hut tax was fixed per district by the tax collector, who may not always have been sufficiently careful in assessing people's ability to pay up. In 1901, for instance, the hut tax was in some areas raised to twelve shillings, an exorbitant amount for the time. No wonder that there was much discontent. In Nsanje, the tax issue focused on the shrine grounds, which under the traditional rules had always been exempt from tribute. This was not fully understood by the tax collectors, who were of the opinion that exemption of the shrine grounds might set a precedent. But although attempts were made by a succession of tax collectors to make the shrine guardians pay, they were unsuccessful. Three of the collectors even met with untimely deaths. Thus A. E. Peile, appointed in 1892, died in January 1894 from a gun accident, while shooting birds. His colleagues H. G. Galt and S. Robins died from fever, in 1896 and 1910, respectively. All these deaths were attributed to Mbona.[35]

Another supposed victim of Mbona's revenge was R. R. Racey, a junior officer in the colonial administration who was stationed in the valley from 1902 to 1905 and who had to be invalided home because of a mental condition. Racey had made extensive investigations about the cult and had even paid a visit to the shrine, about which he wrote a seventeen-page memorandum, dated January 1905. Although he was then already mentally ill, his report contains some rare pieces of information:

Upon learning where the Mbona compound was situated, I decided to pay him a visit. Upon telling some friendly natives [machila men; i.e., palanquin carriers] of my intentions, they begged of me not to go, saying I should die and my death would be upon them for taking me there. The following day after much persuasion my bearers finally arrived near the Mbona gardens. While approaching and still some 500 yards away my attention was drawn to the ground where to my astonishment I saw the spirit of a snake some 100 yards long. It was an inert mass and on looking back the head was seen to have been severed from the trunk.[36]

From Racey's report it is clear that at the time of his visit the shrine and the shrine grounds were in good condition, and there even seems to have been a Salima, possibly the wife of one of the guardians. At first she did not want to be seen, but when Racey persevered, she emerged from her hut, dressed in blue calico:

She had a fine strong almost beautiful face, brilliant black eyes, and a soft musical voice. In answer to my questions Salima replied as nearly as I can recollect that her husband [i.e., Mbona] had been absent a short while; that he came to her as a man, she was not quite sure whether as a spirit or a human being; that he told her what to say to people and how to answer questions; that he had power to transpose himself into one kind of animal or another; to make rain, to cause destitution, famine, punishment and so on; that he was indeed God of the Sena, Chikunda and Amang'anja natives who believed, some having fallen off in their allegiance. She admitted that Mbona had the power to cause or inspire fear. I pointed out that our God who had created all things was Paramount and His rule one of Love, Justice and Truth, proof lying in myself as I showed no signs of fear which she admitted was so.[37]

Thus, in the period following the establishment of the protectorate the cult was once again gaining in importance, this time as a vehicle of Mang'anja resistance against the Kololo and the newly imposed tax rules.

In 1900 the South Africa General Mission (S.A.G.M.) established itself in the district. As early as 1901 the Reverend Edgar Faithful reported that he had been to Khulubvi.[38] His colleague the Reverend E. Price also took a keen interest in the Mbona cult, on which he reported in the S.A.G.M. mission journal on various occasions. In 1911, on the occasion of floods in the Nsanje District, he observed that people were rebuilding the shrine and organizing a major sacrifice for Mbona. Price had nothing good to say about Mbona, whom he reckoned to belong to the "principalities," "powers," and "rulers of the darkness of this world" with which the mission had to contend.[39] He and others were probably influenced by Rowley's books on the history of the U.M.C.A., then standard fare for missionaries going to Malawi, in which the Mbona cult was described as "a painful manifestation of false religion."[40] More particularly, the description by Rowley of the election of a spirit wife from Mankhokwe's village seems to have aroused a strong moral indignation in missionary circles. Captain E. D. Young, leader of the Livingstone search expedition of 1867, also drawing upon Rowley, wrote:

> The hill on which the presiding spirit of the Shire valley reigns, was passed today, the 12th of August. It forms the extreme peak of the Kolubvi hills, and the natives year by year resort to it to listen to the dictates of an unhappy woman who is incarcerated upon it in a hut. She is the wife of a spirit, who once in the human form, as a distinguished chief called M'Bonar [sic], brought the Manganja tribe to listen to his laws. Now, he is supposed to speak through a prophetess, who is constantly being renewed, for death generally relieves the office of its tenant in a year or two. The worst of it is, any man's wife may be seized at a moment's notice as a successor, and great is the dismay when it is known that "Zarima's" life has fled from the lone hill top.[41]

News about the Kololo having destroyed the Thyolo shrine was therefore received with satisfaction.[42] The Scots missionaries in the Shire highlands even took this to mean that the cult had ceased to exist.[43] This, however, was no more than wishful thinking fed by Kololo propaganda. The missionaries in the valley knew better.

In 1912 rumors began to circulate that Mbona's followers were sacrificing young girls to Mbona by throwing them to the crocodiles in the Shire. A. H. Wyatt, then the district commissioner, was convinced that the story was true, but he could not be persuaded to "meddle with the Rain Goddess" (his name for Salima) because his three predecessors had died after having done precisely that. The source of the rumor remains unknown, but it is likely that it originated among the local missionaries and that it was they who urged Wyatt to make investigations.[44]

Around the same time the S.A.G.M. was given permission by the local headman to set up a school at Khulubvi in the immediate neighborhood of the sacred grounds. The wattle-and-daub structure was apparently put up by the villagers themselves, which gave Price the idea that people were beginning to see the light.[45] A year later, when the villages around his mission station were experiencing a drought, there was talk once again among his faithful about going to Mbona. Price for his part speedily organized a service in his own church, and if we are to believe him, rain broke and fell in abundance almost before he had finished. Having heard that Mbona was at that time being neglected, he predicted that Mbona would soon be "a thing of the past," although he foresaw that "the Devil was not going to give in without a terrible struggle."[46] In 1914 he reported that he had been given permission to deliver a sermon on Christ from the door of the shrine hut: "I addressed the people from the door of the hut after getting

permission from the 'priest' in charge. I spoke to them about the great sacrifice of Christ for the world and of God's love for mankind, etc. They
said, 'When we come to believe in Jesus we will be willing to give up our
present worship of Mbona.' 'You see,' they said, 'our fathers taught us all
about Mbona and at present we believe in him. We like you to teach our
children, because they learn good things.'"[47]

Price, whose optimism was apparently inexhaustible, was further heart-
ened in 1916 when Nkhuche, a senior headman and successor of the
Nkhuche who had received Booth, came to the mission to ask for prayers
for rain. "I asked why he had not gone to Mbona as he had previously
done," wrote Price. "He replied, 'We have no longer faith in Mbona. Your
God can give rain, pray for us or our crops will be ruined.'" Price then
asked him if he really believed that the Christian God could give rain. When
Nkhuche said he did, Price arranged for special prayers which Nkhuche
attended daily, having the look, although a heathen, of someone "not far
from the kingdom."[48] It did not occur to Price that Nkhuche was only taking revenge on some of his fellow headmen and more particularly on the
cult officers for not having supported his candidacy for the title of principal headman, which the Nyasaland government had recently introduced.
Among those who had been more fortunate was Chiphwembwe, a pro-
tégé of the mission, who two years earlier had endeared himself to the missionary establishment by setting fire to a *nomi* building, considered by the
mission as representing mere sexual depravity, but who was at the same
time one of the pillars of the Mbona cult.[49] A famous Salima, who was
active in those days, came from his area and had been provided by him.
Whenever she had a revelatory dream, she would first reveal it to Chiphwembwe, thereby contributing to his fame in the cult organization.[50]

THE RESURGENCE OF MANG'ANJA
NATIONALISM

In 1917 the Makombe uprising took place south of the
Zambezi among the Tavara and Barwe peoples of Mozambique.[51] After
the uprising had been defeated, thousands of refugees crossed into the
Nsanje District of Nyasaland, bringing with them tales of horror and
destruction. In the historical memory of the Mang'anja, the rising evoked
echoes of the Zimba wars, as the refugees came from what was considered
to have been the homeland of the Zimba. Mbona was spoken of as the
"father of Makombe," the Barwe paramount and leader of the rebellion,
and as having assisted Makombe in his fight against the Portuguese. This
adaptation of myth expressed Mang'anja sympathy with the refugees and

provided a way in which they could be fitted into Mang'anja metaphysics. Moreover, the idea of Mbona's support of revolt against whites was appropriate enough to the experience of the Mang'anja themselves.

There were various reasons for the Mang'anja to welcome these immigrants. Coming in small separate groups, they posed no direct threat to the Mang'anja political structure, and no group insisted on having its own headman.[52] Headmen were glad to settle strangers in their area, thereby increasing the number of their subjects and adding to their status. Under the traditional system the headman of the village was normally the head of its senior lineage and also related to the junior lineages. Nonrelated persons were incorporated into the autochthonous lineages by a putative relationship with a deceased member. If there was no real blood or affinal relationship between a headman and his subjects, at least the pretense was there. That system, however, could not be followed with the advent of the Makombe refugees. Their different social system and their great numbers did not allow for the application of this principle. Kin loyalty changed to political loyalty, and the authority of the village headmen became more bureaucratic in character.

While all this was welcomed, the headmen needed to define their identity against those foreigners who were thought of as belonging to a lower form of culture. One way of protecting their identity was by consciously preserving Mang'anja social structure, language, and history. The headmen had two channels for cooperation: their meetings with the chiefs, all of whom had remained Mang'anja (at least in the Nsanje District), and, on a separate level, their meetings at the Mbona shrine. It was unavoidable that in the end many headmen were of mixed blood, although they would do everything to pass themselves off as pure Mang'anja. There was little the chiefs could do, since they could not depose a headman officially recognized by the administration. But here the Mbona cult acted as a corrective. There was and is a general prohibition on non-Mang'anja entering the shrine or participating in the rituals. Although this prohibition is not always strictly maintained, it provides the Mang'anja leaders with a means of banning unwanted headmen from participation. The traditional political organization, therefore, remained preserved to a greater extent within the cult than outside it.

The hut tax remained a source of major discontent. To make matters worse, in the very year the Makombe refugees began to arrive in large numbers, plots of land were leased to Europeans in the Dinde Marsh. When in 1921 the hut tax was reduced by half and the European estates gradually closed through crop failures, however, Mbona's continued ability to look after the interests of his people seemed vindicated once more.

Meanwhile, the missionary advance continued. In July 1921 the Catholics established a mission just outside Nsanje township, and its members set out without delay to combat the S.A.G.M. and the formidable Price. The main Catholic interest, as always, was in small village schools, of which they founded a great many.[53] The Catholics were coming in late; the main centers were already occupied or in the process of being occupied by the S.A.G.M. One result of this was that the Catholic church in Nsanje became a refuge for the immigrants from the Portuguese territories, who were looked upon with some disdain by the Mang'anja.[54] The missionaries were well aware of the cult's existence, but the Sena people, who constituted the bulk of the Catholic converts, had no real stake in the cult. Hence the priests felt no compulsion to combat Mbona as their colleagues combatted the *nyau* societies in the Chikwawa District.[55]

Ironically, the missions, far from destroying the cult by their teachings, actually rendered it an important service by helping it adapt to the changing times. People were able to restructure some of the events of Mbona's life along biblical lines. The fact that Mbona's father is not named in most versions of his biography — a consequence of the Mang'anja kinship system which reckons descent through the mother — became positively converted into a myth according to which Mbona was born to a virgin.[56] His food-providing powers, which had hitherto found expression in stories about miraculous rice growing along a well made by him, copious meals found in the sacred thicket, or pumpkins he made to grow on trees for starved refugees, evoked comparison with Christ's food miracles.

At this stage, biblical adaptations primarily reflected positive similarities between Mbona and Christ. The Mang'anja were perfectly prepared to let the two religions exist side by side. Their willingness to let the missionary Price preach in the neighborhood of the shrine was not a renunciation of Mbona but a gesture of genuine if unsophisticated ecumenism. In time some African converts of the S.A.G.M. and of the Catholic mission were appointed to functions in the cult. This was not perceived — except in the case of the medium — as a break with their church but as yet another form of peaceful coexistence.[57] For their part, the missionaries continued to condemn the cult, to denounce it as idolatry and as irreconcilable with Christianity. But beyond sermonizing, they could do little either to suppress the cult or to rival it in its areas of most effective operation. Any drastic attempt to destroy the cult was out of the question, especially since district commissioners occasionally made gifts to the shrine and certainly would not have supported the missionaries.[58] The missionaries did not endeavor to use their spiritual power for the fertility of the land, with the exception of occasional prayers for rain, nor did they encourage the prophetic role. Thus the Mbona cult remained in exclusive possession of ritual services unclaimed by the prevailing forms of Christianity.

THE SEARCH FOR A SALIMA
FROM LUNDU

From 1922 onward, stimulated by the Mwanthota famine which struck the valley in that year, there began a series of attempts to get the classic Salimaship restored with the cooperation of the Lundus.[59] The first tangible result of this movement was the return, in 1926, of the Lundu family to Mbewe, their old site on the right bank. Saizi Lundu was subsequently installed as village headman.

Another attempt was made following the promulgation of the 1933 Native Authority Ordinance, which gave chiefs far-reaching authority over village headmen. In that year the district commissioner for Nsanje, W. S. Phillips, reported that action was taken by the native authorities to resuscitate "the cult of Mbona," which, he said, had lain dormant for a number of years. The shrine had been rebuilt, and attempts were once again being made to obtain a spirit wife from Lundu.[60] At the same time an appeal was being made by the combined Mang'anja chiefs of the Shire Valley to have the Lundu paramountcy restored, but apparently no official reaction followed.[61]

The subject of the Lundu paramountcy was again brought up at the governor's *baraza*, held at Port Herald (Nsanje) in August 1935. His Excellency's answer to the request on that occasion was that if all the chiefs concerned agreed to the desirability of appointing Lundu as paramount chief of the Mang'anja, then something might be done in the matter.[62] As nothing was heard again for a year, eight Mang'anja chiefs, among them the old Chief Thenzwa Tengani, sent a respectful reminder to the governor.[63] As it turned out, they had waited too long, for a younger Tengani was soon to be installed who would have nothing of their plans.

THE TENGANI INTERLUDE, 1936–1961

By 1930 the S.A.G.M. had produced a small group of African preachers and evangelists who took a much less lenient view of the cult. One of these, Molin Tengani, was to be instrumental in upsetting the existing balance of power.

Molin had become a Christian at the Lulwe station of the S.A.G.M. in 1902.[64] For a time he worked as a foreman on the railways, but he afterward joined the mission staff as a teacher, serving successively at Mpatsa, the Tengani headquarters, and Malindi, further south. Following this, he was employed at the Chididi station, where he served until 1936. His uncle Thenzwa, the tenth incumbent of the Tenganiship since Livingstone's visit, had died in 1934, and Molin became a leading favorite for succession. He refused the position at first, but finally gave in and was duly invested in 1936.

He proved to be a stern ruler, and his handling of court matters became notorious. Moreover, unlike the missionaries, he was in a position to threaten the Mbona cult. Upon his accession he refused to make the customary offering at the Khulubvi shrine, and he let it be known that as a Christian he would not continue the obligations to the cult that had formerly fallen to the Tengani chiefs.[65] When the shrine became dilapidated it could not be rebuilt. The cult officers asked Subchief Mbeta, a classificatory relative of Tengani's, to take the latter's place, but he too refused.[66] The guardians who lived at the shrine had hitherto escaped taxation, but attempts were now made to force them to pay.[67] Rumors began to circulate that the waters of the sacred pool at Ndione, said to be reddened with Mbona's blood, had now turned the normal color, a sign that Mbona had withdrawn from the area.

As far as the restoration of the Lunduship was concerned, Tengani wrote a letter to the district commissioner in which he claimed that he was the senior Mang'anja chief in the valley and that his ancestors, not Lundu's, had appointed the other valley chiefs. He claimed that Lundu had no influence left and that the Mbona cult was dead.[68] The district commissioner made inquiries of his own and found that most of his informants agreed with Tengani's version, according to which the only person of consequence to have arrived in the valley before Tengani was Mbona. The first Tengani had been appointed by Kaphwiti, together with the first Lundu, implying that at best they were equals. Tengani's letter was effective in that the Lundu issue was dropped for several decades.[69]

Among the various rules enforced by Tengani, the one which caused the most resentment was that of ridging the gardens before the planting season. This was supposed to lead to increased food yields, but that beneficial effect of ridging had never been proved.[70] Traditionally, the people used a system of shallow cultivation which required far less effort, and they complained that ridged gardens tended to dry out more quickly.[71] The Mbona medium and many of the chiefs protested, but their objections were ignored. Defaulters were either fined or imprisoned, and grudgingly the population had to comply.[72] Garden ridging was first introduced in 1947, but it was enforced only in 1949–50, when the valley was hit by the most serious famine since the one of 1862–63.[73] Emergency feeding programs had to be organized to save people from starvation.

Mbona's medium let it be known that the drought was due to the introduction of garden ridges, to which Mbona was most vehemently opposed.[74] According to Headman Mbangu, senior guardian of the shrine, a delegation from the shrine went to Lundu, then still a subchief, with a black goat — which the headman said was a symbol of the importance and urgency of their message — to ask once again for a spirit wife. Lundu answered, "I have heard the message which you brought from the Nsanje chiefs. All of you know that I have been deposed as the Mang'anja paramount and that Ngabu [Banda] has taken my place. I, as a junior chief, am not in a position to provide Mbona with a Salima. Go to Ngabu with your message. I know that there are no rains because there is no Salima, but I am helpless."[75] The delegation returned to Nsanje to report to the cult principals, who then decided to send another delegation, this time to Ngabu Banda. The latter, however, answered that he was not prepared to take action because he was afraid that the government might no longer tolerate such a custom. In the end, a temporary spirit wife was obtained from Mbangu, and the shrine was rebuilt. Some time later, however, the spirit wife was disowned by the Mbona medium and forced to retire.[76]

Meanwhile Tengani relentlessly expanded his territory. In 1950 both Ngabu and Chiphwembwe died. Instead of appointing successors, the district administration placed the two former chiefdoms and half of Chimombo's chiefdom under Makoko, a relative of Tengani's. A year later, Makoko was made a subchief of Tengani, and in 1953, when Makoko died, he was succeeded by Tengani's son Edwin, who replaced all of Makoko's appointees with personnel from Tengani. A reign of terror now began in connection with the enforcement of garden ridges, and some people migrated to the Portuguese side of the Shire.[77] In that year, also, the Federation of Rhodesia and Nyasaland came into being despite large-scale protests from the population. The powerful chief of the northern Chewa, Mwase, stirred up trouble at Tengani's, and Zambian troops were called in to restore order. Apparently, all this had its effects on the cult also. District Commissioner P. M. Lewis reported that the shrine was being rebuilt that year and that the officers once again intended to approach Lundu. Tengani had been invited but did not take part. If Lundu was unable to send a spirit wife, there would be one from Headman Thunye. Lewis had made it clear also at the meeting of the district council that he had no objection to offer if the cult officers went ahead, saying that he was "all for the revival of these things."[78]

In March 1959, a few months after the return of Dr. Banda to Malawi, a state of emergency was declared. In Nsanje many people were arrested, among them the medium Josef Thom, who had meanwhile succeeded his late brother, Jailos. The day after his arrest he became seriously ill, however, and had to be taken to Nsanje hospital.

In October of the same year a medicine man called Yadi came from

Chikwawa, claiming he had been sent by Mbona to practice at the shrine. He arrived with some twenty people, including his four wives, who installed themselves in Salima's house. At first nobody seems to have reacted, but after a month Yadi was forced to leave the shrine after the guardians complained to the district commissioner. The guardians said they had allowed this because they wanted to see for themselves whether Yadi had truly been sent by Mbona. Only later on did they realize how stupid they had been.[79] This remarkable event can only be understood if it is remembered that there were no cult principals at that moment, since no successors had been appointed. Tengani had taken over their former chiefdoms.

Things changed only in 1961, when the Malawi Congress party won the first general election, and Molin Tengani was subsequently deposed. He was succeeded by his relative Stonkin, who was installed a year later and whose appointment aroused fresh expectations among the Khulubvi officials. Once again attempts were made to have Lundu reinstated and at long last to obtain a Salima from his chiefdom. In 1965 the shrine was rebuilt. Two letters had been written to Lundu, with no result.[80] It was becoming clear by now that Lundu was not in a position to accede to their demands. It was even rumored that the state president had been approached on the matter, but that the answer had been that such an institution could no longer be maintained in our times.

This spirit of malaise was reflected in a rumor which began to circulate in December 1966. According to this rumor, Mbona, tired of the unsuccessful attempts of the shrine officers, had sent a baboon as his messenger to Lundu to ask the latter for a Salima. But Lundu, with the assistance of Headman Mulilima, had seized a gun and killed the animal. Ngabu Banda, who was at that time still Lundu's superior, had sent for Lundu to answer for this atrocity, but the outcome of this was not yet known.[81] The baboon story is a highly symbolic, systematic inversion of the cult's founding myth. Whereas in the founding myth Mbona traveled from north to south, from Lundu's court to Nsanje, where he was killed but given a wife by Lundu afterward, the baboon (Mbona's representative) traveled in the opposite direction. He too was killed, but no wife was forthcoming. On the contrary, the animal was allegedly killed by Lundu to make clear once and for all that he wanted no longer to have anything to do with the cult. The old order had apparently passed for ever. The baboon story reveals a partly conscious, partly unconscious realization that there was no hope ever to revive the classic Salimaship. The organization would have to make do with temporary Salimas, as it had been doing already for several decades. Now secessionist movements set in.

SECESSIONIST MOVEMENTS, 1967–1981

Tengani built his own Mbona shrine in his sacred grove in the year 1967, declaring that he wanted no longer to maintain relations with the Khulubvi organization. Then the medium Josef Thom built his own shrine a year later. When Lundu was finally reinstated as the Mang'anja paramount on July 5, 1959, all the Khulubvi officials were present. Again, Evans Makosana Lundu, the new paramount, promised them full cooperation, but all came to naught. Malemia, the chief jural officer at the shrine, who also had been restored to his rightful position by the new government, had to take action against the medium, who according to the chief had begun to spread nonsensical rumors about Lundu.[82]

In the 1970s the two missions, which from the beginning of the century had been more or less the sole representatives of Christianity in the Nsanje District, were joined by a whole array of new African-led Pentecostal churches and a powerful neotraditionalist movement, which opposed both the old missions and the Pentecostals. The impact of this twin process, which at its peak involved several thousand adults, profoundly altered the religious landscape of Nsanje.[83] It is certainly not an overstatement to say that these new churches disengaged themselves and their followers from traditional religion to a greater extent than the mission churches were able to do. In the mission churches the leaders commanded, although largely unsuccessfully, that the faithful renounce pagan practices. In the Spirit churches, on the other hand, the faithful themselves demanded it. This constitutes the most basic difference between the two.

The Church of the African Ancestors (Mpingo wa Makolo Achikuda) was brought to the district in 1971 by a local man, who had joined it as a migrant laborer in the town of Blantyre, where the headquarters of the movement is located.[84] The movement itself reputedly had been founded some thirty years earlier by Peter Nyambo, a Ngoni from the present Central Region of Malawi, who in his younger years had been known as an active critic of the colonial order.[85] It is one of several neotraditionalist movements in the district,[86] the others being the Ethiopian Church (also known as Topia or Abraham Church) and the African Church, which have, however, remained relatively small in comparison with the Ancestor Church.[87] The main points of its doctrine are set forth in an official circular issued by the headquarters of the movement in Blantyre, which carries the title "The Truth about Jesus, the Savior of the Israelites and the Whites."[88]

Until about 1976 the Ancestor Church had remained a fairly insignificant body with only a few congregations, mainly in the southern and central part of the district. From 1976 onward, however, the movement gradu-

Illus. 21. Subchief Evans Makosana Lundu, 1967. Photograph by G. Zonneveld.

Illus. 22. Installation of Evans Makosana Lundu as paramount chief of the Shire Valley, 1969

ally gained speed, and three years later it claimed a membership of several thousand adults, affiliated with more than sixty congregations in six chiefdoms. In the same period there was also a sharp increase in clashes with the Christian churches and in cases of physical harassment of Christians, leading to occasional police intervention and a number of court cases. Not unexpectedly, it became part of the strategy of the Ancestor Church to gain control of the Mbona cult. The chance seemed to have come in 1976, when it was rumored that the Mbona shrine was in such a poor shape that it was on the point of collapsing. As usual, these rumors led to others purporting that some calamity was about to take place unless action was quickly taken. For the leaders of the Ancestor Church, whose most important congregation was then located in the village of Mbeta, only a few kilometers from the shrine, this seemed an excellent opportunity to offer their services and thereby to gain perhaps some measure of influence in the shrine organization. They therefore paid a visit to the two chief officers of the cult, but these forbade them to set foot inside the shrine grounds, and one even warned them to stay out of his chiefdom altogether.[89] Following this, they decided to approach the principal guardian of the shrine, Headman Mbangu, whose village borders directly on the shrine grounds, but once again they met with firm opposition.

Illus. 23. Modern Roman Catholic village church near Tengani's court, 1965

Some months later, the leaders of the Ancestor Church made a third attempt, by trying to get the cult's medium on their side. Once again they were unsuccessful. Three reasons may account for this. First, the medium was in ill health at the time; he died a year later. Second, he may have been afraid of yet another fray with the two principals of the cult. Third, and perhaps more important, he disagreed openly with the political character of the Ancestor Church. The point here is that he disagreed not so much as an individual but as the personification of Mbona, who is supposed to be superior to any secular power and to stand above secular politics.

Realizing that resistance in the shrine area was too strong, the Ancestor Church leaders now turned to Stonkin Tengani, Molin Tengani's successor, who apparently showed himself more welcoming and who (they said) even made a small contribution to their fund. Among the various topics discussed was the Tenganis' historical position in the Mbona cult, which Molin had abdicated but which the Ancestor people wanted to see restored with a view of gaining entry into the cult along a different route. Tengani's relations with the officialdom at the shrine, however, were such that it was impossible for him to bring any pressure to bear upon them. Other means had therefore to be used, and it is in this light that one should see two

Illus. 24. Blessing a child in a Spirit church, Chikwawa, 1967. Photograph by C. Zonneveld.

extraordinary events which took place in the months following; first, a new Mbona medium emerged near Tengani's own headquarters, and second, three enterprising individuals attempted to create a new cult center to replace the existing one.

Kingy Butao, the new medium, about sixty-five years of age, is said to have become possessed for the first time on September 25, 1977. The event was preceded, as is usual in the case of mediums, by pains in the head, the legs, and the abdomen.[90] When Mbona had entered him, he stumbled, hands outstretched toward a tree, all the while shouting, "I am Mbona!" People gave him a mat to sit on and squatted around him to hear what he had to say. Kingy then told them that Chief Tengani had to inform the Mbona officers that the shrine had to be rebuilt forthwith and that a sacrifice must be made to make the locusts disappear, which were then ravaging the district. Kingy further insisted on Mbona's behalf that Tengani himself had to participate in both these activities as in the days of old.

Kingy was a Mang'anja who had previously been a healing medium and whose forebears had long-standing connections with the Mbona cult. He was also a member of the Ancestor Church. It is therefore more than likely that his possession was provoked partly by the unsuccessful negotiations just described. The event of his possession, however, had few tangible results. The shrine was provisionally repaired one or two months later and a simple ceremony held, but Tengani took no part in it, nor would the cult officials have allowed him to. Meanwhile, Kingy maintained his claims and has, because of his ascetic life and visionary claims, become a sort of sacred figure to the Ancestor movement.[91]

Soon after Kingy's possession, however, in November 1977, a man called Armando appeared on the scene. Like Kingy Butao, he was also a Mang'anja and a traditional healer. This man claimed to have received a revelation from Mbona to the effect that the cult center had to be moved from its traditional place to a forest patch near Tengani's headquarters.[92] This project, much more radical than the first, also looked more realistic, as it bypassed the existing organization and more particularly the two principals of the cult, who had no jurisdiction over Tengani's area. Tengani himself kept a guarded distance, but he did not prevent one of his councillors, nor one of his senior headmen, Lukwa, from teaming up with Armando, whose authority and prestige were thereby considerably increased.

The villagers built a hut for Armando close by the forest patch known as Mtayira ("place of the thrown-aways"), where in former times the corpses of those who had succumbed to the poison ordeal were left to the hyenas. A space was cleared among the trees and the undergrowth, and a shrine was built in the shape of a circular hut, about 1.30 meters high. The entrance to the clearing was marked by a length of dark blue cloth (a traditional symbol of rain clouds), which had been fashioned into a kind of archway through which worshipers had to pass. Armando also ordered some ritual implements to be placed in the shrine next to three large clay pots, which had been sunk into the floor to receive the beer offerings.[93]

The dedication of the shrine was accompanied by much dancing and singing, but no rain fell. Armando then ordered fresh beer brewed for a second attempt, but this, too, was unsuccessful. People then began to doubt his calling, and a meeting was convened at which the councillor and the senior headman were to answer charges of misleading the population. In the meantime Armando fled to Mozambique. The two men were arrested and taken to the police station at Nsanje, where they were charged with withholding the rain under section 471 of the penal code as read with section 2 of the Witchcraft Act. Both pleaded not guilty, but they were detained until March 1978.[94]

It is not easy to assess the role the Ancestor Church played, directly or indirectly, in this project, but it can hardly have been coincidental that the event took place at a time when the Ancestor adherents were concentrating their activities at precisely this part of the district. It is somewhat ironic, though, that while the Mbona cult was visibly declining in its traditional form, it was at the same time being revived in a sectarian form by the Ancestor Church. About the decline of the old shrine there can be no doubt. In 1977 the district administration had discontinued its long-established practice of making gifts to the shrine on the occasion of the annual rain prayers.[95] In May 1978 the medium Josef Thom died, after having held the position for thirty-four years. Although his death was not precisely bemoaned by the other shrine personalities, they nevertheless paid their respects by sending an official representation to the funeral, which attracted a large group of mourners.[96] Although it is impossible to predict whether or not a successor will emerge in due time, it is unlikely that this will happen soon, since the position of territorial medium has become politically well-nigh impossible. In 1981 the shrine lay in ruins, but the sacred grounds were still watched over by a group of elderly guardians.[97]

CHAPTER 5

The Lundu State in the Late Sixteenth and Early Seventeenth Centuries

TWENTY-FIVE YEARS have passed since E. A. Alpers first argued that the Zimba, who are on record as having twice defeated a Portuguese armed force and as having occupied a large part of Makualand in the closing decade of the sixteenth century, were actually a fighting force in the service of a member of the Lundu dynasty of the Lower Shire Valley in Malawi.[1] Alpers' viewpoint has in the meantime come to be accepted by virtually all students of Malawi's precolonial past, including M. D. D. Newitt, who some years ago made his own authoritative contribution to this discussion.[2] Whereas Newitt is prepared to accept Alpers' contention that the Zimba were Lundu's warriors, however, he disagrees on the reputed motive behind the Zimba raids. While Alpers believes that the Lundu state, together with the rival state of Muzura, was already well established in the second half of the sixteenth century, Newitt holds that these states did not materialize as formal systems before the first quarter of the seventeenth century. In his view the overall situation just before and after 1600 was rather one in which powerful groups of invaders, including the Zimba, were still in search of a suitable environment in which to set up a feudalistic state system, modeled after the Portuguese enclaves on the Zambezi. Consequently, Alpers' idea that the Zimba were being employed by the Lundu of that time to strengthen his position as an already established ruler against his rival Muzura would be untenable. Newitt's alternative reading of the early Portuguese documents has far-reaching consequences, for it upsets much of what by now has become standard Malawian historiography. It also considerably weakens the concept of the Maravi states as representing the first clear case of a trade-based as against a tribute-based political power in the East African interior.[3] It is therefore of more than superficial importance carefully to examine the arguments for and against Newitt's argument.

Newitt's alternative reading raises as many problems as it solves. Principally, how do we explain where these powerful intrusive groups came from and why they left their country of origin and moved into northern Zambesia? Newitt himself conceded that there is no direct documentary evidence providing information on these questions.[4] Since it is doubtful that such evidence will ever be forthcoming, the provenance of these groups and the circumstances under which this multiple migratory movement was set in motion are likely to remain forever unresolved problems. The result, then, would be that one theory, said to be weakly supported by documentary evidence, is being replaced by another which seems equally questionable. It is obvious that we have to look for a way out of this impasse.

In this chapter I will argue that Newitt's criticism of Alpers and others does insufficient justice to the available evidence about the existence of identifiable Maravi states from at least the second half of the sixteenth century. Some of the supposed invading bands, I will assert, were either sedentary ethnic groups or armies in the service of established state organizations. As far as the Zimba are concerned, I regard them, as does Alpers, as an armed force under the Lundu incumbent of that time, but I will maintain, against Alpers, that they were not local men, but refugees from south of the Zambezi who operated as a mercenary force under Lundu. Finally, I hope to show that Muzura, Lundu's successor as the most powerful personage in the Maravi state system, was neither a member of the Kalonga dynasty, as maintained by Alpers, nor a predecessor of the Kalongas, as proposed by Newitt, but the ruler of an entirely different state, centered not on the southwestern lakeshore but in the Mwanza area, west of modern Blantyre. This viewpoint, originally argued by W. H. J. Rangeley, has been lost sight of in the course of the discussion.[5] If proved correct, it changes our view of early Malawian history to a considerable extent, since it will no longer be possible to maintain that after Lundu's military defeat in 1622 political dominance shifted directly to the Kalongas on the lakeshore, which has now become the accepted view. Instead, we shall have to get used to the idea that power shifted first to the western Shire highlands, and only several decades later to the lakeshore.

While it is important to get the facts right, it is equally important to develop a theory explaining why these Maravi states became so expansionist and aggressive in the half century before and after 1600. Newitt has decisively shown that Alpers' "ivory thesis," according to which this action was largely due to Portuguese lack of interest in the ivory trade, finds little support in Portuguese documents.[6] Yet his own theory that the turmoils which took place in that period were due to an anarchic *Völker-*

wanderung seems equally untenable. The theory to be developed here is, first, that a number of Maravi states were already in existence in the second half of the sixteenth century (although we shall refrain from engaging in a discussion about their supposed period of origin); second, that some of these states were involved in a process of rapid expansion in the half century before and after 1600; and third, that this Maravi expansionism was set in motion around 1572, when the Portuguese, no longer content with straightforward trade, organized a massive military expedition to conquer the Monomotapa kingdom.

It is not difficult to chart the Portuguese penetration of the Zambesian interior from the early sixteenth century onward, since on that topic a wealth of information has already been made accessible by a number of distinguished scholars.[7] It is much more of a problem to answer the question about what repercussions this had on the Maravi states. The crux as usual is the scarcity of documentary evidence on the internal politics of these states. The only way to solve that problem is to complement the scarce documentary evidence as best one can with data extracted from oral history in the broadest possible sense, including not only narrative accounts about that period, if such are available, but also relics and mnemonics embedded in religious beliefs, rituals, and even the physical landscape. It is fully recognized that the use of oral traditions poses special problems of verification and interpretation, but this need not deter one from making use of them as long as one's sources and methods are open to public scrutiny.[8]

The central question is what developments took place in the Lundu state between the middle of the sixteenth and the middle of the seventeenth centuries in response to the gradual expansion of the Portuguese enclaves. We shall therefore begin with a general overview of Zambesian history, using the relatively few contemporary sources summed up by Newitt and focusing on persons, events, and processes central to our argument.[9] The middle part of the chapter concerns the Zimba, their identity, and their relationship with the Lundu of that period, and it is here that oral history in its various guises will be explored. In the third and final section the results of that exploration will be placed in the broader perspective of Zambesian history to find out if and how the expansionist character of the Lundu state was a logical result of Portuguese politics.

THE PORTUGUESE PENETRATION OF ZAMBESIA

Until the early 1530s long-distance trade in the lower Zambezi region was largely in the hands of Swahili merchants. From then

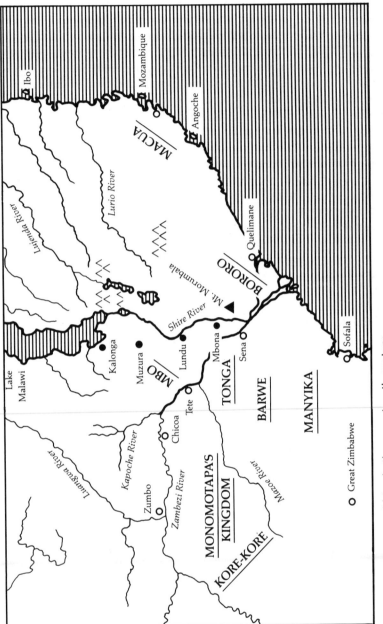

Map 4. Southeastern Africa in the seventeenth century
Source: Adapted from Alpers 1975:3.

onward, however, the Portuguese began to establish their own entrepôts at Sena and Tete and along the main routes into the Monomotapa kingdom. There are no indications that the relationships between the two parties were particularly strained. On the contrary, we learn from Father Monclaro, one of the few primary sources on this period, that in 1572, when he was stationed in Sena, Muslims and Christians were "as mixed as if they belonged to one creed."[10] Generally speaking, both sides traded foreign-made cloth and other luxury goods for slaves, ivory, and the coarse local cloths, known as *machira*. These cloths came mostly from the Shire Valley. Judging from Monclaro's indications, the export to the south bank alone must have consisted of thousands of pieces a year.[11] Although part of the production would have been sold directly to customers on the south bank, it appears nevertheless that by far the greater part was sold to Swahili and Portuguese traders, who acted as middlemen.[12] The successive captains of Mozambique did their utmost to gain control over the inland trade. They deplored especially the collaboration between their compatriots and the Muslims, but they were unable to do much about it.

This began to change, however, with the murder of Father Gonçalo da Silveira at the Monomotapa's court in 1561. The reasons behind the assassination have never become entirely clear, but the general opinion was that Swahili merchants had been able to convince the Monomotapa that Silveira had only come to pave the way for a Portuguese takeover.[13] Apart from that, it was rumored that Silveira had also been accused of sorcery, of bringing drought and famine on the country, and of planning to kill the Monomotapa and set his subjects at war with each other. Accordingly, Silveira was killed in the way a *muroyi* or sorcerer would have been killed. He was first thrown on his face, and then lifted up by his hands and feet. A rope was tied round his neck and pulled from both sides until he was strangled. His body was then dragged by a rope to a nearby stream and thrown into it. This, it is said, was the normal way of getting rid of the body of a sorcerer, so that the poison it was thought to contain could not pollute the atmosphere. According to one account, nothing was left in the darkness but "the empty hut, the smashed crucifix and the trail of blood stretching towards the river."[14]

It is of course possible that things did happen as just described, but one has the impression that a fair amount of conscious and unconscious mythologizing regarding the person of Silveira has taken place as well. It is not without reason that the story focused on the two chief obstacles to the Christian mission, namely Islam and "heathenism," and that it served to legitimate any kind of action against these forces of darkness. One consequence of the murder was that the Portuguese mounted a large military expedition against the Monomotapa under the command of Francisco Ba-

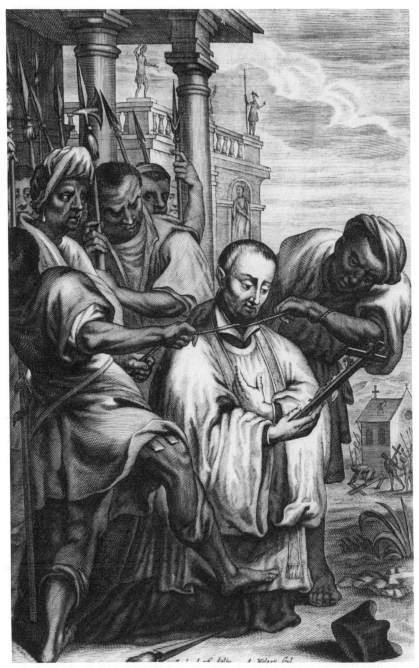

Illus. 25. Martyrdom of Dom Gonçalo da Silveira, S.J., at the Monomotapa's court, March 1561. Artist unknown. From Hazart 1667.

rreto, a former viceroy of Goa and an old friend of Silveira's. It took Barreto almost eleven years, until early 1572, before he and his army set foot at Sena. Barreto had been commissioned to put several requests before the Monomotapa, one of which was for the immediate expulsion of all the Moors from his lands, since they were "enemies of the Christian faith and perpetrators of many crimes."[15]

The first group of Moors the expedition felt it should deal with were those at Sena, who were executed in the most gruesome manner after having been accused by Father Monclaro, chaplain to the expedition, of having secretly poisoned a number of Portuguese. Monclaro reported that the Portuguese soldiers "arrested seventeen of the principal men, among whom was the sheik and one of the plotters of the death of Father Dom Gonçalo. These were condemned and put to death by strange inventions. Some were impaled alive; some were tied to the tops of trees, forcibly brought together, and then set free, by which means they were torn asunder; others were opened up the back by hatchets; some were killed by mortars, in order to strike terror into the natives; and others were delivered to the soldiers, who wreaked their wrath upon them with arquebusses."[16]

The expedition itself was a complete disaster, but it changed once and for all the character of the Portuguese presence in the interior. Instead of continuing to live in small settlements under the protection of local rulers, they now began to carve out autonomous enclaves as outposts of the Portuguese state and the Portuguese church. One of the first missionaries to be sent officially to Zambesia was the Dominican friar Joao dos Santos, author of *Ethiopia Oriental* (1609), which became a classic in its own right as well as one of our principal sources of information on late sixteenth-century Zambesian history.[17] It is clear from Santos that missionary work in those days was limited to the villages and chieftaincies on the south bank over which the captains of the Portuguese forts exercised de facto authority. People on the north bank between Sena and Tete were apparently less receptive to the faith and less easy to subdue. According to Santos, the dominant "tribes" in that area were the Mumbo (Mbo) and the Zimba, both of which had a reputation for cannibalism. Prior to 1590 the Mbo were living inland opposite Tete, whereas the Zimba's main stronghold lay opposite Sena. Both groups were still in a stage of expansion and were trying to extend their control over neighboring chiefdoms.

Chiefs thus threatened might try to conclude an alliance with the Portuguese in exchange for military assistance. One such was the headman of Chicorongo, a place some forty kilometers northeast of Tete, which had been ransacked by Quizura, a chief of the Mbo section. The headman called for help from the captain of Tete, who assembled an army consisting of his own men and those of his eleven vassal chiefs. According to

Santos, his intervention was a complete success, as Quizura and his entire fighting force, amounting to six hundred armed men, were killed.[18] In the course of 1592 a similar incident occurred on the north bank opposite Sena, where a local chief, who was in alliance with the Portuguese, had been overrun by the Zimba and called on the Portuguese for help. This is Santos' account:

> It so happened at the time I was there that the Muzimba Kaffirs, . . . who eat human flesh, invaded this territory and made war upon one of these friendly Kaffirs, and by force of arms took him the kraal in which he resided and a great part of his land, besides which they killed and ate a great number of his people. The Kaffir, seeing himself thus routed and his power destroyed, proceeded to Sena to lay his trouble before the captain, who was then André de Santiago, and to beg for assistance in driving out of his house the enemy who had taken possession of it. The captain, upon hearing his pitiful request, determined to assist him, both because he was very friendly to us and because he did not wish to have so near to Sena a neighbour so wicked as the Muzimba.[19]

When André de Santiago arrived at the place where the Zimba were supposed to be encamped, however, he found that they had ensconced themselves within a strong double palisade of wood, surrounded by a deep and wide trench, which was impossible to take. He therefore called upon the captain of Tete, Pedro Fernandez de Chaves, for reinforcements. The latter immediately prepared to come to the assistance of his colleague with more than one hundred Portuguese and colored men carrying guns, assisted by an African force drawn from his vassal chiefs. In the meantime Santiago and his men may have learned more about these Zimba besides their supposed cannibalism. Thus Santos was told by his informants that they had a special veneration for their king:

> These Zimbas, or Muzimbas, do not adore idols or recognise any God, but instead they venerate and honour their king, whom they regard as a divinity, and they say he is the greatest and best in the world. And the said king says of himself that he alone is god of the earth, for which reason if it rains when he does not wish it to do so, or is too hot, he shoots arrows at the sky for not obeying him; and although all these people eat human flesh, the king does not, to seem different from his vassals.[20]

When the Tete party finally arrived within a few kilometers of the Zimba stronghold, they were ambushed and killed to a man. Father Nicolau do Rosario, who accompanied the expedition as its chaplain, though already severely wounded, was taken to the Zimba fortress, where, according to Santos, he was killed in the most cruel manner. This, it is said, the Zimba did because they held him and the other missionaries responsible for all the misdeeds of the Portuguese, as the latter did nothing without their priests' leave and counsel.[21] One cannot help being reminded here of the massacre of the Muslim merchants, twenty years earlier, at the instigation of Father Monclaro, which took place only a short distance away from the place where the inhabitants of Tete and their priest Nicolau were murdered.

Apparently, André de Santiago knew nothing about the fate of the Tete party until the following day, when

> at dawn they [the Zimba] sallied out of their fortress, the chief clothed in the chasuble that the father had brought with him to say mass, carrying the golden chalice in his left hand and an assegai in his right, all the other Zimbas carrying on their backs the limbs of the Portuguese, with the head of the captain of Tete on the point of a long lance, and beating a drum they had taken from him. In this manner, wth loud shouts and cries they came within sight of André de Santiago and all the Portuguese who were with him, and showed them all these things. After this they retired into their fortress, saying that what they had done to the men of Tete who had come to help their enemies, they would do to them.[22]

Upon seeing this, Santiago and his men decided to retreat in silence under cover of night, but before they could reach the river and safety, they were fallen upon by the Zimba. Together the latter killed one hundred thirty Portuguese and coloreds of Sena and Tete as well as the two captains of these forts. This was a severe blow to the Portuguese presence on the Zambezi, and since the Zimba were now more audacious than before, it was feared they might even do more damage in the future. Therefore Dom Pedro de Sousa, captain of Mozambique, in 1593 decided to put an end to the Zimba threat. Having assembled a war party consisting of two hundred Portuguese and fifteen hundred Africans and taking with him several pieces of artillery, de Sousa went up to the Zimba fort. As the artillery proved useless against the thick earthen walls of the fort, the assailants tried to storm it, but they were easily kept at bay. After two months they decided to retreat and return to Sena. At this point the events of the year before were repeated, for the Zimba caught up with the men who were still in the camp, killed some of them, and seized the greater part of the remaining baggage and artillery.[23]

Santos adds, however, that although the position of the Zimba had become even stronger than before, "he" nevertheless offered peace to the Portuguese of Sena. The fact that Santos at this point uses the singular — no less than seven times in a single paragraph — suggests that he is no longer speaking of the Zimba but of their leader. The person referred to was one Tondo (Tundu), whom the new captain of Mozambique, Nuno da Caunha de Ataide, in 1599 sought leave to castigate, since after having defeated

Dom Pedro de Sousa he had become excessively insolent.[24] When Ataide made his complaint, the Zimba were in control not only of the north bank of the Zambezi but also of much of the coastal area and the land in between. Whether the conquest of the land between the Shire and the Indian Ocean took place before or after Sousa's defeat in 1593 we do not know.[25] We do know, though, that the Zimba had reached the coast in 1595, where Santos was once again able to renew his acquaintance with these warlike folk.[26]

LUNDU AND MUZURA, 1600–1635

One of the key figures in Zambesian politics around 1600 was the Lundu (Rundo, Rondo) of the Lower Shire Valley, despite the fact that he is rarely mentioned in contemporary documents.[27] The power of the Lundus was based partly on the valley's strategic position vis-à-vis Sena and Tete, the principal trading stations on the Zambezi, and partly on its extraordinary agricultural potential due to a combination of wetland and dryland cultivation, which was typical of the valley and which at times of drought gave it a critical advantage over much of lower Zambesia. One of the consequences of this state of affairs was that in periods of prolonged drought the valley attracted many migrants from abroad, who would attach themselves to local chiefs and headmen as serfs or domestic slaves.[28] Another consequence was that the valley became important to the Portuguese settlements along the Zambezi as a granary in times of scarcity. This was as true in the late sixteenth century as it was in Livingstone's day.[29] Commercially, the most important crops were cotton and rice, which were respectively grown on dry land and wet land. We know very little as yet about the organization of the early cotton industry, but it is entirely conceivable in view of its central importance that chiefs and headmen owned several looms and that court fines were paid in *machira*, among other things. Apart from this, we know that traditionally the chiefs and headmen had a right to half of the ivory found in their territories.[30] Taking these various elements together, one may conclude that the Lower Shire Valley constituted an environment in which political power based on trade, given the right conditions, could flourish.

The first mention of the Lundus in a Portuguese document refers to the year 1614, when the then incumbent was approached by Diogo Simoes Madeira, then resident at Tete, to help him recapture the silver mines at Chicoa.[31] The Lundu of that time is described as "a lord with many vassals," and Madeira would certainly not have made his request had the person in question not been an important ruler as well as somebody on whom the Portuguese could rely. The next we hear of him, however, is that in

1622 he was defeated by his rival Muzura in alliance with the Portuguese. Apparently, Lundu had in the meantime become an enemy of the Portuguese, but the reasons for this turnabout remain unclear.

Next to Lundu, the most important person was Muzura, whose name may be rendered "the Uprooter."[32] Father Antonio Gomes, a Jesuit missionary, tells us that Muzura was originally a slave owned by one of the Portuguese settlers on the south bank.[33] Possessed of boundless energy, he left his master for the north bank, where by his prowess as a hunter he gradually built up a following and in the end managed to unite a number of smaller polities into a large kingdom. Gomes, who visited Zambesia in the late 1620s, says that this happened "a few years ago," but as early as 1608 we hear of a Muzura whose power was such that the Portuguese enlisted his help against the rivals of Monomotapa Gatsi Rusere. In 1616 the traveler Gaspar Bocarro was entertained hospitably by Muzura at the latter's headquarters for a full two weeks, another sign that Muzura regarded the Portuguese as his allies.[34] The most important year in his career was 1622, when, together with the Portuguese, he managed to defeat Lundu and thus to become the most powerful potentate on the north bank.[35]

The same event, however, also resulted in a radical break with the Portuguese. Once again the reasons remain unclear, but already in 1623 Muzura had concluded an alliance with the redoubtable Chombe, an expert in the use of European firearms.[36] With Chombe's aid, Muzura attacked a number of Portuguese settlements and raided Karangaland following Gatsi Rusere's death in 1624.[37] Although he was in the end forced to withdraw to the north bank, hostilities continued. In 1629 the Monomotapa Kapararidze, Gatsi Rusere's successor, who had fled to Muzura, persuaded him to join a grand alliance against the Portuguese.[38] This led to the Kapararidze rising of 1631, which very nearly meant the end of the Portuguese presence in Zambesia. Muzura's task was to launch an attack on Quelimane, but he failed to conquer the port, and many of his men were killed. In the next quarter century, however, Muzura's power came to be overshadowed by the Kalonga, whose capital lay on the southwestern shore of Lake Malawi and who was the first to be referred to by a contemporary author as "emperor of Maravi."[39]

TUNDU AND THE ZIMBA IN THE COLLECTIVE MEMORY OF THE VALLEY POPULATION

The foregoing has summarized what is known about the Zimba from contemporary Portuguese sources. We shall now examine additional information, derived from local beliefs, local topography, and various other sources. Our discussion will focus first on the meaning of two composite forms in which the name Tundu has survived, namely Chitundu and Matundu. Following this, we shall examine the relationship between the Zimba and the Lundu of the time and the influence of the Zimba on the process of state formation in the Lower Shire Valley.

Chitundu

In the Shire Valley the name Chitundu refers to a male spirit who is held responsible for heavy storms and whirlwinds, locust plagues, crop-devouring birds, and man-eating lions. The way to appease him is to make an offering of strong liquor (nipa) to him at the shrine of Mbona, who is considered to be a relative of his.[40] People believe that Chitundu's land of origin is not the Shire Valley, however, but the Gorongozi District south of the Zambezi, where he is said to have his own shrine. It is this belief which is referred to in a letter by the missionary E. Price, published in 1927: "It was said a few years ago, after a great storm, that 'Chitundu,' supposed to be a greater rain spirit than Bona, and living near Salisbury [now Harare], had sent Bona back on the great storm; but he did not arrive here, or should we not say that a greater power is working in the minds of the people, and that the gospel is winning its way into their hearts."[41] Although Price mentions Harare as Chitundu's homeland — a reflection of the important place held by Harare in the lives of the numerous labor migrants from the Shire Valley — people whom I interviewed more usually associated Chitundu with the chiefdom of Makombe in the Gorongozi District south of the Zambezi, midway between the valley and Harare. As we have seen, the Makombe chiefdom occupies a prominent place in local oral traditions, not only because of Chitundu but also because of its history of resistance against the Portuguese, which led to bloody reprisals and the flight of many to the Shire Valley.[42] Chitundu is also referred to as kholo la Azimba, which literally means "ancestor of the Zimba" but which can equally be rendered as "founder" or "leader" of the Zimba.[43] The names Chitundu and Zimba have thus become interchangeable, which explains the striking parallelism between people's descriptions of the spirit Chitundu who sends storms, man-eating lions, locusts, and crop-devouring birds and Santos' sixteenth-century account of the Zimba, which describes them in very much the same terms as cannibals in the habit of plundering, killing, and eating their way through all the kingdoms of Kaffraria.[44]

There can therefore be hardly any doubt that the Chitundu who is worshiped in the Lower Shire Valley as a destructive spirit and who is spoken of as the ancestor of the Zimba is a mythologized reference to the Zimba leader Tundu mentioned in the Portuguese documents.[45] His deification is not in any sense unique, for in Zambesia famous persons, even missionaries and Portuguese traders, could become acknowledged territorial spirits (*mhondoro*). D. P. Abraham has rightly described the *mhondoro* cults as "major trace elements precipitated by their history and by their institutional arrangements to perpetuate awareness of the same."[46] This clearly also applies to Chitundu. Hence, when people in the Lower Shire Valley keep affirming that Tundu and the Zimba were historical beings and when, moreover, we possess contemporary documentation about their activities which contains striking overlaps with oral historical accounts, one has to take such information seriously unless one has good reasons for not doing so.[47]

Matundu

Matundu, the other composite form in which the name Tundu is preserved, is a toponym, indicating a range of wooded hills on the southwestern border of the Lower Shire Valley (see map 5), a chief's courthouse, and a sacred grove in the same area.[48] As will be seen, these hills, which range from over seven hundred to over nine hundred meters in height, also play an important part in the Mbona mythology.

The Matundu Hills possess obvious strategic value, since they offer excellent hideouts and since at various points they provide an unimpeded view of the surrounding countryside, making it possible to spot a war party from a considerable distance.[49] Furthermore, the plateaus also allow for the cultivation of a wide range of fruits, vegetables, and staple crops. Throughout the centuries, these hills have been a haven for all sorts of fugitives, and for that reason the area was and is kept under close state surveillance.

Matundu may be translated as "Tundu's people" or, preceded by a locative, as "the land of Tundu's people."[50] There is another "Matunduland" opposite Tete.[51] The fact that both Matundulands were situated across the river from an important Portuguese trading settlement suggests that one of their functions was to control the traffic between those settlements and the Maravi chiefdoms to the north. It is quite likely that the Zimba fortress, described by Joao dos Santos as lying opposite Sena, was situated in the Matundu Hills. The reason for advancing that opinion, as should be clear by now, is the suitability of the place for military purposes and the extraordinarily dense concentration of Zimba mnemonics in and around these hills.

The Zimba and Lundu

If it can be maintained that the Zimba and their leader were immigrants from the south bank, a question arises about their relation to the political

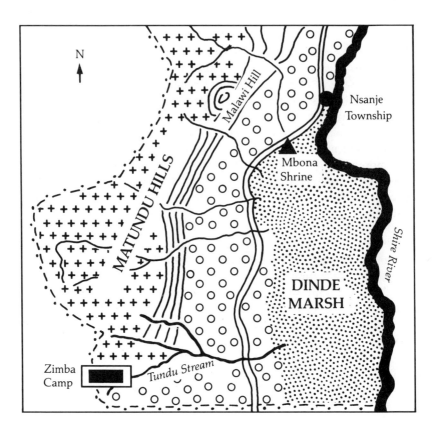

 Plateau or elevated country overlooking the Shire Valley

 Foothills

 Woodland and grassland, the main cultivable areas of the valley floor

 Flood plain, marsh, or dambo

 Zimba base camp near Chididi

—.—.—.— International border

Map 5. The Zimba camp in the Matundu Hills
Source: Schoffeleers 1987b:337.

establishment in the Shire Valley. One possibility is that the Zimba had formed themselves into an army against Lundu's wish and without Lundu's being able to prevent them from doing so. On the other hand, it is also possible that Lundu himself had given his consent to the formation of the Zimba army or that, although it had been formed independently, he was able to use it for his own purposes. The available evidence points to the second possibility, namely that the Zimba were in alliance with the Lundu of that time and that the latter used them to consolidate his power in the Shire Valley and beyond.

That Lundu and the Zimba maintained close relations is suggested by a collection of oral traditions, published by Eduardo do Couto Lupi, which speak of warriors called Marundu, or "Lundu's men," who ransacked Makualand some time in the distant past. Despite their being remembered as Marundu, a name which probably meant nothing to Lupi, he could only conclude that they were the Zimba described by Joao dos Santos, since there were no traditions about another pillaging army.[52]

The idea of a close relationship is also implied in the passage from Santos quoted earlier, in which it was said that the Zimba venerated and honored their king, whom they regarded as "the greatest and the best in the world." Santos does not actually mention the king's name, but if we have to take his testimony at face value, then the reference is in all probability to the Lundu of that time. There was no other dynasty to claim the kingship of the valley, and Santos' description of the ritual performed by the king contains parallels with Mang'anja oral traditions which are close enough to suggest that both refer to the same person. Santos, it will be remembered, reported that this king regarded himself as a god, shooting arrows at the sky whenever it was too wet or too dry. Santos' account supports the idea that the Lundu who ruled at the time of the Zimba wars enjoyed both political and ritual supremacy in the Shire Valley. This meant among other things that on the occasion of a drought or a superabundance of rain he was expected to perform a ritual, which Santos describes as "shooting at the sky." In one of the Mbona biographies reproduced in this volume (Text III/B, secs. 2–3), we are offered an account of what well may have been the same ritual:

> In days gone by, when the rains were late, Lundu Mankhokwe used to call upon his entire family and his subjects to hold a rain ceremony at which he himself would dance. His largest drum was called Kamango. While dancing, the king would point his dagger and leap in the direction of the four winds. In those days God's spirit dwelt in him, which is why he used to make offerings to the Creator of all things when his country was afflicted by a drought or some other calamity.
>
> One year, when Mbona was still a youth, there occurred a devastating

drought. Lundu's subjects came to him, saying, "We beseech you, king, have all your people assembled so that, together with you, they can make a libation, as has been our custom whenever the rains failed to come." The king complied with his subjects' request, arranged for an assembly, and had the rain drums brought out. This done, he set about dancing the way he used to whenever the rains were late, leaping forward, backward, and upward and pointing his dagger at the four winds. But God remained unmoved, for his spirit had withdrawn from Lundu Mankhokwe.

This is the beginning of a narrative which ends with the rain ritual being transferred from the royal court in the northern part of the valley to the Mbona shrine some ninety kilometers to the south. We shall presently return to the political significance of that event, but here we should note once again the striking similarity between the passage in Santos published in 1609, based on data collected in the 1590s, and this piece of oral tradition collected more than three and a half centuries later. Both sources refer to the king as the ritual head of the country and as someone who in that capacity was regularly called upon to perform a ceremony involving "shooting" or "stabbing" at the sky. It is more than likely that Santos, being a remarkable ethnographer, had obtained his information from people who knew the valley and who had firsthand information on the relations between the king and the Zimba. At the very least, the congruence of Santos' account with the above passage from Mang'anja oral traditions about the supposed founder of the Lundu kingdom suggests that Santos' story is not just a product of his or some informant's fantasy but the description of a ritual that actually took place and that for some reason was considered unusual.

These affirmations of the Lundu's ritual supremacy are unusual and noteworthy in that they describe something unknown to the other Maravi states, where rain ceremonies, as far as can be ascertained, were always performed by ritual specialists who were in principle independent of the secular rulers.[53] Although we possess a number of traditions to the effect that the latter did occasionally try to appropriate the rain rituals, we know of no case other than that of the Lundu's in which such an attempt was successful. To reach that goal, armed assistance from outside on a fairly large scale was virtually indispensable. The available evidence leads us to suggest that the Zimba provided Lundu with the means to bring off this feat. That evidence consists first of all of Santos' reference to the king of the Shire Valley (i.e., Lundu) as the king of the Zimba. Second, Santos' reference is extensively supported by local recollections of the Zimba as being called both Marundu and Matundu, that is to say, "Lundu's people" and "Tundu's people."[54] Third, there are many indications that the end of the sixteenth century and the beginning of the seventeenth was a period of repression of such severity as could not have been possible without the help of a mercenary army. For one thing, no other Maravi state possesses a communal cult based on an explicit and elaborate persecution theology. For another, no other Maravi state has apparently managed to wipe out the *nyau* societies within its borders. As for the reasons behind this repression, I suggest that it was a consequence of the Lundu's aim to obtain total control of production and trade in and around the Lower Shire Valley. In sum, then, our findings indicate that the expansionist wars waged by Lundu in the closing decade of the sixteenth century synchronized internally with a massive attempt at centralization of political power by means of reducing a large segment of the population to total subjection and by fundamentally restructuring the system of economic production and distribution.

THE ZAMBEZI VALLEY, 1530–1631

In the concluding section of his article on the early history of the Maravi, Newitt notes that the prime objective of the Portuguese penetration of the Zambezi, which began around 1530, was to participate directly in the trade of the region. In the first half century, that is until about 1580, this process of penetration, as Newitt sees it, developed in four stages. First, there was a time of growing rivalry between Muslim traders and the Portuguese. This may have prompted the second development, which consisted of an attempt to conquer the supposed gold and silver mines of the interior. The failure of this undertaking then contributed to an increased tightening of the trade monopoly of the captains of Mozambique. The fourth development was the growth in Portuguese political control of Zambesia, deriving from agreements made by individual Portuguese with chiefs whom they aided and from whom they obtained commercial and territorial concessions.[55]

On the whole one can agree with Newitt's four-stage model if it is remembered, as Newitt himself suggests, that the four stages cannot be placed in a neat time sequence. Indeed, the distinction between these stages is sometimes so vague that one might equally well regard them as four basic strivings which alternately gain and lose prominence in Zambesian regional politics. Apart from that, it would appear that there is room also for a few minor corrections. Thus where Newitt points to a growing rivalry between the Muslim traders and the Portuguese prior to the attempted conquest of the mines, it would be more appropriate to speak of a growing rivalry between the captain of Mozambique and the inland traders, regardless of whether they were Muslims or Portuguese. Newitt himself reminds us of this basic fact in an earlier study, when he notes that up to the time of the Barreto expedition the majority of the Portuguese traders were backwoodsmen and freebooters who worked hand-in-glove with the Muslims and who had no special desire to cooperate with the captain of Mozambique.[56] As far as the Barreto expedition is concerned, it should be noted that, although it did not achieve what it set out to do and may in that sense be described as a failure, it still heralded the beginning of a new policy with regard to the settlements in the interior. The latter, instead of remaining what they had always been, foreign settlements under the tutelage of local rulers, were now transformed into true Portuguese enclaves, tangibly and visibly connected with the central government and the church in the persons of an officially appointed administrator and one or more officially appointed priests. What Silveira and Barreto had hoped to achieve singlehandedly and in one stroke was in the end achieved only a little more slowly by their successors.

In this situation slavery too became more and more important. Already in 1572 ten to fifteen Portuguese households at Sena possessed an average of several hundred slaves each.[57] With the increase in the number of households and with the increasing expansion of the Portuguese enclaves, one must conclude that the number of slaves increased as well. A logical result of this process would have been that the number of fugitive slaves also grew. Not infrequently, the Portuguese had to appeal to neighboring chiefs to return runaway slaves. If they were not returned voluntarily, the Portuguese might try to use force, as in the case of Chief Chombe.[58] One of the favorite hideouts for escaped slaves until well into the nineteenth century was Mount Morumbala, situated at the southeastern end of the Lower Shire Valley.[59] Although everything was being done to stop the flow of slaves, the effect was negligible, since for the most part they moved when they liked and attached themselves to whomever they pleased.[60] While the majority of escaped slaves would place themselves under the protection of some chief or headman, or perhaps a territorial shrine such as Mbona's, others might band together, build their own fortified settlements, and from there raid the countryside.[61]

It is within this context that one has to understand the origin of the Zimba. Rather than striking out on their own, they apparently preferred to put themselves at the disposal of the local ruler. There are indications in the early Portuguese documents that prior to 1590 sizable centralized states did not yet exist immediately north of the Zambezi. The impression given is rather of a collectivity of relatively small independent polities, bound together by the requirements of regional trade and shifting alliances. Small states which were situated toward the interior at a point where trade routes met, however, were at an advantage and could, given the right situation, outstrip their neighbors. One of these was the Quizura chiefdom, which apparently controlled the overland route from Tete to the Shire highlands. Another was the Lundu chiefdom, which controlled the river route into the Shire highlands. In both cases we see that after 1580 the ruling chief tried to expand in the direction of the Zambezi by absorbing and conquering smaller states lying between himself and the Zambezi. In both cases we also see that the lesser chiefs who were depossessed called on the Portuguese for help and in both cases received it in the form of a Portuguese detachment reinforced with several thousand African troops. The difference, however, is that in Quizura's case the Portuguese intervention was successful, while in Lundu's it was an unqualified disaster. This suggests that the change which had taken place on the south bank from 1572 onward — the Portuguese settlements becoming colonial enclaves with their own armies and vassals — caused the more important state systems on the north bank also to embark on a program of expansion and centralization in order to bring the north bank under their control. While Quizura and Lundu may have begun moving at about the same time, Quizura had the misfortune of having to face the Portuguese when he was not yet sufficiently prepared. This may have given Lundu an opportunity to intensify his own expansionist policy, and it may have been at this point, between Quizura's defeat and Lundu's own encounter with the Portuguese, which is roughly between the mid-1580s and 1592, that Lundu co-opted the Zimba. It is around this time, too, that Lundu wiped out the existing rain cult and other foci of religious resistance such as the *nyau*. After the Portuguese had been defeated in 1592, and again in 1593, it must have been relatively easy for Lundu to occupy the north bank to the west as far as Tete and to the east as far as the coastal settlements.

After 1600 the situation on the north bank became more complex, due to Muzura's rise to power. At first the Portuguese seem to have befriended both sides, for we see that Muzura was approached in 1606 to assist them against the enemies of the Monomotapa and that in 1614 Lundu was asked to help the captain of Tete. Soon afterward, however, the Portuguese must have dropped Lundu, since in 1622 they defeated him with the help of Muzura, who then became the effective ruler of the southern Maravi states. Once this had been achieved, Muzura turned against the Portuguese until the abortive uprising of 1631. There ended the story which began seventy years earlier with the murder of Silveira and which reached its intermediate culmination points in the massacre of the Swahili merchants in 1572 and that of the Portuguese in 1593. The question which remains is Why did Muzura turn against the Portuguese after 1622? A good guess is that he and Monomotapa Kapararidze had come to realize that a continuing Portuguese presence would gradually lead to the total subjection of their

lands. The alternative was to restore the Swahili trade to its former prominence, but this could not be done without exterminating the Portuguese.
This they tried to do in 1631, though without success, because by that time
the Portuguese had managed to build up their own network of alliances
with local rulers on whom they could rely on that decisive occasion. As
Pedro Barreto de Rezende wrote in 1635: "The power of the natives is vastly
greater than that of the few Portuguese who are found in the country, but
the conditions are now very different from what they were in former times,
for we fight them with the same Kaffirs with whom they formerly fought
us, and it is noteworthy that among these slaves or vassals who fight for
us, till the present time there has been no treason, but they fight against
those who are Kaffirs like themselves, with all their might and fidelity."[62]

THE LOCATION OF MUZURA'S CAPITAL

One of the problems in establishing Muzura's identity
is the existing confusion about the location of his capital. Alpers, who
identifies Muzura as a member of the Kalonga dynasty, situated Muzura's
capital on the southwestern shore of Lake Malawi in line with the traditions about the Kalongas.[63] Although its precise location is still a matter
of discussion — indeed it is likely that there was more than one location —
there is general agreement that Kalonga's capital lay somewhere between
modern Kachindamoto and Chipoka.[64] Some twenty years before Alpers,
however, W. H. J. Rangeley argued — on the basis of local oral traditions,
his own extensive topographical knowledge, and a careful examination of
Gaspar Bocarro's travelogue describing his journey to Muzura in 1616 — that
Muzura's capital lay on the banks of the Wamkurumadzi River, in the
Neno/Mwanza area, some 100 to 150 kilometers due south of Kalonga's
Maravi.[65] Consequently, Muzura was not to be identified with the Chewa
paramount Kalonga, but with the Mang'anja paramount Kaphwiti, remembered in oral tradition as the most senior ruler of the southern Maravi.[66]
Although Alpers cites Rangeley's article, he refrains from questioning the
latter's theory about Muzura's identity and the location of his capital, possibly because the Muzura/Kalonga equation appeared to him self-evident.
Yet the matter is not all that simple, and even Alpers cautions his readers
that the Portuguese never made this equation.[67] This is entirely correct,
for as Alpers notes in the same passage, the last contemporary document
mentioning Muzura's name dates from 1648, while the title Kalonga appears for the first time in 1661. To be even more precise, the 1648 document which contains, among other things, Father Gomes' account of his
journey to Zambesia, describes a situation which obtained some twenty

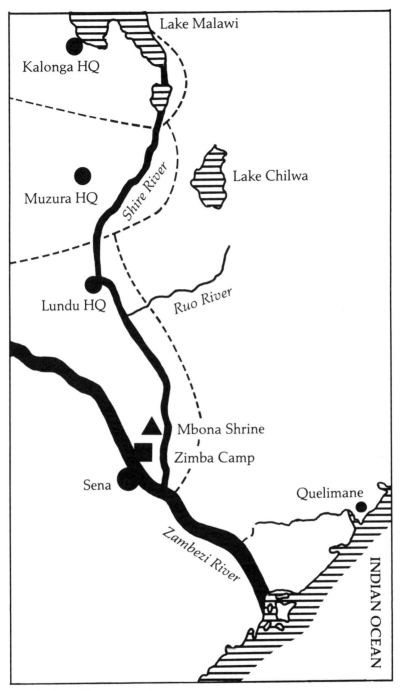

Map 6. Some Maravi capitals
   Source: Schoffeleers 1987b:338.

years earlier.[68] Thus, the time interval between the last contemporary information about Muzura and the first documentation of a Kalonga is rather longer than would appear at first sight.

Newitt tries to solve this problem by suggesting that Muzura was the man who formed the state north of the Zambezi which later became known as the Empire of Maravi, and that the paramountcy which he established later assumed the title Kalonga.[69] Attractive as this may sound, it is a suggestion unsupported by solid evidence. It is to be noted, though, that a similar confusion existed in Muzura's own lifetime, for the Jesuit A. Mariana in a letter, dated 1624, situates Muzura's capital on the southwestern lakeshore (roughly where Alpers would have it).[70] A map by Joao Teixeira, published in 1630, situates it in a mountain range west-northwest of Lundu's capital (roughly where Rangelely would have it).[71] Teixeira's location of the capital is confirmed by Mariana's colleague and contemporary Father Antonio Gomes, who reports that Lake Malawi lies many days' traveling north-northeast of Muzura's place. Gomes' text reads as follows: "The kraal of this king [Muzura] lies at a distance of fifteen days from Sena and at the same distance from Tete, which is sixty leagues upstream from Sena. Many days to the north-northeast from there lies that large lake of which we don't know yet the end."[72]

Supposing that Teixeira and Gomes are right that Muzura's capital actually lay at a considerable distance from Lake Malawi, the question arises why Father Mariana situates it on the lakeshore. The answer is that Mariana had never been to the lake himself and therefore had to rely on the testimony of local informants, whom he may have misinterpreted.[73] Since all Maravi capitals were referred to as Maravi and since lakes and rivers were and are indiscriminately referred to as *nyanja*, there was ample room for confusion.[74] Whatever the case, it is clear that Mariana is the only contemporary source which situates Muzura's capital on the lakeshore, and his information is contradicted directly by Teixeira's map and Gomes' description.

Two further pieces of information provide indirect support for Gomes and Teixeira, however. One of these is a reference to Quizura, chief of the Mumbo (Mbo), who was defeated by the captain of Tete just before 1590. The other is a passage in Schebesta, in which he refers to Muzura as "paramount of the Chipeta." Schebesta's source is an annual report by the Goanese province of the Jesuits, dated 1627, which contains an account by Father P. Mendonça, S. J., of a punitive expedition which the Portuguese had mounted against Muzura and to which Mendonça served as chaplain.[75] The name Chipeta is ethnographically associated with the southwestern Maravi and the modern districts of Dedza and Ntcheu as well as the northern half of Mwanza District. In other words, the Chipeta reference in the

1627 document provides support for the thesis that Muzura's capital was situated at a considerable distance from the lake.

As far as the name Quizura is concerned, the matter is somewhat more complicated, since it has to be established first that Quizura is identical with Muzura. To begin with, a prefix *qui-* (pronounced ki- or kwi-) does not exist in the Maravi dialects. It is a Portuguese misrendering of the prefix *chi-*, which among other things indicates greatness or awesomeness. The name Tundu, for example, is regularly rendered as Chitundu. Chizura (or Quizura) could then be taken to mean the great or redoubtable Zura. While this must remain somewhat speculative, the statement that Quizura/Muzura was a (mu)Mbo is more directly helpful, as the home area of the Mbo is in and around the Kirk Range.[76] Since the Mbo and the Chipeta occupied adjoining geographic areas and since both groups formed part of the Maravi complex, the names were to a certain extent interchangeable, particularly when used by outsiders.

Thus, there is sufficient evidence to posit that Muzura's capital was not situated on the lakeshore and that Muzura himself was not a member of the Kalonga family, but a ruler belonging to a different dynasty. Whether that dynasty was Kaphwiti's, as suggested by Rangeley, or whether he belonged to an altogether different line of rulers is a question better discussed separately.

CHAPTER 6

Oral Traditions and the Retrieval of the Distant Past

SOME YEARS AGO Luc de Heusch criticized Jan Vansina and others for their somewhat overconfident use of legendary chronicles, such as those relating to the first Luba kings, as sources of historical information.[1] If de Heusch were only reacting to overconfidence, there would be little cause for disagreement, for it is commonly recognized that Africanist historians have not always been sufficiently critical in their use of oral traditions. De Heusch's criticism, however, implied considerably more than that. Its tenor was, first, that these chronicles contained little or no historical information, since they were to be considered as no more than the transposition in pseudohistorical terms of a preexisting body of myth, and second, that the only valid approach would be to treat them as myths, that is, as statements about the cosmic order. Even seemingly historical events were in principle to be treated as cosmological metaphors.[2]

It cannot be denied that de Heusch argued his case quite plausibly by pointing, on the one hand, to the striking similarities between the founding myths of a number of Central African kingdoms and, on the other hand, to the parallels between these African myths and the chronicles relating to the first three kings of ancient Rome, which G. Dumézil had already shown to be essentially nonhistorical.[3] But doubt creeps in when one begins to consider some of the implications of this approach. To begin with, it precludes any investigation of possible developments within the body of myth itself, which is presented as timeless. The myths are simply there. They were already in existence before the formation of the kingdoms in the fourteenth or the fifteenth century. Presumably they changed in a superficial manner when the kingdoms came into being by transforming their protagonists into royals, and they continued substantially unaltered till the nineteenth century, when some of the kingdoms vanished and others were fundamentally transformed. The question which this poses is whether structuralism in this unmitigated form extends in another way the classic but erroneous view of a black continent which for countless generations remained unchanged, if not politically, then at least intellectually.

Second, de Heusch's approach to myths, with its assumption of a unitary worldview in which a single text may contain in condensed form all the mythological thought of a people,[4] takes no account of the possibility that different sections of a single society may have different views about the cosmic and social universe and the relations between the two. More concretely, it does not allow for a situation in which people express deep-seated social differences by means of different mythologies. Consequently, de Heusch makes no effort to look for countermythologies among the Luba and their neighbors, although they could in principle have existed among the numerous secret societies, to mention just one possibility. Throughout, however, his attention remains riveted on chiefs and kings as the central aspect of society, thereby perpetuating yet another perspective that in the meantime has come to be considered as lopsided and inadequate.

It is not the intention of this chapter simply to turn the tables on de Heusch. For one thing, his questioning of the way ethnohistorians sometimes treat mythical material is valid and to the point. For another, it is clear that structuralism has its uses for the historian also, as R. Willis notes in his comment on Vansina's work.[5] But the rapprochement insofar as it exists in the field of Africanist studies has remained one-sided, and the structuralists have still to come to the point where they acknowledge the relevance of the historical approach to their own work. It is with this issue that the present chapter is centrally concerned.

I hope to demonstrate the relevance of the historical approach with regard to the Mbona myths — or legendary chronicles, to use de Heusch's terminology — which, like the royal myths of Central Africa, exhibit a great deal of variation. It can be demonstrated that they have their roots in different historical periods and that they can be made to yield substantive information about those periods; that, taken as a whole, they express a crucial development in people's thinking about the social order; and that they represent a dual conception of that order. If these various claims can be substantiated, the chapter will have performed two tasks: it will have shown de Heusch's scepticism in regard to the historiographical potential of myths in principle to be unfounded, and it will have put his structuralist assumptions under scrutiny. The cardinal question naturally is whether and to what extent substantiation will be possible. To answer that question, let me begin by acknowledging that historical reconstruction from mostly oral sources as in the present case is virtually always a matter of circumstantial rather than direct evidence. In addition to this, such information as can be abstracted from these sources is, to use Willis' terminology, primarily of a qualitative kind, referring to social-evolutionary processes rather than discrete events.[6] Given these provisos, however, it would seem that the Mbona material offers a suitable case against which to test de Heusch's central assumptions.

The argument will be developed in three parts. First, I shall introduce the principal versions of the Mbona myth and show how and to what extent they reflect the history we have dealt with in the previous chapters. In the second part, I turn to the cosmological aspects of these legends, asking in what sense they represent different worldviews and what historical factors may have given rise to this differentiation. In the third and final part, I return to de Heusch's assumptions to see how they stand up to these findings.

In the course of my fieldwork and by combing through the scarce literature on the subject, I have been able to collect some twenty versions of the Mbona story, seven of which are reproduced in the second part of this book. Although varying considerably in elaboration and content, they possess a common sequential structure which in essence consists of three elements. First, Mbona is invariably portrayed as a person who had power over the rains and who for that reason aroused the hostility of some rival. Second, all accounts tell us that he had to flee from his rival but that the latter managed to kill him in the end. Third, in all cases, it is mentioned that after the killing a shrine was built to his name and that by this act the beneficial powers he had possessed during his lifetime were perpetuated. This basic structure constitutes the minimal dogma shared by all who have an interest in the cult.

Turning our intention to the variations in these stories, we find that they relate to the location of Mbona's homeland, his ancestry and social personality, and the identity of his main antagonist. Other variations describe events said to have occurred at the time of his flight, the manner in which he was killed, and the manner in which the cult came to be instituted. Taken together, these variations fall into three distinct patterns. Labeling these Mbona I, II, and III, the following picture emerges.

MBONA I

In this stream, represented by Texts I/A and I/B, Mbona is said to have been a Chipeta tribesman from the area of Kaphirintiwa. Mbona was already a married man with several wives when a quarrel developed between him and someone else, one accusing the other of sorcery.

Since the person called upon to arbitrate in the matter was a rain priest (*msumphi*), it is likely that the kind of sorcery referred to had to do with withholding rain. When it remained unclear who the guilty party was, the arbitrator ordered both to undergo the poison ordeal. Some traditions have it that Mbona cheated by secretly taking an antidote which made him vomit; others hold that he objected to the ordeal, declaring it to be a human invention and therefore fallible. Whatever the case, the arbitration effort failed, and Mbona decided to flee to the Shire Valley with some of his followers. Although the two versions reproduced in Part 2 do not mention that he left imprints of his body and his weapons or utensils behind on rocky surfaces along the route, the theme of the imprints should nevertheless be considered as forming part of the Mbona I stream. This appears at its clearest when at the end of his journey he engraves the Chipeta tribal emblem on a rock boulder below Malawi Hill. The local population welcomed him, since he brought them regular rains, but his sojourn among them was not to last, for when his enemies discovered his whereabouts they came down to kill him. After the killing they cut off his head, which they then threw into a thicket, but local villagers buried the head and built a shrine over the place.

MBONA II

In this stream, represented by Texts II/A and II/B, Mbona is portrayed as a member of the aristocratic Phiri clan and a maternal nephew of Kaphwiti, the reputed founder of the earliest state system in southern Malawi. As a married man he was apprenticed to another uncle, who held the position of the chief's official rainmaker. Once, at the time of a great drought, the uncle performed the rain dance, but for the first time in his career without success. Explanations differ about the reason why. Sometimes it is said that Mbona had applied sorcery against him. Others maintain that Mbona made his uncle powerless by accusing him of making improper overtures to the women assisting at the dance.[7] However this may be, Chief Kaphwiti, siding with his senior rainmaker, declared that Mbona merited death, and the latter thereupon took flight. On his way through the Shire Valley he managed time and again to elude his pursuers by changing himself and his followers into a misty vapor, a clump of trees, or a flock of guinea fowl. In the end, however, overcome with fatigue, he was caught. However much his assailants tried to kill him with their knives and spears, though, they were unsuccessful, because as soon as they touched his body they became limp and powerless. In the end Mbona himself told them to cut him with a blade of grass instead, and in this manner they were finally able to kill him. As in the first group of traditions, the head was severed from the body, and a shrine was built over it by Mbona's sympathizers.

MBONA III

In this stream, represented by Texts III/A and III/B, Mbona's homeland is in the valley itself. He is said to have been the maternal nephew of the first Lundu king. Normally he would have been a candidate for succession to the kingship, but there were two obstacles. First, he was considered illegitimate, since his mother, whose name is mentioned as Tundu, had borne him out of wedlock. Second, although already an adolescent, his behavior was still that of a child, for contrary to accepted custom he continued to live in his mother's hut, whereas he should have been staying in a bachelor's hut like other youths. The king therefore despised him, but the ruler did not know that Mbona's mother had conceived him by the power of Mulungu, the Supreme Being, and that he was therefore a son of God.

At the time of a major drought, the king tried to perform the rain dance as he was used to doing, but this time the dance was unsuccessful. Other members of the royal lineage took their turn, also without success. The public then urged the king to let Mbona try, and the long-awaited rains finally began to fall. An accident happened, however, for in the course of the performance a lightning bolt killed the king's young son. The king accepted this as an act of God, but his wife blamed Mbona and refused to sleep with her husband unless he promised to have Mbona put out of the way. The king finally gave in and hired a band of assassins, but when the latter sneaked up to Mbona's hut, they found him and his mother already gone. Sensing the king's evil intentions, the two had decided to flee southward.

On the way Mbona performed a number of food miracles, such as creating a patch of rice, to keep his mother and himself from starving. When they came to the Matundu Hills, which form the southwestern rim of the valley, the mother took leave of her son and was miraculously carried to the south bank of the Zambezi, where she became a priestess with power over rain and drought. Upon her departure Mbona was caught by Lundu's men, but once again they failed to kill him until he told them that this could only be done in the valley below by cutting his throat or the top of his head with a blade of grass. This done, he died, but after the killing he revealed himself as a new territorial spirit. He ordered the king to provide him with a woman who was to be his "wife" at the shrine and to cooperate with his people in making regular sacrifices to him. It was thus that the cult commenced.

Text III/B, just summarized, is a text proper to the commonalty. There exists another version, Text III/A, which contains the view of the court on these events. To avoid undue complications, in this chapter we shall limit ourselves to Text III/B and discuss III/A in the next chapter.

THE THREE STREAMS COMPARED

Each stream tells a somewhat different story, and virtually the only elements that remain unchanged throughout are Mbona's name and the three-phase plot structure. When looked at more closely, however, some of the variations exhibit strikingly regular patterns. To begin with the most obvious example, Mbona's reputed homeland shifts from north to south in an almost straight line (map 7): from Kaphirintiwa, which lies at a distance of more than 300 kilometers from the Mbona shrine, to Kaphwiti's headquarters at about half that distance, and finally to the king's capital in the valley itself. Concomitant with this, one notes that the society into which he is born becomes increasingly centralized, transforming from an apparently stateless system associated with the ethnic designation Chipeta, via an early state system represented by the name Kaphwiti, into a powerful kingdom represented by the name Lundu.

Mbona's de jure status follows a similar upward curve, as in each case he is a close relative and potential successor of the main officeholder. Yet at the same time we see that his de facto status follows a downward curve, for he is first portrayed as an adult with several wives, then as a young man with only one wife, and finally as someone who is socially a child and an outcast. In other words, the pattern is one of an increasing power differential, Mbona becoming more and more powerless in relation to his main antagonist. This, however, appears to be a deception, because the more his outward appearance is that of a helpless victim, the greater his supernatural power becomes. We see this happen in the story of his killing. In the first stream his enemies are able to kill him with iron weapons and at their own initiative, but from the second stream onward iron becomes powerless, or powerless on its own, and has to be substituted by or combined with grass. On the symbolic meaning of that combination we shall have more to say later on; for the moment it is important to note that the initiative is Mbona's, for Mbona himself has to tell the killers that only grass can kill him. This substitution of grass for iron is also a form of mockery, since the arms from which Mbona's adversaries derive their arrogance and power prove worthless and have to be replaced by something that to

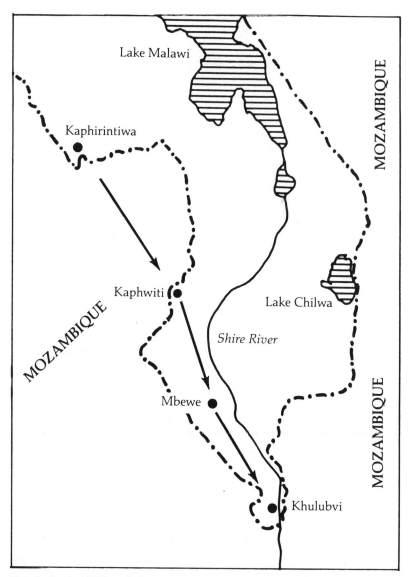

Map 7. Route of Mbona's journeys

them seems nonsensical but allows them nonetheless to achieve their aim.

The increase in supernatural power is equally visible in the account of the cult's founding. In Mbona I, a shrine is built at the initiative of Mbona's followers. In the second stream the shrine is built at Mbona's own initiative, made known by the local medium, but without the participa-

Variation	Mbona I	Mbona II	Mbona III
Homeland	Stateless	Chiefdom	Kingdom
Adversary	Rain priest	Chief	King
Mbona's social status	Adult with several wives	Young man with one wife	Child or childlike person
Manner of killing	With iron weapons	With grass	With grass (and iron)
Founding of cult	Initiative of local population	Mbona's initiative; no cooperation of chief(s)	Mbona's initiative; king ordered to cooperate

Chart 2. Variations in the Mbona traditions

tion of the political elite. Finally, in the third stream the king takes part in the building of the shrine and the organization of the cult, ordered to do so by Mbona himself. For easy reference the variations between the three streams are summarized in chart 2.

MYTHICAL TALES AND FACTUAL HISTORY

Having identified the three streams, we may now ask ourselves whether and to what extent they are to be regarded as reflections of factual history. I am committed to a view similar to Willis' in regard to the Fipa myths: I see the Mbona narratives essentially as a cosmological discourse built upon a number of verbal nuclei that posses definable historical content. It has to be shown therefore that there exist demonstrable correspondences between these narratives and certain historical events and processes known to us from other sources.

This is easiest performed in the case of Mbona III, since the names Tundu and Lundu, which figure so prominently in that stream, also feature in Portuguese documents. Of course, Lundu is a perpetual title which has persisted into our own days and which therefore cannot be pinned down to just one historical period. Tundu, however, is a proper name, which both in Mang'anja oral traditions and Portuguese documentation is mentioned in a specific context, namely the upheavals that took place in connection with the Zimba wars. The fact that Tundu appears in the documentation as a redoubtable war leader and in the narratives of Mbona III as Mbona's mother in no way weakens the evidence. The transformations undergone by Tundu are strictly systematic: from male to female, from father to mother, from bloodthirsty to self-sacrificing, and from someone moving northward to start a military career to someone moving southward

to start a career as priestess. This series of transformations is a perfect il-
lustration of J. Janzen's concept of "ritual inversion," by which he means
a symbolic operation to embrace new or alternative directions of thought
and thus to strengthen the flexibility of the incorporating tradition.[8]

Janzen's paradigmatic example is "Mother Ndundu" (lit., "Mother Al-
bino"), a female overseer in one of the Zairian cults. She is an old woman,
already past childbearing age, who has not given birth to many children;
if she has given birth to children, it is better for ritual purposes if her children have died. Though she is a most unfortunate kind of female figure
in ordinary life, in the context of the cult she is lifted to an elevated position, and all the negative features of her sterile being are brought into the
cult and given central roles. She is made mother of the cult members and
praised in songs as the mother of chiefs. She is thus given a completely inverted and incongruous casting from what would normally be her role.

Ritual inversion is a source of hope, because it signals that things are
not what they seem to be and that there is a power that can turn negative
experience into positive. Janzen considers ritual inversion also one of the
principal mechanisms by which religious systems renew themselves. The
outside, threatening, cruel, or unexpected situation or element can be incorporated into a worldview if it can be made to contrast complementarily
with the inside, secure, old, and routine areas of existence. We saw this
principle at work in the mask of Charlie Chaplin, which reduced the redoubtable American or Western presence in Malawi to human and even
humorous proportions. By absorbing the powerful outsider into our ritual
symbolism, we can cope with him.

The Mbona III mythology in particular contains a number of such inversions. One that immediately comes to mind is the figure of Salima. Very
much like Mother Ndundu, Salima has to be barren or past childbearing,
but she defines earthly fertility by her otherworldly sterility. Another instance is that of Mbona himself, an illegitimate child and on that count
despised, who turns out to be a divine being. Finally, the awesome warrior turns into Mbona's mother and a source of blessing.

Although Tundu is our principal key to a historical interpretation of
the Mbona myths, he is not the only one. Some of the other names and
titles also appear to possess identifiable historical content. The ethnic designation Chipeta, for example, preserves the memory of a stateless system. Perhaps a greater problem is presented by the various feats Mbona
is said to have performed during his flight. It will be remembered that these
consist respectively of a number of rock marks he left behind, a series of
metamorphoses by which he managed for a while to elude his pursuers,
and miracles he performed to provide himself and his mother with food
and drink. The rock marks apparently signify the claims to ownership of

the land made by the keepers of the oldest stream of tradition in regard to the Lower Shire Valley. Once again, this appears at its clearest when Mbona carves his Chipeta emblem on a rock in a strategic place. The accounts of Mbona's metamorphoses in the second stream may conceivably refer to the early state situation, when the valley population, like E. Leach's Kachin, may have oscillated between a stateless and a state-based organization. Mbona's trying to elude the early state builders and making himself repeatedly invisible by becoming part of the surrounding nature seem apt metaphors for autochthonous groups employing a variety of strategies to keep out of the expanding state systems.[9] Finally, the food miracles of the kingdom stream no doubt refer to the condition of famine which then may have prevailed due to large-scale warfare, which made normal cultivation difficult or even impossible.

Careful examination may reveal more such verbal nuclei. It will be remembered, for instance, that only in the third stream is it explicitly mentioned that Mbona's opponent made use of a band of hirelings. This may at first sight seem an irrelevant detail, but against the background sketched in the preceding chapters it is difficult not to recognize in these men a reference to the Zimba mercenaries.

STREAMS AND CONCENTRIC CIRCLES

The verbal nuclei which have just been discussed and others which may still be awaiting identification in no way exhaust the historiographical potential of the various streams, for these can be coupled also with features of the cult organization in a way which makes it possible to elicit further information about the valley's past.

In Chapter 2 it was shown that the cult organization may be conceptualized in the form of three concentric circles around the shrine grounds. Each of these circles was said to be associated with a specific section of the cult's leadership and with a particular phase in the ritual cycle. The innermost circle is the space in which we find the chief ritual and the chief jural officers, who are jointly responsible for the annual rain ceremony. The key figure in the second circle is Chief Tengani, who fulfills a pivotal role in the rebuilding of the shrine. In the third circle, Lundu is the central figure, and the ritual in which he plays the central role is that of electing and installing a new spirit wife. The first circle is activated every year, the second every five to seven years, and the third perhaps every twenty to twenty-five years, the entire cycle theoretically spanning a generation.

There appears to be a certain correspondence between the organizational structure and the ritual cycle, on the one hand, and the several

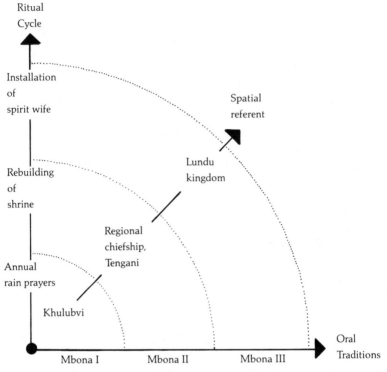

Chart 3. Correspondence between spatial organization, oral traditions, and ritual cycle of the Mbona cult

streams in the Mbona mythology, on the other. Thus, for instance, narratives of the Mbona I tradition, that is, narratives declaring Mbona to have been a muChipeta who came to the valley before there were any chiefdoms, are found exclusively in the inner geographic circle and more specifically among the family of the chief ritual officer, Ngabu, and his immediate associates. Text I/A, for instance, which is representative of this tradition, was recorded around 1907 by a European tax collector, the then Ngabu being the principal informant. Some sixty years later I recorded Text I/B, another instance of this tradition, and Chapirira, Ngabu's deputy, was my principal informant. This appears to lend credence to Ngabu's claim, referred to in Chapter 2, that his office is the oldest in the cult hierarchy.

Narratives of the Mbona II tradition, that is, of the tradition associated with an early state system, are found in the inner and middle circles. In the inner circle the chief jural officer, Malemia, and his associates are the keepers of the tradition. Two of these associates are Headman Mphamba,

	Circle I	Circle II	Circle III
Mbona I	Chief ritual officer and associates		
Mbona II	Secondary officials	Regional chief and associates	
Mbona III	Chief jural officer and associates		King and associates
	Population at large		

Chart 4. Social location of the various streams in the Mbona narratives

author of Text II/A, and Mr. B. A. Phiri, Malemia's chief councillor, who has also composed a biography in the Mbona II mode.[10] The other narrative in the Mbona II tradition reproduced in this book (Text II/B) stems from the middle circle and was obtained from a person whose family hailed from the Tengani chiefdom. A hypothesis following from these texts and the offices connected with them would be that Tengani's may have been the first state structure which the early cult organization had to confront and that in the wake of that confrontation a dual power structure developed, represented in the organization by a chief ritual officer and a chief jural officer.

In order to establish more concretely the historiographical potential of these traditions, let us return to Chapter 3 and the quarrel between Ngabu and Malemia about which of the two offices should be given historical primacy. Briefly, Ngabu claimed that his apical ancestor had been made a priest by Mbona himself, who also granted him secular jurisdiction. The Malemias came some time later at the request of the Ngabus, who were then in need of administrative assistance. After a while, however, the Malemias made themselves independent by monopolizing the administrative and jural side of the cult. Malemia's version is the opposite. His forebears, he asserted, were the first to lead the shrine organization. After a while they called in the Ngabus to help out with the rituals, but in the end the Ngabus monopolized that part of the cult.

Nothing in these contradictory viewpoints gives us a clue about whose claim to primacy is correct. Territorial cults often existed before state organizations, though, and consequently Ngabu's priestly office may have preceded Malemia's administrative office. But even that is not to be considered an iron rule, because according to the Chewa historian S. J. Ntara, newly established chiefdoms did occasionally invite priests from outside if they had none of their own.[11] As a matter of fact, the only real clue may be Ngabu's claim that Mbona was a muChipeta and that the priestly office dated from the Chipeta period. It has all the appearances of a real clue, because it refers to an identifiable phase in the early history of the valley and because the Chipeta identity is claimed by nobody else. Though Malemia claims that his apical ancestor possessed sacerdotal powers, which were later delegated to the Ngabu lineage, he or his associates do not claim any link with the Chipeta culture. On the contrary, they emphatically deny that Mbona ever was a muChipeta. In fact, this was one of the first lessons they tried to teach me, although it took me a long time to understand its true meaning.

The reader will recall the passage in the Introduction to this book where I speak of the interviews I had with two different groups of shrine officers in 1964 and 1966. I said there that to my amazement the second group contradicted virtually everything their colleagues had told me about Mbona. The bone of contention was Mbona's ancestry. Whereas the first group emphasized that Mbona was a muChipeta (Text I/B), the second group upon being confronted with this piece of information retorted angrily that this was a lie made up by people "who tried to belittle Mbona." Apparently, being called a muChipeta carried negative connotations, which makes Ngabu's claims to historical primacy all the more convincing. At any rate, the Chipeta issue is far from dead.

The Mbona III narratives are represented in this volume by a folk text (Text III/B) and a text from Lundu's court (Text III/A). Both texts form first and foremost part of the outer circle, where the court is situated. Since the folk text is not bound to any particular office, however, variations of it are found throughout the valley. As will be made clear in the next chapter, the court text and the folk text together constitute a dialogue or even a dispute between the court and the commonalty about the blessings of a centralized state and the limits of centralization.

One of the most striking aspects of the three streams is that the keepers of these various traditions (with the exception of the folk tradition) are of the same type as the authority figures in the successive streams, namely a rain priest (Ngabu), a chief (Tengani), and a king (Lundu). How is this parallel to be explained? An obvious possibility is that the streams function as *post factum* charters in regard to the offices concerned, but considering everything that has come to light about the Chipeta, the Zimba, and so forth, one has to dismiss this as too simplistic. Certainly the traditions kept by the various officials do function as charters, but that need not necessarily mean that they are *post factum* inventions. As a matter of fact, the most obvious and at the same time also the most logical interpretation would be to view the different streams and corresponding organizational circles and ritual phases as rooted in the same historical periods. This should not be taken to mean that they originated in the precise form that they have today. Rather, the suggestion is that the biographical streams, the organizational circles, and the three-phased ritual cycle reflect successive stages in history in which the valley population had to seek accommodation with different power structures. In these accommodative processes, their rain cult, like rain cults elsewhere, would have played a crucial role. These processes of centralization and resistance against centralization seem to be graphically symbolized by Mbona's person, who at first appears to form part of the emerging power structure but who by means of a series of stereotyped events, represented by the sequence "conflict-flight-murder" comes to be identified also with the preexisting community. The outcome in each case, then, is the emergence of a mediating figure with whom both sides can identify and who thus becomes capable of symbolizing the resulting accommodation.

THE MANG'ANJA WORLDVIEW

Having considered some of the links between the Mbona narratives and the political and cultic history of the Mang'anja, we can now discuss their relevance in relation to Mang'anja intellectual history. The claims made at the beginning of this chapter were, first, that we could infer from these narratives a crucial development in the Mang'anja worldview and, second, that the Mbona narratives represent not one but two worldviews, which are respectively those of the aristocracy and the commonalty. To substantiate these claims, we shall begin by distinguishing between the various imageries used to describe Mbona.

In the first two streams Mbona is sometimes openly portrayed as a sorcerer, while this is not (or less clearly) the case in the third stream. In the first stream Mbona has to face the poison ordeal, which implies that there had been a sorcery accusation. In the second stream we are told that he used sorcery against his uncle. Neither stream, however, is unambiguous on this point, for each also contains versions which cast Mbona's opponent in the role of sorcerer.

The traditions of the third stream, particularly those of the folk version, are of a different kind. There, Mbona is described in the imagery of a child, or sometimes even of an infant, thereby in principle excluding the possibility of his using sorcery. Translated into power relations, this means that in the sorcery streams Mbona is portrayed as the equal of his antagonists, since in principle their roles are interchangeable. Either may be sorcerer or victim. Not so in the infancy stream, where the crucial point seems to be the absolute unevenness between the two parties, who face each other as adult and child. It seems to me that the division of power in each case, namely more or less symmetrical power relations and decidedly asymmetrical power relations, fits the political situation of the historical period which it purports to reflect. This requires little clarification as far as the prestate situation is concerned, for there the power relations were in theory symmetrical. Intervillage warfare regularly resulted in a temporary splitting up of the entire populace in two halves. But even during the early state period, power relations were not overly asymmetrical, since institutions such as the *nyau* societies kept the power of the aristocracy in check. In the Shire Valley, however, most of these checks appear to have been destroyed during the Zimba period, and the resulting powerlessness of the commonalty found an apposite expression in the imagery of the defenseless and innocent child.

This said, let us examine once again the accounts of the founding of the cult, which was ascribed in the first two streams to the initiative of the local population and Mbona's followers and in the third stream to Mbona's own initiative. At first sight there seems to be no connection between this and the two imageries just referred to, but this may be misleading. Let us begin by considering the infancy stream. The logic underlying the plots of these stories appears to be that there are two kinds of reality, that which is immediately perceptible and that which is hidden but which will reveal itself when it is vitally challenged. In the latter case, not only does it reveal itself, but it also establishes its superiority over the other type of reality. Thus Mbona, who at first appears as a child, defenseless against the king, in the end manifests himself as a powerful supernatural being, capable of forcing the king into submission. We are here in the presence of a further example of the principle of ritual inversion as formulated by Janzen. It is not difficult to see that the plot would be inconclusive and its message incomplete and ineffective without this final theophany, for without it we would never have known the true nature of the child. But what do these two realities refer to in sociopolitical terms?

In view of the widespread warfare at the time of the first Lundu kings as described in the previous chapters, an obvious suggestion would be that the contrast refers to the daily reality of oppression and violence as against the ideal of peace. The message which the stories of the third stream seem to convey is that violence is self-defeating or, put differently, that peacefulness in the end is stronger than violence. The king may seem all-powerful and the child totally defenseless, but when things have run their course the roles are reversed: the king has become the weaker party, and the child has become the stronger. The reversal of roles, however, does not amount to a simple inversion. The child does not kill the king but inaugurates a new order in which the king's role, too, will be a peaceful one.

Historically, Lundu came to be defeated by Muzura, but the Lundu dynasty remained in power until the nineteenth century. The power relations in the Lundu kingdom, however, remained demonstrably different from those in the other Maravi polities, where the *nyau* societies continued to provide a powerful instrument of opposition to the ruler. Since this was no longer the case in Lundu's kingdom, abuse of royal power was a more realistic threat.

It seems to me that the infancy stories and the "two realities ideology" of which they are an expression would be functional in precisely this type of power structure. The reality of kingship cannot be and is not questioned, but its destructive power is believed to be kept in check by a higher order. The condition of subjection in which the population finds itself is thus acknowledged at one level of consciousness but denied at another, and what at first sight seems unacceptable in the end becomes acceptable.

The sorcery stories are of an entirely different nature. They do not propound a doctrine but describe a conflict between two more or less equal parties. In accordance with this, the building of the shrine is not presented as the beginning of a new moral and political order. Mbona does not force his killers into submission. They just go back where they came from, and the two parties which confronted each other throughout the story remain separated even when events have run their course. This continuing separation is not only the conclusion of the stories themselves, but it is also, and in a sense much more forcefully, brought out by the existence of opposing traditions within these streams, namely one which holds Mbona guilty of sorcery and one which declares him innocent. This is the kind of ambiguous reportage one expects when two sides vie for power without a victor clearly emerging.

THE HOMINIZATION OF THE SNAKE

At this point we shall take up a question which needs to be answered, if only to round out the argument: What makes Mbona different from other Bantu deities symbolized by a water serpent? This mythical animal forms part of one of the great themes of Bantu mythology, namely the eternal conflict of the lightning and the rainbow.[12] Christopher Wrigley writes, "The point about the lightning and the rainbow is that, since the primeval separation, they have been the only surviving links between earth and heaven. Both are highly ambiguous powers. Lightning brings the life giving rains but is himself a killer. Rainbow, in African thought, is a great snake which lives in water, but when it rears into the sky it holds apart the waters of earth and the waters of heaven, and must therefore be severed, beheaded, to release the rains."[13]

Wrigley has expressed doubt about my historical interpretation of the

Mbona stories, arguing that they can only be viewed as part of the mythical complex based on the theme of the rainbow and the water snake, as described by de Heusch for Central Africa. More concretely, his suggestion is that Mbona, like his Central African and interlacustrine counterparts, has for centuries been conceived of as a malign, rain-withholding power, needing constant propitiation. Only after the upheavals of the 1860s did his death acquire a new significance, making him a member of a group of suffering deities. In sum, the martyrdom theme that I see emerging around 1600 is said to have been nonexistent before the second half of the nineteenth century.

Wrigley's objections do not differ substantially from those of de Heusch against Vansina, which makes it worthwhile to consider them carefully.[14] In essence, the allegation is that the historical information I think can be derived from those stories, particularly from the Mbona III traditions, finds little support in the historical facts insofar as they are known to us. Put somewhat more mildly, even if my historical interpretation of the Mbona stories were correct, there is no way to "prove" its correctness. Perhaps not, but it may be worth trying.[15]

Unfortunately, Wrigley's article makes it appear as if in my view the entire Mbona tradition derives from the early Lundu state. This is not so, for as I have made clear in the present chapter and elsewhere, there are three sets of Mbona biographies. Of these three sets, only one presents Lundu as Mbona's main antagonist, but it does so consistently. It is therefore misleading to assert, as does Wrigley, that the name or title of Mbona's antagonist varies "from version to version," thereby creating the impression that the Lundu connection is not in any way solid or historically meaningful. Second, I have demonstrated on the basis of internal textual criteria that the Lundu versions are substantively different from the others. In only those texts does Mbona himself order a shrine to be built, and in only those texts is Mbona's death given explicit salvific meaning. Third, that salvific dimension is not a mid–nineteenth century development, but something which must have originated at some earlier stage. If it were a mid–nineteenth century development, it would be hard to explain why the Lundus play a central role in these texts in view of the fact, emphasized also by Wrigley, that by the mid–nineteenth century their power had dwindled to insignificance. The origin of this particular set of Mbona biographies has therefore to be located further back in time, and the time around 1600 is the only period which corresponds with the historically identifiable elements in the narratives we are discussing.

My principal argument has been the name Tundu, which appears both in a contemporary written document and in some of the Mbona texts. In an effort to dismantle this crucial piece of evidence, Wrigley hypothesizes that Tundu was a war god, whom the Portuguese mistook for a real general. Helpful as this may be to bolster his theory, it is methodologically unsound to reject contemporary firsthand evidence in favor of mere hypothesizing. Moreover, I wish to repeat that the posthumous divinization of historical individuals is an important cultural feature of Zambesia, as evidenced by the *mhondoro* cults. Tundu became a "war god" only after his death, and it is thus that he became a major trace element to perpetuate awareness of the Zimba episode.

Another argument for dating this set of Mbona traditions to the period just before and after 1600 are the striking congruences between Santos' documentation and the oral traditions of the Shire Valley. One instance of such congruences is Lundu's rain dance as described in one of the major texts of this set (Text III/B, secs. 2–3) and Santos' description of the ritual performed by the king of the Zimba, whom we hold to have been one of the early Lundus. The importance of these testimonies lies not only in the fact that they are analogous but also, and even more so, in the fact that they provide testimony, independently from each other, that Lundu was both king and rain priest. I have maintained throughout that such a combination is and was most unusual among the Maravi. Kings and senior chiefs had priests whom they asked to perform the rain rituals. They took part in the ceremonies, but they did not officiate themselves. We see this illustrated in Text II/A, which describes how the reputed founder of the first Maravi state, Kaphwiti, relied on his priest, Mlauli, to perform the rites on his behalf. The fact that in the 1590s someone gave Santos precisely this piece of information to illustrate Lundu's power suggests also that the combination of kingship and priesthood in one person was considered unusual.

Another striking congruence between Santos and Mang'anja traditions is provided in the way they describe the destruction wrought by the spirit Chitundu and the Zimba.[16] These similarities seem to me too close to be dismissed out of hand. It is possible and even likely that before the Zimba period Mbona was conceived of as a zoomorphic and ahistoric rather than an anthropomorphic and historic deity, much like his Central African and interlacustrine counterparts.[17] The central thesis of this book is that the Zimba experience resulted in a profound transformation of a preexisting mythical discourse in the sense that it changed Mbona from an ahistorical into a historical deity and from an essentially malign or at least highly ambiguous deity into an essentially benign deity. In a nutshell, this constitutes the most profound difference between Mbona I and II, on the one hand, and Mbona III, on the other.

Let me summarize what has been achieved so far. First, we have been able, on the basis of internal textual criteria, to identify three streams in the Mbona narratives, each of which describes a different set of power relations between Mbona and his adversary. Second, it has been argued on the basis of oral and documentary evidence that these streams reflect political processes which took place before and during the closing decade of the sixteenth century. The picture which emerged was one of a three-phase development represented respectively by an acephalous organization, relatively centralized chiefdoms, and a highly centralized kingdom. Third, we have seen that the three streams exhibit certain parallels with the cult organization as evidenced by the types of authority — priestly, chiefly, and royal — that successively play a role in the rites. These correspondences have been interpreted as deriving from the charter function that the traditions undeniably exercise, but also as reflecting the historical development of the organization itself. More concretely, the suggestion was made that the three streams and the three types of authority are to be regarded as precipitates of the same historical events and processes.

Fourth, we have noted also that the biographies contain continuous and discontinuous features. The former is exemplified by the gradual increase of power on the part of Mbona's main adversary and the corresponding decrease of power on the part of Mbona himself, and the latter is exemplified by the imagery used to describe this power differential and by the accounts of Mbona's killing and the subsequent foundation of the cult. The discontinuity in the third group of narratives suggests that the core message of these narratives was different from that of the other streams. That message, then, was seen to refer to a fundamental difference between political relations in the kingdom and prekingdom periods and to a fundamental difference in the religious reaction to these relations. As far as the nature of political relations is concerned, the contrast between the two situations was found to be that between relative symmetry (the sorcery imagery) and pronounced asymmetry (the infancy imagery). As far as the religious reaction is concerned, the opposition appeared to be between the view that religion is part of the power play and the view that religion denies the validity of the power play.

The final observation was that the latter view developed during the early kingdom period among the commonalty in reaction to the aristocratic view which continued as the philosophy of those in power, thus establishing a dual worldview which has persisted into our days.

Considering these various findings, we may, I think, claim with Willis that we have made a case for the validity of the historical approach in respect to a body of genesis myths, in the sense that they may in principle be made to yield qualitative historical information.[18] But we have also gone beyond Willis by arguing that it may even be possible in some cases to retrace the historical development of the myths themselves and thereby to reconstruct part of a people's intellectual history. Assuming that our exposé, despite the gaps that an exercise of this kind necessarily contains, is essentially plausible, the question arises whether there exists a logical contradiction between the structuralist and historical approaches.

My doubts about de Heusch's structuralism relate primarily to his assumption of a unitary ideology underlying the mythical constructs of a people or, as in his case, a congeries of peoples. One would think that the possibility of a unitary worldview existing among a certain population at a certain stage of its political and cultural history cannot be reasonably denied, but the opposite possibility is not to be dismissed either. In fact, what I am trying to demonstrate is the existence of precisely such a situation among the Mang'anja, where the nobility and the commonalty from the seventeenth century onward seem to have held different views about the nature of social reality, differences which in my view resulted from historical events that led to an unusually sharp cleavage between rulers and subjects. Structuralism seems unable to say much about the political reality underlying the conceptual contrasts it attempts to identify and interpret. Human reality includes also reacting to political oppression, and it is these aspects which the structuralist approach leaves undiscussed or which it even obscures.

CHAPTER 7

Ideological Confrontation in Oral Tradition

EVER SINCE B. Malinowski formulated his concept of myths as political charters, there has been a tendency among anthropologists to regard origin myths as *post factum* constructs designed to legitimate existing privileges and positions.[1] A classic example of this pragmatist view is Leach's study of political systems in Highland Burma, in which he attempts to demonstrate that origin myths change with clocklike regularity in response to shifts in the political constellation.[2] More recently, however, voices have been raised, particularly among historians, which insist that a society's past is not manipulated at will but that it is treated circumspectly, the way one deals with any scarc resource.[3] Oral traditions contain records of a group's special rights, and it is only to be expected that strong indirect sanctions are at work for their preservation.[4] From this it may be inferred that accounts of the past, when they concern important aspects of a society, are constructed in such a way that the original event is preserved and in principle recoverable. The assumption, then, is that oral tradition, if it is to be functional, must be subject to certain rules preventing it from completely losing its historical moorings, and the question which logically follows is whether it is possible to explicate those rules. In this chapter an attempt will be made to answer that question in relation to the two versions of the Mbona myth which pertain to the kingdom period (Texts III/A and III/B) and which are crucial to our understanding of that period.

Both texts deal with the restoration of the cult, but the basic difference between them is that Text III/A does so from the viewpoint of the court, and Text III/B from the viewpoint of the commonalty. Since the parties involved have different interests in accordance with their different positions in the political structure, the texts can be read as an ideological confrontation. Whereas the court version conveys the message that without the king there would be chaos, the folk version, while not directly challenging the king's right to rule, counters by intimating that the king, instead of preventing chaos from arising, created chaos himself by grossly abusing the authority entrusted to him. By destroying the cult he undermined the foundation on which a balanced form of cooperation between king and people could have taken shape.

One of our aims will be to establish what use our two texts have made of objective history. Since they represent different political interests, one naturally expects them to have made different selections from the historical material or to have chosen different emphases. If such divergences can be identified and if they can be explained in the light of known historical facts, it will become possible to find out how the selective mechanism operated and, following that, in what sense manipulation of the objective past has taken place. That type of investigation has been made possible in our case by the fact that names and events which play a role in our two mythical tales figure also in contemporary Portuguese documents. Thus, we have at least some idea about the time when and the historical circumstances under which these myths emerged. We shall begin our exposé with a schematic presentation of the two mythical texts, and from there we will proceed to an examination of their similarities and differences and of their relationship to objective history.

THE COURT VERSION (TEXT III/A)

This text is tightly structured and consists of three clearly demarcated sections, each of which contains an account of four journeys. The northbound journeys are made to obtain a bride or to recruit followers. The southbound journeys are made in connection with the founding of the kingdom and the cult.

Mbona is born in the southern part of the Shire Valley at a time when Lundu still lives at Kaphirintiwa in central Malawi and when a formal state system has not yet developed in the valley. Unable to find a wife in the valley, Mbona travels northward to try his luck among his kinsmen at Kaphirintiwa. He is then given a spouse by his maternal uncle Lundu, who is the chief of those parts.

Accompanied by his newly acquired wife, Mbona returns to his native country, where the couple intends to make a home. Due to chronic civil strife, of which he is held to be the cause, however, Mbona and his wife are regularly forced to hide in caves.

In the end, realizing that this cannot last, Mbona returns to Lundu, who provides the young couple with a house and a piece of land.

While at Lundu's, a drought occurs against which the rainmakers are powerless. Mbona, though their junior, succeeds in making rain with the help of two ritual spears and thereby arouses the ire of his uncle and the official rainmakers. He flees again to the south, but his uncle and his men manage to track him down. Mbona tells them to tie a blade of grass around his neck before killing him. The blood gushing from the wound immediately turns into water. After the killing the head is severed from the body and buried separately.

After Mbona's death Lundu returns to his home in the north, but while en route he discovers a place, called Mbewe, in the middle of a wilderness, which has good soils and which therefore seems to him a suitable location to settle. Upon his arrival in the north he finds his chiefdom once again in the throes of a drought.

Being held responsible by the population (as he had killed the only competent rainmaker), Lundu and his wife decide to migrate to Mbewe, where Lundu builds a hut of poles strong enough to keep out the "wild animals" (i.e., *nyau* dancers) prowling there.

After a successful farming season Lundu returns to his former headquarters in the north to cede the chieftaincy to one of his kinsmen and to recruit followers from among his lineage.

Together with these he moves for good to the Shire Valley, where he builds a capital at Mbewe and thus becomes the ruler of a large and prosperous kingdom. He appoints local and regional chiefs exclusively from among his kinsmen.

When Lundu has established his new capital, Mbona's messengers travel to it to ask the king for a shrine hut to be built at Khulubvi.

Lundu agrees and sends junior kinsmen to oversee the shrine's construction and to help with the organization of the cult.

When the shrine hut has been completed, Mbona's messengers once more travel to Mbewe, this time to ask Lundu for a spirit wife.

Lundu agrees again. He sends one of his own sisters, who is duly installed. Then the cult formally commences.

THE FOLK VERSION (TEXT III/B)

Mbona is born at Mbewe, Lundu's capital, in the heyday of the kingdom. His mother, called Chitundu, is the king's sister and still a virgin, because she conceived and gave birth to her child in a miraculous way.

Lundu, unaware of this, considers Mbona an illegitimate child who is disqualified for succession to the kingship. Moreover, Mbona is still a bachelor and contrary to customary law continues to live in his mother's house, although he should already be married.

A serious drought occurs. Lundu performs a spectacular rain dance the way he always does, but on this occasion he is unsuccessful. His councillors conclude from this that Mulungu (God) has turned away from him for some reason and that Mulungu has already taken possession of one of Lundu's maternal nephews and potential successors.

In order to find out who this might be, Lundu orders his nephews to dance, one after the other, but none of them is successful. The king concludes from this that none of his potential successors has found favor with Mulungu, but his councillors remind him that Mbona too is one of his nephews and therefore also ought to be given a chance. At first Lundu refuses, but in the end he allows himself to be persuaded, and he asks Mbona's mother to transmit the invitation to her son.

Mbona refuses at first, because he has a premonition that both he and his mother will be in serious danger, but his mother tells him that they have to endure this for the sake of the people, who otherwise will have to die of starvation. In the end, Mbona is persuaded and begins preparing himself by manufacturing two ceremonial daggers, besides other implements.

Mbona moves to the dancing ground dressed as a powerful medicine man and carrying impressive magical objects. At first nobody recognizes him, since the metamorphosis is almost perfect, but in the end everyone has to conclude that this can be nobody but Mbona. No sooner has he pointed his ritual daggers at the four points of the compass and the sky above him than lightning flares and the crash of thunder is heard, followed by torrential rain. The public is mad with joy and gives the youthful rainmaker a huge applause.

Before the dance Mbona had asked Lundu to order his people to keep the small children locked up in their mothers' huts. This was done, but when the small ones hear the jubilation outside, they become impatient. At long last Lundu's little son, the child of his junior wife, manages to escape from his mother's hut, but the moment he finds himself outside he is hit by lightning and split asunder. The public is terrified, but the rains continue.

At the conclusion of the mourning period it is customary that the parents of the child cohabit "to set the mourners free." The child's mother, however, refuses to cooperate, since she regards Mbona as a sorcerer and her son's killer. She therefore demands that her husband have him executed. Lundu refuses at first, but later he gives in and calls a few hirelings together who agree to execute Mbona at daybreak.

Mbona, who in some mysterious manner has overheard this conversation, flees with his mother the moment the king's hirelings surround the hut. The latter immediately begin the pursuit, but they are unable to find anybody.

Having reached the Matundu Hills in the southern part of the valley, Mbona performs food miracles. He creates a well of water on a flat rock and makes rice grow around it, which cannot be planted elsewhere.

In these hills Mbona says farewell to his mother, Chitundu, who crosses the Zambezi and becomes a rain prophetess south of the river.

Now his killers come upon him. They try to kill him with their spears and arrows, but they are unsuccessful. Mbona then tells them that the only way to kill him is to cut his throat with a blade of grass.

Mbona is killed on the bank of a stream, which becomes a river of blood.

After his death Mbona, through his medium, asks Lundu for a shrine hut and a wife. The wife is obtained by capture. When the shrine is built Lundu serves as the center pole around and upon which the shrine is constructed.

A PRELIMINARY ANALYSIS

At first sight our two stories seem to have little in common with the events we are familiar with from the Portuguese documents. There we read of wars between African states and between these and the Portuguese enclaves of the interior, whereas that subject does not seem to be touched upon at all in our two texts. Yet despite this we are able to note some parallels. Both in the Portuguese documents and the Shire Valley myths we come across the name Tundu. That name was commented upon extensively in Chapter 6, where it was argued that Mbona's mother, Chitundu, is a systematic transformation of the Zimba leader Tundu, who constitutes the principal, but by no means the only, bridge between the oral traditions and documented history. If this is correct, the question may be raised what the function of this transformation might be. There are a number of answers to this, one of which has already been suggested: it is a symbolic inversion serving to accommodate a novel and traumatic experience by widening the explicative potential of the incorporating tradition. About this change in the explicative potential of the Mbona myth we shall have more to say later on in this chapter.

On a more pragmatic level, the Zimba episode may have been so damaging to the reputation of the Lundus that it became a forbidden topic, only to be touched upon in a veiled and inverted manner. It should be remembered, though, that even in its inverted form the Tundu image is in a sense historically objective, for if it is true that the Zimba general was directly responsible for the destruction of the earlier cult organization, then he was by the same token indirectly responsible for the emergence of a new cult organization and a new theology. It may therefore rightfully be claimed that he gave birth to the cult and thus became its "mother" in a symbolic sense.

What has just been said about the name Tundu constituting a bridge between the Portuguese documents and the folk version of the Mbona story does not hold for the court version. The name Tundu is nowhere to be found in that text, nor is there any reference, veiled or otherwise, to mercenaries. When Mbona is persecuted and killed, Lundu and the elders perpetrate the act, not some hirelings. The court version remains silent also about Lundu's career as chief rainmaker, another crucial element explicitly referred to in the folk text. In other words, there appears to be little connection between the court story and the Portuguese documents, and we may therefore ask ourselves with some reason whether it refers to the same events as the folk version. This brings us to the next step, a systematic comparison of the two texts.

First, both versions contain all the crucial episodes of the story: the conflict with the king, the flight to the south, Mbona's death, the building of a shrine, and the king's gift of a bride to Mbona. Therefore, a fundamental unity exists between the two texts at the level of plot structure. Also, the two versions cover different periods in the formation of the Lundu kingdom. The court version covers the period from the founding of the kingdom to its heyday and ends there. The folk version, on the other hand, starts from the period when Lundu's power is past its apogee and ends when he finally cedes ritual power to the cult. From the viewpoint of the process of state formation, then, the two versions are strictly complementary: one begins where the other ends. But their complementarity does not end there, for even where the two versions refer to the same episodes, one version reveals what the other omits. Thus, in the court version we miss all references to Tundu and the Zimba mercenaries as well as to Mbona's food miracles. Furthermore, the impotence of iron weapons is referred to in a weakened form: in order for them to become effective, a blade of grass has to be tied around Mbona's neck. Again, it is possible that the Lundu dynasty did not want to be reminded of these details and that for this reason they were filtered out of their reminiscences. The hired killers may have reminded the Lundus that they came to power with the aid of a mercenary army, which became notorious for its cruelties. Mbona's food miracles would have evoked the idea of famine and thus of a failure on the part of the Lundus to provide their people with food. Finally, it is imaginable also that the court was not particularly inclined to portray Mbona (i.e., the cult organization) as having been more powerful than the Lundus, hence the weakened reference to the impotence of iron weapons (i.e., of armed force).

On the other hand, it was in the interest of the population at large to expatiate precisely on these details and to keep the memory of Tundu, the Zimba, their cruelties, and their final defeat alive. There are thus profound differences between the two versions, but these differences are complementary rather than contradictory. Summarizing, then, we may say that the folk text is closest to the Portuguese documents and that it serves as a heuristic bridge between the latter and the court text. Without the folk text we would probably have had no means of linking the court text, or parts thereof, with definite items in documented history. The complementary character of our two texts weakens somewhat, however, when we consider the principle of desynchronization, for here we discover the first indications of contradiction.

THE PRINCIPLE OF DESYNCHRONIZATION

In processes of state formation, rain cults usually come under attack when the state organization is expanding and intensifying its control over the population and the forces of production, not when the state organization is in decline. This is only logical in view of the fact that rain cults, as we have seen, often function as rallying points of opposition against the state, particularly the nascent state. Once a rain cult has been incapacitated by the emerging state, it may reappear in the same or some adapted form when the state is past its apogee. The reemergence of a rain cult after a period of forced absence signifies that effective opposition against the state has once again become possible.

Comparing the pattern just sketched with our two texts, we see that both texts contain a striking anomaly. Thus the folk version has Mbona (symbolizing the cult) persecuted and killed when Lundu has been "deserted by Mulungu" (i.e., when the king's power was already on the decline). The court version, on the other hand, has Mbona's death where it logically belongs, as part of the rise of the kingdom, when the Lundu dynasty tries to get rid of all institutions standing in the way of increasing centralization. The court version makes it appear as if the restoration of the cult (i.e., the building of the shrine and the installation of a spirit wife) took place at the apogee of the Lundus' power, whereas the folk version puts it where one would expect it logically, when the power of the Lundus is in decline. By making it appear that the restoration of the cult took place when the state was at its strongest, the court version creates the impression that the restoration was an event entirely controlled by the court. Messengers come with a petition from the cult organization without any threat of force vis-à-vis the king, and the latter sends his kinsmen to oversee the construction of the shrine and the conduct of the cult. Later on, when the shrine folk ask him for a spirit wife, he gives them no less a person than his own sister. All this exudes nothing but harmony. The folk version, on the other hand, makes clear that the request to have a shrine built is urgent and that the king is not at all free in his decision. Furthermore, when the shrine is built, the king has to play the role of center pole, a ritual role which in the Mbona cult is associated with both centrality and servitude, as we saw in Chapter 2. When the shrine folk demand a spirit wife for Mbona, the king answers in despair that he has none to offer and that a bride must therefore be captured. In the folk version, the restoration of the shrine is therefore anything but a matter of harmony: it seals the defeat of royal absolutism.

I must confess that I have more difficulty explaining why the folk text makes Mbona's persecution take place when the king's power is on the point of diminishing instead of letting it take place when the young kingdom is on the rise. The commonalty may perhaps have found it difficult to admit that the cult has been inactive for a rather longish period. By making destruction and restoration appear as more or less immediately succeeding each other, the impression might be created that this had not been the case. Apart from this, presenting the birth of the cult as having taken place directly after the persecution may have also been a way of reinforcing the idea of divine intervention.

The ideological confrontation becomes even more explicit when we consider the information given by the two versions about Mbona's marriage partner. According to the court version Mbona was unable to find himself a suitable bride in his home country, and for this reason he had to turn to his uncle Lundu, who at that time lived in Malawi's Central Region, well to the north of the Shire Valley. Lundu, so the story goes, provided Mbona with a wife, and at a later stage also with a hut and a piece of land. The folk version, on the other hand, maintains that Mbona was not married and that he still lived in his mother's hut. The text also suggests that this was due to his uncle, who did not consider him a legitimate member of the lineage, and therefore not entitled to be given a wife by the head of the lineage. Thus, whereas the court text says that Mbona could not find a bride in his homeland and that he therefore had to be given one by the (future) king, the folk text suggests that the king refused to do this.

To understand the significance of this contradiction, one must know that it refers to the distinction between elders and youngsters in the kinship system and also to the distinction between free men and slaves. In both types of relationship marriage was a crucial item, for both the younger males of a lineage and its male slaves depended on permission given by the head of the lineage, with the one difference that a young free man had a right to marriage which the slave did not have. Otherwise, their treatment was not much different. Both were pawns in the hands of the elders, who controlled the lineage and decided who should be allowed a spouse and when.[5] Hence what the folk version appears to be saying in symbolic form is that when the Lundus came to power the basic rights of the commonalty (symbolized by Mbona) were no longer recognized and that the inhabitants of the kingdom were treated like slaves. In view of the atrocities perpetrated by the Zimba, who acted as Lundu's strong arm, that message hardly needs explanation.

The message of the court version is the exact opposite. It says that in an acephalous system people hardly have rights or that they are unable to make use of their rights. This is illustrated by Mbona's being unable to find himself a bride in his chiefless homeland. He finally receives one in his uncle's country, but when he returns with her to his home country, life there is made impossible for the couple, and once again they have to take refuge with Lundu. In other words, only under the protection of a centralized state are people able to exercise their basic rights. Hence, when the two versions contradict each other clearly and squarely, they do so with regard to the value and the functioning of particular political systems.

THE RULES FOLLOWED IN THE USE OF ORAL TRADITIONS

Having surveyed the similarities and differences between the two versions, we are now in a position to formulate the rules which apparently have been operative in relation to objective history. First, it is clear that historical facts may be presented in symbolic form. Human groups or institutions associated with such groups, for instance, may be personified. Thus the name Lundu may stand for the aristocracy as a whole, Tundu may represent the Zimba and their activities, and the name Mbona may stand for the commonalty and the cult organization, which was temporarily eliminated but later restored. The right to marry stands for being a free person. The word *drought*, the nonfunctioning of the climatic cycle, appears to be symbolic shorthand for the nonfunctioning of society on account of endemic conflicts. Conversely, regular rains appear to signify a proper functioning of society.

The second rule appears to be that a discussion such as the one engaged in here between the aristocracy and the commonalty requires a shared historical framework. In our case, that framework consists of a combination of state history and cult history pertaining to the same set of events. This allows for the simultaneous formulation of opposite views, since the aristocracy dominates one and the commonalty dominates the other.

The third rule to be inferred from the two histories is that historical facts which throw an unfavorable light on one of the parties may be concealed by that party. The opposing party, however, may react by preserving and even emphasizing precisely those elements. When this becomes dangerous, the elements in question may be inverted in such a way that they simultaneously conceal and reveal the truth. We have seen this illustrated by the transformation of Tundu from bloodthirsty warrior to loving mother. Inversion, apart from serving to widen the explanatory power of a symbol, may therefore also function as a safety device.

Fourth, processes and events may be desynchronized. Concretely, this means that a crucial event in the history of the cult may be linked with a phase in the process of state formation with which that event has no logical connection. The result is that the event in question is given a different meaning from the one it had originally. Formal contradiction occurs only when the two parties express their opinion on a matter of ideological importance, such as the value of kingship and the role of the cult.

Summarizing our discussion so far, we may say that the Mang'anja treat that part of their history which evolved between 1580 and 1622 with great care. Although one party may leave important facts unmentioned, the opposing party may unmask this by revealing or emphasizing precisely those events. One may even shift an event to a different point in time where it is logically out of place, which means that the deviation from history can be noticed and corrected. It is apparently not permitted to say of events which did happen that they did in fact not happen or, conversely, to maintain that events did happen which actually never took place. Where something of that nature occurs, as in the episode of Mbona's marriage — one version asserting that he was given a wife by his uncle, the other version denying it — the event referred to forms part of the ideological contestation.

The discussion, as we have seen, ultimately does not concern the question of whether or not Mbona was given a marriage partner, but whether a person's rights are better guaranteed in a centralized state than in an acephalous society. That the Lundus did organize a strongly centralized state system is denied by neither party. It is considered a historical fact which is above denial. What can be questioned, though, is the proper functioning of that state. That questioning process takes place at two levels. One level is that of practical politics. It is at this level that the cult medium confronts the chiefs in regard to problems which are of immediate concern to the population. The other level is that of political philosophy. There, the question is posed whether there should be a centralized state system at all and, if so, what conditions should be met for it to function properly. It is this philosophical discussion which informs our two texts.

POLITICAL TRACTS AND COSMOLOGICAL TREATISES

It will have become clear by now that the kingdom texts can be read both as political tracts and cosmological treatises. The two belong together in the mentality of the Mang'anja, since in their thinking the correct movement of the seasons depends on the correct management and control of society. Usurpation of power by the king ends in drought. This is unavoidable, as it means that the king failed to respect the principle of dual sovereignty.[6] Ritual and secular power have to be in balance. Restoring that balance appears to be of special concern in the folk text, which opens with the story of the king usurping the role of the rain priest. After the king fails, dual sovereignty is temporarily restored when Mbona takes over the role of rain priest, but he is soon challenged anew by Lundu, who understandably feels threatened. The permanent restoration of dual sovereignty sets in with Mbona's flight, which creates the necessary physical distance between court and cult, and it is brought to completion by his death and reappearance as a powerful supernatural. From then onward, there are once again two complementary sovereigns: Lundu in the north of the valley and Mbona in the south.

This is also the moment when the suppressed sections of the population, notably those known as Banda or Chipeta, are restored to their rights. This does not necessarily mean that there has been a general and complete return to the pre-Zimba situation. Such a thing may have been impossible in view of the many Banda/Chipeta that had been killed or forced to flee, but it meant that those who had remained behind regained a measure of freedom, which was once again guaranteed by the cult. But the cult was no longer dominated by the Banda/Chipeta as it had been in the past. It had now become a totalizing duality, bringing both the older population segments and the Maravi together in a system of contrasting and complementary positions.[7] The king became wife-giver in relation to the chief priest, Ngabu Banda, and the latter became wife-receiver in relation to the king. At the shrine itself, the two principals formed a similar pair, Malemia being the jural and Ngabu the ritual head; one represented the Phiri/Maravi, the other represented the Banda/Chipeta.

THE IRON AND THE GRASS

The creation of what amounts to a form of antagonistic cooperation seems graphically represented by the two instruments, iron and grass, with which the killing was effected.[8] Thus we read in the folk text that Mbona himself tells his enemies, after they try in vain to kill him by means of spears and arrows, that only vegetal matter can do that (Text III/B, sec. 20). Indeed, following his advice, they finally manage to cut his throat with a blade of grass. The court text (Text III/A, secs. 15–16) mentions the same two substances, but according to that text Mbona tells his enemies to tie a blade of grass around his neck before killing him, implying that otherwise they would not be able to perform the killing. According to that text, therefore, iron is not altogether powerless, but only when applied on its own.

Starting from the folk text, we note that the replacement of iron by grass is one of the inversions that are so characteristic of this profoundly religious text. The facts that Mbona cannot be killed by the usual weapons and that he alone decides how the killing is to be carried out establish him as superior to his persecutors. This is further enhanced when the heavily armed men are told that the only way to kill their enemy is to drop their weapons and use a blade of grass instead.

There is more to it, however. In a subtle way the contrast also refers to the division of labor between the major sections of the population: the Banda/Chipeta and the Phiri/Maravi. The Banda/Chipeta are commonly associated with valleys, grass, and a grassland economy. The Phiri/Maravi, on the other hand, are associated with hills—the places where iron ore is mined—and fire, which is essential for smelting and smithery. The two groups are said to have formed a totalizing duality at two levels, namely of the polity and of the marriage system. At the level of the polity the Phiri/Maravi were the rulers, and the Banda/Chipeta the ritual specialists. At the level of the lineage they were each other's wife-givers and wife-takers. It was a way of saying that for Mang'anja society to function properly, some sort of balance ought to be maintained between the two population components. Lundu upset that balance by denying the original population its long-established rights. The grass symbol of the Banda/Chipeta disappeared from view, as it were, when Lundu decided to suppress them by force. Interestingly enough, we see the grass symbol reappearing in the scene of Mbona's death as one of two agents by which he is killed.

One might possibly interpret the grass symbol in the murder scene as a way of ridiculing violence (symbolized by iron) or as a statement to the effect that violence is not the ultimate authority, in other words, as a moral statement. Second, it may also be interpreted as a statement about objec-

tive history, for inasmuch as iron was unable to kill Mbona, the Phiri/
Maravi were unsuccessful in perpetually subduing the Banda/Chipeta. It
is the Banda/Chipeta land which provides the instrument with which the
invaders kill one of their number, making him into a deity that belongs
to both groups. By mixing with the valley people, the incoming Maravi
lost part of their own aristocratic religion to a preexisting earth cult. That
earth cult, however, also changed in the process, because it became the
cult of two peoples, for which it acted as a unifying factor.[9]

PART TWO

Mbona Biographies

GENERAL INTRODUCTION

THE STORY of Mbona's life and death has no formal liturgical function in the sense of being recited as part of a religious ceremony. Nor is there any person who may be regarded as the official narrator, keeper, or interpreter. The story is transmitted from person to person and from generation to generation as a form of entertainment and as a kind of informal education much like common folk stories. As demonstrated in Chapters 3 and 4, however, the story may also be used to assert or dispute claims to certain rights, positions, and functions in the cult. The story may also be used to conceptualize and explain important meteorological, social, and political events. A drought, for instance, will always occasion a marked increase of interest in the Mbona story, not just because drought is a central theme in the accounts of Mbona's life but more so because each drought is viewed as a repetition of the original event which brought the cult into being. If there was social disorder then, there is social disorder now. If Mbona provided the explanation then, he provides it now. If he was active then, he is active now. It is clear, therefore, that apart from its entertainment value the story also has a pronounced theological, moral, and cosmological significance.

Although travelers, missionaries, and colonial administrators from the 1860s onward have had a more or less continuous interest in the cult, not until 1922 did the first Mbona biography appear in print. That version, predominantly in the Mbona I mode, is being reproduced here as Text I/A. The second published text, a folk variant of the Mbona III mode, appeared in 1936 in the Netherlands.[1] The author, Elias Chakanza from the Nsanje District, was then being trained as a primary school teacher. The Dutch version is a careful translation of the original Mang'anja text by Father

J. Eyssen. The third biographical text was published in 1953 and consists of a compilation of traditions collected two or three years before from informants, mainly chiefs and senior headmen, up and down the valley.[2] Due to this variety of informants from different locations, the author, the colonial administrator W. H. J. Rangeley, was the first to note the existence of different traditions or patterns of traditions. Instead of treating them as distinctive modes and as precipitates of different political configurations, however, he tried to combine them all into a kind of master version. Despite this, Rangeley's lengthy article has remained a most valuable source of information, not only on the story of Mbona's life but also on many aspects of the cult. The fourth published biography, which is quite distinctly in the Mbona III mode, was published in 1980 by the present author. It is reproduced here in amended form as Text III/B.

The remaining texts in this book (I/B, II/A, II/B, III/A, IV) are published for the first time. They have been selected from a total of some twenty texts, most of them rather brief, collected between August 1964 and December 1967. I decided that the book should include two representative texts for each of the three streams or modes. Texts which demonstrated the characteristics of an individual stream in a particularly enlightening way were preferred over others, and more detailed texts were preferred

Illus. 26. Blind storyteller, Nsanje, 1967. Photograph by C. Zonneveld.

over less detailed ones. In the case of Mbona I, however, there was little room for selectiveness, since that tradition is kept alive only by a tiny group surrounding the chief priest Ngabu. I have simply reproduced the two brief biographies at my disposal, one collected in 1907, the other in 1964. Text IV, the last biographical text in this book, has been included because it is a compilation by a Malawian which sums up the major themes in the three streams besides adding some of its own. For reasons of economy this concluding text, like the two short ones in the Mbona I mode, are published in English only, whereas the four texts in the Mbona II and Mbona III modes are reproduced here both in English and Chimang'anja.

THE MBONA I TRADITION

TEXT I/A
Ngabu and Chiphwembwe (1907)

THE PRESENT TEXT, first published by S. S. Murray in the 1922 edition of *A Handbook of Nyasaland,* was copied from the Lower Shire District Book (vol. 1, 1907), now in the National Archives of Malawi. The informants, Ngabu and Chiphwembwe, are described by the author as "Mbona's 'High Priests.'" Chiphwembwe was in 1907 still an underling of Malemia's, although in later days he came to supplant Malemia, as we saw in Chapter 3. The account brings out some of the major characteristics of the Mbona I stream. It tells us, for instance, that Mbona hailed from the country of the Chipeta, and it mentions the name of his father. The account does not mention any chief as having played a role in Mbona's life and death, thereby suggesting that the cult came into existence before the first chiefdoms.

TEXT

The Amang'anja of the Lower Shire District are said to have come from the Chipeta country in Central Angoniland,[1] many generations before Livingstone's visit in 1859, under a chief named Mbona, whose story has now passed into a superstitious legend. Another section came a little later from Lundu, west of the Shire,[2] under the original Tengani, who was a vassal of that chief, then paramount over all the Amang'anja, whose representative is now an unimportant village headman in the West Shire district.[3]

The chief superstition among the natives is the belief that the spirits of the dead can influence nature for the good or the ill of the living, and those spirits are propitiated by making sacrifices (nsembe) to them, generally of native beer. This belief is especially strong as regards Mbona, who is considered to be the "patron saint" of the district, with control of the rainfall, and consequently of the food supply. Mbona lives in Mlawi hill, which is considered sacred to him, but his "temple" is a hut in a thick clump of forest known as Kuluvi, in section C, almost at the foot of Mlawi. A woman lives in this hut who is known as Mbona's wife. Offerings must be made in this hut only and must consist of blue or black coth. The persons making the offering, or anyone who approaches the hut, must be clothed in blue or black. Europeans are not encouraged to visit this "temple," and very few have done so.

There are several versions of the history of Mbona which differ in many particulars, but the following notes were communicated by Ngabu and Chipwembwe (principal headmen),[4] who are Mbona's "High Priests," and who received the tradition from their fathers. It is impossible to ascertain, even approximately, when the events occurred. Mbona probably is not credited with possessing any special powers himself, but he intercedes with "Mlungu"[5] on behalf of the Amang'anja people, when he is pleased, and leaves them to suffer from droughts and floods when they have neglected or offended him.

Mbona came from Malawe, Kukambiritiya,[6] near the Achipeta country. His father's name was Chingale and his mother's name Chimbe.[7] He had four wives called Sawawa, Samisanje, Chungwe and Tiza.[8] Mbona came down to this country on account of a "Mlandu"[9] regarding an accusation against someone of being a witch, to whom a headman named Msumpi[10] ordered "mwabvi"[11] to be given. The accused drank the mwabvi and did not die, so the headman ordered a feast to be given to celebrate the event, and Mbona refused to take part in it as he objected to the ordeal trial. He told the people that he had power from "Mlungu" to tell when people were guilty and that poison was unnecessary.[12] They wanted to kill him, so he ran away and came towards this country, and across the Shire into what is now Portuguese territory. He wanted to make a village at Zambawe[13] in that country, and planted rice there which the people still grow every year. There is a peculiarity about this rice that it cannot be removed from the locality in which it was first planted by Mbona.

People have gone there to buy it, but have always forgotten to take it with them when they left. Mbona left Zambawe as he heard that his pursuers from his own country were close by, and he recrossed the river, but he was overtaken by them at Ndione forest, in Chipwembwe's section, on the Ndindi marsh. They killed him there, but before he died he asked that his body should be buried at Ndione, but his head taken to

Kuluvi forest near Mbango's village, and Mbango, who was one of his slaves,[14] was to look after the place. The latter appointed Mbukwa to be the headman in Kuluvi forest. Mbona had a brother called Kupatikana, who wanted to succeed him and take his name, but Mbona told him in a dream that he did not want him to do so in case he might also be killed,[15] so Mbona had no successor, but Kupatikana remained here and made sacrifices (Nsembe) to Mbona every year. After he died Ngabu (Mbona's son) and Chipwembwe (Mbona's brother)[16] made sacrifices and continue to do so to this day, or rather their descendants do. The principal chief, Tengani, agreed to this arrangement, but he is not related to Mbona.[17] When there is no rain Nsembe is made to Mbona, who intercedes with "Mlungu" and rain comes. This "nsembe" is always made at Kuluvi, where his head is buried.

TEXT I / B

Chapirira and Kumbiwanyati (1964)

The following text is part of a tape-recorded interview I conducted on August 24, 1964, with village headman Chapirira, official deputy to the high priest Ngabu Phiri, and Kumbiwanyati, cleaner of the shrine grounds. It was my first interview with any of the shrine officials, hence the question-and-answer format, which was avoided on subsequent occasions. The interview, excerpts of which were reproduced in Chapters 2, 3, and 4, ranged over a variety of topics, including the organization and the more recent history of the cult. Here, we confine ourselves to the passages which deal with Mbona's biography and the beginnings of the cult. The text, brief as it may be, is nevertheless crucial. It stems from a source close to Ngabu, and it shows significant parallels with Text I/A, recorded more than fifty years earlier.

TEXT

1. Qu.: Whereabouts was Mbona born?
"Mbona was born far to the north of the Shire valley. It is sometimes said that he came from Lundu's village near Chikwawa, but he was born somewhere in Zambia.[1] From there he moved to Lundu's, where he lived for a while with relatives because his own people, the Chipeta, were after him in connection with some quarrel they were then having among themselves. But when he found out that even at his new place he was not safe, he fled to these parts via Dzambawe and Chididi.[2] We were pleased with him and regarded him as God's son whom we had to respect."

2. Qu.: What made people think he was God's son?

"Before he came we used to experience a lot of hardship, but he ended that. When we speak of hardship we are thinking particularly of droughts which in those days occurred almost every year and which inevitably meant famine. If food could be found at such times, it certainly was not much. That is why we welcomed him when he came to these parts, and why we called him a son of God."

3. Qu.: Can you tell me when Mbona was born?

"We know little about the time he was still living in his native country, but he was certainly born before the arrival of the Goanese.[3] We don't know the names of his parents, but we believe that he was born like the Lord Jesus whose mother conceived from the Holy Spirit."[4]

4. Qu.: Who killed him?

"His own countrymen. They tracked him down to this place and, when they did not find him immediately, decided to wait until they would get a chance to kill him."

5. Qu.: Why did they want to kill him?

"They told us they were after him because he was the cause of the quarrels they were having among themselves. We on our part replied that we did not understand this, since he had brought us nothing but good. For instance, the day he offered prayers we would have rain and there was no longer scarcity in our country. But those people had already made up their minds, and when they finally came upon him, they killed him for fear that one day he might return to their country."

6. Qu.: Why is it that Mbona, though a Chipeta, chose to live among the Mang'anja?

"Because the Mang'anja belonged to his own kind, since like him they had originally come from Zambia. He knew, therefore, when he came to the valley that he would be among his own folk, which is another reason why we did not turn him away."

7. Qu.: What happened after his death?

"In accordance with his last wish we buried his head in Khulubvi thicket and his body in the Ndione thicket on the edge of the marshes, at the place where he was executed. Ndione too is a sacred place."

8. Qu.: Why was a shrine built?

"We built a shrine hut over the place where we buried his head, for he was a man of great wisdom, and his head was the source of that wisdom. We hoped that by building that hut and by making offerings there, his spirit might stay with us forever and bestow its blessings upon us, which is indeed what happened. Droughts became a rarity."

THE MBONA II TRADITION

TEXT II/A

M. E. Rambiki (1960)

THIS TEXT was composed by Mr. M. E. Rambiki from Mphamba, a village situated along the main district road in the neighborhood of the Mbona shrine. The author kindly gave me permission to use it here. Although the manuscript bears no date, internal criteria, such as spelling, indicate that it was composed in the early 1960s, when there was a general upsurge of public interest in the precolonial past in connection with Malawi's forthcoming independence. From his early adulthood until his retirement, Mr. Rambiki served as a primary school teacher in the South Africa General Mission (S.A.G.M.), which was later renamed the Africa Evangelical Fellowship (A.E.F.). He is a member of the Mphamba family, which controls an important headmanship and has historical links with the shrine organization. In 1976 the author himself succeeded to the Mphamba title.

The text consists of two parts, one of which describes the migration of the ancestral Mang'anja from a supposed homeland in Uganda, while the other concerns itself with Mbona's biography. It is a text which essentially belongs to the Mbona II complex, since it describes the origin of the cult in relation to the formation of an early state system. It also contains elements, however, which derive from the prestate and kingdom traditions.

In accordance with the early state traditions, then, Mbona is said to have been a kinsman of Kaphwiti, the supposed founder of the first chiefdoms in and around the valley. These chiefdoms, so we are told, employed their own rain caller, Mlauli by name, who belonged to the aristocratic Phiri clan. This man, who also was Mbona's mother's brother and guardian, took Mbona into his household to instruct him in the art of rain calling. Mbona is said to have been such a clever apprentice that in due time he became his uncle's equal, which apparently gave him the idea of usurping the latter's position. This he tried to do by means of sorcery: when his uncle performed the rain dance on the occasion of a particularly severe drought, no rain fell. Mlauli, sensing that this was Mbona's doing, flew into a rage and swore that he would kill his sister's son, but Mbona, seeing that he stood little chance to win, took flight, pursued by his uncle. After a long and eventful journey, which took Mbona to the southern part of Nsanje District, Mlauli finally caught up with him, killed him, and returned home. Mbona's friends and kinsmen, however, decided to build a shrine to his name so that his spirit would remain with them, and thus it was that the cult came into being.

At base this story tells us that in the early days of the Kaphwiti state the original Maravi system of rain calling came to be replaced by another. The original system is described as centering around a living rainmaker and as being the property of an aristocratic group living in the highlands area. The second system, Mbona's, which is said to have sprung from the first, focuses on a deified person and is associated with the commoner population of the valley. At first sight, this seems to contradict the idea subscribed to in this book that regional rain cults were already in existence before the rise of the early state systems. The introduction of the early states, however, may well have had such profound effects on the preexisting cults that one can justifiably speak of a transformation or second founding. Their new form may be viewed as in some way generated by the state system, as indeed the present version does. Organizationally, this implies the creation of new offices which allowed the new rulers to affiliate with and obtain a certain amount of control over the cult. This, as we have seen, appears to have been a normal pattern in many parts of Africa, and the possibility that a similar process developed in the present case is not to be dismissed out of hand. It is possible that the Mphamba title was one of those new offices.

In the course of a later visit to Malawi in December 1981 and January 1982, I was allowed to peruse another manuscript, which also deals with the Kaphwiti period and which contains some interesting variations on the text presented here. Its author, Mr. B. A. Phiri, whose family also has traditional ties with the shrine, kindly permitted me to use it. In my explanatory notes it is referred to as MS 2.

MANG'ANJA VERSION

1. Mu chaka cha 15 hundred, kale-kale ndithu, mtundu wa Amang'anja (Amalawi) unali ndi mfumu yao yaikulu ndithu; dzina

lache linali Chiridzodzwe. Kuti tinene za Mbona tiyenera kufotokoza za ufumu wa Amalawi poyamba.

2. Chiridzodzwe uyu dzina lache linali Undi. Chiridzodzwe anali ndi abale ache, ndiwo awa: Kaphwiti ndi Mlauli. Mlongo wao anali Nyangu, wamkazi. Chiridzodzwe pokhala mfumu ndi abale ache ndi anthu ao, poyamba anali kukhala ku Urundi, m'dziko la Uganda. M'bale wa Chiridzodzwe (Undi), Mlauli, anali wolosa (kunenerera) zakutsogolo. Choncho anthu amenewa anayamba kumveka mbiri yao ku Urundi'ko.

3. Pafupi ndi dziko lao, kumene anali kukhala, kunali mutundu wina wa anthu, achi-Mahomedi. Amahomediwa, mtsogoleri wao anali kugonjetsa anthu ambiri ku Urundi kuja. Ndipo anafunanso agonjetse mfumu Chiridzodzwe (Undi) ndi abale ache Mlauli ndi Kaphwiti. Choncho poyamba analetsa Amalawi kuti asamvere zimene Mlauli anali kulosa. Akatero adzawapha onse Chiridzodzwe, Mlauli ndi Kaphwiti pamodzi ndi anthu ao onse.

4. Amalawi onse (Amang'anja) ndi mfumu wao Chiridzodzwe (Undi) anakhala pansi kudya mtondo (kupangana chochita). Chiridzodzwe ndi Mlauli ndi anthu ao adatsimikiza zochoka kuti athawire kwina, pafupi ndi Urundi, m'dziko lomwelo.

5. Koma kunalibe zakudya zokwanira. Zolima za anthu zinali mchewere okha pa malo amenewo; dzina lache akati kuti dziko la Munga. Choncho anasamukanso kudza ku Tanganyika.

6. Koma ku Tanganyika kunali mfumu yina dzina lache Kavalo. Ena akum'cha Kafara. Iyeyo sanamvane ndi Amang'anja (Amalawi). Mfumu Chiridzodzwe, Kaphwiti ndi Mlauli ndi anthu ao onse anapangana kuchokanso pa zifukwa ziwiri: 1) Anali osamvana ndi mfumu Kavalo (Kafara); 2) Dziko la Tanganyika linali lopanda mitengo. Ilipo, inde, koma njaifupi-ifupi. Mfumu Chiridzodzwe anakonda kukhala m'dziko la mitengo yaitali-tali.

7. Chomwecho mfumu Chiridzodzwe anachoka ndi anthu ache, nadzakhala ku mtsinje wochuka, ku mpoto kwa thamanda lalikulu lija, amati Nyasa pena Malawi. Mtsinje umenewo ndiwo Songo, ena amaucha Songwe. Amang'anja (Amalawi) anakhala pambali pa mtsinje umenewo. Ndipo linali tsidya lino la Songo ataoloka.

8. Atakhala pa malo amenewa, mfumu Chiridzodzwe (Undi) anafuna kudziwa ngati panali malo ena okoma koposa pa Songo. Choncho anatuma nduna yache yochedwa Changamire. Iye anayenda ndi gulu lache la nkhondo nafika ku phiri la Zomba, chifukwa phirilo likaonekera kutali. Akali pa Songo Chiridzodzwe anapatsa ufumu Chungu ndi mthandizi wache wa unduna waung'ono, Muilang'ombe, kuti abagwirizira ufumuwo chifukwa iye adayamba kukalamba.

9. Changamire uja pofika ku Zomba adapezako anthu a mtundu wina,

Akamfupidolo (Mwandionerakuti), ena amawacha Abatwa. Changamire anali wamkali kwambiri. Anthu afupi misinkhu awa anafuna kum'chita chiwembu (kum'chita makunje) pofuna kum'pha (Changamire). Pokhala Changamire anali wamkali ndiponso ngwazi, choncho anaphapo Abatwa khumi, nadula mitu yao, naipfeka ku mipani khumi, napita nayo kukaionetsa mfumu Chiridzodzwe. Chiridzodzwe anakondwere kwambiri ndi mbiri imene Changamire anabwera nayo. Chotero Chiridzodzwe anasanduliza ngwazi Changamire akhale Karonga, kuthanthauza kuti mkulu ndi mtsogoleri wa nkhondo.

10. Chiridzodzwe anauza Chungu amene anagwirizira ufumu, kuti auze anthu asamukire, kutsikabe ndi dziko, adze ku malo ena kumene adafikapo Changamire. Pochoka ku Songo kuja anthu onse anadzamanga pa Phirintiya. Ena amachula phiri limeneli Kaphirintiya, ndiko kuti kaphiri ka thya-thya-thya. Pamenepo mfumu Chiridzodzwe (Undi) anamwalira. Koma asanafe, anafotokozeratu kuti malo amenewo ndiwo adam'konda. Ndipo anafuna anthu ache akhale pamenepa.

11. Pa nthawi imeneyo ndi kuti mwana wache anakula mokwanira kuti alowe ufumu, ndipo anam'cha dzina la bambo wache lomwelo, lakuti Undi. Undi atalowa ufumu m'banja mwache munabadwa ana amuna ndi akazi. Mwa ana amuna awiriwa, woyamba anali dzina lache Kaphwiti, kutenga dzina la ambuye ache ang'ono aja. Ndi wachiwiri anali Chingale. Kaphwiti anakwatira msanga ndi m'banja mwache munabadwa mwana wamkazi wochedwa Chitimbe. Monga mwa mwambo wachiMalawi anakwatira pa chisuwani. Choncho Chingale, mbale wache wa Kaphwiti, anakwatira mwana wa Kaphwiti, Chitimbe.

12. Ndipo ufumu wa Kaphwiti unakulabe ndi ku nyanja ndi ku mtunda komwe, mpakana ku mapiri. Ndipo chifukwa cha kukula kwa dzikolo, ufumu naonso unayamba kugawanikana. Maina a abale achifumu atatu aja ana ao anatenganso maina a makolo ao: Undi, Kaphwiti ndi Mlauli. Ana a Mlauli analipo ndipo analowa ulauli wa zochita za bambo wao. Koma m'banja la mlongo wao wa Undi, paja tinati Nyangu, munali mwana wochedwa Mbona.

Ufumu wa Mbona uyamba

13. Mbona anali mwana wamkamwini wobadwa ndi mlongo wache wa Undi, Nyangu. Ana onse achiMang'anja amalamulidwa kwa amai ao. Choncho Mbona anali kukhala ndi mbuye wache, Mlauli. Ndipo pa unyamata wache anali kuphunzira zonse za matsenga a Mlauli, mbuye wache. Inde, anali wa luso kwambiri pa nkhani ya matsenga monga mbuye wache Mlauli.

14. Anthu amaopa Mlauli kwambiri; ndipo anali kumperekera mitulo yambiri, monga nsembe. Anthu akasowa mvula, chaka cha chilala, ankadza

kudzafunsa nzeru kwa iyeyo. Iyeyo anali kulaula, nabvina (kugiya) pa bwalo, ndipo pakumatero, ndi kusolola mpeni wachiMang'anja wakuthwa uku ndi uku, amaucha kandranga, kuusolola m'chibete (chimache) ndi kuloza ku mpoto, pena kumwera, kunja kwang'anima mphezi. Pakutha kutamba pa bwalopo, kawiri-kawiri kunali kugwa mvula. Pochita izi zonse, Mlauli anali kumphunzitsa mwana uja, Mbona. Choncho Mbona anaphunzira nzeru zonse za ambuye ache, napambana kukhala wa matsenga kuposa Mlauli amene.

Kuthawa kwa Mbona

15. Mbona ndi mdzukulu wa Undi, Mlauli ndi Kaphwiti, chifukwa anali mwana wa mlongo wao wamkulu, Nyangu. Kotero ataphunzira matsenga a Mlauli, mbuye wache, chaka china mvula inasowa. Ndipo anthu anadzalamba kwa Mlauli kuti awapatse mvula. Iye anati kuti mmawa bwache adzatamba pa bwalo kuti mvula ibwere.

16. Pa nthawi imeneyo ndi kuti Mbona atakwatira kale posachedwa. Mkazi wache anali kuchedwa Chitundu. Pa nthawi'yo anali ndi mwana Mwana wache woyamba dzina lache Ngabu. Mwana wina Nyanguru. Mwana ameneyo atakula anadzicha Magombe, amene patsogolo anthu anamucha Makombe. Mwana wina ndi Mphamba.

17. Mmawa mwache, anthu onse atasonkhana, Mlauli anayamba kutamba kuja. Mlauli atagiya (kutamba) pa nthawi yomweyo Mbona anakonza tsenga lache kotero kuti Mlauli posolola mpeni wache uja m'chimache kuloza kumpoto, kunja sikung'anima, ai. Anthu anadodoma kwambiri. Anayamba kugiya ndi mphamvu yache yonse, naloza kummwera ndi kumpoto, koma osang'anima konse, kufikira analema Mlauli. Ndipo anali ndi manyazi ambiri poona kuti sikudzafika mvula.

18. Anthu akali chidabwire choncho, Mbona naye anafika, nayamba kuthandiza mbuye wache kugiya kuja. Kudangotero, atangobvina pang'ono pokha, anasolola mpeni wachenso wa kandranga, naloza kumpoto ndi kummwera. He! Kunamveka kuti phe-re-re-re-re-re! Ng'ani . . . ng'ani! Thiri-ri-ri-ri, kamtambo lezu . . . Mbona anayamba kuimba nyimbo yoti:

> Mtambo uwu ndi uwu,
> wanya mvula nguti?
> Wanya mvula ndi
> uwu!

19. Pakuloza kachiwiri mpeni wache wakandranga mvula inayamba kunyotha. Pa nthawi imeneyi akazi achifumu ndi ena onse a m'mudzimo ananyamuka ndi nthungululu ndi ufa m'manja mwao, natsira ngati nsembe pa mutu pa Mbona. Mlauli pakudziwa kuti ulemu wache ud-

zatha, kuti anthu sadzamuopanso monga kale, anapsya mtima, naturuka m'bwalo, nalowa m'nyumba kuti akonzere zida za nkhondo. Pa nthawi yomweyo Mbona anadziwiratu chomwe chidzachitike. Choncho anapotoloka, nabisala.

20. Anthu am'mudzimo anayamba kulekana. Ena anakhala mbali ya Mlauli; koma ena ambiri anakhala mbali ya Mbona. Mlauli anafuna kumpha Mbona kuti anthu am'tsate iye. Mbona analibe njira yina yothetsa udaniwo, koma kuthawa ndiko. Iye anachoka pamodzi ndi mkazi wache ndi ana ache, nayenda chakutsama mapiri okha.

21. Mlauli anadziwa kuti Mbona anathawa limodzi ndi mkazi wache ndi ana ache, kudzanso ndi anthu ena. Choncho sangathe kuyenda mwamsanga. Ndipo anayamba kuwalondola. Koma Mbona akaona kuti Mlauli ali pafupi, iye anali kuzemba pochita matsenga odabwitsa: mwina amasanduka kukhala nkhalango; kuchokera nkhalango kusandulika mpingo wa nkhawena, kumveke kwere-kwere-kwere, kuuluka.

22. Pakasowa madzi anali kufika pa thanthwe ndi kuyamba kufukula mchera (chitsime) pa thanthwe paja, nayamba kumwetsa ana ache, mkazi wache ndi anthu ache. Pakuwerama chogwada pa mwala paja, mogwada maondo ndi mogwirizira manja, maziru anali kungotsala; maziruwo ndi mopondera mapazi pa mwalapo. Pofika pa malo otere Mlauli anali kungodziguguda pa mtima, nati, "Suyu anali pano; anapuma pano."

23. Chokha-chokhacho anafika ku mapiri akuno, monga kuswa malire ndi Apwitikizi, natsikira ku mtsinje wa Chimwala, nadzakhala pa Khulubvi. Pa malo pamenepa anasanduliza nkhalango yokha ya kankhande ndi lunguzi, ndi nkandankhuku. Pofika Mlauli anadziwa kuti ndi Mbona anachita icho, namudzimbula.

24. Kuchokera apa anapitikitsana kwa ndiwe yani, ndidike ndikuphe. Choncho Mbona analotetsa nkhope yache ku Chiriwakufa. Koma anali atalema kwambiri, nabisala pa nkhalango yina ya pa dambo, pakati pa Khulubvi ndi Chiriwakufa. Malo amenewa anawacha Ndione, kuthanthauza kwache kuti: Ndiri pano, ndigwire.

Imfa ya Mbona

25. Mlauli anasolola mpeni wache wakandranga kuti amlase nao Mbona, koma mpeni uja unapindika monga chofewa chiri chonse. Anayesa kuti kapena atam'cheka pa khosi, monga amachitira ndi nkhuku. Mbona anangoseka kuti, "Ambuye, mwana mnzako mpachulu: usangoti ndikupha, koma kulinga utakwerapo!"

26. Anapitiriza nati, "Ukafuna kundipha ine, usanditengere chitsulo chiri chonse, ai, chinsonga chachitsulo, kaya nthungo kapena mipeni, siziri ndi mphamvu pa ine; ndinazidyera kale. Kaya munditengere mjere wa

phesi ya chimanga kapena dzani (yani), tsamba la bango, ndizo ndiopa; muona ndidzafa ngati nkhuku. Koma ambuye, ndikupemphani kuti ndikadzafa, inu mutenge mutu wanga ndi kukauika pa Khulubvi, pamene ndinafikira. Koma mtembo wanga uikidwe pompano!"

27. Mlauli anauza ankhondo ache akhwatule yani la bango kapena kusuwa mjere wa phesi, monga Mbona ananenera. Atangokhwathula yani la bango, anaona kuti Mbona anayamba kupfuula kuti, "Ambuye mundipheranji? Ndikufa ine! Mayo!" Pompo anapendeketsa tsamba lija pa khosi pa Mbona. Dzi-dzi-dzi! Anangoona nsonga kuti chiii . . . m'mwamba, potero pansi mwaziwo, ndiye kungoyeyeketsa pansi di-di-di mtsinje mbeee . . . madzi a mwazi.

28. Pa nthawi yomweyo anthu onse anangoona kuti akulowa m'kati mwa mwazi. Apo Mlauli anati, "Inu chotsani mutuwo, tiutenge, tidzipita." Onse aja anabwerera atatenga mutu wa Mbona, nafikanso pa Khulubvi, nautaya m'nkhalangomo. Koma ana ache a Mbona ndi Mphamba anamva kuti bambo wao anaphedwa pa Ndione, ndipo kuti mutu wache unataidwa pa Khulubvi. Ndipo choncho iwo anabwera pamodzi ndi abale ache ena, natenga mutuwo, naukwirira, pa tsinde la mtengo wa mtondo, nacha mtondowo Chitupira.

29. Ndipo anawo anati kuti pano sitingachokenso, koma timange pompano. Ndipo anasankha nduna zina za m'gulu la Mbona kuti zidzisunga mudzi wa Khulubvi. Koma mkazi wache, Chitundu, pokhala kuti anali wa ku Chipiloni, sanafune kukhala ndi abale a mamuna wache ndi ana ache. Iye anabwerera kwao.

30. Abale amene amasunga mudzi wa Mbona ndi awa: Mbukwa, Chilamwa, Kambalame, ndi Kombe. Anthu ena onse amene akakhulupirira Mbona chifukwa cha zinchito zache anatsatirabe Mbona ndi kum'pembedza kwambiri. Ndipo m'mudzi uwu, wa Khulubvi, anamanga nyumba yache ya Mbona, pokhulupirira kuti iye sanafe, koma mzimu wache uli moyo. Ndipo pa usiku mzimuwo umabwera kudzacheza ndi anthu ache.

31. Choncho wina pachibale cha Mbona anali kuyamba kunenera kumalota zonse zofuna Mbona. Akati Mbona afuna nsembe ya mowa, ali ndi ludzu. Anthu onse omutsatira amasonkha mapira, nakapereka kwa nduna zosunga mudziwo, monga Mbukwa ndi Chilamwa. Pophika mowayo, tsiku loyamba kubviika chimera, mvula inali kugwadi. Tsiku lowira mowawo, popita kukatsira nsembe, anthu anali kubwerera kwao atabvumbwa.

32. Anthu ena amachokera kutali kwambiri, monga ku Mbewe, koma anabalalikira, ankabwera kudzalambira Mbona ndi kumapempha mvula. Ena ankachokera ku Chipiloni, Morumbala, ndi Ncheu kumene anachokera Mbona, ku Malawi, ku mudzi wa Kaphwiti.

33. Choncho anthu achiMang'anja sanaiwale mbiri ya munthu womve-

kayu, Mbona; chifukwa cha zamphamvu zache zimene anazichita angakhale atafa. Anthu okhala m'mudzi uwu wa Khulubvi amalandirabe
mitulo yochokera madera akutali odzapereka nsembe, monga: zirundu
za nsaru zakuda (biriwita), mitambala ya nsomba kudzanso zakudya
zamitundu-mitundu.

Zochitika pomanga nyumba ya mbona

34. Pomanga nyumba ya Mbona amaitana mmodzi wa adzukulu a Mbona
mu ufumu wa Tengani. Ndipo akamanga tsindwi la nyumba ya Mbona
pa mutu wa Tengani, nchito ya Mbona itatha, Tengani pobwerera ku
mudzi anali kufa. Tidzipitirira ndi mbiriyi mtsogolomo.

ENGLISH VERSION

1. Long ago, in the year A.D. 1500,[1] the Mang'anja or Maravi people had a great chief whose name was Chiridzodzwe.[2] If we are
to tell the story of Mbona, we must begin by saying something about
the Maravi state system.

2. This Chiridzodzwe, then, was also known as Undi.[3] He had two male
relatives named Kaphwiti and Mlauli, and a female relative called
Nyangu.[4] During the first years of his rule, he lived in Urundi, a place
in Uganda, together with his kinsmen and his people.[5] Chiridzodzwe's
relative, Mlauli, was a man who could dream about and foretell the future, and this caused the Maravi to be much spoken about in Urundi.[6]

3. Not far from their place lived another group of people, known as the
Mohammedans.[7] Their leader brought many inhabitants of Urundi under
his rule, and he also intended to subject Chiridzodzwe together with
his kinsmen, Mlauli and Kaphwiti. He therefore forbade the Maravi to
listen to Mlauli's prophecies, saying that, if they did, he would kill Chiridzodzwe, Mlauli, Kaphwiti, and all their people.

4. The Maravi and their chief, Chiridzodzwe, thereupon went into council[8]
to decide on a course of action. The ultimate decision was to leave and
seek refuge at another place, some distance from Urundi, but still in
the same country.

5. In their new homeland food was not plentiful, since people could grow
only bulrush millet there.[9] They therefore called it Munga ("thornbush
country"). This led them to migrate once again, this time to Tanganyika.

6. In Tanganyika, however, they met a chief called Kavalo, whom some
call Kafara, who was unsympathetic toward them.[10] Chief Chiridzodzwe,
Kaphwiti, Mlauli, and their people decided to move once more, for not
only did they have trouble with Chief Kavalo, but the country of Tangan-

yika was also treeless. There were trees, but only small and spindly ones, whereas Chiridzodzwe preferred a country with tall trees.[11]

7. He therefore moved with his people to a well-known river at the northern tip of that great expanse of water called Nyasa or Lake Malawi. They crossed this river, variously known as Songo or Songwe, and established themselves on its south bank.[12]

8. Having lived there for a while, Chief Chiridzodzwe wanted to know if there was perhaps a more favorable place for a settlement, and he thereupon sent his lieutenant Changamire on a scouting trip.[13] Changamire went southward with his band of warriors as far as Mount Zomba, which is visible from a great distance.[14] While still at the settlement near the Songo, Chiridzodzwe delegated his powers to Chungu and the latter's assistant, Muilang'ombe, because he had become too old to carry out the duties of his office himself.[15]

9. Upon arriving at Zomba, Changamire came across people of a different type, known as Kamfupidolo, Mwandionerakuti, or Batwa.[16] These dwarfish people tried to ambush Changamire and kill him. But Changamire, being a fierce man and a *ngwazi,* or hero, killed ten of them, cut off their heads, stuck them on poles, and had them carried to Chiridzodzwe for his inspection. Chiridzodzwe was so pleased with Changamire's report that he promoted him to the position of *karonga,* or general.[17]

10. Chiridzodzwe now told Chungu, who was the acting chief, to move his people southward to the place which Changamire had explored. Leaving Songo, the entire group went to settle at Phirintiya or Kaphirintiya, which means a low, flat-topped hill.[18] Chief Chiridzodzwe died there, after having stated that he liked the place and wanted his people to remain there.

11. By that time his son was old enough to take over the chieftainship, and he was henceforth called Undi like his father before him.[19] After his enthronement, sons and daughters were born to him. He had two sons, the firstborn named Kaphwiti after the younger of his two maternal uncles, while the second was named Chingale. Kaphwiti married at an early age and had a daughter by the name of Chitimbe. In accordance with the Maravi custom of marrying one's cross-cousin, Chingale, Kaphwiti's brother, took for his wife Chitimbe, who was Kaphwiti's daughter.[20]

12. Kaphwiti's chiefdom expanded until it reached from the lowlands and the foothills to the high mountains.[21] Because of its extent, it had to be divided among the descendants of Undi, Kaphwiti, and Mlauli, who also succeeded to their fathers' titles. Mlauli's sons, moreover, inherited their father's prophetic ability. Undi's first sister, Nyangu, whom

we have mentioned earlier on, married a man from a different lineage. They had a child whom they called Mbona.[22]

The Beginnings of Mbona's Power

13. As all Mang'anja children come under the authority of their mother's kinfolk, Mbona went to live with his mother's brother Mlauli.[23] In his boyhood he learned from his uncle everything about rain magic. Indeed, his talents in this field were as great as his uncle's.

14. People had great respect for Mlauli and brought him many gifts as ritual offerings. Whenever they needed rain in a year of drought, they turned to him for advice. He would then utter his prophecies and perform a rain dance in the village meeting place.[24] When he pulled his Mang'anja dagger, called kandranga,[25] from its sheath and pointed it to the north or the south, lightning would start flashing. Often rain would be falling by the time he finished dancing. It was thus that Mlauli taught the youth Mbona, who learned so well that he became even better at it than Mlauli himself.

Mbona's Flight

15. Mbona was a maternal nephew to Undi, Mlauli, and Kaphwiti, as he was the son of their elder sister Nyangu. It so happened that after he had studied under his uncle Mlauli, there was a year of drought. People came pleading to Mlauli to give them rain. He told them that early the next morning he would perform the rain dance in the meeting place.

16. By that time Mbona had already married the woman Chitundu,[26] who had borne him a son by the name of Ngabu. Two more sons were born, the elder of which was first called Nyanguru. He renamed himself Magombe after he had grown up. Still later, people came to call him Makombe. The name of the younger son was Mphamba.

17. At daybreak when all the people had assembled, Mlauli began to perform his dance. At the same time, however, Mbona used sorcery against his uncle so that, when the latter drew his dagger and pointed it to the north, no lightning flashed.[27] He tried again with all his might, pointing to the south and the north until he became exhausted. The public was in despair, and seeing that no rain fell, Mlauli was filled with shame.

18. While people were still wondering what had gone wrong, Mbona came in place of his uncle. After the first few movements of the dance he drew his dagger, pointed it to the north and south, and lo! there were peals of thunder and flashes of lightning. Then a small cloud appeared in the sky, and Mbona began to sing:

Illus. 27. Mang'anja ceremonial dagger (*kandranga*), 1860s.
From Rowley 1866:245.

This cloud or that cloud;
which one relieves itself of rain?
That one relieves itself of rain![28]

19. When he pointed the second time with his *kandranga* dagger, rain began to pour. Thereupon the chief's wives and all the women from the village ululated for joy and rushed toward Mbona, their hands full of corn flour, which they poured on his head as an offering in thanksgiving.[29] Mlauli, seeing that his reputation was lost and that he could no longer command people's respect, flew into a rage, stalked away from the meeting place, and went to his hut to get his weapons ready. Mbona, having had a sense of foreboding, turned on his heels and went into hiding.[30]

20. When the villagers began to take sides, some with Mlauli, but the majority with Mbona,[31] Mlauli decided to kill Mbona to prevent anybody from following him. Mbona, seeing what would happen, turned away and went off into hiding. Thus, he left with his wife and children, keeping all the time to the hills.[32]

21. Mlauli knew that Mbona had fled with his wife, his children, and some other people, and he realized that he could not be traveling very fast.[33] He therefore started following them, but each time Mbona saw Mlauli closing in, he and his followers escaped from sight by some astonishing feat of magic. Sometimes he would turn into a forest thicket; on other occasions he would change into a flock of guinea fowl, which could be heard whirring away in flight.[34]

22. Whenever his children, wife, or followers felt thirsty, Mbona would scoop out a water hole in the bedrock so that they could drink.[35] Wherever he knelt on, took hold of, or walked over bare rock, imprints of his knees, hands, and feet would remain.[36] Mlauli, when coming upon such places, would beat his chest in a rage and exclaim, "It must have been that man. He took a rest here!"

23. In such fashion did Mbona manage to reach the southern hills, keeping close to the Mozambique border. He came down the valley of the Chimwala Stream[37] and stopped at Khulubvi, which place he turned into a tangle of different thorn shrubs. When Mlauli arrived there, he realized once again that this was Mbona's doing, and he grew exasperated with him.

24. From now on the chase was on in earnest. Mlauli being more than ever determined to kill Mbona. It had been Mbona's intention to make for the Chiriwakufa tributary, but overcome with fatigue, he hid himself in a thicket on the marshland between Khulubvi and Chiriwakufa.[38] He gave that thicket the name Ndione, which means "I am here; try to catch me!"[39]

Mbona's Death

25. Mlauli drew his *kandranga* dagger to stab Mbona, but its blade bent as if it were something utterly soft. He thought that he could cut Mbona's throat like a chicken's, but Mbona told him mockingly, "Uncle, when your rival stands on an anthill, never say 'I have caught you' until you are up there yourself."[40]

26. He went on, saying, "If you want to kill me, do not bring against me anything made of iron such as an arrowhead or spears and knives. Those have no power over me as I have eaten medicine against them.[41] Instead, use the sliver of a maize stalk or the leaf of a reed: those are the things dreadful to me.[42] You will see that I shall die like a chicken. However, uncle, when I am dead, I beseech you to bury my head at Khulubvi, where I ended my journey. But my body is to be buried here."

27. Mlauli told his warriors to take a blade from a reed or crush a maize stalk as Mbona had told them. They then tore a blade from a reed, and presently Mbona was heard crying out, "Uncle, why are you killing me? Woe unto me, I am going to die!" When the leaf was bent around Mbona's neck, making sharp sawing sounds as it began to cut, they noticed that it had become straight and rigid. Blood flowed in profusion, and splashing to the ground, it turned into a dark stream, a river of blood.[43]

28. When they found themselves sinking in this rising tide of blood, Mlauli said, "Cut off his head and take it along with you; we must be going!" They all joined him carrying Mbona's head, and when they came to Khulubvi, they tossed it into the undergrowth. Mbona's children, including Mphamba,[44] however, came to know that their father had been killed at Ndione and that his head had been disposed of at Khulubvi. They therefore came with some relatives to take the head for burial at the foot of a *mtondo* tree, which from then on they declared sacred.[45]

29. His children then said, "We must not leave this place again; let us settle here!"; and they chose from among Mbona's followers some to be in charge of the village of Khulubvi.[46] His wife Chitundu, however, who hailed from the Chipironi area,[47] returned to her own people because she did not wish to stay with her late husband's kinsfolk and her children.

30. The kinsmen in charge of Mbona's village are Mbukwa, Chilamwa, Kambalame, and Kombe.[48] All those who had believed in Mbona because of his great deeds remained faithful to him and were devoted to his worship. They built a hut for him at Khulubvi village, trusting that he had not died and that his spirit was still alive. That spirit comes by night to visit its people.[49]

31. One of Mbona's kinsmen began having possession experiences during which he revealed Mbona's wishes. When he said that Mbona was

thirsty and wanted an offering of beer, all of his followers would collect millet and take it to the guardians of the village, such as Mbukwa and Chilamwa. When they prepared the beer, rain would already be falling the day they began soaking the millet used for making malt.[50] The day the beer had matured and was being poured out as a libation, people would return to their homes amid downpours.

32. Some worshipers would come from as far away as Mbewe. After having made their entreaties to Mbona for rain, they would once again disperse. Others came from Chipironi, Morumbala, and Ntcheu, Mbona's homeland where Kaphwiti's capital, Malawi, was located.[51]

33. The Mang'anja never forgot the story of that famous man, Mbona, because of the mighty things he did, even after his death. The people of Khulubvi still receive offerings from faraway districts in the form of lengths of black or dark blue cloth, bundles of dried fish, and food of every kind.[52]

The Rebuilding of the Shrine

34. Whenever Mbona's hut was to be rebuilt, they summoned a member of Mbona's lineage from the chiefdom of Tengani.[53] It was customary to build the roof of Mbona's shrine upon the head of Tengani. When the work for Mbona was finished and Tengani returned home, he would die. We will continue this story some other time.

TEXT II/B

S. Chimbuto (1966)

The narrator of TextII/B was Mr. Stole Chimbuto, a retired primary school teacher, who had turned to cash crop farming. The Chimang'anja version was tape-recorded at his home near the township of Ngabu, Chikwawa District, in October 1966. The text consists of two main parts, which concern Mbona's life and death (secs. 1–16) and the cult organization in precolonial days (secs. 17–23). Both the plot and the symbolism of this text exhibit a relatively simple structure which lacks the ambiguity and complexity of the other texts, with the exception of those in the Mbona I mode, which are also relatively simple. There is, for instance, in this text not the remotest hint that Mbona could possibly have been guilty of sorcery himself. On the contrary, the name Mbona is said to mean exactly the opposite: someone who is always good and kind to everybody and who is rightfully loved by everybody (sec. 4).

At the time of the cataclysmic drought he is still a little boy who bursts into tears when he has to meet the elders and whose tears finally unleash the rains (secs. 3–4). The two leaders of the community, Kaphwiti and Lundu, decide to kill him, although he is still a child, and to this end they set out on a long journey which takes them from the central Chewa area to the Shire Valley (sec. 7). They are, however, unable to kill him until he tells them to stab him with a blade of grass rather than an iron weapon (sec. 8). When he dies, a heavy storm breaks, and his blood turns into a river (sec. 9). Seeing this, his killers become paralyzed with fear, but Mbona, speaking through the mouth of one of their number, orders them to go to Lundu — who was not present at the killing — and arrange for the building of a shrine and the procurement of a spirit wife (secs. 10–11). At this point the narrator briefly interrupts the plot to mention the names of the chief cult officers (sec. 12). Then he continues with the killers reporting to Lundu (sec. 13) and with some data on the beginnings of the cult (secs. 14–16). The remainder of the text is devoted to brief accounts on the organization of the smaller and larger shrines in the area (sec. 17), the logistics of a major rain ceremony (secs. 18–19), the intertwining of cult and kingdom (secs. 20–21), and the shrine guardians (secs. 22–23). The text concludes with the observation that this was the way it was in the past and that the cult still exists.

It will have become clear from our summary that a large part of this text is composed in the Mbona III mode, as evidenced by the extensive references to Lundu and the Lundu kingdom and by the childhood symbolism, the theme of the powerless iron, and the theophany following the killing. At the same time, however, one also notes a number of Mbona II elements, such as the role played by the early state builder Kaphwiti and the fact that the conflict starts in the central Chewa area before the foundation of the Lundu kingdom. Typically of Mbona II, Mbona is killed by his direct opponent and not by a band of hirelings as in Mbona III. The decisive criterion for considering this a Mbona II text, however, is that Mbona is killed by Kaphwiti and not by Lundu.

MANG'ANJA VERSION

1. Lero tiri kunena za Mbona. Mbona ndiye anali mulungu wa Amang'anja, amene iwo anali kum'pembedza, Amang'anja atachokera ku mpoto, ndi mkulu wao Undi, wachiwiri Kaphwiti, wachitatu Lundu.

2. Onsewa anafika ku Kaphirintiya. Pa Kaphirintiya anali kudzala mbeu zao. Ndiye chaka china mvula sinagwe, mvula sinabvumbe. Chonco Amang'anja anali kubvina, kusauka, nayesa-yesa kuti mvula ibvumbe.

3. Mvula ikulephereka chonchija, panali kamwana kena, mdzukulu wao wa Lundu, Kaphwiti ndi Undi. Iye anali mwana wa mlongo wao, ndipo dzina lache anali Mbona. Anthu ananena kuti, "Akulu-akulu, muleke kubvina, ayambe kubvina mwanayu." Ndiye mwana uja atabvina anamulowetsa m'bwalomo, mwana uja anali kuchita mantha ndi kukana kulowamo. Pa nthawi imene anali kuti iye alire, ndiye nthawi yomwe anthu anamva mphezi kuti pha-la-la. . .

4. Misozi yache inapanga mvula. Ndiye anthu onse anakondwera, nadzala mbeu zao, za mayere, chitowe, nzama ndi nanyera. Izi ndizo zimene zinali mbeu zao. Atadzala izi, ai, zinachita bwino ndithu, mpakana anthu nakondwera. Choncho anthu onse anayamba kutama mwanayo, namati, "Mwana ameneyu ndiye wopambana ndithu, ameneyu ndi Mbona."

Dzina la Mbona ndiye kuti: Angomuyamika munthu aliyense, pali ponse, ngakhale munthu woipa; ngakhale pali chiani choipa, iye angobvumbitsa mvula. Ndiye munthu amene amangokoma pali ponse. Ndiye choncho anam'cha Mbona. Choncho Amang'anja onse anakondwera naye, namutama kwambiri.

5. Akulu-akulu, ambuy'ache, aLundu, aKaphwiti, onse amene anayamba kumuda, chifukwa chakuti onse anayamba kutama mwanayo. Choncho iwo anaganiza za kum'pha mwanayo. Ndipo mai wache atamva, anamuuza mwanayo kuti, "Ambuye ako alikufuna kukupha chifukwa chakuti uli kutamidwa, pamene iwe uli kugwetsa mvula. Ukabvina mvula ili kugwa. Anthu ambiri ali kukutama, ndiye akuti akufuna akuphe." Ndiye mwanayo anathawa.

6. Kuthawa kwache, anayang'ana chakum'wera. Kumwera kwache anatulukira ku Chikwawa; napitirirapo, napyola nkhalango muja, napita dziko la Nsanje. Ndipo anayendayenda, napyola, nazungulira phiri lija lichedwa Malawi, ku Nsanje. Anapyolera pang'ono; koma'nso nabwerera, nafika pa malo pafupi ndi Nsanje. Atakhala pansi pa Nsanje'po anali wotopa tsopano. Choncho ali kukhala pansi. Iye anali nao akazi ache awiri, galu wache, ndi nthungo yache. Zonsezo anali nazo. Tsopano atatopa, anakhala pansi.

7. Ambuye ache, akam'tsatira aja, anachokera komwe ali kungom'tsabe mpaka zaka. Iwowa anali ndi zakudya zao, monga malambe, matondo, bwemba, mipinji-pinji ndi zina zache zokumba-kumba pansi. Ndi iwo anthu aja anali kungonka, nam'tsatirabe, mpakana kum'peza.

8. Atam'peza anatenga nthungo zao kuti amlase, koma analephera. Ndipo anatenga'nso mibvi yao kuti amlase, koma analephera'nso. Iye mwini ananena kuti, "Inu, tengani nansongole, udzu uja wochedwa dzina lache nansongole, muutenge umenewu ndipo mulase pa mutu panga."

9. Ndipo atalasa pa mutu paja, iye anafa. Koma tsiku lomwelo kunauka chimphepo chachikulu ndipo'nso chimvula chachikulu. Magazi ache anapanga mtsinje, ndipo dzina la mtsinje umenewu ndi Nyamadzere. Uwowu unayenda ngati ufuna kupita ku Nyanja ya Matope. Nyanja ya Matope ndi imene inapatsidwa dzina ndi Azungu, dzina loti Shire. Koma ife kale tinali kuichula kuti Nyanja ya Matope. Mtsinje umenewu uli kupitabe choncho, ndipo uli kuyandikira kuti ufike komweko, pafupi pache unapanga thamanda. Thamandalo dzina lache ndi Ndione. Kufikira mpakana lero thamandalo liripobe.

10. Choncho kunja kutacha, anthu onse aja, amene anam'tsira aja, pamene mphepo idaomba ndi mvula yambiri, adachita ngati kukomoka ndipo sadadziwe chochita. Adaona kuti pamene iye Mbona anali panasanduka mtsinje, "Aa, nanga titani tsopano?" Ndipo mmodzi mwa iwo anagwa, nachita ngati masomphenya. Anakhala ngati mlauli, nanena

kuti, "Koma munthu uja alipo. Ine ndiripo, Mbona. Ndapanga mtsinjewu. Ndiye ndiri kuno, pa thamanda pano, dzina lache Ndione. Choncho ine ndiri kukuuzani kuti mubwerere ku Mbewe." Chifukwa mbuya'che yekhayo, Lundu, amene anali kum'tsatira pambuyo, anaima pa Mbewe, dziko la Chikwawa.

11. Wakugwa uja anapitiriza kuti, "Kumeneko mukatengeko mkazi. Mukatenge mkazi ndi mwamuna. Abwere kuno. Mudzandimangire nyumba. Mkaziyo adzikhala m'nyumbamo. Koma asakhale mkazi wobala, koma wosiya kubala. Si namwali, ai." Choncho anthu aja adatuma ena.

12. Eni ache anali kumeneko, anali olamulira ndi awa: Khambani, Mbukwa, ndi Mithanje. Pa mtunda pachepo ndiye Mbango, kwinako Ngabu, kwinako Malemia. Awa ndiye anali ansembe, oyang'anira mizimu, mzimu wachiMang'anja, Mbona, ku Nsanje. Koma wotsira nsembe m'katimo, ndiye Mbukwa, Kambalame ndi Mithanje.

13. Tsono ofuna kutenga mkazi aja atapita kwa Lundu anati, "Mphwanu uja, mdzukulu wanu uja, tidampeza koma adatilaka kum'pha. Ndipo ndi iye yekha adatilamulira kuti, 'Tengani nansongole, mulase pa mutu panga.' Koma titamlasa, zimene zidagwapo ndi zakuda, zosaneneka, zosaoneka ndi maso. Tonse tinakomoka kufikira kunja kutacha. Koma mmodzi mwa ife anasanduka mlauli, monga masomphenya. Ndiye anafotokoza zonse, chifukwa mzimu wache wa Mbona unam'kutira munthuyo. Ndiye choncho anayamba kunena kuti, 'Pitani kwa mfumu Lundu, mukatenge mkazi kumeneko, msuweni wache wa Mbona.'" Ndiye Lundu anam'patsa. "Ndi munthu m'modzi tim'funa'nso." Ndiye adampatsa, nabwerera anthu aja, nafika komwe ku Khulubvi.

14. Ndiye adamanga nyumba, nalamula kuti munthu aliyense atenge mtsiki umodzi-modzi, wina mphano imodzimodzi. Asaphatikize ziwirizi, ai. Uwu unali mwambo wache wonenedwa ndi Mbona. Ndiye nyumba yacheyo inali yozungulira. Choncho itamangidwa nyumba ija, iwo anatenga munthu wamamuna uja, amene anachokera kwa Lundu kuja, nam'mangira chindu chache cha nyumbayo pa mutu. Ndipo chitatha chindu chija, anachiika pamwamba pa nyumba.

15. Ndipo itatha nyumba ija, anatenga mkazi uja namuika m'nyumba mommo. Mkaziyo dzina lache ndi Salima. Ngati mkazi uja amwalira, anali kupita'nso komwe kwa Lundu, natenga mkazi wina, nati dzina lache'nso Salima. Koma iye Mbona sanali kuoneka, ai. Koma kungoti pamene mkazi afika m'menemo, amati mwini wache anali kukondwera kwambiri. Ndipo ati amafika nthawi ya usiku, koma anthu sam'uona, ai. Chifukwa ati iye ndi mzimu wa ife Amang'anja.

16. Choncho mamuna uja, amene anamangiridwa chindu pa mutu uja, basi, chaka chomwecho anali kufa. Pa chaka china nyumba ikafunika'nso anali kutenga'nso mamuna wina konko, nabwera naye kufika kuno. Koma

akam'mangira chindwi cha nyumba ya Salimayo, iyeyo anali kufa'nso chaka chomwecho.

17. Kunja, kunena kuno kwa Amang'anja, dziko la Nsanje, Chikwawa kufikira Thyolo, anapatula mudzi wina, nati kumeneko kukhale kom'pembedzera. Uwu unali mudzi wa Changata, ku Thyolo. Monga momwe achitira Azungu, kuti kumakhala college, ndipo'nso pena pamakhala centre, choncho college yaikulu ndi imene inali ku Khulubvi, ku Nsanje kuno. Ndipo centre yache inali kwa Changata ku Thyolo, ndipo kumeneko'nso anali kum'pembedza. Monga achitira'nso Azungu kuti village school, ife'nso malo amene ali ku Michiru, kufupi ndi Blantyre, ndipo kumeneko anaikako munthu wina, dzina lache Mbalale. Iye'nso nchito yache inali ya kupembedza'nso kumeneko.

18. Dziko lino, kukapezeka kuti kuli matenda, pali uliri, kuti anthu onse ali kungobvutika kwambiri, munthu uja, wokhala kwa Mbona uja, mlauli uja, amanena-nena, nagwa, namati, "Eee, ndiri kufuna kuti dziko lonse lino, mutenge ngala imodzi-imodzi ya mapira, kapena maere ngala imodzi-imodzi; chakudya pang'ono-pang'ono, mubwere nazo kuno." Izi zinali kuyambira komwe ku Michiru, ku Blantyre; kufikira pa Changata, ku Thyolo; kufikira Ngabu, ku Chikwawa; nazipitirira mpakana Chapananga, mpaka ku Nsanje, nakasiyako katundu ameneyo. Choncho iwo anati, "Tipangireni nsembe." Ndipo akonkunowa anali kupanga nsembe, kuti matenda amenewo athe.

19. Mvula'nso 'ngakhale inali kubvuta, sikabvuta'nso ai. Tsono iwo anali kuchita chimodzimodzi, kupanga nsembe, kuti, "Tiyenera kupanga nsembe." Choncho anthu anali kupanga nsembe m'midzi. Choncho anali kulamulira kuti mudzi uli wonse upange makumbi ao, monga tinyumba tating'ono-ting'ono, monga muja azungu amapanga masukulu ang'ono-ang'ono. Choncho nawo'nso anali kupanga m'mudzi uli wonse timakumbi pang'ono-pang'ono mopembedzeramo. Iwowa anali kutenga chimanga chao, kapena kupanga mowa wao, ali kutsira nsembe. Ndipo pa nthawi yomweyo ali kubvina, nyimbo ziri pakati, choncho anali kuona kuti mvula inkabwera, onse anali kukondwera kwambiri. Koma matsoka, zaka zina mvula sinali kubwera. Koma 'ngakhale zinthu zinali choncho, iwo anali kudziwa kuti tichitebe choncho, basi. Kufikirana anali kuchitabe chomwecho, mpakana mwina anali kukomana nazo.

20. Sikuti zinali kokha kuno, ai, koma 'ngakhale'nso ku Nyanja ya Mchenga yonse. Inali yache ya Lundu, ndipo anthu onsewa anali kupembedza chimodzi-modzi. Nyanja ya Mchenga ndi imene anthu masiku ano akuiti Zambezi. Kuli mfumu ina yache'nso imene inaitanidwa ndi Lundu, ndipo dzina lache ndi Chituwi. Ena amafunsa kuti, "Kodi iye Lundu'yu anali kupita monsemu?" Eee, iye anali ndi mkulu wache, dzina lache Lipiti. Ameneyu ndiye amene anali kutuma kuno, kuti, "Chab-

wino, pitani." Nthawi imene iwo anali ku Mbewe kuti, "Pitani mukagawe maiko onse, ndi kukapita m'maiko onse ndipo mukaikemo mafumu akuti-akuti." Izo zinali kuchitikadi. Ndiye chifukwa cha ichi, onsewa nsembe yao yaikulu inali kuchitika ku Khulubvi. Uko ndi kumeneko anali kutenga iwo ulamuliro wonse, 'ngakhale ku Mulanje komwe, 'ngakhale'nso ku Chipironi. Maiko onsewa anali mu ulamuliro wache wa Lundu. Ndiye mzimu wache ndi kumakhala Mbona.

21. Mbona anali mzimu, koma wolamulira wache anali Lundu, amene anali ambuye wache ndi amene'nso anali m'dziko lino kale. Choncho Amang'anja onse kumucha iye mulungu wao. Kufikira lero 'ngakhale pang'ono-ng'ono anthu saiwala, ai. Makolo omwe aja, amene anali kukhala kwa Mbona, alipobe, ndipo ine ndinapitako ndi kuwaona ndi maso anga. 'Ngakhale'nso ndiri mwana, ndidapitako kuti ndikaonetsetse bwino, ndipo ndinacheza nao. Choncho kufikira lero iwo alipobe.

22. Koma nyumba zao ziri zonga zomwe zija zimene adali kumanga kale-kale za chiMang'anja, zosakometsera. Alibe mipando, alibe zigowi. Iwowa anali kuopa. Ndipo pakuwafunsa, anati, "lai, koma tiri naye mfumu wathu, ameneyo ndiye ayenera kukhala m'mipando, ndipo mpando ndiwo chiguwo. Siwamitengo, ai. Ameneyu angathe kukhala ndithu pamenepo, osati ife kukhala pa chiguwo, ai." Anakanika.

23. Ndiye akulu-akulu okhala m'menemo, 'ngakhale lero, msonkho sakhoma, ai. Kale sanali kukhoma, koma Azungu anadza m'menemo ndi kuti, "Ayenera kukhoma." Tsono nzeru yao imene idapanga iwo ndi iyi: anyamata onse amawatulutsa kupita kunja, koma akulu-akulu okha, okalamba, ndiwo amene amakhala mommo. Chifukwa iwo salola kuti m'dziko mwaomo mulowe msonkho. Opembedzao akalipobe ku Khulubvi. Umo ndi m'mene Amang'anja anali kum'pembedzera mulungu wao, ndi kufikira lero, iwowa ali kum'pembedza Mbona.

ENGLISH VERSION

1. Today we are going to talk about Mbona, the godhead[1] of the Mang'anja, whom they began to worship after they had arrived from the north under the leadership of Undi,[2] with Kaphwiti and Lundu as second and third in command.

2. They had all settled at Kaphirintiwa and had begun growing crops, when one year there was no rain. The Mang'anja performed their rain dance, suffered hardship, and tried everything to make the rains come.

3. At the time of the drought there lived among them a little boy, a nephew of Lundu, Kaphwiti, and Undi. He was the son of their sister, and his name was Mbona. People said, "Elders, stop dancing and let this boy

try!" When the child had finished dancing, they wanted him to enter [i.e., return to] the dancing arena, but he was scared and refused to go. When he was on the point of bursting into tears, people heard the crash of thunder.

4. The boy's tears made rain.[3] Everybody rejoiced and began planting finger millet, sesame, and groundbeans,[4] which was what people cultivated in those days. The crops did well, and people were happy. So they began praising the child, saying, "This child is the greatest. His name is Mbona indeed!" The name Mbona means someone who is praised and thanked by everyone, even by an evil person. Someone who makes the rains fall, however bad the situation, or someone who is unfailingly goodhearted.[5] That is why they called him Mbona, and that is why the Mang'anja loved him and held him in such high esteem.

5. But the leaders, among whom were his uncles Lundu and Kaphwiti, without exception began to hate him because of his popularity with the people, and they thought of killing him. When his mother heard of this, she told him, "Your uncles are plotting to kill you because you are being praised for making the rains come. When you dance, rain falls, and many people pay you homage. That is why they want to kill you." The boy then took flight.

6. Fleeing, he made for the south till he found himself at Chikwawa. Thence he traveled through thick forests to Nsanje. Skirting the hill called Malawi, he went on for a while, but then turned back until he came to a place in the neighborhood of Nsanje township. Overcome with fatigue, he sat down to rest. With him were his two wives[6] and his dog; he himself carried a spear. All these he had with him. Since he was tired, he sat down.

7. In the meantime his uncles, who had left their homes to track him down, had been following him for years. Living on such things as monkeybread, tamarinds, wild plums, and edible roots and tubers,[7] they kept wandering about following him until they finally found him.

8. When they came upon him, they poised their spears to stab him, but they failed to harm him. They also shot arrows at him, but once again they failed. Mbona then said, "Take the kind of grass they call *nansongole,* and cut me on the head with it."[8]

9. When they had cut him on the head, he died, but the same day a storm broke, and rain fell in torrents. Mbona's blood turned into the stream we know as Nyamadzere,[9] which slowly began winding its way to the Mud River. The latter came to be called Shire by the Europeans, but in the olden days it was known as Mud River. While the new stream was still making its way to the Mud River and just before it reached its destination, it formed the Ndione Pool,[10] which is still there today.

10. When the storm broke and the heavy rains fell, Mbona's pursuers were petrified, not knowing what to do, and when at daybreak they saw that the place where Mbona had died had changed into a stream, they exclaimed, "What are we to do now?" Then one of them fell into a trance as if possessed — as if he were a spirit medium — saying, "That man is still alive. I, Mbona, am still here.[11] I made this stream, and I am staying here at this pool called Ndione. It is my will that you return to Mbewe." This he said, because Lundu, one of the uncles who had been following him, had remained behind at Mbewe in the area of Chikwawa.[12]

11. The entranced man continued, "Go, fetch a woman from there. Bring a woman and a man here. You shall build a house for me, and the woman shall live therein. She shall not be a woman still capable of bearing children, but one who has ceased to bear. Nor do I want a young maiden." Thereupon messengers were sent.

12. The headmen in charge of the place were Khambani, Mbukwa, and Mithanje.[13] Above the marshland one finds at some distance from each other the villages of Mbango, Ngabu, and Malemia,[14] who were the priests and overseers of the cult of Mbona, the guardian spirit of the Mang'anja at Nsanje. The ones making offerings inside the spirit hut, however, were Mbukwa, Kambalame, and Mithanje.

13. When those who had been sent to Lundu arrived there, they said, "We found your nephew, but he outwitted us when we tried to kill him. He then told us, 'Take *nansongole* grass, and cut me on the head.' What happened afterward was something terrifying and indescribable, something no eye has ever seen. All of us were in a faint until daybreak, when one of us began to have visions and turned into a spirit medium. He explained everything to us, as it was Mbona's spirit which had taken possession of him. He also told us, 'Go to Chief Lundu to find a wife for Mbona from among his cross-cousins.'"[15] Lundu then gave them a woman, but they said, "We also need a man," and he gave them one. This done, they went back to Khulubvi.

14. They built a hut for Mbona and made a rule that each person should contribute only one stalk of grass or one sliver of bamboo, and no one should contribute both. This had been ordained by Mdona himself. After they had built the walls of the hut, which was circular in shape, they fetched the man who had come from Lundu and built the roof upon his head.[16] Once it was finished, it was lifted onto the walls of the hut.

15. When the hut was ready, the woman, whose name was Salima, was made to live in it. If she died, they went to Lundu to ask for another woman, whom they also called Salima. Although Mbona remained invisible, it is said that he was greatly pleased with his wife. They also

say that he comes to her during the night, but nobody sees him, for he is the guardian spirit of us, the Mang'anja.

16. The man upon whose head the roof was built would die the same year. Whenever they built a new spirit hut, they went to look for a man at Lundu's and brought him here. And when the roof of Salima's hut had been built upon his head, he would also die within a year.[17]

17. Outside the country of the Mang'anja — that is to say, the districts of Nsanje, Chikwawa, and Thyolo — they chose yet another village as a place to worship Mbona. That village was Chief Changata's on the slopes of Mount Thyolo. You may compare this with the European system of building a college in one place and a central school in another. The college in our case would be the Khulubvi shrine near Nsanje, while the central school would be Changata's shrine at Thyolo.[18] Finally, the village school under the European system would correspond to the Michiru shrine near Blantyre,[19] where they put a man called Mbalale in charge. His duty was to worship Mbona there too.

18. Whenever there were dangerous diseases or epidemics about and people went through a lot of suffering, that person at Mbona's shrine — the medium we just mentioned — became possessed and began to make utterances, saying, "I want everybody in the land to contribute some grain — no more than a head of millet or Guinea corn or some other food — and I want those gifts brought here." Gifts were collected at Michiru near Blantyre, Changata's in Thyolo, Ngabu's and Chapananga's in Chikwawa, and thence taken to Nsanje, where all the offerings came together. The medium would thereupon say, "Prepare an offering!" and the inhabitants would make an offering so that their sufferings might come to an end.

19. Whenever the rains were late, it would no longer be a problem. They would act in the same way, saying, "We must make a libation." This they would do in their own villages. Orders were given to each village to build its own shrine in the form of a small hut. These may be compared with the village schools built by the Europeans. Every village would build its own hut as a place of worship, where the inhabitants would take their maize, or the beer they might have brewed, as an offering. Rain would already begin to fall when they were still performing the rain dance and singing their rain songs, and all would rejoice. If sometimes they were less fortunate and rain did not fall, they still kept to this custom, trusting that another time they would have better luck.

20. These things were not only done here, but also in the area of the Sand River, which equally formed part of Lundu's domains and where people worshiped in the same way. The Sand River is the one known

nowadays as the Zambezi. There was a certain chief in that area, Chituwi by name,[20] who had been appointed by Lundu. People often ask, "Did Lundu himself make the rounds of all those places?" As a matter of fact he made use of somebody whose name was Lipiti.[21] When still at Mbewe, Lundu would send him to this place, saying, "All right, go!" Or he might tell him, "Go, divide the various areas and appoint such and such persons to be chiefs in those places." That is how is was done, and that is also why their most important sacrifice was made at Khulubvi. It is from Mbewe that chiefs received their authority, those at Mulanje as well as those at Chipironi, for all these districts fell under the authority of Lundu, and Mbona was their guardian spirit.[22]

21. Mbona was the spirit, but Lundu was his senior, since he was Mbona's mother's brother and since he also had come to the country long ago. It is for this reason that the Mang'anja called him their god. To this day people remember him, and he is not forgotten, not for a moment. Those elders, the ones who lived at Mbona's place, are still there. I went there myself to see them with my own eyes. Though still a child, I went there to have a close look at everything, and I had a chat with them. To this day they are still there.

22. Their huts are like the ones that the Mang'anja used to build in the olden days, that is to say, very plain. They have no wooden chairs, not even clay benches on which to sit. These things they abstain from out of respect for Mbona, for when questioned about this, they said, "We have our chief who may use a seat. Not a wooden chair; only a clay bench.[23] We ourselves cannot use it." They were quite firm on this point.

23. Nor do the elders living there pay taxes, which continues to this day. That is an old custom, but when the Europeans came to the country, they said, "You must pay." The problem was solved by moving all the young men out, while the older ones stayed,[24] for they could not allow taxes to be paid in their village. Those cult officers still live there at Khulubvi. This is the way the Mang'anja used to worship their godhead Mbona, and to this day they continue worshiping him.

THE MBONA III TRADITION

TEXT III/A
Che Ngwangwa (1967)

Text III/A, "the story of the twelve journeys," was collected in Kadzumba's village, a short distance away from the headquarters of the Lundu paramountcy, on August 24, 1967. The narrator was Che Ngwangwa, an elderly subsistence farmer, and the person who recorded it was Stephen Mbande, youngest son of Senior Headman Mbande, then a young man in his early twenties with a primary school background. Since the structure and the message of the text have been extensively discussed in Chapter 7, no further introduction will be necessary.

MANG'ANJA VERSION

Kumene anabadwira Mbona

1. Mbona mbiri yache inamveka kutali m'dziko lonse lino la Malawi. Uyu anali munthu wamamuna. Ndipo anabadwa mwa munthu. Koma iye sanabadwire ku Kaphirintiya, ai. Koma anabadwira kwa Apwitikizi, ku Mozambique ndiye kwao kweni-kweni. Atakula anafuna kuti akwatire mkazi. Koma anaona kuti kwao kunalibe mkazi yemwe anali kum'konda. Choncho anayamba kubwera kuno, nalonda phiri limene lichedwa Kaphirintiya.

Mbona akwatira kwa Lundu

2. Ndipo anafika ku Kaphirintiya, dziko la Amang'anja ndipo lokongoladi. Ndipo iye atafika kumeneko, anali ngati mlendo kwa iwo. Ndipo ali kuti amai ache a Mbona kalelo anabadwira ku Kaphirintiya kwa Kabvina.

Ndipo iye analibe mlendo, koma akuti anali ndi mkulu wao, mwana wa mlongo wao.

3. Ndipo Mbona anaona mkazi amene anafuna kuti apange naye banja. Ndipo ataisimba nkhaniyi kwa mfumu Lundu, popeza kuti anali mdzukulu wao, anam'patsa mkaziyo. Ndipo Lundu anati, "Eee, ife takupatsa mkazi, ndipo takulola kuti umunyamule ndi kupita naye kwanu." Ndipo Mbona ananyamula mkazi wache, napita naye kwao kwa Apwitikizi. Ndipo atafika kwao anakhala ndi banja labwino. Ndipo pamenepa anapatsa chitsanzo kuti ana akazi apite ndi kukhala ndi mwamuna wao. Mbona sanapereke ndalama kwa Lundu, ai, koma anangopatsidwa mkaziyo ngati kuloola kapena mphoto yache.

Mbona achoka ku Mozambique kupitanso kwa Lundu

4. Ndipo kwao, kumene iye anabadwa, kunafika nkhondo zambiri chifukwa zomwe zinali kuchitika pa makhalidwe ache. Ndipo nthawi zonse anali kuthawira ku mapanga a miyala pamodzi ndi mkazi wache yemwe. Ndipo ataona kuti nkhondo zinachuluka, anaganiza zopita komwe anatenga mkazi wache. Ndipo anabwerera kwao ku Kaphirintiya. 5. Mfumu Lundu atawaona, anakondweranso, nawamutsa. Ndipo iye anafotokoza za chidani chonse chimene chinkaoneka kwao. Ndipo mfumu Lundu anam'patsa malo ache, a pa yekha, kuti iye ndi mkazi wache akhalepo. Ndipo Mbona ndi mfumu Lundu anakhala pamodzi.

Chilala chioneka kwa Lundu; nsembe: akulu alephera

6. Koma patapita zaka zina kumeneko kunaoneka chilala, chifukwa mvula ndi imodzi yomwe sinafike. Ndipo Lundu anauza anthu ache ndi abale ache kuti achite nsembe yopempha mvula. Ndipo atatero, anadziwitsa akulu onse ndi anthu ena za msonkhanowo. Analalikira kuti ukhale tsiku lamulungu. Ndipo unyinji wa anthu unasonkhana kuti udzaonere katsiridwe ka nsembeyi kwa mizimu. Ndipo anatenga ng'oma zazikulu, naziika pa bwalo. Ndipo pamenepo panali mtengo waukulu ndithu kotero kuti anthu onse anakhala ndi kukwanira mu mthunzi wache. 7. Ndipo anayamba kubvina mkulu mmodzi-mmodzi, nyimbo ili pakamwa; anthu ali kubvomera ndinso ng'oma ziri kuimbidwa. Mkuluyo anayamba kutandala-tandala mkatimo, koma mvula sinabwere konse. Anthu onse anayamba kudandaula ndithu, ndipo mkulu woyambayo ataona kuti walephera, anauza mkulu wina kuti alowemo ndi kubvina ndi kuyangalanso. Ndipo onse anaturukamo ndi manyazi popeza kuti anazolowera kale kuti, pakutsira nsembe ya mvula, nthawi yomweyo anali kuponda matope a mvula. Ndipo analowanso wina wachitatuyo. Ndipo atabvina-bvina, iyenso anadabwa ndithu, nalephera ndi kutulukamo ndi manyazi.

8. Ndiye akulu-akulu anzao amene anaitanidwa aja anadabwa kwambiri. Ndipo unyinji wonse wa anthu unati, "Nanga popeza kuti tiri kusowa ndi madzi akumwa omwe, nanga ife timwa chiani? Chakudya tiribe. Nsembe ziri kukanidwanso!" Ndipo akulu aja anayamba kufunsana kuti ngati alipo wina amene angathe kulowamo. Akulu aja anakana nati, "Palibe, koma amene alipo ndi kamwana kamene kakhala panoka." Ndipo anati, "Kalekeni kuti nakonso kayese kubvina pa nsembeyi!"

Mbona adzetsa mvula

9. Ndipo anali ndi nthungo zache ziwiri, mpeni ndi nkhwangwa yache. Ndipo atalowa m'nyumba anatulukamo, ali kuimba nyimbo, ng'oma ili kulira, ndipo nthawi yomweyo anayamba kubvina, nasonyeza nthungo yache kumwamba ndipo anaona kuti pomwepo mphambe inayamba kugunda kwakukulu, ndipo kachiwiriko mvula yamaile inabvumba.

Chidani

10. Kuyambira nthawi yomweyo anthu anadabwa nati, "Kodi ameneyu ndi munthu wotani?" Tsopano akulu-akulu anayamba kubvina aja anachita dumbo nauza anthu kuti, "Ameneyu sangabweretse mvula, ai. Koma wabweretsa mvula ndi ife pano, chifukwa cha kubvina koyamba komwe kuja. Tisiyeni tilowenso kachiwiri." Ndipo atalowa mkatimo anabvinanso molimbika, koma analephera. Mvula sinabwere konse, ai. Ndipo atayesa-yesa akulu onseo, anaona kuti alepheratu.

11. Ndipo anamuuza kuti abvinenso kachiwiri ngati mvula ingabwere. Ndipo atangolowa mkati, nasonya-sonya ndodo yache kumwamba, nthawi yomweyo mvula inabwera yoopsya. Ndipo akulu aja anachita naye dumbo loopsya, nati, "Kodi iwe mphamvu zimenezi wazitenga kuti? Iwe mwana wamng'onowe?" Ndipo kuyambira pamenepo anafuna kuti am'phe, chifukwa anali kuopa kuti anthu adzamkhulupirira iye. Ndipo mvula sinaleke kubvumba. Inabwera nthawi yonse chifukwa nsembe yache inalandiridwa.

Mbona ayamba kuthawa

12. Ndipo iye anazindikira kuti akulu aja amafuna kuti am'phe. Ndipo anthu ena achisoni anam'simbira za imfa yache. Ndipo iye ndi mkazi wache anafuna kuti abwerere kwao kumene kunachokera iye, kwa makolo ache, napangana kuti achoke pa nthawi yausiku. Ndipo kunja kutada anayamba kuthawa, nanyamula zakudya pang'ono, naziika m'nsengwa ndi chibvundikiro. Ndipo iye anatenga zipangizo zache chifukwa konse kumene anali kukhala iye sanali kusiya zache, ndipo anayamuka ulendo wao.

13. Ndipo akulu aja ataona kuti wathwawira mdani waoyo, anapangana

kuti amulonde kufikira komwe ati alekeze iye. Ndipo anayamba ulendo wakum'thamangira Mbona kuti ngati ati am'peze, am'pheretu. Ndipo atatero, anayenda ulendo ali kuthamangabe, koma analephera osam'peza pafupi, ai. Ndipo akulu aja anadabwa kwambiri, nati, "Timati kuti tim'pezere pafupi; munthu ameneyu ali kuyenda bwanji?" Koma iwo (Mbona ndi mkazi wache) sanali kuthamanga, ai. Anali kungoyenda ndi mkazi wache, koma anthu m'mbuyo muno, thukuta mbuu, kuti tim'peze. Ndipo anadziwa bwino kuti munthuyo anali ngati mzimu.

14. Ndipo mmene mukaponda mapazi ache simunali kuuma kapena kufafanizika, ai. Ndipo akangoponda kamodzi kokha, inkasanduka njira yoyera. Ndipo udzu sunali kutha kumera ndi pang'ono pomwe m'njira mmene anali kuyendamo iye Mbona. Ndipo atafika ku dziko la Nsanje, anadziwa kuti tsopano ndayandikira kwathu, koma adani ache anali kumulondabe. Ndipo anauza mkazi wache kuti ayambe kukhala pa mwala, kuti adzipuma bwino pang'ono.

Mbona agwidwa

15. Ndipo ali kupuma choncho, adani ache anatulukira. Koma iye sanali kufuna kuti achite nao nkhondo, ai kapena kuti awathawe; izo sanafune. Anangowayang'ana. Ndipo iwo anam'gwira kuti am'phe. Koma iye anawaletsa, nati, "Ngati mufuna kundipha, ai, ine ndabvomera kale chifukwa sindinakuthaweni. Koma tsopano mverani zomwe ndiri kufuna kukuuzani. Pa malo pano sindinafune kuti mundipherepo, ai. Munditenge pano ndi kupita nane pafupi ndi kwathu, phiri limene muli kulionalo. Ndipo musakandiphe msanga, ai. Mukayambe kuyembekezera. Ndipo mukatenge kaudzu ka nansongole ndi kundimanga m'khosi mwangamu, ndipo mundiphe bwino." Ndipo atangotha kulankhula, anthu aja anam'nyamula pa mapuzi pao.

Imfa yache

16. Ndipo atafika naye pa malopo, anam'goneka pansi, natenga udzu umene anaunena ndi kum'manga pa khosi pache, natenga mpeni ndi kum'dula. Ndipo pomudula, anatuluka magazi, amene anasanduka madzi eni-eni nthawi yomweyo, ndipo madziwo anachulidwa dzina loti Ndione. Atatero, anatenga mutu wache ndi kuika pa msitu ndi kuukwirira. Atatha izo, anthu aja anapita ali okondwa kwambiri ndithu.

Kubwerera kwao

17. Ataona zonse zatha, anati, "Tsopano uyu wafa, tiyeni tidzibwerera kwathu." Ndipo akubwerera akulu ambiri mwa iwo anafa. Ndipo nthenda yache inawapha sinadziwike. Pa ulendo wao otsala analipo anai

okha kudza iye mfumu Lundu. Mkazi wache yemwe wa Mbona sana-
yende nthawi kuchokera pamene anafa iye Mbona.

18. Ndipo Lundu pakuona kuti nthawi imene anali kuthamanga sanali
kuona za nthaka ya dzikolo, anaona pobwerera nthaka imene anaiko-
nda, nati, "Aa, koma ili ndilo dziko labwino!" Anaima pakati pa Mbewe,
nati, "Pano koma ndidzamangapo!" napitirira ulendo wache.

19. Ndipo atafika kwao anapeza mmera wonse utatha kupsyerera ndi
dzuwa, nati, "Nanga titani?" Anthu onse anali kudandaula kwambiri.
Ndipo anali kuyesa kutsira nsembe zambiri kuti kapena mvula n'kugwa,
koma ai, sinabwere. Ndipo anthu ambiri anafuna Mbona, nati, "Kodi
mwam'pheranji munthu uja? Ali ndi moyobe mvula inali kubwera bwino."

Lundu athawira ku Mbewe

20. Ndipo Lundu pakumva zodandaula za anthu anachita manyazi,
nathawa nthawi ya usiku, ndi kupita ku Mbewe kuja kumene anaonako
malo. Ulendowu unali wa iye ndi mkazi wache, basi. Ananyamuka nthawi
ya usiku atatenga phoso lao lokwanira. Ndipo analonda mapazi a mbale
wao amene anaphedwa kale. Ali kuyenda, anali kupuma, chifukwa uwu
unali ulendo waufulu, osati wothawa nkhondo. Ndipo atafika pa malo
omwe iye anasiya, anapezapo pali bwino, ndipo panalibe ndi munthu
ndi mmodzi yemwe. Ndipo iye anauza mkazi wache, "Malo amene
ndifuna kuti ndikhale ndi ano!" Ndipo anatula katundu wao, nayamba
kutsira nsembe pa tsinde la mtengo kuti malowo akhale a mtendere.

21. Ndipo anamanga nyumba yache ya mitengo yokha-yokha, kuchitira
kuti mu msitumo munali zirombo zambiri. Choncho Lundu anakhala ku
Mbewe'ko. Ndipo analima zao ndi kucha bwino zakudya zao, nadzala
mbeu zomwe anali kudzala kwao ku Kaphirintiya. Ndipo atatha chaka
kapena mvula imodzi, anauza mkazi wache ayambe kupita ku mudzi ndi
kukatenga abale ache. Choncho atamvana ndi mkazi wache, anayamba
ulendo wopita kwao ku Kaphirintiya, nati, "Iwe mkaziwe, tsala kuno. Ndi-
dzakupeza mwezi wamawa."

Lundu asamusa abale ache ku Kaphirintiya

22. Ndipo Lundu atabwerera ku Kaphirintiya, abale ache anamlandira
bwino. Ndipo iye anayamba kuwasimbira za ubwino umene anaupeza
ku Mbewe, nati, "Ine ndabwera kuno kudzakunyamulani, inu abale anga.
Ndipo tidzapita tonse kuti tikakhale limodzi kumeneko. Kulibe mfumu
yina, koma ine ndekha." Ndipo anakhala kumeneko kudikira kuti ayambe
kukonza akatundu ao. Atatero, anamanga akatundu ao, ndipo mfumu
Lundu anatsira nsembe kuti adzukulu ache akafike nao bwino. Ndipo
anatsazika abale ache amaere amene anawasiyira ufumu wachewo.

23. Ndipo ali kubwerera, anauza mbale wache wina, dzina lache Kabvina, kuti ayambe kukhala pa yekha. Kumeneko kunali kum'gawira ufumu wache. Anam'patsa abale ache ena pang'ono kuti atsale naye. Ndipo atayenda pang'ono, anauzanso mbale wache wina, dzina lache Kaphwiti, kuti atsalenso ndi ufumu wache pafupi ndi kwa Selemani, kwa Apwitikizi. Kaphwiti ndi Kabvina anakhala mafumu akulu kumeneko. Ndipo kufikira lerobe ufumu umenewu ulipo. Ndipo ena anapitiriza ulendo wao, mpakana onse anafikira ku Mbewe.

Pofika ku Mbewe; Lundu atsira nsembe

24. Ndipo pofika, Lundu anatenga ufa umene unatsala pa ulendo pao, napita m'thengo, natsira nsembe kuti anao akhale bwino pa mudzi watsopanowo. Ndipo atatero, anawaonetsa malo onsewo, nati, "Eee, malo onsewa ndi anga, palibe mfumu yina yoposa ine, ai. Ndipo kuyambira kwa Apwitikizi mpakana ku mapiri, dziko lonseli ndi langa!"

25. Ndipo Lundu anatenga abale ache ena, namapita nao kwa Apwitikizi, nawagawira maufumu. Chifukwa dziko la Lundu malire ache anali Zambezi, popeza kuti iye sanaoloke Zambezi ndi kupita patsidya, ai. Ndipo Lundu analibe kuuma mtima, ai. Anali kufuna kuti mtundu wache wonse ukhale wa mafumu okha-okha. Ndipo mbumba yache inachuluka, nakhala ali kukondwa ku Mbewe. Ndipo kawiri-kawiri anali kukonda kuphika mowa wa mapira.

Kufuna nsembe kwache kwa Mbona

26. Pamene anaona kuti Lundu ndi abale ache analonda mapazi a Mbona, anadziwa kuti abale ache (a Mbona) ali pafupi tsopano, ndipo anafuna kuti am'dziwe. Anagwa komwe ku Khulubvi, nati, "Ine ndifuna kuti Lundu andimangire nyumba, ndipo atatha nyumbayo, andifunire mkazi. Ndipo asachedwe. Ndiri kuifuna nthawi yomweyino." Ndipo mmawa kutacha, amthenga anali kupita ku Mbewe kuti akafotokoze zonse zimene Mbona anali kufuna kuchokera kwa Lundu. Ndipo Lundu anali kutuma ana ache kuti apite ku Khulubvi ndi kukamangitsa nyumba. Ndipo atatero, nyumba yonse inali kumagidwa bwino.

27. Ndipo pomanga nyumbayo panali malamulo akuti mfumu yekha ndiye anayenera kumangiridwa denga lache la nyumbalo pa mutu pache. Mamangidwe a nyumbayo anali a dzira. Ndipo Lundu anali kuuza Tengani kuti akamangiridwe denga la nyumbayo pa mutu pache. Ndipo atatero, nyumbayo inali kumangidwa mwaudongo ndithu.

28. Nyumba ija itatha kufoleredwa ndi nsaru ya biriwita wa madzi, monga momwe adanenera mwini wache, akulu aja anali kuuzidwanso ndi Mbona kuti akam'tengere mkazi wache: "Chifukwa ine sindifuna kuti ndidzikhala ndekha ngati mwamuna wakutha akazi, ai. Ndifuna kuti

Lundu andipatse mkazi wanga monga anachitira poyambe ndikali moyo. Asakatenge kapolo wa Lundu kuti akhale mkazi wanga, ai. Ine sindidzalola. Ndipo musakatenge namwali, kapena nchembere imene iri kubalabe, ai. Kome nkhalamba yomwe kwa amuna singapiteko, ndiponso akhale mfulu."

29. Ndipo atabwerera ku Kaphirintiya wakumwera ndi kupita ku Mbewe, anali kum'peza Lundu, nati, "Ife takupeza Lundu, kholo lathu, uku ku Khulubvi, nyumba ya Mbona yatha, koma tsopano akufuna mkazi!" Apo ayamba kufotokoza zonse monga iye, Mbona, ananenera. Ndipo Lundu anali kutenga mlongo wache apo chi! nati, "Ameneyu, m'nyamuleni, mupite naye!" Ndipo atatero, mkazi wa Mbona anali kuyenda pa chikuku, ndipo poyenda ngati apeza mtengo utadula njira, sanali kuloledwa kulumpha mtengowo. Ngati aulumpha, aonela mkazi wa mfumu. Ndipo Mbona nthawi yomweyo anali kugwa ku Khulubvi, nati, "Mkazi ameneyo abwerere kwao chifukwa wandionera mwano."

30. Ndipo atapeza mtengo kapena phesi, anali kuitumba yonse ndi kupitira kumbali. Ndipo kunja kutada, anali kufuna malo abwino kuti agoneka maiyo. Ndipo atayandikira ku Khulubvi, nati afika lero, anali kuyamba kugwa, nati, Adziwa kale kuti mkazi wache afika pa tsikulo, nati, "Ndiye mkazi ameneyu, ndifuna kuti akhaledi muno mu Khulubvi!"

Makhalidwe a mkazi wa Mbona

31. Mkazi wa Mbona akafika ku Khulubvi, anthu anali kumlemekeza kwambiri, chifukwa iye wonyoza mkazi wa Mbona anali kuona mabvuto ambirimbiri. Ndipo iye Mbona sanali kufuna kuti mkazi wache anenedwe miseche ndi anthu ena. Ndipo atafika naye, anali kum'phera ndiwo zabwino za mbuzi. Ndipo anali kupita kukamulowetsa m'nyumba mwache nthungululu ziri kubvina. Ena anali kuwaza maufa pa mitu, ndipo anali kumuloweza m'nyumba mwachemo mwaufulu ndithu.

32. Ndipo mtundu wa Chikunda sunali kuloledwa kuti apite ndi kukaona nsembe za Mbona. Atatengera khama, anali kudwala pang'ono ndi kufa. Ngakhale lero, munthu wamba sangathe kupita kukaona nyumba ya Mbona. Akatero abwerako ali m'manda. Malowo ngobvuta kwambiri. Ngati kuli msonkhano, Achikunda onse anali kuwaletsa kupitako, koma Amang'anja okha.

Khulubvi

33. Ndipo anali kuwauza kuti, "Kusapite munthu ndi mmodzi yemwe kuti akaone mkazi wanga. Otha kupita kumeneko ndi nkhalamba zimene zilibe amuna, izo zitha kudzachezeka mkazi wanga!" Ndipo akatero, anali ndi muitanitso wambiri. Ana ang'ono ndiwo amene akatha kupitako kukacheza naye. Ndipo nthawi zonse anyani anali kubwera pafupi ndi

nyumba yache ndi kucheza ndi mkaziyo. Ndipo atatero, mfumu anali kukonza zakudya zabwino ndi kupatsira ana ang'ono, napita nazo ndi kukam'patsa mkazi wache. Ndipo timitsuko ta madzi tinali kukhala ndanda-nda, osasowa madzi. Ndi madzi akumwa omwe anali kubwera ndi atsikanao. Ndipo nkhalamba zokalamba kwambiri zinali kubwera kudzam'chezetsa.

34. Ndipo ngati alaka-laka kanthu kena, iye sakalankhula, koma Mbona ndiye amene akagweratu m'mudzi ndi kunena zonse zimene mkazi wache anali kuzifuna nati, "Zipezeke msanga!" Ndiye ngati afuna thumba la mpunga, nthawi yomweyo mpunga unali kugulidwa ndithu. Kanthu kenanso ndi kuti Mbona sanafune kuti mkazi wache agwire nchito ya mtundu uli wonse, kuyambira kutunga madzi, kulima, kuphika; nchito zonse Mbona anali kuzikana kuti mkazi wache asazigwire, ndiye chifukwa chache mkazi wache woyamba anali Salima, chifukwa chakuti panalibe ndi nchito ndi imodzi yomwe imene mkazi wache anali kuigwira. Anali kungodya, basi.

Mbona achezera Salima

35. Ndipo pa nthawi yausiku anali kufika akuluwo, kudzacheza ndi mkazi wache. Ndipo nthawi zambiri anali kum'gonetsa tulo takufa nato, kuti ngati angadzuke, ndi kuchita mantha ndi kuthawa. Atalowa m'nyumbamo, anali kum'tseteka thupi lache lonse, sete sete sete, kufikira atatha kum'tseteka mkaziyo. Ndipo mau ambiri anali kumuuza m'maloto, ali m'tulo. Ndipo iye atapita, anali kudzuka, nazindikira kuti mamuna wache anabweradi, ndipo anali kukumbukira maloto ache onse amene iye anam'lotetsa.

36. Ndipo mkaziyo, nthawi zina ali m'tulo, anali kum'dzutsa, nakhala m'maso, koma ali chigonere. Ndipo anali kuona nsato ili kulowa m'nyumbamo, koma yaikulu, iye popeza kuti anadziwa kale kuti anali mamuna wache, anakhala wosafuna kuti achite mantha ndi pang'ono pomwe. Ndipo anali kuona chirombocho chitam'zunguniza mkhosi mwache, nam'seketa-seketa, kuyambira ku mutu mpakana ku miyendo. Nthawi yomweyo anangolowa m'nyumbamo, mkazi wache anali kugweratu nafotokoza zonse zimene iye anali kuzifuna. Ndipo atatha kucheza naye, anali kupita ku malo ache amene anali kukhala iye, pobisika ndithu.

Zochitika pa Ndione

37. Chinsatocho chinali kukhala m'madzi amene anachita kusandulika. Ndipo madziwo ndi a mizimu kufikira leroli. Ndipo ngati munthu angapiteko nthawi yakummawa, aona zinsaru zakuda mapesa, mapesa ali phe phe phe pa mphepete pa madziwo. Koma amene wabwera nazo wosam'dziwa bwino. Anali kupeza nkhunda ziri bii, kumwa madzi koma

zamitundu-mitundu. Apo anthu anali kudziwa bwino kuti malowo ali akulu ndithu.

38. Ndipo munthu wofuna kadzawedza nsomba pa Ndione anali kufika pafupi kuti apatsidwe nsombayo. Ndipo ataponya ng'ambo yacheyo yoyamba, anali kumutsa chinsomba chache chachikulu bwino kotero kuti iye sanali kutha kuchinyamula. Ndipo atafuna kuti aponyenso ng'ambo, anali kulephera, osapha ndi imodzi yomwe, nati, "Takupatsa kale nsomba yako yaikulu." Ndipo atatero mmawa ngati apitanso kuti akawedzenso yina, lero kapena tsiku lachiwiri, anali kuona zobvuta chifukwa sanali kupatsidwa nsomba, ai, koma kawiri kawiri anali kupatsidwa mutu wa mwana wa munthu. Ataona zodabwitsazo, anali kusiya mbedza m'madzi, nathawako. Ndipo munthu woteroyo sanali kutha kunena kanthu. Zimenezi ziri kuoneka mpakana pa masiku ano. Nsomba ndi zambiri m'madzimo koma ndi za Mbona, chifukwa madzi ali patali ndi dziwelo. Ndipo thamandalo silimaphwa ndi pang'ono pomwe.

Cifikire cha azungu

39. Pamene azungu anayamba kubwera, anamva bwino za ku Khulubvi, ndipo kufikira leroli malowo ngobvuta kwambiri. Kuyambira leroli Mbona ali kulirabe nsembe zache za ku Khulubvi. Koma ziri kulephereka.

40. Mfumu Lundu anamwalira ku Khulubvi asapondeko ndi pang'ono pomwe. Anthu amene anali kupita kukatsira nsembe ya Mbona anali atsabwira ache a Lundu, amene anali ndi mifunda ya Abanda okha. Awa ndiwo amene anali kuloledwa kuti akapereke nsembe yache ya Mbona. 'Ngakhale mfumu Lundu anamwalira, Mbona anali kuitanitsa nsembe yache. Ndipo ali kuti Lundu ayenera kuti akamangitse nyumba ndi kupereka mkazi wache. Izi zinayamba kusiidwa pamene azungu anayamba kuchuluka kuno ku Malawi.

41. Ndipo pamene makolo onse anatha kufa, zinthu zinayamba kuiwalika. Koma masiku onsewo Mbona anali kukumbukira miyambo yonse. Ndipo ana onse amene anali kutumidwa ndi Lundu, anatha kukwezedwa m'mipando yapamwamba.

ENGLISH VERSION

Where Mbona Was Born

1. Mbona's fame was known far and wide over here in Malawi. He was male and born of a human being. He was not born at Kaphirintiwa but in the Portuguese territory; his original home was in Mozambique.[1] When he had grown up, he wanted to marry, but in his own country he could not find a woman whom he liked. That is why he first came

to these parts[2] and why he went on from here to the hill called Kaphirintiwa.

Mbona Married at Lundu's

2. He went to Kaphirintiwa, that lovely country of the Mang'anja people,
but when he got there, he was like a stranger to them. It is said, though,
that, many years earlier, his mother was born there, in Kabvina's village.
He was therefore not a real stranger, but their sister's son, since it is
also said that he had an uncle there.

3. When Mbona had found a suitable partner, he informed Chief Lundu,
whose maternal nephew he was, and the woman was given to him. Lundu
said to him, "We give you this woman and we allow you to take her home
with you!"[3] Mbona thereupon took her to his village in Portuguese territory, where they raised a fine family. By so doing he established the
practice of girls moving to their husband's village. Mbona did not pay
Lundu anything; he was given the woman without cost or charge.[4]

Mbona Leaves Mozambique for Lundu's Village

4. Mbona's personality and doings, however, gave rise to a great many
brawls in his home village.[5] Each time this happened he and his wife
took refuge in a cave, but when he realized that the situation was going
from bad to worse, he decided to return to his wife's natal village, and
thus the couple went back to Kaphirintiwa.

5. Chief Lundu was pleased to see them again and asked them what
had happened. Mbona thereupon told him all about the hostilities they
had met with, and Lundu gave him a place of his own where he could
stay with his wife. Mbona and Lundu thus lived in the same place.

Drought and Rain Dance at Lundu's: Failure of the Elders

6. After a few years there occurred a serious famine in those parts
because not a single shower had fallen. Lundu told his subjects and
kinsmen to organize a rain ceremony. All of the elders and some other
people as well were notified of the coming event. Word was spread that
it was to take place on a Sunday,[6] and a large crowd turned out to witness this ceremony in honor of the spirits. The big drums were brought
out and taken to the dancing place under a tree so large that all of those
present could find a place in its shade.

7. Each of the elders took his turn in the dance and in leading the rain
songs, while the audience chanted the responses and the drums were
beaten. When the first of them had completed his whirling movements
in the midst of the gathering without any rain falling, however, people
began to express their disappointment. Acknowledging failure, the elder
now told number 2 to move in and dance, but he too met with failure.

Both had to withdraw in shame because in the past, whenever a rain ceremony was being held, they used to end up dancing in mud.[7] Then a third person tried, but much to his dismay, he was not successful either and had to make a shameful exit.

8. The other elders who had been invited now felt quite uneasy, and the crowd shouted with one voice, "Since there is no water at all, what are we to drink? There is nothing to eat either. Even our libations are no longer accepted!" The elders thereupon began questioning each other whether there might possibly be someone else who could enter the dancing ground. The answer was, "There is no one except this youngster[8] sitting here!" They said, however, "Let him come so that he too may try his luck at this ceremony!"

Mbona Makes the Rains Come

9. Having gone to his hut, Mbona came back carrying two spears,[9] a knife, and an axe, and chanting a rain song to the throbbing of the drums. The very moment he started dancing and pointing his spear to the sky, there was a flash of lightning followed by a terrific thunder clap; and when he repeated that movement, torrential rains began to fall.

Conflict

10. When this happened, everyone began to exclaim in surprise, "What kind of person is this?" But the elders who had danced first were jealous of him and said to the bystanders, "This man cannot make the rains fall at all. The ones who caused them to fall are we who danced before him. Allow us therefore to move once more into the dancing ground!" Entering it, they danced with all their might, but to no avail, for not a drop of rain fell, and when all had taken their turn, they knew that their case was hopeless.

11. Mbona too was ordered a second time to the dancing ground to see if the rains would fall again, but the moment he made his way to the center pointing his stick at different parts of the sky, there was a tremendous downpour. The elders now became possessed of a frightful jealousy, asking him, "Little baby that you are, where did you get those powers from?" From then onward they looked for a way to kill him because they were afraid that he would get the population on his side. The rains, however, did not stop. They continued throughout the season because his libation had been accepted.[10]

Mbona's Flight

12. Mbona knew that the elders intended to kill him, for some people who sympathized with him had told him about it. He and his wife therefore thought of going back to his parents' village, where he was born,

and they decided to leave by night. When darkness had fallen, they set out on their journey carrying a little food in a covered basket.[11] Mbona also took his utensils,[12] for he never left those behind, wherever he had been staying.

13. Seeing that their enemy had escaped, the elders swore that they would pursue him until he gave up. Thus it was that they began giving chase, their mind set on killing him the moment he would be caught. They hastened on their way, but success was denied them as they failed to find him anywhere near. In their astonishment they exclaimed, "We keep telling ourselves that we shall come upon him before long, but how can this man travel so fast?" In reality, however, Mbona and his wife were not at all in a hurry. They were walking at a normal pace, but since those chasing them had to run themselves into a sweat trying to find them, they became convinced that he was a kind of ghost.

14. Wherever Mbona set foot, the soil would never dry up, nor would his footprint ever be deleted. On the contrary, even if he trod there only once, a clear path would appear, and not a blade of grass would sprout where he had been walking.[13] Having reached Nsanje District, he knew that he would be home shortly. His enemies on their part were keeping up their pursuit, but despite this Mbona told his wife to take a short rest on a rock.

Mbona Is Captured

15. While they were thus resting, his enemies appeared on the scene, but Mbona had no intention whatever either of fighting or fleeing. He just looked them over, and when they grabbed him in order to kill him, he stopped them short, saying, "If you want to kill me, I submit, since otherwise I would have run away. Listen therefore to what I am going to say. I do not wish to be killed at this spot. Instead, take me to the hill you can see in the distance, close by my home. Furthermore, don't kill me in haste, but wait until you have found a small blade of *nansongole* grass,[14] which you must tie around my neck if you are to kill me properly." Only when he had finished speaking did they carry him off on their shoulders.

Mbona's Death

16. Having reached the place he had pointed out, they put him down, fetched the type of grass he had mentioned, tied it around his neck, and cut his throat with a knife.[15] The blood which gushed from the wound immediately turned into water, and the pool which it formed was given the name Ndione. Following this, they took his head to a forest patch, where they buried it, and when everything was finished they cheerfully set out on their return journey.

Their Return Journey

17. Seeing that they had accomplished everything, they said, "Since that man is now dead, let us go home!" On their way home, however, many of the elders died of a mysterious disease. In the end only four survived together with Chief Lundu.[16] Even Mbona's wife did not survive her husband for long.

18. When they were still chasing Mbona, Lundu had found no time to pay attention to the soils of the country he was traveling through, but on his way back his eye was caught by a type which looked good to him, and he exclaimed, "My, this is fertile country indeed!" Halting in the middle of the Mbewe area, he declared, "This is the place where I am going to build my village," and he continued on his way.

19. Back home he found all the newly planted crops scorched by the sun and people who were complaining bitterly. He asked, "What are we to do?" They made one libation after another, but to no avail. Not a few people said, longing for Mbona, "Why did you kill that man? When he was still alive, there was no lack of rain!"

Lundu Flees to Mbewe

20. Listening to the reproaches of his people, Lundu lost his confidence, and when night had fallen, he left secretly for Mbewe, where he had found a place for his village. No one accompanied him on this journey except his wife. They left by night, and taking enough food with them, they retraced the footsteps of their kinsman who had been killed. They rested from time to time, for this was a journey of their own choice and not a flight from some war.[17] Coming to the place he had discovered on his previous journey, he found that it was suitable and that no one else lived there. He therefore said to his wife, "This is the place where I want to live!" Thereupon they put down their belongings and made an offering to the spirits at the base of a tree so that the place might favor them.

21. He built a house with walls made of poles, because there were many wild animals living in that forest.[18] Thus it was that Lundu established himself at Mbewe. He worked his land, planting the same crops he had planted at Kaphirintiwa, and food was not lacking. After a year, or maybe after one wet season, he announced to his wife that he intended to return to his former village to bring his kinsfolk back with him. Having arranged everything with his wife, he set out for his homeland Kaphirintiwa with the words, "You my wife, stay behind. I shall be back in a month."

Lundu Moves His Kinsmen from Kaphirintiwa

22. When Lundu arrived back at Kaphirintiwa, his relatives bade him welcome, and he began telling them of the marvels of Mbewe. "My kins-

men," so he said, "I have come here to take you with me. We shall all leave to make our home at that place. There is no other ruler there but me!" He stayed on until they were ready to move, and when they had packed their belongings, Lundu made an offering to the spirits so that his sisters' children might arrive safely in his company. He then ceded the chieftaincy to some maternal kinsmen and left.

23. While they were still on their way, he told one of his relatives by the name of Kabvina[19] to stay behind and establish his own place, which meant that he had granted him a chiefdom; and he also let him have a few of his relatives. Having traveled some distance again, he told another relative, whose name was Kaphwiti, to stay behind as a chief near Selemani in Portuguese territory.[20] Kaphwiti and Kabvina became big chiefs in those parts, and their titles have survived to this day. The others continued their journey until they arrived at Mbewe.

Upon His Arrival at Mbewe, Lundu Makes a Sacrifice

24. After their arrival, Lundu took the flour which was left over from their journey and entered a thicket, where he made an offering so that his dependents might prosper in their new settlement. This done, he showed them around the place, saying, "See, this whole place is mine. There is no greater ruler here than I. From the country of the Portuguese to the Shire highlands all this land is mine!"[21]

25. He then took some of his kinsmen to the country of the Portuguese, where he gave them chieftainships, but since the Zambezi River formed the border of his country, he did not cross over to the south bank. Lundu, far from being a selfish man, wanted all men of his lineage to be chiefs. His dependents grew numerous. They lived a happy life at Mbewe, and they often brewed millet beer of which they were very fond.

Mbona Wants His Own Cult

26. When Mbona saw that Lundu and his kinsmen had retraced his own footsteps and were now living nearby, he wanted them to acknowledge him. He therefore took possession of someone at Khulubvi, saying, "I want Lundu to build a hut for me and afterward find me a wife. Let him not tarry, for I want this without delay!" Early next morning messengers were already on their way to Mbewe to relay everything Mbona wanted from Lundu. Lundu thereupon sent some of his younger kinsmen to Khulubvi to see to the construction of the hut. They did as they were told, and a solid hut was built.

27. There was a rule in connection with that hut — which always had to be round — that while they were making its roof, it had to rest on the head of a chief. Lundu therefore ordered Tengani to go there and have

the hut built upon his head.[22] This having been arranged, they built a good and solid hut.

28. When the hut had been covered with dark blue cloth[23] according to his own instructions, Mbona also ordered the elders to find him a wife. "Since I do not want to live alone like a man shunned by women,[24] I want Lundu to provide me with a wife, the way he did when I was still among the living. You shall not take one of Lundu's slaves to be my wife, for I am not going to allow that. Nor shall you take a young maiden or a woman still capable of childbearing. Instead, bring an elderly person, who no longer lies with men, and who is born free besides."

29. Upon their arrival at Mbewe from the "Kaphirintiwa of the south,"[25] they went to Lundu with the message, "Hail, Lundu, our father! Mbona's house at Khulubvi is finished, and he now wants a wife." They then went on to explain everything Mbona had said. Lundu thereupon fetched one of his sisters[26] and said, "Take this one here and depart with her!" Following this, Mbona's wife made the journey on a litter screened off from public view. Whenever the bearers saw a tree that had fallen across the track, they had to go around it, for it they tried to jump over it, Mbona's wife might be exposed to view.[27] Should such a thing happen, Mbona would take possession of someone at Khulubvi, saying, "Let that woman return to her home, for she has been exposed!"

30. Hence, whenever they came across a branch or even a stalk, they avoided it and went around it. At nightfall they looked for a place where the woman could be bedded down decently. On the day of her arrival, when she was approaching Khulubvi, Mbona, knowing that this would be the day, took possession of a person, who then exclaimed, "This is a fine woman indeed. I want her to live at Khulubvi!"

Rules Regarding Mbona's Wife

31. When she had arrived at Khulubvi, people paid her much respect, for anyone who failed to show respect to Mbona's wife would be in great trouble. Nor did Mbona allow people to speak evil of her. After they had come with her, a goat was killed to provide special relish for her; and when they took her to her hut, there was ululating and dancing. Women strewed handfuls of flour on the heads of their companions,[28] and she was installed amid great rejoicing.

32. The Chikunda people were not allowed to attend the libations at Mbona's shrine. If someone had that temerity, he would get sick and die after a while Even nowadays ordinary persons may not see Mbona's shrine. If they do so nevertheless, they will die soon after, for it is a dangerous place. When they were having a meeting, only Mang'anja were bidden to it, and the Chikunda were all kept away.[29]

The Khulubvi Shrine

33. Mbona had ordained, "Let no one come to see my wife except elderly widows. Only those may visit her!" Despite this, she still attracted many visitors. Little girls, too, were allowed to see her, and there would always be baboons coming to her hut to entertain her.[30] The headman of the village saw to it that decent food would be prepared for Mbona's wife, which the little girls then carried to her. She had no lack of drinking water either, for this was brought by the same girls and kept in small jars which stood lined up in a neat row.[31] There were also some very old ladies around to keep her company.

34. If she wanted anything, she did not have to ask, for Mbona would take possession of some villager to let it be known what it was that his wife wanted, and he would say, "Let it be found quickly!" If, for instance, she wanted a sack of rice, rice would be brought without fail. Apart from this, Mbona did not want his wife to do any kind of work such as drawing water, hoeing, or cooking. He refused to let his wife do any of these chores, which is why the first of their line was called Salima, meaning someone who does not perform menial tasks. She ate without having to work for it.

Mbona Spends the Night with Salima

35. When darkness had fallen, the great one himself would come to visit his wife. Often he would make her sleep very deeply lest she wake up and flee for fear. Having entered her hut, he would lick her whole body, making soft sibilant sounds until he had finished.[32] Meanwhile he would tell her many things in her dreams. After he had gone, she just would wake up realizing that her husband had been there, and she would remember everything he had made her dream about.[33]

36. Sometimes, though, he would wake her up when she was asleep, and she would be lying there with open eyes. She would see a large python slipping into the hut, but realizing that it was her husband, she did not experience the slightest fear.[34] She would feel the animal coiling itself around her neck and licking her everywhere, from her head down to her legs. The moment he entered, she would fall into a trance, and he would tell her everything he wanted. His visit over, he would return to his own place, which was well hidden.

Events at Ndione

37. That python lived in the pool, which was formed when Mbona's blood turned into water and which to this day is a place of the spirits.[35] If anyone goes there at daybreak, he will find lengths of black cloth spread

out along its banks, one after another, but it remains a mystery who puts them there. People have also seen large flocks of doves of various kinds drinking there, which made them aware that this was a holy place.[36]

38. If a man wanted to go fishing at Ndione, he could go near the pool to get his fish. The first time he threw his lure, he would land a fish so big that he could not carry it by himself, but if he wanted to try a second time, he would catch anything at all, but Mbona would say to him, "I have already given you a big fish!" If after that kind of incident the same person would come back either that morning or the next, he would not catch a single fish. Instead, as often happened, he would land the head of a child.[37] Having glanced at the dreadful thing, he would leave his hook in the pool and run, but he would be unable to tell his story. Things like this happen to this day. There are many fish in that pool, but they belong to Mbona. The water in the pool never diminishes, despite the fact that there is no stream nearby.

The Arrival of the Whites

39. When the Europeans came, they heard much about Khulubvi, and there have been problems ever since. To this day Mbona cries for a sacrifice at Khulubvi, but nothing is done.

40. Chief Lundu died, having never even set foot in Khulubvi.[38] Those who went there to sacrifice were his ritual friends, all of them members of the Banda clan.[39] Even after Lundu's death Mbona kept demanding that sacrifices be made and that Lundu's successor provide him with a house and a wife. All this gradually stopped when the Europeans became too numerous in this country.

41. When the ancestors were still alive, they always remembered to worship Mbona, but when they had all died, things began to be forgotten. Lundu's underlings — those sent by him to serve at the shrine — were all raised to the rank of chief.

TEXT III / B

Che Chapalapala (1967)

THIS TEXT was recorded on August 13, 1967 at the village of Misomali, Chapananga chiefdom, in the northwestern part of the valley. Misomali is about 35 kilometers by road from the present headquarter of the Lundu paramountcy, and some 125 kilometers from the Mbona shrine. The narrator, Chapalapala, was a middle-aged subsistence farmer, and the person who recorded it, Eustace Chaziya, was a secondary school student from the same village.

The text as it stands clearly represents the Mbona III complex, of which it possesses all the major characteristics. Thus, for instance, Mbona's chief opponent is no longer a sibling or one of the early chiefs but the first king, and his homeland is no longer in the highlands to the north of the Lower Shire Valley but in the valley itself, which formed the geographic center of the kingdom. Again, in contrast with the Mbona I and II complexes, which invariably describe him as a married man, he is here portrayed as a child, or childlike person, to emphasize the inequality of power between him and the king. Also, the cult is not founded and Mbona's divine status not proclaimed by some third party (his kinsmen or the local villagers), but by the martyr himself. Finally, state and cult are no longer separate as in Mbona I and II, but formally integrated in a single organizational system, and the king is held co-responsible for maintaining the shrine and a spirit wife.

After an introductory statement on Mbona's genealogy, the story opens in the usual manner by mentioning the occurrence of a drought, which as we have seen, is a common Mang'anja metaphor for a condition of social unrest. The text implies that the cause of the unrest is the king, who has therefore lost favor with God and has consequently become incapable of performing the rain dance (sec. 3). He is then urged by some of his underlings to let his potential successors try, but they are equally unsuccessful, and the only conclusion the king can draw is that the dynasty is doomed (sec. 5).

When inviting his potential successors to perform the dance, however, Lundu has deliberately excluded his nephew Mbona, whom he considers ineligible, not only because Mbona is considered an illegitimate child since his father is unknown but also because he still sleeps in his mother's hut, though already an adolescent or adult (sec. 16). To understand the king's behavior one has to remember that under Mang'anja customary law a man's sisters and their children are answerable to him, particularly in the matter of marriage, but neither Mbona nor his mother seem willing to conform to customary practice. Both have remained unmarried for no ostensible reason, and to add insult to injury, she has borne a son out of wedlock who in his turn develops a quasi-incestuous relation with her. Yet as we saw in Chapter 6, Mbona's unmarried state is also to be explained as a consequence of the king's unwillingness to provide him with a spouse.

The narrator explains what the king could not have known, namely that Mbona, like Jesus, was born directly of God, without the mediation of a physical father (sec. 1). Instead of the king, Mbona is now blessed by God, something which already becomes clear when as a small boy he astonishes his friends by making clay figurines of goats and cattle come to life (sec. 4). Here then lies the principal contrast between the leading actors in this drama. On the one hand, there is a king who is still the mightiest person in the country but whose ritual power has been taken away from him. On the other hand, there is Mbona, who is considered socially abnormal and who is therefore treated as an outcast, but who — unknown to the world — possesses the very power that the king now lacks.

Since the narrative has made it clear that the king himself would not think of inviting Mbona to perform the rain dance, one or more intermediaries capable of making the king change his mind are needed. These are found in the persons of a few underlings, maybe the king's counselors, who insist that Mbona as a member of the royal lineage should also dance. The king at first strongly resists the suggestion, but eventually he has to give in. He has Mbona's mother (his own sister) called in and tells her to inform her son that he, too, is to perform the rain dance. Now it is Mbona's turn to object: he reminds his mother of the evil treatment he always receives from the family and tells her of his foreboding that their lives will be endangered. Nevertheless, she is able to persuade him by telling him that their own fate is unimportant as long as the present crisis can be resolved and people will again be able to live in peace (sec. 7). Mbona, however, only agrees on the condition that the king issue an order to the effect that at the time of the dance all children between the ages of five and nine must be locked up in their parents' huts, lest they come to grief. The king consents, and the stage is set for the performance (sec. 9).

Mbona, in preparation for the dance, forges two daggers — normally only one dagger is used in the rain rites — and collects such other paraphernalia as are needed for the occasion (sec. 8). When he finally makes his way to the assembly, everybody, including the king, is overawed. At first, nobody even knows who he is (sec. 10). The text conveys at this point the idea of a total transformation of Mbona's person. He is no longer the youth who in the eyes of the king has never grown up and who considers himself an outcast, but a man with an overpowering presence. He has now effectively become the king himself, doing what the king used to do. The success of the dance qualifies Mbona as the only person fit to rule the kingdom, but toward the end of his performance an accident occurs which steers events in an altogether different direction.

It so happened that among the children locked in for the occasion was a little son of the king, who had been born to his junior wife. Eager to see what was going on, the boy apparently managed to unfasten the door, but the moment he stepped outside a lightning bolt split him asunder (sec. 13). The king seems to accept this as an accident for which Mbona bears no responsibility, but the child's mother thinks differently. She holds Mbona guilty of sorcery and exacts a promise from her husband that Mbona will be executed (sec. 14). The king then hires a band of assassins, and the roles are once again reversed: the king is the powerful ruler, and Mbona is the defenseless person who can only escape death by taking flight. But the king's power at this stage no longer derives from his authority as head of state but from his use of naked violence. We have now moved into the second part of the story.

An obvious question to be asked is why children between five and nine years of age should be locked in, and not, say, children who are either younger or older. To understand this, we must first realize that the Mang'anja distinguish three phases in childhood. The youngest children, up to about age five, are still allowed to sleep in their parents' huts. The second group, here identified as children between the age of five and nine (although these figures are just approximations), usually stay with grandmothers or elder sisters. Finally, the third group, consisting of children above age nine, have their own sleeping quarters (*gowero*), where they are strictly separated according to sex. The difference between the middle group and the two others seems to be that the middle group is, sexually speaking, very much betwixt and between. They no longer share the intimacy of their parents' hut, and they have not yet reached the stage where boys and girls are rigorously separated as in the *gowero* system. As a number of anthropological studies have shown, persons who do not clearly belong to one or the other category, or who share in the properties of several categories at once, are often avoided, particularly when a community finds itself in crisis. The rationale behind this avoidance behavior seems to be that such beings are reminiscent of confusion and social chaos.

Applied to our case, we may then interpret Mbona's rain dance as an activity or event designed to move the community out of a state of chaos. This requires that the symbols indicative of such a state be hidden or destroyed, hence the taboo on that particular age group and the killing of its chief representative, the king's own son. That interpretation seems to accord with the fact that the child is not just killed but split asunder, suggesting a radical separation of right and left, male and female, and perhaps also secular and ritual power.

Another question which poses itself is why the major representative of the betwixt and between group is killed by someone who himself is very much part of that group. For Mbona is both a grown-up and a child, a human being and a deity, and son and husband to one and the same woman. The answer is that from the moment Mbona accepts the invitation to perform the rain dance, he sheds all this indeterminacy. He decks himself out and behaves in a way which no longer leaves any doubt about his status as an adult male, a member of the royal lineage, and the king's potential successor. As stated before, the text itself suggests that a radical transformation has taken place, for the audience at first does not recognize Mbona. This first transformation (another is to follow later) takes place the moment he leaves his mother's hut for good. True, he will return once more to collect his belongings, but the confusion of categories is then already over.

This symbol of the hut points to a parallel between Mbona and the king's son. The boy, too, steps outside his mother's hut, but unlike his counterpart he has not yet shed his indeterminacy and thus confronts Mbona with the very condition from which the latter is trying to free himself. Mbona therefore has no other choice, so to speak, but to kill the child. The killing thus carries a double symbolic load, referring respectively to the king and Mbona. For the king, the death of the child may be viewed as symbolic of the cessation of his ritual power. For Mbona, the child's death may be seen as confirming the end of his own indeterminacy. Yet the full meaning of the event cannot be grasped until we have discussed Mbona's own death and its aftermath. Let us therefore once again pick up the thread of the story.

According to custom the chief mourner and his wife are the first to resume sexual relations at the end of the mourning period. Only then are the other kinsmen of the deceased person free to resume their normal lives. The event may, however, be postponed when it is felt that certain conditions have not been met. This is the case, for instance, when the cause of a person's death remains unclear, which is what happens in this version of the Mbona story. Although the king appears satisfied that his child's death was an act of God, his wife does not agree. Hence, when Lundu goes to her to end the mourning period, she refuses to sleep with him unless he promises to have Mbona executed. The king, who at first seems unwilling to comply with her wish, is finally persuaded to hire a band of assassins, who decide to murder Mbona at the first cock's crow.

There is a striking parallel here between Lundu's wife and Mbona's mother. Both have to persuade a man to do something which he does not want to do. Mbona's mother persuades her son to dance and is thus instrumental in ending a drought. Lundu's wife persuades her husband to have Mbona disposed of and thus becomes instrumental in establishing a cult which holds out the promise of breaking the drought cycle once and for all. But the two women also represent a number of contrasts. Mbona's mother very much acts as the unselfish person, who puts the public good before her own, while Lundu's wife seems to do the opposite. Unimpressed by the fact that the drought has ended and a major disaster has been averted, she exacts vengeance for her dead child and refuses to accept that his death is the price she and the king have to pay for the well-being of the population. Yet she does not exactly play the role of an evil genius, for whatever her motives for inciting her husband to have Mbona murdered, the killing heralds the beginning of a new era in which the population will be assured of regular rains. Nor is Mbona unequivocally portrayed as the innocent youngster he appears to be at the beginning of the story. For a brief spell he is also the powerful magician whom people fear because he may be in alliance with the dark forces of the universe. The story is therefore not a simple account of good people versus evil people, with the good ones winning in the end, but a complex narrative in which the good and the bad seem to shade into one another.

The key concepts that come to mind in this story are undeniably separation and purification. Confused categories, as we have seen, have to be unravelled. The king mixes things up: he is both the secular and the ritual head of the country. Apparently, this is too much for one person to do, because he may become a potentate. Therefore, he has to be "unmixed." His ritual power is to be taken away from him and confided to a different agency. Mbona, too, is a mixture. Being predestined to something quite different, he is nevertheless tempted to imitate the king and adopt the trappings of secular power. He, too, has to be "unmixed" and purified so that he can once again be the representative of the Supreme Being. The story ends with the two powers being neatly separated yet cooperating for the good of the whole community. Let us see how this happens.

The killers come to Mbona's hut at the first cock's crow (sec. 16). This is the time when important rituals such as sacrifices to the ancestors are performed, and it seems therefore not altogether accidental that our text emphasizes this time aspect, for Mbona is in a sense a sacrifice to be offered for the good of the population. But the time to perform the sacrificial act has apparently not yet come, for Mbona is able to escape and flee to the southern part of the valley, where his murderers will finally catch up with him.

We can now see how Mbona's flight fits in with the logic of the story, which as we have suggested turns around the ideas of separation and purification. By his flight Mbona physically separates his own ritual power from the center of secular power. He could not be sacrificed in the king's capital, since this would mean once again that the two powers might become mixed up by being part of the same place. It had to be done elsewhere, in a different part of the country, where the ritual organization would be in a position to develop a certain measure of autonomy.

During the final stage of his flight, Mbona performs several miracles (sec. 17), which recall the miracles of his childhood and stress his role as a provider of food and fertility. He also takes leave of his mother, who goes to some part of Mozambique, south of the Zambezi, where she becomes a spirit wife in her own right (sec. 18). The possible historical meaning of this event was discussed in Chapter 6. Here we simply note that the parting of the two brings the process of separating Mbona from his mother to its completion. First, he has left her house, which makes it possible to occupy a house of his own, namely the shrine soon to be built for him. Next he takes leave of her person, which makes it possible for him to marry a woman who is not his mother, namely the spirit wife, who will be given to him when the shrine is finished.

When his enemies finally catch up with him, we encounter the usual themes of the Mbona III complex. Spears and arrows are powerless, and his killers have to use vegetal material to kill him (sec. 20). Then there is the theme of the stream. Usually, it is said that Mbona's blood turns into water, which then forms a stream. Here it is said that his blood fills an already existing stream, suggesting the inverse process of water taking on the color of blood. Last, there is the theme of the pool teeming with fish, which we find mentioned in most versions. What we miss in this text is the decapitation scene, although it is implicit in the story, since the entire third part is devoted to the Khulubvi shrine, where the head lies buried. Had the decapitation episode been made explicit, it would have made an interesting contrast with the killing of Lundu's little son, who in a sense was Mbona's alter ego. For the boy, as we have seen, was killed in such a way that his left and right parts were separated. In the case of Mbona, however the upper and lower parts of the body are separated. In other words, the difference between the two is that between horizontal and vertical cleaving. This brings the sorting-out process to an end, for once left and right, above and below, have been separated, the main categories have been delineated and the new positions have been indicated. What remains to be done is to work out a structure which allows the community once again to function peacefully. This is the subject of the final part of the story.

The third part of the story opens with the announcement that after his death Mbona became a spirit (his second transformation) and that he himself instituted the cult by giving orders to the king through a spirit medium. First, the king had to build a shrine for Mbona (sec. 21), and once this was finished, he had to provide him with a spirit wife (secs. 22–23). This, then, completes the tranformational process, for king and cult have now become fully distinguishable agencies, which are nevertheless bound together in a system of mutual recognition and cooperation. As long as that system was maintained the annual rites were always successful (secs. 24–26).

The narrative suggests quite strongly that the emergence of the cult was a humiliating experience for the king. The roof of the hut had to be built upon his head (sec. 21), and the selection of a spirit wife was apparently also a problematic affair for him (sec. 23). In fact, no Lundu king ever set foot in the shrine grounds, which the dynasty had to avoid, being Mbona's wife-givers and fathers-in-law. This avoidance relationship, combined with the creation of a considerable physical distance between the secular and the ritual centers of the kingdom, made it possible for the Lundus to continue operating for several centuries afterward.

I am in possession of a summary of a strikingly similar text, recorded on my behalf by Mr. E. C. Mandala at an interview with Chief Stonkin Tengani on August 23, 1973. The fact that two versions of this text have been recorded both in the north and the south of the valley suggests that it may have enjoyed popularity. The main difference between the two texts is that in the version recorded by Mandala all people had to remain inside their huts for the duration of the dance and the rains resulting from it, which lasted several days. At this time Lundu stayed with his senior wife. His junior wife, however, who resented this, told her little son to go outside and call his father over to her hut. The boy refused at first, but when his mother kept insisting, he obeyed. The moment he was out in the open, he was struck by lightning and killed. The same moment the rain ceased to fall, and people were once again free to leave their huts. Despite the fact that Lundu's junior wife herself causes the death of her son, she manages to convince the king that it was Mbona's fault. The story then unfolds in the same manner as its counterpart.

MANG'ANJA VERSION

1. Mbona ndi mdzukulu wache wa mfumu Lundu Mankhokwe, mwana wa mfumukazi, mlongo wache wa mfumu Lundu'yo. Koma mfumu Lundu sanasamale Mbona ngati mdzukulu wache weniweni chifukwa Mbonayu analibe bambo wache: anali kuchulidwa mwana wa chigololo. Iye anangobadwa popanda bambo wache monga muja anabadwira Ambuye Yesu.

2. Ndiye kuti kale mvula ikabvuta, mfumu Lundu Mankhokwe anali kusonkhanitsa ana ache onse ndi anthu ache kuti adzaimbitse ng'oma zopempha mvula; iye mwini anali kubvina. Ng'oma yache yaikulu inali kuchulidwa dzina lache kamango. Kabvinidwe kache ka mfumu kanali kolumpha-lumpha ndi kutosa-tosa ku mphepo zinai. Pa masiku amenewo mzimu wa Mulungu unali mwa iye, mfumu Lundu. Ndiye chifukwa chache kanthu kali konse kakabvuta m'dziko, kaya ndi mvula, Lundu anali kutsira nsembe kwa Mulungu wao, mlengi wa zonse.

3. Chaka china, nthawi imeneyo Mbona anali mnyamata, kunadza chilala chosaneneka ndi choopsya kwambiri. Ndiye anthu adadza ndi kudandaulira mfumu Lundu, kuti, "Chonde, chonde, mfumu, itanitsani anthu anu onse kuti pamodzi ndi inu adzatsire nsembe ya mvula monga tidazolowera chaka chiri chonse mvula ikabvuta." Mfumu idamva madandaulo a anthu ache, nayamba kuitanitsa onse ndi kusonkhanitsa ng'oma za kamango. Ndipo mfumu Lundu anayesera kubvina monga adazolowera chaka chiri chonse mvula ikabvuta. Anayamba kubvina ndi kupita chakutsogolo, chakumbuyo ndi chamlenga-lenga. Anayesera'nso kutosa-tosa ku mphepo zinai, koma Mulungu sadamumve. Chifukwa mzimu wa Mulungu unali kutali ndi mfumu Lundu Mankhokwe.

4. Mbona anali kuchita zinthu zodabwitsa kwambiri pa ubwana wache. Akapita kukasewera ku madzi anali kuomba dothe ndi kuyerekeza mbuzi kaya ng'ombe pa maso pa anzache onse. Ndipo iye akati, "Ndifuna kuti ichi chisanduke mbuzi kapena ng'ombe," nthawi yomweyo chinali kusandukadi chomwe akachifuna ndipo chinali kuyenda. Anzache anali kudabwa kwambiri ndi zomwe mnzao anali kupangazo, ndipo pobwerera ku mudzi anali kuuza makolo ao, namati, "Haa, zikupanga mnzathuzi ndi zosasimbika. Akati kuti mbuzi kapena ng'ombe ibwere, inali kubweradi kuchokera ku zinthu zimene anali kuzipanga ndi manja ache."

5. Nsembe ija itakanizika chonchi, anzache aja a mfumu Lundu ana-

muuza kuti, "Mfumu, apa tikuona kuti mzimu wa Mulungu wathu wa-thawa mwa inu. Koma ife tikudziwa kuti mzimu womwewo watsika mwa mmodzi mwa adzukulu anu. Choncho uzani adzukulu anu onse kuti ayambe kubvina, mmodzi-mmodzi, kuti tione amene ali ndi mzimu wa Mulungu wathu." Choncho mfumu ija inasonkhanitsa adzukulu ache onse amene anali kuwakhulupirira kuti, ngati iye amwalira, mmodzi mwa iwo adzakhale mfumu pa malo pache. Choncho adzukulu onse amene anali kuwakhulupirira anabwera ndi kubvina, koma sipanaoneke kan-thu kali konse. Lundu anatembenukira mafumu ang'ono aja, nati, "Ma-fumu ndi anthu nonse amene mwasonkhana pano, mwaona nokha kuti palibe ndi mmodzi yemwe mwa adzukulu angawa amene ali ndi mzimu wa Mulungu, choncho, kuti palibe amene angalowe ufumu wanga ine nditafa. Onse anabvina, koma palibe wapambana."

6. Koma mafumu onse anadziwa bwino lomwe kuti Mbona anali mwana wa Lundu, ngakhale iye analibe bambo wache. Pa nthawi imeneyo ana onse obadwa m'chigololo, angakhale anali adzukulu ache a mfumu, sanali kuloledwa kulowa ufumu wa amalume ao. Choncho mfumu Lun-du atamva kuti Mbona ayenera kubvina, anati, "Kodi mukuti Mbona anayenera kubvina? Kodi abvina ndi njira yanji popeza kuti iye ndi chi-tsiru chopanda nchito, ndipo'nso ndi mwana wa chigololo amene sa-ngalowe ufumu?" Koma ena anati, "Ai, mfumu, Mbona ayenera kubvina." Choncho mfumu inabvomereza kuti Mbona abvine. Choncho anaitana mai wache wa Mbona, anati, "Mai, mwana wanu ndiye wotsiriza kuti abvine m'bwalomo. Choncho mukamuuze kuti abwere kuti adzabvine kuno."

7. Mai uja unafika kwa mwana wache Mbona, namuuza kuti abvine. Chon-cho Mbona anati, "Amai, muti ndikabvine? Nanga ine sindine chitsirizira kwathunthu?" Ndipo mai wache anati, "Inde ndiwe chitsirizira; ndiye chifukwa chache ukukabvina potsirizira." Apo Mbona anati, "Koma ine ndiri kuopa kwambiri, chifukwa ndikabvina padzaoneka zinthu zoopsa kwambiri ndipo moyo wanga udzamwazika pamodzi ndi wanu, mai." Koma mai wacheyo anati, "Palibe kanthu mwana wanga, ngakhale ife tione zobvuta, koma anthu amene ati adzatsaleo adzapeza mtendere."

8. Mbona anati, "Chabwino, ndakumverani, Ndiye tsopano tengani nsatsi, muziphike ndi kuzisungunula kuti mupange mafuta, ndipo mafutao muwaike m'nsupa bwino." Iye Mbona anasula mipeni iwiri, yakuthwa konse-konse, yochedwa kandranga. Ndipo anapanga'nso chinthu cho-khala ngati lamba wamkulu wam'chuno. Anatenga mafuta aja napaka-paka nao mipeni ija ndipo yonse inakhala ili noni-noni, mafuta okha ndithu.

9. Iye Mbona asanabvine anati kwa mfumu Lundu, "Inu mfumu, tumi-zani mthenga ndi kuuza anthu anu onse kuti ana onse a zaka zisanu,

kapena zisanu ndi ziwiri, kapena zisanu ndi zitatu, kapena zisanu ndi zinai, atsekeredwe m'manyumba." Ndipo mfumu Lundu anatumiza asilikari ache pa dziko lonse ndi kudziwitsa anthu onse kuti ana a zaka zisanu kapena zisanu ndi zinai atserekedwe m'manyumba; asatuluke konse panja. Ngati aturuka adzaona zoopsya ndithu. Asilikari aja atatha nchito yao, anabwerera, nati kwa mfumu, "Tadziwitsa banja liri lonse lokhala m'dziko muno kuti asamale ana ao a zaka zisanu kapena zisanu ndi zitatu."

10. Mbona tsopano anatumiza mthenga kwa anthu aja anasonkhana kuti iye akubwera. Choncho anayenera kuyambiratu kuimba ng'oma za kamango. Itayamba kulira ng'oma, Mbona anaturukira ndipo anali kuyenda modabwitsa kwambiri kotero kuti anthu ena ambiri anachita mantha pomuona. Mafumu onse, ngakhale mfumu Lundu yemwe, anachita mantha poona zinthu zimene Mbona anazibvala m'chiuno mwache ndi nsupa imene inali m'manja mwache. Zoona, zinthu zimene Mbona anali nazo zinali zochititsa mantha ndithu. Anthu ena anayamba kufunsana, nati, "Kodi uyu ndani? Ameneyu ndani? Abale anzanganu tandiuzani zonse."

11. Anthu onse anatsimikiza kuti anali Mbona pomuona ali m'bwalo. Pofika m'bwalo muja anazolomitsa mutu wache, nagwira ku maso kwache. Atatero, anaweramuka, nati kwa mafumu, makamaka kwa mfumu Lundu, "Kodi mfumu, mwadziwitsa banja liri lonse kuti asamale ana ao a zaka zisanu mpaka zisanu ndi zinai kuti atsekeredwe m'manyumba mwao?" Ndipo mfumu anati, "Inde, onse atsekeredwa." Ndipo Mbona anati, "Zikomo kwambiri ngati mwachita zimenezo."

12. Ndipo kamango anayamba kulira ndipo naye'nso ndi kubvina kutsatira monga momwe muja mfumu Lundu anali kubvinira. Anali kulumpha chakutsogolo, chambuyo, chamlenga-lenga, natsira momwe muja amalume anali kuchita. Anasolola kandranga wache, nayamba kusonya ku mmawa, ndipo, taonani!, nthawi yomweyo mphezi inang'anima. Atasonyeza'nso chakumadzulo, chimphezi china'nso choopsya chinagunda. Ndiyetu azimai anatulutsa nthungululu, azibambo akugubuduzuka ndi mantha, ndipo anali kukondwera podziwa kuti mzimu wa Mulungu wao unachoka mwa Lundu ndi kulowa mwa mdzukulu wache mmodzi, Mbona. Ndipo Mbona atatulutsa'nso kandranga wache, chimphepo cha mvula yoopsya chinabwera.

13. Nthungululu zinaluluta koopsya ndithu ndipo ana aja anatsekeredwa sanapeze bwino pakumva nthungululuzo. Anangofuna ataona kabvinidwe ka Mbona. Koma iye mwini sanafune kuti ana abwere ndi kudzaona kabvinidwe kache. Koma iye Mbona sanasiye kusolola chimpenl chache chija ndi kusonyeza ku madzulo ndipo nthawi yonseyi chimvula ndi zing'ani-ng'ani zinali kubwera. Pa nthawi imeneyo mwana wache wa

Lundu wochokera m'nyumba ya mkazi wache wamng'ono, anatuluka kuti aone. Mai'ne! Cing'ani-ng'ani chinam'ng'amba, ndipo mwana uja anafera pompo. Ndipo anthu ataona mmene mwana anamwalirira anachita mantha akulu ndithu. Koma chimvula chamaere chinadza m'dziko lonse la mfumu Lundu.

14. Mbona atatha kubvina anapita kwao. Ndipo mfumu Lundu limodzi ndi mafumu ena onse ang'ono anasonkhana ku nyumba kwache kuti akaike maliro a mwana uja. Atatha kuika maliro mfumu Lundu anapita ku nyumba ya mkazi wache wamng'ono kuti akalonde maliro. Koma mkazi uja anati, "Ai, ine ndiye toto, sindifuna. Sindifuna kuti ine ndikhale nanu malo amodzi, chifukwa mdzukulu wanu wapha mwana wanga dala. Pa chifukwa chimenechi ndifuna kuti ukwati wathu uthe, ndipo ngati simufuna kuti uthe, muyenera kupha Mbona, chifukwa sindifuna'nso kuti ndimuone ndi maso anga. Ine toto." Apo mfumu Lundu anaziganiza, nati atha kutumiza anthu kuti akaphe Mbona. Anthuwa anabvomereza za kuti aphe Mbona. Choncho anthu aja anasonkhana ku nyumba ya mfumu, namvana kuti akam'phe Mbona tambala woyamba atangolira.

15. Muja mkazi wamng'ono wa Lundu anali kuuza mwamuna wache za chiwembuzi, Mbona anali kuzimva nthawi yomweyo. Ndipo anauza amai ache kuti, "Amai, sindinali kukuuzani kuti pambuyo pa kubvina kwanga tidzaona mabvuto akulu? Choncho pambuyo panga, madzulo ano, padzafika amaliongo ofuna kundipha ine ndi inu. Koma amai, musadandaule. Konzani katundu ndi phoso kuti amaliongo, akadzafika pa khomo, ife tidzatuluke ndi kuthawa." Amai ache anatenga khambwe (dengu) nalongeza zonse zofunika pa ulendowo. Mbona anakonzeratu: anatenga uta wache ndi mibvi kudza'nso nthungo.

16. Tambala woyamba atangolira, amaliongo aja anafika, nazungulira nyumba yonse ya amai ache a Mbona popeza kuti, ngakhale Mbona anali wa msinkhu waukulu, anali kugonabe ndi amai ache, m'nyumba imodzi. Mbona atangotsekula chitseko, anaona amaliongo aja atazungulira nyumba ya amai ache, namuuza kuti, "Amai, senzani katundu kuti tidzipita, adani athu afika." Ndipo anayamba kutuluka, koma amaliongo aja sanaone konse anthu awiri aja kutuluka kwao. Potuluka iwo, anapingiza chitseko chija. Ndipo anthu aja, amene ankafuna kugwira Mbona, natsekula chitseko mwamphamvu ndithu, koma sanapezemo munthu aliyense mkatimo. Iwo anati, "Haa, Mbona wathawa pamodzi ndi amai ache." Apo anaganiza zotsatira anthu awiri aja, ndipo anaterodi. Koma kunawatengera nthawi kuti awagwire anthu aja.

17. Mbona anayenda-yenda ndi kufika ku Chididi. Pamenepo analenga munda wa mpunga. Anapita'nso kwa Karonga. Kumeneko analengako khola la nkhunda, ndipo nkhunda zimenezi ziripobe mpaka lero. Anapita'nso ku Nyakalambo. Nyakalambo ndi nkhalango yaikulu kwam-

biri imene ikupezekabe mpakana lero. Mu nkhalango imeneyi muli nyama za mitundu yonse imene ingapezeke m'dziko la pansi pano: muli njoka zosawerengeka ndipo'nso apusi ndiye zinyalala. Akuyenda choncho anafika ku malo ena kumene kuli thanthwe lalikulu. Apo Mbona analatsitsa nthungo ndi mibvi yache pa thanthwepo. Ndipo amai ache anatula pansi khambwe lija, nagwada pansi ndi Mbona yemwe, kuti akumbe chitsime. Ndipo kuti amwe, anagwada pansi, ndipo pamene maondo ache ndi pamene anasiya khambwe ndi zida zache patha kuonekabe mpakana lero lino.

18. Pa thanthwe limeneli ndi pamene Mbona anatsadzikana ndi amai ache. Amai ache analowera ku dziko la Apwitikizi ku malo ochedwa Chitundu. Ndipo anthu akumeneko amatsira nsembe zao ngati pali chilala kapena mabvuto a mtundu uli wonse. Ngati amai ache a Mbona, dzina lache Chitundu, ameta mpala, chaka chimenecho kumakhala chilala choopsya. Ku dzikolo Apwitikizi amati Chitundu, kunena amai ache a Mbona. Koma ku Malawi kuno timati Salima.

19. Mbona atachoka apo anapita ku dziko la Malemia chakumwera kwa Malawi. Anafika'nso ku chimwala chachikulu chochedwa "Mphini za Achipeta." Chimwala chimenecho chinalembedwa mphini za mtundu wa Achipeta. Mphinizi ziripobe mpakana lero lino. Atachoka apo, ndiye anafika m'dziko lija la Malemia.

20. Nthawi yonseyo ndikuti amaliongo ache anali kum'tsatabe. Ndipo Mbona anafika pa mtsinje wochedwa Ndione. Atafika pamenepo anangoona kuti adaniwo anam'gwira, nafuna kuti amlase ndi nthungo ndi mibvi yao. Koma iye anati, "Ngati mufuna kuti mundiphe musandilase ndi nthungo kapena mibvi, koma mukatenge mnjere (chibade cha mizimbe, mphesi za chimanga kapena udzu), ndipo mudzandicheke pa khosi." Anthu aja anakatenga mnjere, ndipo Mbona anati, "Tiyeni pa mtsinje wa Ndione kuti mukandiphe bwino." Anapita naye ku malo aja, ndipo anam'cheka pa khosi ndi mnjere. Ndipo pa khosi pache panatuluka madzi oopsya kwambiri, natsikira mu mtsinje wa Ndione, ndipo mtsinje wonsewo unadzaza ndi magazi ache. Ndipo kumatsirizo a mtsinje umenewo kuli dziwe ndipo mu dziwemo muli nsomba zambiri-mbiri.

21. Ngakhale Mbona anafa, mzimu wache sunafe, ulipobe, ndipo mlauli mmodzi anati, "Abale, mzimu wa mbale wathuwo ukufuna kuti tim'mangire nyumba ku malo ena ochedwa Khulubvi. Ndipo munthu aliyense ayenera kudula bango limodzi-modzi, louma kapena laliwisi." Ndipo anthu onse anachita monga momwe Mbona anafunira. Mfumu Tengani ndi Maere ndiwo anatenga nsichi zoyamba za pa khomo ndi kuziika poyambirira zina zonse zisanaikidwe. Nyumba yache ndi yadzira (yozungulira). Pomanga chindwi anali kuti chindwilo lidzamangidwe pa mutu pa mfumu Lundu Mankhokwe. Anthu onse anasungadi miyambo

yonseyo. Nyumba itatha mthenga unali kupita kwa mfumu Lundu Mankhokwe kuti nyumba tsopano yatha, latsala ndi chindwi kuti lima-
ngidwe. Litatha kumangidwa kulikweza pa nyumbayo.
22. Nyumba itatha, anali kufunabe mnzache woti ndi kum'sangalatsa.
Choncho anali kulankhula mwa alauli kuti anali kufuna mkazi. Alauli
aja anali kutumiza wamthenga, dzina lache Kambalame, amene anali
kupita kwa Tengani ndi kukamuuza kuti Mbona anali kufuna mkazi.
Tengani naye'nso anali kutumiza Kambalame yemweyo kuti apite kwa
Lundu kuti akafune mkazi woti amutumize kwa Mbona, ku Khulubvi.
23. Koma mfumu Lundu anadodoma kwambiri kuti, "Ndidzatani ine kuti
nditenge mkazi wachikalambire ndi kukam'pereka kwa Mbona?" Apo anthu ena anzeru anangoganiza kuti angogwira mkazi woteroyo mwachif-
wamba, ndipo anaterodi. Anatenga chinsaru choyera chachikulu ndithu
nagugudiza mkaziyo, nam'tenga mwaupandu, mpakana anafika naye
kwa Mbona ku Khulubvi. Mbona analandira mkaziyo ndipo anthu anam-
cha mkaziyo dzina loti Salima. Salima akakonda ana ango'ono okha kuti
adzicheza nao. Salima anaguliridwa nsaru za mitundu iwiri: zakuda ndi
zoyera. Thanthauzo la nsaruzo: nsaru yakuda inkathanthauza mvula, kuti
chaka chimenecho anthu apha dzinthu dzambiri. Ndi chaka chautendere.
Nsaru yoyera ithanthauza chilala chamoto-moto. Ngati Salima abvala
nsaru yoyera, chaka chimenecho kuli chinjala choopsya.
24. Ngati mvula ibvuta kwambiri, alauli amayankhula kuti, "Mbona wa-
kwiya kwambiri chifukwa simufuna kum'tsirira nsembe monga munazo-
lowera kale. Tiyeni tikapereke nsembe kwa Mbona." Kambalame ama-
tenga mthenga umenewu ndi kupita nao kwa Tengani, ndipo Tengani
amautumiza'nso kwa Lundu Mankhokwe. Banja liri lonse linali kupereka
dzinthu, monga chimanga, ndi kuchikonola. Atatha kuchikonola, anali
kuchiika mabvuwo, koma osaikamo madzi. Usiku chimvula chinali
kubwera kuti chibviike chimera cha nsembeyo. Mmawa mwache anthu
onse anali kukondwera poona kuti mphale yonse yabviikidwa ndi madzi ochokera kumwamba. Mowa utalusulidwa, anthu onse amakhala
okondwa kwambiri podziwa kuti posachedwapa adzalandira mvula.
25. Mowa utapsya amautenga ndi kupita nao ku Khulubvi kukaupereka
nsembe kwa mulungu wao, Mbona. Wansembe wache anali munthu
wina wochedwa Maere, ndipo iye, popemphera, amkati:

> Cho cho cho!
> Mnjale sukweredwa.
> Masamba a mu msitu,
> akazi sawazinga nkhata;
> akazi sawaumba nkhata!

Atatsira nsembe, anthu amabwerera akuimba nyimbo yao yakuti:

Kamtambo ndiyako ndiyaka!
Kanya mvula nkoti?
kanya mvula ndiyako.

Chilamwa ndiye amaimba nyimbo imeneyi. Pa nthawi imeneyi mvula
inali kugwa mosaneneka pa dziko lonse la Lundu.
26. Potsira nsembe anali kuchula maina a akulu-akulu akale, monga
amachitira akhristu achiRoma, pochula maina, akuti, a anthu oyera. Iwo
amati, "Inu, Mbona, mutipatse mvula, ife ana'nu amene tikusauka
chifukwa chosowa mvula." Iwo anali kuchula maina a anthu amene anafa
kale kuti akawanenere kwa Mbona, mulungu wao. Ndipo pa nthawi imeneyo pankaoneka kuti mvula inali kugwa nthawi yoyenera, ndipo anthu akati adzale mbeu zao, zinali kukula bwino ndithu. Ndipo pa nthawi
yokolola, dzinthu dzinali kuchuluka bwino, ndipo pa dziko lonse panali
mtendere wokha-wokha.

ENGLISH VERSION

1. Mbona was one of King Lundu Mankhokwe's neph-
ews, the son of his elder sister.[1] But Lundu did not really treat him as
his nephew, because Mbona had no known father and was therefore
considered illegitimate. He was born without a father the way the Lord
Jesus was.
2. In days gone by, when the rains were late, Lundu Mankhokwe used
to call upon his entire family and his subjects to hold a rain ceremony
at which he himself would dance. His largest drum was called Kamango.[2]
While dancing, the king would point his dagger and leap in the direction of the four winds. In those days God's spirit[3] dwelt in him, which
is why he used to make offerings to the Creator of all things when his
country was afflicted by a drought or some other calamity.
3. One year, when Mbona was still a youth, there occurred a devastating
drought. Lundu's subjects came to him, saying, "We beseech you, king,
have all your people assembled so that, together with you, they can
make a libation, as has been our custom whenever the rains failed to
come." The king complied with his subjects' request, arranged for an
assembly, and had the rain drums brought out. This done, he set about
dancing the way he used to whenever the rains were late, leaping forward, backward, and upward and pointing his dagger at the four winds.
But God remained unmoved, for his spirit had withdrawn from Lundu
Mankhokwe.
4. Mbona was someone who could perform astonishing feats even as

a child. When he went playing by the riverside, he would make clay figurines resembling goats or cattle in the presence of his friends. The moment he said, "I want this to change into a real goat or cow," the figurine would change into the animal mentioned and begin moving. His companions marveled at Mbona's feats, and back in their village, they would tell their parents, "My, what that friend of ours can do is beyond words. Whenever he says there should be a goat or a cow, that animal appears without fail out of the clay things he makes with his hands."

5. When Lundu's libation had thus been rejected, those close to him said, "Majesty, we can only conclude that God's spirit has withdrawn from you. We do know, though, that the selfsame spirit must now have descended upon one of your nephews. Therefore, order all of them to dance, one after the other, so that we may decide which one now possesses God's spirit." The king thereupon called those of his nephews whom he thought to be likely candidates for succession when he would be dead.[4] All of them came and danced, but not one was successful. Lundu then turned to his underlings with the words, "Chiefs, and all of you gathered here, you have been able to see with your own eyes that none of my nephews is in possession of God's spirit and that therefore none of them will be able to take my place, when I shall be dead; for all have danced, but none was successful."

6. The chiefs, on the other hand, knew quite well that Mbona belonged also to Lundu's house despite the fact that his father had remained unknown. In those days, illegitimate children, even if they were a chief's nephews, were not allowed to succeed their uncle. Therefore, when Lundu heard their request that Mbona should also be given a chance to perform the rain dance, he said, "Are you suggesting that Mbona should have danced, too? How can he possibly, since he is a fool, a good-for-nothing,[5] and a child born of adultery, who can never succeed to the throne?" Yet some of them kept insisting, saying, "With due respect, your majesty, Mbona must dance!" The king thereupon gave in, and having summoned Mbona's mother, he said to her, "Sister, your son shall be the last to dance at our gathering. Tell him therefore to come and perform!"

7. The woman went to her son and told him that he was to dance, but Mbona answered, "Mother, do you really mean that I should dance? Am I not the one whom they always think of last?" To this his mother replied, "You are right; they always think of you last, which is why you will be the last one to dance!" But Mbona said, "I am scared, for when I dance, dreadful things will happen, and they are going to kill both me and you." His mother then said, "That is of no importance, my son. we

may have to suffer, but those remaining behind will live in peace."[6]

8. Thereupon Mbona said, "Very well, I am persuaded. Now fetch some castor beans, cook them, and carefully collect their oil in a medicine gourd."[7] He then forged two daggers of the *kandranga* type,[8] and he also made himself a kind of large waist belt. The oil he used to polish the daggers until they were smooth and shining.

9. Before he began his dance Mbona said to Lundu, "Majesty, tell your subjects to keep all children between the ages of five and nine safely locked up in their mothers' huts." Lundu thereupon sent his guardsmen to the far corners of his kingdom in order to make it known to all that children between the ages of five and nine must be locked up in their huts and that on no condition should they come outside. If they did, the most dreadful things would happen to them. When those guardsmen had carried out the order, they reported back to the king with the words, "We have told every family in the country to take care of its children between the ages of five and nine!"

10. This done, Mbona let it be known to those assembled that he was on his way and that the rain drums should be beaten forthwith. As soon as they began to roar, Mbona strutted out, and the view he presented was so awe-inspiring that many people became terrified. Even the chiefs, including Lundu himself, took fright when they saw the objects tied around his waist and the medicine gourd in his hands. And right they were, for the things Mbona carried on his person were quite fearful. Everywhere people began to ask one another, "Who is this man? Who is he? Please, brethren, tell us!"

11. Everyone had to admit, though, that it was Mbona they saw moving into the dancing ground. Upon reaching the center Mbona made a deep bow, touching his forehead with his hands. Following this, he stood upright and addressed the chiefs, turning to Lundu in particular: "Your majesty," he said, "did you tell everyone to take care that all children between the ages of five and nine be locked up their huts?" The king answered, "Yes, all have been locked up!" To which Mbona replied, "Thank you very much for doing this!"

12. Once again the drum Kamango began to roar, and Mbona started dancing, leaping forward, backward, and upward and performing the rite just like his uncle Lundu used to. But as soon as he drew his dagger, pointing it first to the east—lo and behold!—that same moment lightning flared; and when he pointed it to the west,[9] a terrific flash of lightning hit the earth. Thereupon, the women began their ululations, and even the men rejoiced, though trembling with fear, for they were now certain that God's spirit, after having withdrawn from Lundu, had come to dwell in Mbona, one of his nephews. When Mbona drew his

dagger once more, a storm broke, and rain began to fall in torrents.

13. There were mad ululations, and when the littles ones who had been locked up in their mothers' huts heard these, they grew restless. They longed to see Mbona dance, although he himself had said that he did not want them near. Meanwhile, Mbona continued drawing his dagger, pointing it to the west, and each time thunder and lightning would follow. While all this was going on, one of Lundu's children by his junior wife managed to get out to see what was going on. But alas! a flash of lightning split him asunder, and the child was instantly killed. When people saw in what manner the child had been killed, they were terrified, but abundant rains fell in the whole of Lundu's kingdom.

14. Having finished the dance, Mbona went home, while Lundu stayed behind with all his underlings to bury the dead child. When the mourning period was over, he went to the hut of his junior wife to end the rites, but she would have none of it, saying, "No thank you, I do not want to. I have no desire to sleep with you, because your nephew has killed my child on purpose. Therefore I want a divorce, and if you do not agree, you will have to kill Mbona, for I do not want to set eyes on him again. That's final!" Having pondered this, Lundu replied that he might send others to kill him. Those who showed themselves willing to do this assembled in the king's quarters, and they agreed to strike at the first cock's crow.

15. While Lundu's junior wife was busy inciting her husband, Mbona could hear what she said. He told his mother, "Mother, did I not warn you that we would be in serious danger after my dance? This very evening a gang will come to kill both you and me. Do not be upset, though; pack our belongings as well as some food, so that when they come to our door we shall be ready to flee. His mother took a basket into which she packed everything they might need on their journey. Mbona, too, brought himself in readiness, taking with him his bow and arrows as well as a spear.

16. At the first cock's crow, the assassins drew a cordon around the hut of Mbona's mother, for although Mbona was already a grown-up, he still slept under the same roof as his mother. The moment he opened the door, he saw that their hut had already been surrounded, and he therefore said to his mother, "Mother, lift our luggage onto your head so that we may go; our enemies have arrived!" Thereupon, the two of them left the hut, unnoticed by those who had come to kill them. Once outside, they put the door back and fastened it to its post. Those who were after Mbona now forced their way in, but finding nobody inside, they exclaimed, "My, Mbona and his mother have escaped!" They then

decided to go after the two, and they did so, but it would be some time before they were able to lay hands on them.

17. Mbona traveled continuously until he reached Chididi, where he created a rice field.[10] He then proceeded to Karonga, where he created a coop full of doves, which can be seen there to this day.[11] He also went to Nyakalambo, which is a large forest, still existing, where one finds animals of every kind under the sun — among them countless snakes and monkeys — but all of them harmless.[12] Traveling further, he came to a place marked by a large rock into which he struck his spear and arrows. His mother put down her basket and knelt down together with Mbona to dig a hole in that rock and drink from it.[13] The imprints of their knees and the basket can still be seen there.

18. On that rock, too, Mbona bade farewell to his mother, who went to a place called Chitundu in the country of the Portuguese.[14] People there make offerings whenever there is a drought or some other calamity. The year Mbona's mother, Chitundu, shaves her head, there will be a major drought.[15] In the land of the Portuguese they know Mbona's mother as Chitundu, whereas in Malawi they call her Salima.

19. From there Mbona went to the country of Chief Malemia, south of the hill called Malawi. On his way, he came upon a large rock boulder, which is known as the Chipeta Tatoos, because the tatoos of the Chipeta people have been carved on its surface.[16] From those marks, which are still extant, he went to Malemia's chiefdom.

20. In the meantime his enemies were still following him, and when Mbona found himself near a stream called Ndione, they were finally able to capture him. When they tried to use their spears and arrows against him, he said, "If you really want to kill me, spears and arrows will be useless. Use the rind of sugar cane, a maize stalk or a blade of grass, and cut my throat with that." When they went looking for such an item, Mbona told them, "Let us go to the bank of the Ndione, so that you may kill me properly." They then took him to that place and cut his throat with a blade of grass. An enormous gush of water spurted from his throat into the stream, which came to be filled with blood. Along its lower reaches there is a pool teeming with fish.

21. Although Mbona died in the flesh, his spirit did not die and is still alive. One day a certain medium said, "Brethren, the spirit of our kinsman Mbona wants us to build a hut at a place called Khulubvi. Nobody may come with more than one reed stalk, whether dry or green." All did as Mbona had ordered. Chiefs Tengani and Maere[17] each put in a door post and held it in position until the other posts were put into place. Mbona's hut is circular in shape. The roof had to be made upon the head

of King Lundu Mankhokwe.[18] Everyone followed these rules. When the circular wall of the hut was finished, a message was sent to Lundu to inform him of the progress made and to remind him that the roof still had to be made. When the roof was completed, it would be lifted onto the walls of the hut.

22. When the hut had been built, Mbona wished for a companion to gladden his heart. He made it known through his medium that he wanted a wife. The medium then sent a messenger by the name of Kambalame ("Little Bird") to Chief Tengani, informing him that Mbona wanted a wife. Tengani in his turn sent the man on to Lundu, for it was Lundu's duty to find a woman to live with Mbona at Khulubvi.

23. Lundu, for his part, not knowing what to do, asked, "How can I get an elderly woman to be sent to Mbona?" A few ingenious people then suggested he take one by force, which is what happened.[19] Taking a large piece of white cloth, they threw it over a woman and forced her to go with them to Khulubvi. Mbona approved of her, and people gave her the name Salima. Salima liked to be visited by small children only. They brought her two types of cloth: one black, the other white. This is what those two cloths signified: the black one indicated a year of plenty, in which people would reap an abundant harvest. The white one, however, meant much hunger, and the year Salima dressed in white there would be a serious famine.[20]

24. When the rains are late, the medium says, "Mbona is angry, because you no longer remember to make libations as you did in the past. Come, let us make a libation to Mbona!" Kambalame then takes the message to Tengani, who sends him on to Lundu. Each family gave a bit of grain, such as maize, which they would pound. After pounding it, they would put some of it in potsherds without adding water. At night rain would fall in torrents, soaking the grain and making it sprout.[21] When waking up, people would rejoice, because the potsherds had been filled with water from the sky. When the beer was fermenting, everybody would be at peace, for they knew that the rains would not be long in coming.

25. When it was ready for consumption, the beer would be taken to Khulubvi as an offering to Mbona, their great spirit. His priest, whose name was Maere, would then intone the following hymn:

> Cho, cho, cho!
> The mnjale tree cannot be climbed!
> From the leaves of the sacred forest
> Women do not fashion headpads![22]

On their way back from the ceremony, people would sing the following song:

> This little cloud!
> That little cloud!
> Which of you
> Relieves itself of rain?[23]

The one who led this song was Chilamwa.[24] When it rang out, the whole of Lundu's country would be drenched in rain.

26. When pouring their libations, they would also call out the names of the great ancestors, much as the Roman Catholics do when they invoke the names of their saints. They would say, "Mbona give us rain! We your children are suffering for lack of rain!" They then called out the names of those long dead to intercede for them with their God, Mbona. In those days, rain would always come at the appointed time. When people said it was time to plant, their crops would grow without fail; their harvest would be abundant, and the country knew nothing but peace and prosperity.

A MALAWIAN SYNTHESIS

TEXT IV
J. E. Chakanza (1967)

THE PRESENT TEXT was composed in Chimang'anja in 1967 by a young man, Joseph Chakanza, who was preparing for the Roman Catholic priesthood and who for that purpose had to serve a probational year on one of the mission stations. The one assigned to him was Ngabu, situated in the chiefdom of Ngabu Banda (to be distinguished from his namesake at the shrine), which occupies the entire central part of the Lower Shire Valley. Chakanza formed part of the first generation of Malawian seminarians trained to take a positive view of their country's traditional culture rather than condemning it wholesale, as had been customary. In line with this new attitude, students were encouraged to collect information about traditional religion and to write papers on the subject. The author, a native of the valley, focused on the Mbona cult, which may have seemed to him attractive both from a theological and an ethnohistorical viewpoint. Some thirty years earlier his father had also recorded a version of the Mbona story.[1]

It is particularly against this ethnohistorical background that one has to read the present text. The author tries to separate fact from fiction by comparing different accounts of the same fact or episode and opting for the one that seems the most plausible. He was not the first to use that method. W. H. J. Rangeley, a colonial administrator and an ethnohistorian of considerable local renown, had tried the same method some fourteen years before.[2] The difference between the two is that Rangeley, occupying the position that he did, was able to collect his data from the length and the breadth of the valley and from the most important members of the traditional political establishment, whereas Chakanza had to confine himself largely to the central section of the valley and to the commonalty. Consequently, Rangeley's account contains considerably more information about the relationships between the political and the religious establishments, but the two accounts both contain extensive compilations of Mbona I, II, and III traditions. As noted in the introduction to Part 2 of this book, practically no version of the Mbona story is "pure" in the sense of representing one tradition only at the exclusion of the two others. Virtually all versions are therefore to be regarded as combinations of several traditions. What sets the Rangeley and Chakanza accounts apart is that they are exercises in conscious comparison or attempts at establishing a kind of critical ethnohistory. Neither author thought in terms of Mbona I, II, and III as we have been doing in this book, but it is significant that their comparative exercises have resulted in two accounts with a strikingly balanced representation of the three streams that we have identified. As we have considered Rangeley's Mbona article in the first part of this book, we will now examine Chakanza's.

To begin with, Chakanza's text is in several important respects typical of Mbona I: It names Mbona's father, it expatiates a great deal on the imprints ("boundary markers") Mbona is supposed to have left behind on various rocks, and Mbona's chief adversary is a sibling and not an uncle. As far as Mbona II is concerned, three or four points are to be noted. First, the story begins at a time when Kaphwiti, the reputed founder of the earliest Mang'anja state, is the supreme political authority. Second, Mbona is apparently married to one wife only, which though seemingly trivial is nevertheless characteristic of Mbona II. Third, there is an emphasis on Mbona's metamorphoses during the flight. Finally, there is the theme of the tug-of-war between Mbona and his pursuers. With regard to Mbona III themes, one may point to Lundu's position as Mbona's maternal uncle and wife-giver, the killing being done by hired assassins, the rice miracle, the episode of Mbona parting with his wife, and the powerlessness of iron, which, although it appears also in Mbona II, receives more emphasis in Mbona III. Superficially, one might be tempted to consider Chakanza's to be a Mbona III text, but it lacks the "bite" of Mbona III in that it omits the entire childhood symbolism and virtually all references to the theophanous episode. Mbona's murderers return home unharmed, as they do in streams I and II, and Mbona does not reveal himself in a storm or through a medium to establish a cult. The question to be asked is whether this is to be regarded as something accidental or as something rather more structural. The latter seems to be the case.

The chiefdom of Ngabu Banda, where Chakanza collected his information, is a major cotton-growing area which has, especially since the flooding of the Dinde Marsh in the late 1930s, attracted thousands of immigrants from the overpopulated Nsanje District. Comparing the kind of information he was able to get from the autochthonous population and the immigrants, Chakanza found the latter by far the more knowledgeable. He explicitly tells us that nearly everybody who had something worthwhile to tell was an immigrant from Nsanje, implying that many of these immigrants came from the neighborhood of the shrine, where cult affairs were much more part of everyday talk than elsewhere. This seems to be borne out by the descriptions of the shrine grounds and the sacred pool (secs. 19–29), which contain the kind of detail that can only be provided by people familiar with the situation. More important, though, one can see it illustrated in the prominent place given to Mbona I and II motifs, which, as argued in the first part of this book, point to a source or sources close to the major shrine officials. Yet specific central or northern motifs are not lacking either. Thus, for instance, the incident of the missionaries barging into the shrine grounds, becoming mad, and dying afterward (sec. 21) is without doubt a reference to the Anglican missionaries who in August 1862 went looking for a more suitable location for their mission station in the neighborhood of the Thyolo shrine and who on that occasion met with the most determined resistance on the part of the local shrine officials. One finds this episode extensively described in the journals of several of the missionaries.[3] Although the folk version recorded by Chakanza is not correct in every detail (for instance, the missionaries who died were not the same as those who had been to the shrine, as Chakanza's text suggests), one can nevertheless maintain that it is a recognizable recollection of a historical event documented more than a century ago. The difference between the northern and southern traditions is that when people from the southern part of the valley tell stories about Europeans violating the prohibition to enter the shrine grounds and being punished for it, the culprits are tax collectors instead of missionaries.

Yet despite such differences, the traditions collected by Chakanza also represent a synthesis of northern and southern data. That synthesis is not only to be regarded as a conscious construct on the part of the author — which of course to a great extent it is — but also as the outcome of largely subconscious processes by means of which the autochthonous and immigrant sections of the local population have tried to weave the two types of data into a logical and generally acceptable account. To illustrate this, one need only to look at Mbona's pedigree in the present text. As far as his mother is concerned, there is nothing unusual. In line with other accounts, especially within the Mbona III tradition, she is described as Lundu's sister. This, as we have seen, is a way to symbolize the close relationship between and interdependency of the royal dynasty and the cult. The unusual element is rather that Chakanza's text mentions Tengani as Mbona's father, and Tengani, as we know, is the perpetual title of the southern dynasty. In other words, Lundu and Tengani — two names representing two autonomous state systems — are linked together by Mbona's name, Tengani being Mbona's father and Lundu being his maternal uncle.

In a subtle yet complex way this genealogical construct describes the position of the southern immigrants in the chiefdom of Ngabu Banda as it obtained until fairly recently. Under the Maravi kinship system the maternal uncle has priority over the father, but clashes are difficult to avoid, especially in situations in which patrilineal descent becomes more and more emphasized. Although immigrant familes (many of them from Tengani) had already lived in Ngabu Banda's chiefdom for one or two generations and although they had in the meantime made a not inconsiderable contribution to the local economy, they still tended to be considered culturally and politically inferior to the autochthons. Second, most of the southern immigrants maintained a patrilineal system of descent, while the host group remained largely matrilineal, though this is no longer the case to the degree that it used to be. This, too, used to create problems, particularly when immigrants intermarried with autochthons. The portrayal of Tengani as Mbona's father and Lundu as Mbona's maternal uncle and the tensions and conflicts suggested or evoked by that combination may thus be regarded as a reflection on some major social contradictions through the prism of conflicting kinship systems (matrilineal and patrilineal) and conflicting social roles (maternal uncle and father). Since the contradictions referred to were most acutely felt by the immigrants, it stands to reason that they were also the ones making the greatest efforts symbolically to solve them. By the same token, they would have had a more direct interest in the Mbona cult and its oral traditions than would the autochthons. The suggestion to be made, then, is that the immigrants' knowledgeability in regard to the Mbona cult, on which the author of the present text puts so much stress, may have been a consequence of their geographic origin as well as their present social position. For even if they hailed from the cult's heartland, they could have ignored it if it was in no way functional to them.

TEXT

I am of the opinion that the events I am about to describe did actually take place, although it is difficult to say when. Many people in the Shire Valley know about them, but as they occurred long ago without anybody recording them, our only sources of information are oral testimonies. But when history has to be passed on by word of mouth only, certain elements tend to be omitted, while others are continually added. That elements have been added is clear, and that others are no longer remembered is also clear, for no two or three people among those I interviewed recounted the story in the same manner, although there were occasional similarities. I have also met people who muddled up everything. When that was the case I have only retained such bits of information as seemed to fit in with the present account.

In the chiefdom of Ngabu, where I collected most of my material, people who are knowledgeable on this subject are rather rare. Quite a few told me that, if I wanted to know more, I ought to go to Nsanje. As a matter of fact, nearly everybody who had something worthwhile to tell came from there. Yet people at Ngabu remain convinced that it is a true story, and for them it has meaning, even if they do not remember every detail. It is this conviction of theirs which makes me also believe that something did indeed take place in the distant past, even if it was different from what we are being told now.

Mbona's Parentage

1. We have no reliable information about Mbona's parentage, although there seems to be evidence of some kind of connection between Mbona, Lundu, Tengani, and Kaphwiti. It is said, for instance, that in the beginning the four of them lived together in a place called Kaphirintiwa, where they became involved in a quarrel with a Chief Changamire,[4] and that it was this which eventually made them decide to migrate to the Shire Valley.

2. More specifically, it is said that Mbona held the position of diviner[5] vis-à-vis Kaphwiti, Lundu, and Tengani. As regards these three, the general conviction is that Lundu and Tengani were Kaphwiti's maternal nephews and that Kaphwiti divided the country between them after they had arrived here from Kaphirintiwa. Lundu was thereby granted authority over the Chikwawa District and Tengani over Nsanje. Mbona, for his part, is said to have been the son of Lundu's sister, born to her after she had married Tengani.[6]

The Conflict

3. As said earlier on, many people are convinced that Mbona was a historical person. The general opinion is that he lived in Lundu's chiefdom, some say even at Mbewe, Lundu's headquarters. Whatever the case, being a married man he had settled in his elder brother's village section much like everyone else.[7]

It sometimes happened that in a particular year the rains failed. Whenever this was the case, people tried various means to make the rains come, such as making a libation at the base of a tall tree or performing the rain dance. Often enough, their attempts would be unsuccessful, but it is said that the day or the year Mbona performed the dance, rain would come without fail. No matter how long people had been suffering, their misery would always end when Mbona danced [in my opinion, the dance referred to was a form of magic].[8]

4. Because of this, Mbona became well known, and his fame spread far and wide. His elder brother, however, was none too pleased, and filled with envy he said to himself, "Since my younger brother is becoming a celebrity around here, everybody will move to his side and join his followers. Maybe they will even make him their chief." There are those who say that the elder brother was himself the ruler of those parts and that his hatred was caused by his fear of being deposed. He therefore secretly arranged with certain people to have his younger brother killed.[9]

Mbona's Flight

5. As soon as Mbona learned that his elder brother by the same mother had conspired with others to dispose of him, he began to think about taking flight. Taking his bow and arrows, a spear, a little rice, and a few other things (some mention his dog), he made off. When the evil brother discovered that Mbona had escaped, he told his hirelings to go after him and not to rest until they had killed him.

6. Mbona, however, was superior to any human being. He traveled south through British territory[10] with those men doggedly following in his trail. It sometimes happened that they came quite close but that they still failed to see him. On such occasions they would stand there looking at an anthill, or they would find themselves enveloped in thick fog or darkness. Or they might be staring at a thicket, a huge tree, an animal, or suchlike.[11] But each time it happened to be Mbona who was hiding behind those obstacles, and they were able to proceed only when he decided to clear the road again.

7. Leaving the British domain, he turned west into Portuguese territory until he came to Dzambawe near the site of the old mine, which has now been closed because of the poor quality of the coal found there.[12] Some people told me that Mbona's wife is still alive and that she lives there. It is also said that she will never grow older and that she is a famous diviner, but as all this is hard to believe, let us forget about it.[13]

8. It was there that Mbona began to feel thirsty, but it was a dry and waterless place. He therefore put his belongings down and began to scoop the rock with his bare hands. In a short while he managed to dig a well, which filled itself with fresh water,[14] but since he had no cup, he had to kneel to drink. Leaning on his hands, he bent over the well and drank straight from the water. This done, he scattered the rice he

had brought with him along the rim of the well, where it began to sprout. It still grows there every year, when its season has come again, yielding a fine crop.[15] The imprints of his various belongings can also be seen there to this day.

9. After leaving Dzambawe, we are told that he returned to British territory, traveling in a southerly direction until he came to Ngabu's chiefdom.[16] His footprints are still visible in the neighborhood of the school in Chituwi's village and along the upper course of the Chingadzi Stream in the Nsanje District.[17] I have not been able to ascertain what he did at Makande, but some people told me that it was the home area of one Bandawe, about whom I cannot say much except that he may have been the local cult leader, somewhat like Tengani in Nsanje.[18] Since people in Ngabu's chiefdom also believed in Mbona, Bandawe may have been the one escorting them whenever they went to worship at Nsanje. I also heard that on his way to Nsanje, Mbona passed close by Tengani's village, where, according to some, there are also imprints to be seen.

Mbona's Arrival at Nsanje

10. When Mbona got to the stream called Nyamadzere,[19] which flows by the Chididi mission station, he stepped onto a rock, leaving an imprint of his foot behind. He also took a brief rest there, laying his bow and spear beside him, and those too left imprints that can still be seen.

11. In the meantime his enemies did not think of giving up and kept on chasing him. He himself continued in a southerly direction toward Malawi Hill, which he then ascended. It is said that, when he reached its top, he left yet another footprint behind on a rock. He made a water hole there too and drank from it in exactly the same manner as at Dzambawe, leaving the imprints of his knees and hands on the rock on which he had been kneeling.

12. As his enemies were still pursuing him despite the distances involved, Mbona traveled down the eastern slope which faces Nsanje township until he came to a place called Khulubvi at the foot of Malawi Hill. From there he continued eastward to a place called Ndione on the edge of the marshes.

13. Upon reaching Ndione, Mbona felt very tired, but his enemies were still following him. It is true, he had been using magic so that they had not been able to do anything as yet, but they were far from giving up. Feeling utterly exhausted and sympathizing with his enemies,[20] he finally told them to do as they liked. They were overjoyed when they heard this, and snatching a bow, they tried to shoot an arrow at him. People say, however, that the arrow, instead of wounding Mbona, became strangely twisted. Next, they tried to wound him with an axe, but the axe reportedly

broke. Following this, they tried a large bush knife, but it bent double. They ended up by firing a gun at him, but what a shameful sight that was, for it ejected water instead of a bullet![21]

14. Yet his enemies were not prepared to give up, and a tremendous fight now ensued, which lasted a very long time. Grabbing him and forcing him to the ground, they once more tried to cut his throat with a knife, but the knife became limp like a maize leaf and was of no use. The fight continued the whole day, and only when everybody, including Mbona, felt utterly exhausted and every available weapon had been tried did he reveal his secret. Having told them first that they would never succeed no matter how hard they tried, he added, "But if you are still determined to kill me, take a leaf of the *nansongole* grass[22] and use that to cut my throat. In that case I shall die without fail!"

15. He also said to those present, "When I shall be dead, bury my body at Ndione and my head in Khulubvi thicket at the foot of a *mnjale* tree."[23] The tree he referred to is very tall and stands in the middle of Khulubvi. He continued, "When my head has been buried at the foot of that tree, a pot of the *phiso* type is to be placed over it [*phiso* is the Sena term for the large earthen pots used by women to brew beer].[24] People shall also build a hut there in which my wife shall live and my belongings shall be kept, for I must always have a wife. If you do not obey these commands, you will experience a great many troubles and, most important, you will have no rain."

16. When Mbona had finished speaking, his enemies fetched a *nansongole* leaf, grabbed him, and pinned him to the ground. This done, they cut his throat and killed him. People say that where his blood flowed, a deep well was made, which filled itself with an enormous quantity of blood before spilling over to form a river.[25] Upon seeing this, those present were awestruck. We also hear that along the well and the stream, which contain blood instead of water, one finds medicinal trees and plants of every description.

17. It is said, though, that after the murder these people never did what Mbona told them to do. They just went home and lived like everyone else without giving it further thought and unafraid of what might happen to them for having killed Mbona without fulfilling his last wishes. We hear that the consequences were dreadful indeed, for when the time came to plant, there was no rain at all. Not even the smallest cloud could be seen. There followed a frightful drought which led to an equally frightful famine, and only when they were suffering thus did people begin to remember Mbona's words and commandments.[26]

18. They took his head for burial at the base of a *mnjale* tree in the middle of Khulubvi, where it was covered over with a pot. Next they built

a reed hut with a thatched roof over which they spread a blue cloth,[27] and they concluded everything by installing Mbona's wife in the hut together with his personal belongings. Only when all this had been completed did Mbona unleash the rains, and people no longer needed to be uncertain about whether they should plant or not. There were abundant crops that year because there was plentiful rain, and all around there was great rejoicing at the time of the first fruits and the harvest.

Khulubvi

19. The village of Khulubvi is surrounded by a fence of thorn shrubs.[28] Within are the huts of the guardians, and Mbona's shrine is in a clearing. It is said that all wild animals found there, such as monkeys, baboons, snakes, and the like are harmless. They used to come to the doorways of the huts or to the village meeting place without people chasing them away, and on occasion people let them even eat with them. It is forbidden to kill them, an injunction which also applies to the marabous in the neighborhood.[29] In days gone by, Mbona's hut had to be rebuilt every year or every few years, and if this was not done there would be no rain, or there might be an invasion of locusts or some other pest making people suffer and go hungry.[30]

20. There had to be a woman in his hut, who was known as Salima. When one Salima died, another had to be fetched from Lundu's area, but she always had to be an elderly person or someone whose husband had been dead for a while. Some people say that the woman had to come from the village of Dzimbiri,[31] which forms part of Changata's chiefdom in the Thyolo District. Others maintain that she had to come from Ngabu's chiefdom.

21. Of Mbona's cloth and other possessions, it is said that they are still extant and that they are not subject to decay. There is also an ancient rule to the effect that no European should be allowed into Khulubvi since Mbona himself has forbidden this. Despite this, it once happened that a few well-known missionaries forced their way in, staying there for hours on end despite the prohibition. But they were to know what they had done, for as soon as they had returned home they began running about, shouting at the tops of their voices like madmen, and in the end they died without even being buried.[32] At least that is what people say. If one wants to visit the place, one needs the permission of the guardians. Children are not allowed in at all.[33]

22. In the olden days they kept the following procedure when rebuilding Mbona's hut. First, a message was sent to Chief Tengani, who would then come with his people. Before reaching Khulubvi they spent the night at Malemia's village,[34] which lies close by at the foot of Malawi

Hill. Early the next morning all of them assembled and proceeded to Khulubvi, where they would be met by Chief Ngabu and Headman Mbangu, whose village is adjacent to the shrine. There they would find chiefs and headmen from other places as well as people bearing gifts. 23. Having discussed whatever needed to be discussed, the building of the hut began. Everybody had to work hard, and while going about one's task, one had to take off one's clothes and remain naked.[35] When the walls of the hut were finished, they began building the roof upon the head of Chief Tengani. Some say that every Tengani who had taken part would die soon after, which is also why some incumbents absconded to Mozambique when being bidden to the rebuilding.[36]

24. After finishing the roof, they would spread a blue cloth over the grass thatching. But before lifting it onto the walls, they invited the rains by swaying it in the direction of the four points of the compass, beginning with the east in the direction of Ndione. The moment they had finished their work, peals of thunder would be heard, lightning would flash, and a storm would break accompanied by heavy downpours, so that on their way home people would be drenched to the bone.

Ndione

25. Ndione was a place where quite unusual things happened. It was, for instance, customary every year to take a young boy and kill him there as a sacrifice to Mbona.[37] Offerings of flour and beer were also made there. Whenever there were problems concerning the land, the village headmen would go to Khulubvi with their elders to make this kind of offering. Upon approaching Khulubvi they would halt in silence at a place nearby, and the headman alone would enter the grove to make an offering on behalf of his people.[38]

26. There lived many big and tasty fish in the well and the stream at Ndione. In the olden days people used to go fishing there, but there was a limit to the number of fish they were allowed to catch.[39] A person could catch one, two, or three fish and no more. If you said, "These fish are lovely and quite easy to catch. Come on, let us try a fourth one!" you might drag up a child instead of a fish. That child would be crying and would tell you, "Take me and eat me, for those fish are apparently not enough for you!" The fisherman would then become frightened and start running around in circles without ever finding his way home again. 27. Or he might drag up three knobkerries, which made for him the moment he landed them, to give him a sound thrashing, and again he would begin aimlessly running around. On some other occasion he might drag up a sable antelope, which is a forest animal and which would say, "Are those fish not enough? Take me and eat me!" and the outcome would

be the same as in the other cases. People therefore took great care. When they had caught one, two, or three fish, they went home without trying any further.

28. In the forest around Ndione there are vegetal medicines in the form of trees and all sorts of herbs. Everybody knowing something about medicines goes there to collect them.[40] Adjacent to Ndione one finds the villages of Nkhukuime, Mmanzi, and Chilembwe.[41]

The Decline of the Cult

29. In the year 1935 or 1936, when Chief Tengani (the one who recently abdicated) had been installed, he refused to pay homage to Mbona, and he also refused to have the roof built upon his head, because he had become a Christian.[42] When he stuck to his decision despite pressure and protests from the population, things at Khulubvi began to change. The waters at Ndione changed from red to colorless.[43] People began catching fish there as they liked, and they moved about the place without any trace of fear. At Khulubvi, too, things took a turn for the worse. Everybody, including Europeans, could go inside and look at things. The inhabitants who had never paid tax before, as they were Mbona's people, now had to pay like everyone else.[44]

Mbona's Manifestations

30. This is how Mbona communicated with his people after his death: he made someone from Khulubvi or from the villages of Mbangu, Ngabu, Chiphwembwe, or Nthole dream.[45] It is said that when such a person had a dream he or she was able to tell people everything they needed to know. People therefore were quick to do as they were told, even if it was something difficult, for fear that otherwise they might find themselves in great trouble.[46] I have also been told in connection with Mbona's miraculous powers that he could turn into a snake (or that after the murder he turned into a snake) and that he would come to his wife by night to tell her things such as "This year there will be famine!" or "This year there will be food in abundance!"[47] Others again say that Mbona was in the habit of visiting a *mtondo* tree, which they called "the tree of the spear."[48]

31. People from Ngabu would travel to such places as Nyathana and Kalambo, or even to Tengani and Khulubvi to hear those prophecies.[49] According to some, the person who conveyed Mbona's utterances about what was to be done in a certain year lived at Mitseche,[50] but others maintain that it was his wife, the one in Mozambique who is said never to grow old. One also hears that everything Mbona foresaid came to be fulfilled, which is why so many people had faith in him and why some

still have it. That Mbona's memory is not altogether dead, not even in our days, becomes clear when one interviews people in Nsanje and Chikwawa. Though the story may be mixed up in many ways, it is surprising to see the remarkable attraction it still exercises on people, including little children.

NOTES

SOURCES

INDEX

NOTES

INTRODUCTION

1. The Shire River runs through three valley areas, respectively known as the Upper, Middle, and Lower Shire Vallies. In this study the name Shire Valley refers to the lower valley, which borders directly on the Zambezi.

2. The word *lundu* has the general meaning of "chief" (Scott 1892:294), but in the Shire Valley it refers specifically to the paramountcy of that name, which was officially established in 1969. With regard to the precolonial period, the phrase "Lundu kingdom" will be used. When referring to the king or paramount himself, we shall use the title as if it were a personal name. When it is necessary to specify the incumbent, the latter's personal name will be added (e.g., Lundu Mankhokwe).

3. Interview, Chapirira and Kumbiwanyati, Aug. 24, 1964.

4. Interview, Mbukwa, Khombe, and Kambalame, Oct. 9 and 12, 1966.

5. I interviewed the medium Josef Thom, locally known as Chambote, on five occasions (Oct, 31, 1966, Dec. 4, 1967, Sept. 5, 1968, Dec. 24, 1971, and April 1, 1972). On two further occasions (Dec. 22, 1967, and Sept. 18, 1972), interviews were conducted on my behalf by Elias Mandala, then a student at the University of Malawi. All the interviews took place at the medium's residence in the village of Thole, Malemia chiefdom, Nsanje.

6. Vansina 1985:23.

7. Vansina rejects the notion of a "middle period" and prefers to speak of a "floating gap," which, as it were, moves on with the passage of time (Vansina 1985:24).

8. For the Tallensi of Ghana, see Fortes 1964; for the Lovedu, see Krige and Krige 1943; for Mwari, see Abraham 1966, Ranger 1967, Daneel 1970, Bhebe 1979, Schoffeleers 1979d; for Chaminuka, Karuva, and Dzivaguru, see Gelfand 1962, Garbett 1969, Bourdillon 1979, and Lan 1985. For a collection of essays on south central African territorial cults, see Schoffeleers 1979a. Additional instances of territorial cults and a useful bibliography can be found in Heintze 1970.

9. Schoffeleers 1979b:1. Although territorial cults may cover land areas of various sizes, I have in mind only cults such as those mentioned in n. 8 which are of regional importance.

10. Mitchell 1961:31.

11. Ibid., 33.

12. Rau 1979.

13. Gluckman 1964:31.

14. On the Mwari cult among the Kalanga, see Bhebe 1979. The Ngoni, who at first ignored and even suppressed the Chisumphi cult of central Malawi, later on developed psychiatric symptoms, which could only be cured by adepts of that cult; see Rau 1979.

15. Schoffeleers 1979b:27ff.

16. Turner 1974:185.

17. Werbner 1977:xiv.

18. E.g., Ranger and Kimambo 1972.

19. There are a few exceptions (e.g., Abraham 1966 and Rennie 1979), but even these fail to pay attention to traditions other than those of chiefs and mediums.

20. Malinowski 1948:93–148.

21. Fortes 1945; Cunnison 1951, 1959; Beidelman 1970.

22. de Heusch 1975, 1982a; Wrigley 1988.

23. A detailed discussion of Vansina's theoretical position can be found in Willis 1980. Willis' major criticism is that Vansina fails to indicate how mythical and symbolic meaning is to be distinguished from historical fact in narrative data.

24. Feierman 1974; Willis 1976, 1981; Miller 1978.

25. Wrigley 1988.

26. de Heusch 1982a:34–75; 1982b:331–75.

27. For an extensive discussion of the latter period, see Mandala 1990.

28. Miller 1973:124–25.

29. Hamilton (1987) has made a number of points which fit in very well with the foregoing. Drawing on the theories of Gramsci and Laclau, he too argues that effective ideologies seldom reflect solely the interests of the dominant or ruling group of a society. Insofar as they seek to neutralize the antagonism of the subordinate groups, ideologies also reflect their interests and their struggles. He further argues that ideological artifacts such as oral traditions reflect the conflict between the interests underlying different worldviews. Finally, he emphasizes the particular importance of oral traditions in precapitalist African societies, not only because the transmission of ideas in such societies is almost entirely by word of mouth but also because oral traditions concerning important subjects are often connected with the cult of the ancestors or local deities and as such acquire additional authority.

30. Kopytoff (1987) has shed further light on the issue of traditional African state ideologies, first, by noting that their dualistic character is a common trait and, second, by suggesting that their dualism manifests itself not only in two paradigmatic stories about the foundation of the polity, namely that of the ruler and that of the subjects, but also in a dual view of its constitutional legitimation, namely the idea that the king has a right to rule and the opposite idea that he rules by the will of his subjects. The standard myths of the subjects depict the founders as intruders. The myths of the rulers, for their part, see the subjects in the metaphor of the late-coming adherents to the polity the rulers had founded. This accomplished a crucial reversal of chronological primacy: the original inhabitants could be seen as "immigrants" into the new society, for they were incorporated into it after its creation. "Political chronology" thus dominates "real chron-

ology." This difference in chronological perceptions corresponded to the difference in the conception of the essential character of the polity. In the ruling groups' view, it was their private estate that had only grown larger. Hence the ruler's ideology of rulership was patrimonial: the polity was an extension of the ruler's household. Yet the perspective of the subjects lingered on, and in that perspective the ruler remained a stranger who, followed by others, insinuated himself into power and legitimated his regime by appropriating local ritual symbols. Consequently, the ruler may be blamed for a variety of ills, from drought to civil unrest. Particularly in the earlier phases, when the two perceptions of the ruler's office have not yet come to constitute an articulated whole, this may make the ruler a readily available scapegoat. Kopytoff thereby proposes a sociogenesis for the (African) scapegoat king that invites comparison with René Girard's controversial theory on the same subject (Girard 1977).

31. Schoffeleers 1977, 1975, 1985c, 1987b, 1985a, 1987a, 1980.

CHAPTER 1: THE SHIRE VALLEY AND ITS POPULATION

1. Details in Pike and Rimmington 1965:27–29 and Robinson 1973:55–58.

2. In the first week of January 1982 I noticed fine stands of maize in the neighborhood of the shrine, whereas a little to the west the maize plants were much smaller and had to be interplanted with sorghum. Often there is even the possibility of a second maize planting (*mulopi*) in June or July, allowing for a harvest in September. This striking feature may have been one of the reasons why Khulubvi became the center of a rain cult.

3. Much detail on the valley's agricultural potential in precolonial times is to be found in the publications of the Livingstone expedition and the first Universities' Mission to Central Africa (U.M.C.A.) missionaries. Cf. Bennett and Ylvisaker 1971; Foskett 1965; Livingstone and Livingstone 1865; Rowley 1866; Wallis 1952.

4. Morgan 1953:465.

5. Morgan 1953; Colman and Garbett 1973:8–9; extensive descriptions in Mandala 1990.

6. Buchanan 1885:117–19.

7. Chafulumira 1948:3–5.

8. For the Barwe rebellion, known as the Makombe rising, see Ranger 1963 and Isaacman 1976.

9. The 1907 figure is based on data from the *Handbook of Nyasaland* (1910); the 1931 figure is taken from Pike and Rimmington (1965:135); the 1966 and 1977 figures are from the official census reports. In recent years, tens of thousands of refugees have once again moved in from Mozambique due to RENAMO atrocities.

10. Monclaro (1569) 1899:229, 234; Mandala 1990, chap. 1.

11. For the Malawian iron technology, see Van der Merwe and Avery 1987. For its economic and political aspects and for details on the salt industry, see especially Mandala 1990.

12. Livingstone and Livingstone 1865:93.

13. Isaacman 1972:34; Duly 1948:21.

14. Murdock 1959:258; Rita-Ferreira 1966:14.

15. Rattray 1907:45–48; Chafulumira 1948:9–10. Chafulumira renders the plural as *mavimba*.

16. Interview, B. Nhlane, former district commissioner at Nsanje, May 15, 1966.

17. Port Herald District Annual Report 1945, p. 2. The place where they came from in Zimbabwe is specified elsewhere as Mtoko, northeast of Harare, on the road to Tete (Duly 1948:21).

18. The name Maravi as an ethnological designation for that congeries was reintroduced by Tew (1950:30).

19. Tew 1950; Marwick 1965; Rita-Ferreira 1966; Phiri 1983.

20. Mitchell 1956; Mandala 1990, chap. 1.

21. Chafulumira 1948:28.

22. Ntara 1973:98–101; Rangeley 1963:36–40.

23. Clark 1972:23; Cole-King 1973:9; Roberts 1976:25, 66.

24. Clark 1972:25.

25. Ntara 1973:99; Text II/A, sec. 9.

26. Thus Sir Harry Johnston found that around Mt. Zomba the Kafula were referred to as *alungu* (Johnston 1897:52–53), which is a generic name for spirits or the spirit world. Senior Headman Mbeta from Nsanje referred to the Kafula on Malawi Hill as *zinzimu* or *zinyau*, terms which may both be translated as "powerful spirits" (Interview, Group Village Headman Mbeta, Nsanje, Oct. 19, 1966).

27. Interview, Group Village Headman Nkhuche, Sept. 21, 1973. The interview was conducted by Mr. F. Msambalima.

28. Murray 1922:121; Tew 1950:31; Rita-Ferreira 1966:14.

29. Ntara 1973:156.

30. Tew 1950:31.

31. *Handbook of Nyasaland* 1910:22.

32. Jackson 1972:38; Scott 1892:89, s.v. *chipeta*.

33. Gamitto 1960, 1:67.

34. The Xhosa and a large number of Shona groups in the Zambezi Valley name as their original home a place whose appellation literally means "long grass." Lan (1985:77–79) explains this largely in symbolic terms as referring to a "source of fertility." Whilst that interpretation may be fully acceptable, the Chipeta case suggests that, more concretely, the "long grass" may also refer to a particular ecosystem and a people's acephalous past.

35. The pattern of Ngoni occupation, however, was not everywhere the same. In Dowa the Chipeta were able to keep separate from the Ngoni (*Handbook of Nyasaland* 1910:22). In Dedza they became subjects and serfs of the Ngoni (Shepperson and Price 1958:403, 474). In Ntcheu the Ngoni intermarried with the Chipeta, who in the end became culturally dominant (*Handbook of Nyasaland* 1910: 37).

36. See Langworthy 1972:28–35; Phiri unpubl. 1975.

37. One of these questions is what relationship there was between the *chipeta*

ecological system and the acephalous organization of the populace. My suggestion is that the *chipeta* system was the product of an agricultural technology which predated the emergence of the centralized states. Apparently, the rulers of these states have not always been able to bring these economically valuable areas under their control.

38. See also Rangeley 1953:8.

39. See Text III/B, sec. 19 and n. 16. Rangeley (1953:14) notes that this fact alone "goes far to strengthen the story of those who say that Mbona has fled from the Cipeta country." The "tattoos" consist mainly of a series of undulating furrows. For a detailed description, see Price 1953:62.

40. Ntara 1973:6. W. S. K. Jere's translation is not altogether satisfactory, but I have decided to use it, since it is the only English translation of Ntara's *Mbiri ya Achewa* which is available and since the essence of the text has in this case not been tampered with. See Schoffeleers 1974, however, for criticisms of this particular edition of Ntara's main work.

41. One version of this tradition is contained in a four-thousand-word manuscript composed in 1967 by Stephen M. Tengani, youngest son of the late Chief Molin Tengani. The manuscript deals with the early history of the Mang'anja, but it also contains rare information on Mang'anja royal rituals. Mr. Tengani kindly allowed me to make a copy of the manuscript. The same story has also been recorded by Dr. H. Bhila, who obtained his information from Chief Chapananga in the northwestern part of the valley (Bhila unpubl. 1977:13). This suggests that it functioned as a standard myth among the southern Maravi.

42. Hamilton 1955:220.

43. Marwick 1965:22.

44. Schoffeleers 1972.

45. Murray 1922:43; Rangeley 1953:8; Ntara 1973:8–9.

46. Ntara 1973:30–43; Rangeley 1952; Schoffeleers 1979c.

47. Macdonald 1882, 1:279; Scott 1892:215, s.v. *kapirimtiya*, and 589, s.v. *takadzo*; Murray 1922:48; Ntara 1973:8–9; Schoffeleers 1985b:19–20; Darot MS 1930; Hovington MS, n.d. See Werner 1906:73–74 for a similar myth recorded among the neighboring Yao.

48. For a detailed analysis of this myth, see Schoffeleers unpubl. 1968:194–214 and Schoffeleers 1971.

49. Cf. Texts I/A; II/A, sec. 10; II/B, sec. 2; III/B, sec. 1; IV, sec. 1.

50. Kaphirintiwa, for instance, can only be reached after hours of strenuous climbing. The same goes for the Thyolo shrine, the remnants of which are to be found nearly one thousand meters above the valley floor.

51. Ntara 1973:40; Rangeley 1952:39.

52. Interview, Headman Nkhuche, Sept. 21, 1973. When the Maravi became dominant, oral traditions averred that they had founded those shrines at Kafula settlements. Headman Eliazer Nsadzu, of Nsadzu village in the Central Region of Malawi, explained this as a means of "consolidating their conquests, just as the British used to build churches in places where Africans had been living" (interview, April 10, 1974, by Dr. N. E. Lindgren and E. C. Mandala, cited with their permission).

53. Interview, Headman Mwanda, Sept. 23, 1972, at Mwanda village, conducted by E. C. Mandala. Mwanda's statement implies that Mbona did not belong to the earliest Chipeta group in the valley (see also Text I/B). Apart from oral traditions which explicitly state that there existed an early shrine on Malawi Hill, one may point to a body of traditions which hold that, while fleeing from his enemies, Mbona moved from Malawi Hill to the valley, or that he was captured on Malawi Hill and from there taken to the plain below (Texts III/B, secs. 17–19; Text IV, secs. 10–12). I take these traditions to be symbolic of the shrine's transferral from Malawi Hill to the plains below at the reinstatement of the cult, probably in the first half of the seventeenth century.

54. Ntara 1973:22; Wallis 1952:93–95.

55. See Bruwer (1952:179) for the Chirenje shrine in Malawi's Central Region. At the time of the Ngoni attacks, the population sought refuge at the old Kaphirintiwa shrine, taking the sacred drum with them (interview, Headman Chikafu Mbewe, Lilongwe District, Sept. 16, 1967). The Thyolo shrine also served as a refugee camp during the slave raids in the 1860s.

56. Schoffeleers 1979c:152.

57. Rowley 1866:265–66; Rangeley 1953; Ntara 1973; Amanze unpubl. 1986.

58. Ntara 1973:38: "It has already been seen that our ancestors did not have chiefs at first and that their priests were always women." A more adequate translation of the original Chewa text would have been: "We have already seen that our ancestors had no chiefs, but they had spirit wives instead."

59. See Linden 1979:191 for the shrine of Mankhamba; Rangeley 1952:37–38 and Ntara 1973:22 for Msinja; Racey (British Public Record Office, C.O. 525/7, Jan. 24, 1905) for Nsanje. The presence of a Mbewe priesthood at the Chirenje shrine was confirmed by its officers (interview, Sept. 30, 1969). At the Thyolo shrine, it was confirmed by the local spirit wife and Chief Changata, in whose territory the shrine is situated (interview, Moses Kalitsiro Mpuka, then Chief Changata, and others, April 13, 1971, conducted by E. C. Mandala at the chief's headquarters).

60. Rangeley 1952:37–38; Linden 1979.

61. On *nyau* among the northern and western Maravi, see Hodgson 1933; Rangeley 1949–50; Makumbi 1964; Marwick 1968; Rita-Ferreira 1968; Linden and Linden 1974; Yoshida 1991 and forthcoming. On *nyau* among the southern Maravi, see Schoffeleers unpubl. 1968:307–416; Schoffeleers and Linden 1972; Schoffeleers 1976; Kubik 1987.

62. Details on charges in cash and kind made by three *nyau* branches in the Chikwawa District are to be found in Schoffeleers unpubl. 1968:332 (table 25).

63. There is an intricate symbolic correspondence between female puberty rites, the final mourning rites, *nyau* performances, and the June–August period (cold season) in the climatic cycle. See Schoffeleers 1971.

64. Gamitto 1960, 1:106–7. *Batuke* (*batuque*) is a common Portuguese term for African dances. *Kateko* is danced with a drum (Scott 1892:218). In the Lower Shire Valley it is executed by men on festive occasions. *Pembera* (*-pemphera:* "to pray") refers to a dance in honor of the spirits also known in the Shire Valley. The name may also refer to the *nyau* dance, which is called *pemphero lalikulu* (great prayer). *Gondo* is danced at mourning rites (Gamitto 1960, 1:102).

65. Schoffeleers unpubl. 1968:321; Kubik 1987:23–33.

66. I have observed, for instance, that in those villages of the valley where the Chipeta variant of the *nyau* was active (mostly in the Chapananga chiefdom), there were no Spirit churches, while in villages where the Mang'anja variant of the *nyau* was active (in the Kasisi and Lundu chiefdoms), such churches did operate. These churches being even more strongly opposed to the *nyau* than the mission churches, a likely explanation for their nonexistence in the "Chipeta area" is that they are not tolerated there by the *nyau*. See Wishlade 1965 for a different interpretation.

67. There are several reasons for considering the Kololo chiefs as the initiators of the "softer" version of *nyau*. First, its main concentration is in the Kololo-controlled chiefdoms. Second, oral traditions insist that the Kololo chiefs were great supporters of the *nyau*. Finally, the *nyau* are never mentioned in the diaries of the U.M.C.A. and the Livingstone expedition, who lived in the valley prior to the Kololo takeover.

68. The symbolism of the masks and the zoomorphic structures is more extensively discussed in Schoffeleers unpubl. 1968, chap. 5. Photographs and technical descriptions of Lower Shire Valley masks and zoomorphic structures may be found in Blackmun and Schoffeleers 1972. Kubik 1987 contains photographs of *nyau* masks from the Shire highlands. Nurse (1988) makes the important observation that the zoomorphic structures always assume the same patterns, while the masks vary considerably from one group to another. He suspects that the masks have a mainly satirical and outward purpose, while "the real matter" of *nyau* is carried on by the zoomorphs.

69. Illustrations in Lindgren and Schoffeleers 1978:52.

70. Historical clues, apart from the masks' stylistic characteristics, may well be contained in their names, the songs that accompany the performances of particular masks, and the dancing styles typical of individual masks. I have been told that some forty different dance sequences have been identified (personal communication, Dr. D. Kadzamira, University of Malawi).

71. A full description of the initiation rites and specimens of *nyau* vocabulary and passwords appear in Schoffeleers unpubl. 1968, chap. 5.

72. A list of 103 *nyau* branches active in the Lower Shire Valley in the years 1966–67 can be found in Schoffeleers unpubl. 1968:322–23. Kubik (1987) estimates that in the mid-1980s there were "probably over one hundred" branches in Malawi. My Lower Shire Valley list as well as lists from the Central Region in my possession show that his estimation is far too conservative.

73. Kubik, for one, denies the *nyau* all religious significance (1987:21). Yoshida, on the other hand, demonstrates how intimately the *nyau* is connected with people's ideas about the spirit world (1991 and forthcoming).

74. Foà 1900:40–44. Yoshida (1991 and forthcoming) provides a myth from eastern Zambia which confirms and elaborates Foà's interpretation.

75. Schoffeleers unpubl. 1968:413–14.

76. Phiri 1983:24, cited by Kubik 1987:16, 60; Rita-Ferreira 1968:20. The most explicit formulation of this function is Nurse's, who maintains that "it is now more openly acknowledged what many of us used to suspect it was: a set of ceremonies created and maintained by deracinated men to uphold their dignity in matrilineal

society, tolerated and encouraged by women in the interests of social stability" (Nurse 1988).

77. Hovington MS, n.d.:61.

78. The reference is to Chief Kasisi of the Chikwawa District.

79. Malawi Government 1964:4; Ntara 1973:14; Price 1963.

80. Lévi-Strauss 1970.

81. Personal communication from Dr. F. Mnthali, University of Malawi.

82. The tradition is contained in a manuscript entitled "Notes écrites a Nambuma en 1930," by Father Darot of the White Fathers. In the kingdom of Undi these mats were taken to the court as a form of ritual tribute (Langworthy 1972:116). There is a popular belief that the clouds caused by the annual bush fires turn into rain clouds. The same belief may help explain the burning of the mats, because the end of the initiation ceremony coincided with the end of the dry season.

83. Schoffeleers 1971:98–99.

84. Lane-Poole 1938:2; Winterbottom 1950; Marwick 1963:378. Langworthy 1971:104.

85. Roberts 1976:83.

86. See Chapter 5 for details.

87. This periodization, which was originally proposed in Schoffeleers 1973a, has in the meantime received explicit support from the archaeologist Phillipson (1976:195).

88. Langworthy 1972:29–30. See also Texts II/A and II/B.

89. Details on the Lundu and Muzura periods will be provided in Chapter 5. On the Karonga kingdom, see Phiri unpubl. 1975.

90. Livingstone and Livingstone 1865:198: "Formerly all the Mang'anja were united under the government of their great Chief, Undi, whose Empire extended from Lake Shirwa to the River Loangwa; but after Undi's death it fell to pieces, and a large portion of it on the Zambesi was absorbed by their powerful southern neighbours the Banyai." Headman Zandia, one of Livingstone's informants, told him that Undi still ruled over the Shire Valley when he was a child (Wallis 1952, 1:172).

91. Details in Schoffeleers 1973b.

92. This theme will be more fully discussed in Chapter 7.

93. Tengani MS 1967:14; Gamitto 1960, 1:102; Scott 1892:453, s.v. *nkhondo.*

94. De Souza 1881:508. De Souza's source is Father Boym, a seventeenth-century Polish Jesuit. Since there were regular contacts between the Portuguese, especially those resident in Tete, and Kalonga (Axelson 1969:153–54), who was then the principal ruler, it is likely that the reference is to Kalonga.

95. Langworthy 1972:113.

96. Ibid., 114.

97. Barreto de Rezende (c. 1635) 1899:408; Gamitto 1960, 1:70–72.

98. Gamitto 1960, 1:71.

99. Barreto de Rezende (c. 1635) 1899:419.

100. Langworthy 1972:106.

101. See Texts II/A, II/B, and III/B.

102. This is graphically illustrated by an oral tradition associated with the now-

defunct Mwalanduzi shrine in Thyolo District. Apparently this shrine was also dedicated to a python deity which lived in a swamp. One day a lion appeared which wanted to take possession of the swamp, but while attempting this it was drowned in the mud (oral communication with Mr. P. Cole-King, director of antiquities, Malawi).

103. Linden 1972.

104. Langworthy 1972.

105. Ntara 1973:22.

CHAPTER 2: THE RITUAL CYCLE OF THE MBONA CULT

1. The visit was made with permission from the principals of the cult, who ordered me to arrive with an offering of two bottles of local liquor and a few lengths of black cloth. For an additional eyewitness account of the shrine's layout, see Rangeley 1953.

2. The number of huts (and therefore of guardians) has apparently remained the same for over a century, for in 1862, when a member of the U.M.C.A. mission visited the place, there were seven also (Bennett and Ylvisaker 1971:305).

3. See Text III/B, sec. 25 and n. 22. The flora of the sanctuary proper is described in Kathamalo 1965.

4. These are poles of the *kalembo* tree, which I have been unable to identify botanically.

5. Interview, Headman Mwanda, Sept. 23, 1972.

6. Interview, Chapirira and Kumbiwanyati, Aug. 24, 1964, sec. 23.

7. I do not mean to say that at one time people chose to use this perishable material because it tied in so well with their etiology. Rather, the nature of materials chosen for a variety of historical and practical reasons happens to tie in with a particular etiology.

8. For traditions about the roof of the shrine being built upon Tengani's head, see Text IV, sec. 23 and n. 36; also Text II/A, sec. 34. According to Rangeley (1953:19), it was Tengani's task to place the central pole in position and hold it upright until the roof was firmly in position. This need not contradict the information that the roof was built upon his head before he placed the central pole in position. Mr. Tom Price once collected a tradition according to which it was built on Tengani's penis (T. Price, personal communication). The riddle raised by this somewhat unusual tradition can be solved when it is seen that there is a tendency to substitute head, penis, and snake for each other, all three being archetypal symbols of maleness. This is expressed, *inter alia*, by a number of traditions according to which a snake or termite hill, both phallic symbols, emerged from the place where Mbona's head was buried.

9. Rangeley 1953:19; on the person of Mariano, see Chapter 4.

10. According to Headman Mphamba (interview, Dec. 22, 1972), this wooden structure is called *ntalimba*, and it is made of *ntalala* or *nthongololo* wood, which I am unable to identify botanically.

11. See Text II/B, sec. 22.

12. Rangeley mentions that the spears were part of the offerings made by Mariano to the shrine as a sign of reconciliation after his men had destroyed it (Rangeley 1953:24). The fact that Mbona has two spears places him symbolically on par with the king, who was the only person allowed to carry two spears (see also Text III/B, sec. 8). The person of Mbona thereby symbolizes the meeting of the dry and the wet seasons.

13. I was once told by a veteran missionary that until the 1940s important persons, and they alone, were offered *nipa* in these wooden "eggcups," which may explain why this one was reserved for Mbona.

14. The drum Kamango is also mentioned in Text III/B, sec. 2, as being used at a rain dance performed by Lundu Mankhokwe. On a visit to Tengani's headquarters in Nov. 1966, I was shown a similar drum, also called Kamango, which was used to call people together for important occasions.

15. The monitor lizard (*m'nganzi, gondwa; Varanus niloticus*) is associated with the sky, thunder, and rain, and it is also called by one of the divine names, Mulungu, Chiuta, or Mphambe (Stannus 1910:299, 301). It occurred to me that the lizard's habit of plunging into rivers and pools from overhanging trees may be one of the factors accounting for these associations.

16. These trees were identified as *ngagaga* (*Acacia scorpioides*), *ntangatanga* (*Albizzia gummifera*), *mpingo* (ebony; *Dalbergia melanoxylon*), *tamya, nsehese, nangali,* and *nkiriza*. The four unidentified names are Sena and do not appear in Topham's *Check List* (1958). The theme of forests growing up on treeless land after the death or burial of some prominent person is well known in Maravi traditions. It is a mythical elaboration of the traditional form of a chief's burial. When the chief died, he was often buried in his own hut, which was deserted after the ceremony. It slowly turned into a forest patch which was held sacred and in which later incumbents would also be buried.

The fact that some of these species are said to have come from the hills may refer to Mbona's flight from the hills to the marsh. It may also refer to Mbona's being a member of the Phiri, or hills, clan. The most likely explanation for the occurrence of these dryland trees in the marshes is that they are a remnant of the preinundation flora. The permanent inundation of the Dinde Marsh began in 1936.

17. On Molin Tengani, see Chapter 4. More normally, it is said that the waters of the pool used to change to red when some disaster was imminent but that this no longer happens due to the cult having lost its authority. Others, however, maintain that the color of the waters continues to change even in our days.

18. See, for instance, Text IV, secs. 26–27.

19. Interview, Chapirira and Kumbiwanyati, Aug. 24, 1964, secs. 47–48. See also Text IV, sec. 25, which states that this type of sacrifice was an annual event.

20. Interview, Chapirira and Kumbiwanyati, Aug. 24, 1964, sec. 49.

21. Cf. Chapter 4 on the rumor of Lundu's having shot one of Mbona's monkeys.

22. Guyot 1895:56: "Le territoire de Mbona est une terre indépendante, c'est-à-dire que son chef ne relève d'aucun capitao-mor."

23. I have collected five detailed lists provided by various officials in the course of my research, from which it has been possible to identify some nineteen different

hereditary titles in the Mbona organization, varying from chief ritual officer ("high priest") to shrine sweeper. Some of these titles are now defunct.

24. The chiefdoms of Tengani and Dobvu, respectively to the north and south of Khulubvi, functioned as the direct representatives of the Lundu kingdom, much as the district organization of later years represented the colonial and postcolonial states.

25. For Ntcheu, see Text II/A, sec. 32; for Maganja da Costa, see Price 1963:75.

26. Interview, Headman Mphamba, Dec. 22, 1972.

27. Interview, Chief Ngabu Phiri, Sept. 24, 1972. Bororo used to be the general name for the north bank of the Zambezi east of the Lower Shire Valley. Marromeu lies south of the Zambezi estuary, as does Phodzoland. Pilgrimages from Phodzoland are confirmed by traditions from those parts: "All Phodzo *nyakwawa* [headmen] used to visit her" (interview, A. Marianno, Mopea, Zambesia, Oct. 28, 1976, by H. L. Vail and L. E. White, who kindly put a copy of the interview at my disposal). It is to be noted that at the time of Livingstone's travels Khulubvi harbored a sizable colony of Phodzo rice growers (Wallis 1956:105; Foskett 1965:210).

28. Interview, Chapirira and Kumbiwanyati Aug. 24, 1964, sec. 50.

29. Schebesta 1929:6.

30. Interview, Chapirira and Kumbiwanyati, Aug. 24, 1964, sec. 47. The *prazo* referred to belonged to the Mariano family (see Chapter 4), and the overseer in question is named as Chagunda, the leader of the anti-Portuguese insurrection of 1884 (cf. Mandala 1990:84).

31. See Ranger 1967; Daneel 1970.

32. Rowley 1866:268–69.

33. Rattray 1907:43–44, 118–19, 204–5.

34. Bruwer 1952; Rangeley 1952, 1953.

35. Gwengwe 1965:19–30.

36. van Breugel unpubl. 1976:53–71.

37. Amanze unpubl. 1986. A number of rain hymns are discussed also in Chimombo's study of Malawian oral literature (1988:133–52).

38. Text II/B, secs. 18–19.

39. Interview, Chapirira and Kumbiwanyati, Aug. 24, 1964, sec. 12.

40. Ibid. sec. 13.

41. See Text III/B, sec. 25.

42. Interview, Chapirira and Kumbiwanyati, Aug. 24, 1964, sec. 45.

43. Rowley 1866:269. Lying on the back symbolizes the community's willingness and readiness to receive the rains, the divine semen. For a similar ritual among the Nyamwezi, see Tcherkézoff 1987:39.

44. Amanze unpubl. 1986.

45. Interview of the medium Chambote (Josef Thom) by E. C. Mandala, Dec. 22, 1967. The medium was angry because Mbukwa had accepted money from visitors attending the ceremony and from the district council with which to buy twelve bottles of local liquor, one goat, and one umbrella. The umbrella, symbolizing a darkened sky, is part of Salima's outfit and is held over her head during processions.

46. See Text II/A, sec. 34; Text IV, sec. 23.

47. Interview, Chapirira and Kumbiwanyati, Aug. 24, 1964, secs. 61–65.

48. Text IV, secs. 23–24.

49. Interview, Chief Stonkin Tengani, by E. C. Mandala, Aug. 23, 1973.

50. From the verb -lima, "to hoe." Like so many etymologies, however, this one too may be a post factum construct.

51. Wallis 1956:93–94.

52. Text III/A, secs. 28–29.

53. Interview, Chapirira and Kumbiwanyati, Aug. 24, 1964, secs. 39–41. The ideophone we indicates something straight or smooth or a path without turns; cf. Scott 1892:664.

54. Rangeley 1953:23.

55. Text III/A, secs. 29–31.

56. Interview, Chapirira and Kumbiwanyati, Aug. 24, 1964, secs. 31–32.

57. See, e.g., Text IV, sec. 30.

58. Interview, Chapirira and Kumbiwanyati, Aug. 24, 1964, sec. 30.

59. Interview, A. Marianno, Oct. 28, 1976.

60. Rangeley 1953:22.

CHAPTER 3: THE PRINCIPALS AND THE MEDIUM

1. I have opted for the term principal to avoid terms such as leader — which seems more appropriate when speaking of a movement than an institution — or priest, which suggests that both possess ritual authority, whereas only one (Ngabu) may be described as such.

2. Interview, Headman Mphamba, Aug. 19, 1973; interview, Moshtishu, Chiphwembwe village, Sept. 21, 1972.

3. Interview, Headman Mphamba, Aug. 19, 1973.

4. Interviews, Chief Malemia, Oct. 20, 1966, Aug. 20, 1967, and Jan. 4, 1980.

5. Interviews, Chief Ngabu Phiri, Sept. 24, 1972, Aug. 16, 1973, and July 13, 1974.

6. Mandala unpubl. 1973–74.

7. Rangeley 1953:20.

8. This was the ceremony described in the preceding chapter.

9. Schoffeleers unpubl. 1977.

10. Instances cited in Schoffeleers unpubl. 1977.

11. Josef Thom built his own shrine in 1968 at the height of his conflict with the principals. Like Mbona's shrine hut, it was circular in shape and of normal proportions, but the materials were those used for ordinary huts. Its entrance faced east. Opposite the entrance, two small mounds of black clay were fashioned on an east-west axis, each about one foot in diameter. The one on the eastern side was said to be Kaphirintiwa and had a hole in the middle; the one on the western side was said to be Malawi and had been flattened. The medium himself could not explain this arrangement except that such was the tradition. On Sept. 5, 1968, I was present when the medium made a libation in Mbona's honor. Kachasu (strong local liquor) was poured into the hole of "Kaphirintiwa," and a cone of maize flour was made on top of "Malawi."

12. Mr. B. A. Phiri, councillor to Chief Malemia, who knew Josef well and had great respect for him, told me once that building this rival shrine had been a major mistake, since it might well have split up the entire cult community (interview, Jan. 2, 1979).

13. Interview, Chief Ngabu and councillors at Ngabu's headquarters, July 13, 1974.

14. In the early hours of March 3, 1959, the security forces were given the task of arresting every influential nationalist sympathizer in every district of the country. This operation, code-named Sunrise, caused violent reactions everywhere, including the Nsanje District. Although the medium was arrested on suspicion of political activism, it is unlikely that he ever was politically active, since he used to say that "Mbona was above politics." He had to be hospitalized and then sent home after a few days because of a mysterious illness, however, which he got immediately after his imprisonment and which he attributed to Mbona's intervention (interview, Oct. 31, 1966).

15. Interview, Fraser Falamenga, Aug. 30, 1973.

16. Interview, Josef Thom, Oct. 31, 1966.

17. Interview, Mbangu and Mbukwa, Jan. 10, 1980.

18. See Text III/B, sec. 24.

19. The reference is to Josef Thom.

20. Ideophone for the act of raving (*-bwebweta*).

21. I have not been able to identify the title Mkanjawe.

22. More usually, pests and the like are attributed to Chitundu, a companion spirit of Mbona, to whom offerings are made on such occasions. Details on Chitundu will be given in Chapter 5.

23. Interview, Chapirira and Kumbiwanyati, Aug. 24, 1964, 35–41.

24. See Chapter 4 for more details about this rumor.

25. The colonial government on various occasions tried to introduce the obligatory ridging of gardens in an effort to stem soil erosion. Each time, however, this met with considerable resistance from the population, which was of the opinion that ridging of gardens, at least on the valley floor, contributed to soil erosion rather than preventing it. For details, see Mandala 1990.

26. This seems to contradict the idea that the red color of the pool has positive connotations. For instance, it is said that before the accession of Molin Tengani the pool was always red, lending curative qualities to the flora around it.

27. Lienhardt 1975:130.

CHAPTER 4: THE QUEST FOR A SPIRIT WIFE AND THE STRUGGLE FOR MANG'ANJA POLITICAL SUPREMACY, 1859–1983

1. Interview, Headman Kadinga Banda, representative of the Mankhokwe family, Aug. 27, 1971.

2. Rowley 1866:151, 266. Actually, Mbona was not the name of the tutelar deity, as Rowley would have it, but of the local spirit wife. The Thyolo shrine,

like most of the Maravi shrines, was dedicated to the High God under his python manifestation, and the mythology of Mbona the martyr played no role there. Nevertheless, the two shrines were viewed by the population at large as parts of one and the same cultic complex, though the Nsanje shrine at Khulubvi was considered the more important (cf. Text II/B, secs. 18–19).

3. Kabvina used to be Kaphwiti's most important subchief and a member of the royal lineage. Chibisa, though the most amply documented Mang'anja ruler of the period, remains a rather shadowy figure due to the fact that he used to spin all sorts of tales about his person. Local traditions remember him as Kabvina's "younger brother." He was shot in early 1863 (Newitt 1973:239–40).

4. For the attitude of Tengani and Mankhokwe toward the Portuguese, see Livingstone and Livingstone 1865:76, 96; for the alliance of Chibisa with the Portuguese, see Wallis 1956:188 and Newitt 1973:139–40.

5. Livingstone was in contact with the Mang'anja for a period of nearly five years, from Jan. 1859 to the end of 1864. During this time he undertook six journeys through the Shire Valley. In its later years the expedition was joined by members of the Universities' Mission to Central Africa (U.M.C.A.), who also established themselves in Mang'anja country. The result has been an unusually rich documentation on the Shire Valley in the early 1860s (e.g., Livingstone and Livingstone 1865; Rowley 1866; Wallis 1952, 1956; Foskett 1965; Tabler 1963; Bennett and Ylvisaker 1971).

6. Livingstone and Livingstone 1865:93, 108.

7. Wallis 1952:93–94.

8. Ibid. Rowley renders the husband's name as Chimbeli, adding that he was regarded as Mankhokwe's ambassador and that the woman who had been selected was his senior wife. Mankhokwe apparently wanted to punish him for "playing the chief" at some villages to which he had been sent (Rowley 1866:411–12).

9. Wallis 1956:188.

10. Rowley 1866:401.

11. Cf. Text IV, sec. 21.

12. Rowley 1866:430–53.

13. Livingstone and Livingstone 1865:456.

14. Kirk, one of the members of the Livingstone expedition, found Khulubvi destroyed in May 1863 (Foskett 1965:521). The raid itself may have taken place in March of that year, when Mariano's men pillaged the area around the shrine after defeating and killing Tengani (Wallis 1956:288).

15. Newitt 1970:93.

16. Interviews, Headman Mbeta, Oct. 7, 1966; Chapirira and Kumbiwanyati, Aug. 24, 1964, secs. 14–18; Headman Mwanda, Sept. 23, 1972.

17. Mandala 1990:84.

18. Faulkner 1868:27.

19. Newitt 1973:280.

20. Interview, Chapirira and Kumbiwanyati, Aug. 24, 1964, secs. 14–18.

21. Interview, M. E. Rambiki (Headman Mphamba), Jan. 5, 1980. *Chiwalawala* was said to be derived from *-balalika*, "to scatter" or "to disperse."

22. Pringle 1884:162–63.

23. Guyot 1895:56. I owe this reference to Dr. W. Rau.

24. Newitt 1973:282–85; Mandala 1990:83–84.

25. Kerr 1886, 2:282.

26. Group interview, B. A. Phiri, Chief Malemia, and Headman Chiphwembwe, Jan. 4, 1980.

27. Macdonald 1882, 1:196–203. The fullest treatment of this period is to be found in Mandala 1990.

28. Rangeley 1959:89.

29. Buchanan 1885:33–34; Hanna 1956:65–66; Newitt 1970:98–105; Ambali 1931:12.

30. Rangeley 1959:98.

31. See details of the Booth episode in Shepperson and Price (1958:59–63), who base their argument on Booth's manuscript "The Call of the Mang'anja People for Pacifists."

32. On Jan. 3, 1982, I interviewed the then headman Chataika (at that time some seventy years old) and two of his sons on the Booth/Chilembwe episode, but it appeared that the family had no recollection about it. The reason for this may have been a break in the line of succession, due to an earlier Chataika's having been deposed for allegedly having forged a postal order.

33. The taboo on the shedding of human blood applies to all territorial shrines. It also serves as one of the reasons forwarded by the population to explain why the *nyau,* whose performances sometimes lead to brawls and bloodshed, are forbidden in the vicinity of such shrines.

34. *Central Africa: A Record of the Work of the Universities Mission* (1895), 13:66–67.

35. Society of Malawi Library, Rangeley Papers, File 1/1/3, "Correspondence on Maravi History," M. Metcalfe to W. H. J. Rangeley, Aug. 9, 1952. According to local traditions, Peile had against all rules been shooting birds at Khulubvi. It is said that he committed suicide upon returning home by shooting himself (interview, B. A. Phiri, Jan. 4, 1980).

36. British Public Record Office, C.O. 525/7: Case of Mr. R. R. Racey, 3d assistant, enclosure in B.C.A., no. 35, Jan. 24, 1905. The beheaded snake may be a reference to Mbona's beheading.

37. Ibid.

38. *South African Pioneer* 14 (1901):208.

39. Price 1911.

40. Rowley 1866:267; also Rowley 1881:151.

41. Young 1868:91.

42. Pringle 1884:162–63.

43. Hetherwick 1917:420.

44. Society of Malawi Library, Rangeley Papers, File 1/1/3, "Correspondence on Maravi History," M. Metcalfe to W. H. J. Rangeley, Jan. 13, 1952. Wyatt's information was at that time confirmed by R. Macdonald, who had for some twenty years been customs officer at Port Herald. District Commissioner Lewis, who was asked to Rangeley to check the story in 1953, reported back that it was totally unknown to the local population (P. M. Lewis to W. H. J. Rangeley, Oct. 4, 1952).

It must therefore have originated among the local Europeans, among whom the missionaries stood to gain most from any measures against the cult.

45. Price 1916:82.

46. Price 1913:104–5.

47. Ibid. It is inconceivable that Mr. Price could have addressed an audience from the door of the shrine hut. This would have meant that not only Price but also a whole crowd of people would have entered the sacred enclosure, something tantamount to sacrilege. There being no reason to suppose that rules were not as strictly followed in the beginning of the century as they were at other times, certainly with regard to Europeans, I take it that Price actually delivered his sermon at some place nearby.

48. Price 1916:83.

49. The term *nomi* refers to mixed working parties of boys and girls who offer their services to villagers against payment in cash or in kind. During the hoeing season they construct a communal grass shed in which they live promiscuously. The missions were understandably opposed to the *nomi*, but they could do nothing without the cooperation of the local chiefs (Schoffeleers 1973c).

50. Interview, J. Chiriwekha and Headman Nthole, Aug. 25, 1973.

51. For details on the Makombe rising, see Ranger 1963 and Isaacman 1976.

52. An exception is to be made for the aristocratic Mwenye ("Indian") families, who claim descent from the Sena Muslims. Their number, however, is very small.

53. Nsanje mission diary, consulted at the Nsanje mission station.

54. The Nsanje baptismal register shows that of the early converts only 10–20 percent were Mang'anja, whereas around that time the Mang'anja still constituted around 67 percent of the population of the Lower Shire District; cf. Murray 1922: 72–73.

55. Schoffeleers and Linden 1972.

56. Traditions to this effect were collected both at Nsanje and Chikwawa (cf. Text I/B, sec. 3, and Text III/B, sec. 1).

57. In the earlier period of my research, four of the leading functionaries of the shrine were members of the S.A.G.M., while the medium, Josef Thom, was a Catholic. He died in May 1978. In Jan. 1982 I found that Ngabu was the only traditionalist left among the senior cult officials. The late medium was the only one who felt he could not be both a Christian and Mbona's representative.

58. According to information obtained from the late Headman Mbeta (interview, Oct. 7, 1966), which was confirmed by the district commissioner's office at Nsanje, the custom of making gifts to the shrine was still practiced in the 1960s. The contribution consisted of a small amount of cash to be used for the purchase of a piece of black cloth and a black umbrella. The practice has since been discontinued.

59. Chanock 1973:27.

60. Malawi National Archives, Nsanje Annual District Report for 1933, in NSP 2/1/4.

61. Malawi National Archives, File NSP 1/15/1, "Correspondence between D.C., Port Herald, and P.C., Southern Region (1936/37)."

62. District commissioner, Port Herald, to senior provincial commissioner, Southern Province, Blantyre, March 4, 1936 (archival index, n. 4).

63. Archival ref., n. 4: Jan. 21, 1936.

64. Details from Tengani's curriculum vitae are from a manuscript written and kept by his son Stephen (Tengani MS 1967), who kindly allowed me to make use of it.

65. Interview, Mbukwa, Khombe, and Kambalame, Oct. 9, 1966; see also Text IV, sec. 29.

66. Interview, Headman Mbeta, Oct. 19, 1966.

67. Text IV, sec. 29. According to most informants, the attempts to make the shrine guardians pay hut tax remained unsuccessful. Tax exemption was reconfirmed in 1966, according to information provided by the district commissioner's office (May 10, 1967).

68. Molin Tengani to district commissioner, Port Herald, Jan. 1938 (Archival ref. n. 79).

69. District commissioner, Port Herald, to provincial commissioner, Southern Province, March 23, 1938.

70. Vaughan 1985:64.

71. See Chapter 3, n. 25. The traditional cultivation method is briefly described in Duly 1948:15.

72. Information provided by Fryton Malemia, agricultural instructor at that time (interview, Aug. 8, 1967).

73. *Njala ya Nkhozi*, the "Nkhozi famine," named after the Nkhozi stream in Chief Dobvu's area, where people went to collect water lily tubers for food.

74. Interview, B. A. Phiri, Jan. 4, 1980.

75. Headman Mbangu, interviewed by Mr. D. S. Jelemani on the author's behalf, April 2, 1978.

76. Interviews, Headman Mbangu, April 2, 1978, and Jan. 5, 1980. The dismissal was probably inspired by the medium's intention to reopen discussions with Lundu.

77. Malawi National Archives, Malawi Government, "Calendar of events, Nsanje District." This document was drawn up at the first population census after independence to help establish the age of people who did not know their birth dates.

78. Society of Malawi Library, Rangeley Papers, File 1/1/3, "Correspondence on Maravi History," Lewis to Rangeley, Nov. 28, 1953.

79. Interviews, Josef Thom, April 1, 1972; Mbangu and Mbukwa, Jan. 10, 1980.

80. Interview, Headman Mbeta, Oct. 7, 1966. According to this source, Lundu had answered that he could find no one, as all were afraid they would die.

81. Interview, Rev. Mark Mangeya, Dec. 29, 1966.

82. Interview, Chief Nyachikadza, Aug. 20, 1973.

83. Schoffeleers, 1985c.

84. Interview, Mr. D. D. Forty, secretary of the Nsanje division of the Church of the African Ancestors, Mbeta village, Jan. 6, 1979. The local founder was one Zuze J. Alufinali from the village of Mphomba, which lies a short distance from the Mbona shrine.

85. Peter Nyambo was born in 1884. He traveled extensively through Europe and parts of Africa in the service of the Seventh-Day Adventist Mission. Later on

he went to South Africa, where he became actively engaged in a small movement which aimed at drawing the British government's attention to the abuses of the colonial government in what was then the Rhodesias and Nyasaland. In that function he sailed to England in May 1914 to present a petition to the king, once again returning to South Africa in 1917. The Church of the Black Ancestors was reportedly founded soon after his definitive return to his native district around 1942 (Shepperson and Price 1958:203–9; Wishlade 1965:20–21).

86. The term *neotraditionalist* is used here in the same sense as Linton's "nativistic movement" and thus refers to "any conscious movement on the part of a society's members to revive or perpetuate selected aspects of its culture" (Linton 1943). I prefer *neotraditionalist*, however, because it expresses more clearly the character of the Nsanje movements, which aim at making traditional features relevant to the present situation.

87. There is some confusion about the use of the name "Ethiopian Church." Wishlade (1965) uses it as an alternative appellation for the Church of the African Ancestors, but in Nsanje the two names refer to two different church bodies.

88. "Zoonadi zacheza Mpulumutsi wa aIsraeli-Azungu: Yesu" (3pp.; n.d.).

89. Interviews, B. A. Phiri, Jan. 2, 1979; D. D. Forty, Jan. 6, 1979; Headman Mbangu, Jan. 5, 1980.

90. Interviews, D. D. Forty, Dec. 31, 1978; A. Kamfula, Jan. 3, 1979. Notebook, D. D. Forty.

91. Territorial mediums usually lead a normal married life, but Kingy maintains that Mbona commanded him to live in celibacy from the time of his possession.

92. Group interview, Petro Thom, Catholic church elder; A. Kamfula, Catholic catechist; D. D. Forty, Ancestor leader, Jan. 13, 1979. Also Nsanje police, civil case no. 121/77. The three interviewees maintained that the incident took place in the month of November, which is a normal time for rain rituals, but the police report states that it happened "between August and September."

93. When I visited Armando's place on Jan. 3, 1979, the "shrine" was still partly intact, but his hut, which stood at a little distance, had been razed to the ground by the villagers.

94. Nsanje police, civil case no. 121/77. Section 2 of the Witchcraft Act (1968) reads: "Trial by ordeal of *muabvi* or other poison, fire, boiling water, or by any ordeal which is likely directly or indirectly to result in the death of or bodily injury to any person shall be and is hereby prohibited." How this section came to be applied in Armando's case I am unable to explain, except that the forest patch in which he erected the shrine had a long historical link with the poison ordeal. It is also possible that Armando at one time or another had suggested that people undergo the ordeal.

According to the police report, Lukwa stated that he and Armando were descendants of Mbona and that it had been their intention "to travel by night to the place where Mbona is believed to be [i.e., Khulubvi] and take him to their own place so that people at Tengani would enjoy a regular supply of rain."

95. Interview, B. A. Phiri, Jan. 2, 1979. Mr. Phiri is a former member of the district council, Nsanje. The official reason for its discontinuation was that the district council no longer made provision for occasional contributions to deserv-

ing causes. It no doubt also reflects the shrine's diminished importance in the life of the district at that time.

96. Interviews, Jimu Thom, the late medium's brother, Jan. 1, 1979; B. A. Phiri, Malemia's deputy at the funeral, Jan. 2, 1979.

97. Interview, Lusiano Rice, Dec. 31, 1981. Mr. Rice, a catechist at Nsanje Catholic Mission, had been allowed to visit the place together with three companions on Sept. 29, 1981. He told me that on that date little remained of the shrine except a few poles stuck in the ground. The roof had caved in and, like the reed walls, had been eaten by termites.

CHAPTER 5: THE LUNDU STATE IN
THE LATE SIXTEENTH AND EARLY
SEVENTEENTH CENTURIES

1. Alpers 1967, 1968:21; 1975:51–53. Alpers and Ehret 1975:517.
2. Newitt 1982.
3. Curtin et al. 1978:172–73.
4. Newitt 1982:158.
5. Rangeley 1954; Bhila unpubl. 1977.
6. Newitt 1982:149.
7. Schebesta 1966; Axelson 1969; Isaacman 1972; Newitt 1973; Alpers 1975; Bhila 1982.
8. Willis 1976; Miller 1978.
9. Newitt 1982:151.
10. Monclaro (1569) 1899:235.
11. Ibid., 229, 234–35.
12. Ibid., 234; Santos (1609) 1902:234–35.
13. Schebesta (1966:75), for one, suggests that one of the reasons behind Silveira's murder may have been the latter's disapproval of the cordial relations between the local Portuguese and Swahili communities. Newitt (1973:40) expresses his opinion that the Muslims at the Monomotapa's headquarters must have realized that Silveira was going to upset the existing modus vivendi between the two parties. As for the reasons why they entertained such good relations, Schebesta states that "for the traders it was advantageous, as is known from many sources, to maintain such trading relations with the Moors" (1966:75).
14. Rea 1960:32–35.
15. Monclaro (1569) 1899:247.
16. Ibid. 236.
17. Santos, who was born around 1560 in Portugal, became a member of the Dominican order in 1584. Two years later he was appointed to the Southeast African missions of the Dominicans, where he worked eleven years before returning home to write his magnum opus. According to Schebesta (1966:93), Santos' first term on the Zambezi lasted only ten months, from Sept. 1590 to July 1591, after which he left for Mozambique, but Santos' own text implies that he left for Mozambique only in the course of 1593 (cf. Santos (1609) 1901:299). Having seen

through the publication of *Ethiopia Oriental,* he returned to the Zambezi missions, where he stayed until 1616 or a little later. He died in Goa in 1622 at the age of sixty-two.

18. Santos (1609) 1901:292.

19. Ibid.

20. Ibid., 295.

21. Ibid.

22. Ibid., 296.

23. Ibid., 297–99.

24. Alpers 1975:53.

25. Both Alpers (1975:50) and Newitt (1982:156) assume that there were two Zimba campaigns, one before and one after 1590. If we leave out the Zimba horde which ravaged Kilwa and Mombasa as unrelated to Lundu's Zimba, however, there is no evidence left of any Zimba action in Makualand prior to the 1590s. Even Lupi's account, which is one of Alpers' main sources, implies no Zimba activity on the east coast before that date. It is therefore likely that the Zimba conquest of Makualand took place only after 1590 or even 1593.

26. Santos (1609) 1901:368–69.

27. The principal reason why Lundu receives less attention in Portuguese documents than Muzura is that the latter, whose final political breakthrough coincided with the return of the Jesuits to the Zambezi (1615), was considered much more of a threat to their missionary work.

28. Newitt (1973:188), quoting Antonio Pinto de Miranda, a Zambezi settler who wrote in the 1760s, mentions that the greatest number became slaves in time of famine, when selling themselves and their children was the only alternative to starvation.

29. Santos (1609) 1901:268: Wallis 1956:268.

30. Gamitto 1960, 1:127; Chafulumira 1948:20.

31. Bocarro (1676) 1899:395.

32. The name Muzura may have been derived from the verb *-zula,* "to pull up by the roots"; *mu-* is a common actor prefix; the consonants *r* and *l* are interchangeable in Chiman'anja. Cf. Scott 1892:681, s.v. *zula.*

33. Gomes (1648) 1959:199–200.

34. Bocarro (1676) 1899:461–19. The location of Muzura's capital is discussed in the final section of this chapter.

35. The year 1622 is mentioned by Schurhammer (1920:349), whose source is Father Sebastian Barreto's annual report to the superior general of the Jesuits from Goa, dated Dec. 15, 1624.

36. Bocarro (1676) 1899:387–95; Axelson 1969:41–42.

37. Axelson 1969:67; Newitt 1973:52; Newitt 1982:160; Alpers 1975:83; Schebesta 1966:118; Courtois 1889:13. There is apparently no unanimity on the year of Gatsi Rusere's death, some sources mentioning 1623, others 1624.

38. Newitt 1982:160.

39. Barreto (1667) 1899:480.

40. Interviews, Mbukwa, Khombe, and Kambalame, May 4, 1967; Josef Thom, April 1, 1972. According to the officials, an offering of strong liquor (*nipa*) had

been made to Chitundu a few days earlier to drive away huge swarms of birds, which were causing considerable damage to the rice fields in the nearby marshes. Mr. Thom told me that two months before the interview the roof of the Mbona shrine was partly blown off by a whirlwind, which in his view had been caused by Chitundu "because people had been neglecting Mbona."

41. Price 1927.

42. The relationship between Makombe and the Zimba in oral historical accounts is somewhat complex. The following statement may be regarded as typical: "The Zimba were great hunters. Their leader was Makombe, who lived near Gorongozi Mountain. The overall name of the tribe was Nyanguru [Makombe's royal clan name]. One section called itself Tonga, deriving its name from the verb *tonga*, which means 'to command,' for wherever they went, they took command of the place. Others again called themselves Barwe, but they formed one group only" (interview, Stole Chimbuto, Oct. 18, 1966).

43. Interview, Fryton Malemia, Aug. 8, 1967. On the different meanings of *kholo*, see Scott 1892:227.

44. Santos (1609) 1901:300.

45. The prefix *chi-* is commonly used in the Mang'anja language to convey the notion of something big or redoubtable. Chitundu may therefore be translated as "the fearsome Tundu."

46. Abraham 1966:46.

47. See my rejoinders to Newitt in Schoffeleers 1987b and to Wrigley in Schoffeleers 1988.

48. Livingstone's logbook for Jan. 3, 1859, mentions Matundu as the name of the range of hills west of the Shire (Wallis 1956:76). Rangeley notes that Chief Ndamera has a sacred grove called Matundu, to the north of the Tundu Stream. The same source also mentions the name of Subchief Chimombo's court as Matundu (Society of Malawi Library, Rangeley Papers, File 2/1/17). See also Malawi National Archives, District Maps, Dept. of Surveys, Blantyre, sheet 10, Nsanje (1975).

49. A likely location for the Zimba fortress would be the Lulwe Plateau, on the southwestern corner of the Matundu Hills, which at an altitude of around five hundred meters extends several miles into Mozambique in the direction of Sena. This plateau is drained by the Tundu Stream, which carries water for most of the year (Murray 1922:65, 68).

50. On the use of the prefix *ma-* in Chimang'anja, see Scott 1892:299. Also see Price 1963.

51. Gamitto 1960, 1:28, and route map attached to vol. 2.

52. Lupi 1907; Alpers 1975:51–52.

53. See Bruwer 1952; Rangeley 1952, 1953; Gamitto 1960, 1:76–77; Amanze unpubl. 1986.

54. It can hardly be coincidental that the Zimba were known both as Matundu and Marundu. Whether or not these two names were used interchangeably by the same speakers is not known, but there can be little doubt that the two names referred to the same group of people.

55. Newitt 1982:161.

56. Newitt 1973:34–38.
57. Ibid., 37.
58. Bocarro (1676) 1899:388.
59. Gomes (1648) 1959:180; Barreto (1667) 1899:475.
60. Newitt 1973:201–2.
61. Ibid., 202.
62. Barreto de Rezende (c. 1635) 1899:408.
63. Alpers 1975:49.
64. Price 1952:76; Rangeley 1952:32; Ntara 1965:19; Linden 1979:188.
65. Rangeley 1954.
66. Cf. Texts II/A, secs. 11–12; II/B, sec. 5.
67. Alpers 1975:68, n 46.
68. Gomes (1648) 1959:157, n. 5.
69. Newitt 1982:159–60.
70. Beccari 1912:112–14. Aloysius (Luis, Luigi) Mariana (also rendered as Mariano) was born in Brescia, Italy, in 1581. He joined the Jesuit order in 1600 at the age of nineteen. Before his ordination he was sent to Goa, where he completed his theological training. In 1614 he went to Southeast Africa, where the Jesuits had opened a new mission field five years earlier. He took part in a reconnaissance expedition to Malagasy, which earned him some fame as an explorer and which may have been one of the reasons why he was being asked to provide geographic information about Lake Malawi. He taught for a while at the newly established college of St. Francis Xavier on Mozambique Island. In 1620 we find him among the Jesuit community at Sena, where he was still working in 1625.

By 1620 the Turks were in possession of all the Red Sea ports, making it virtually impossible for missionaries to travel to Ethiopia along the eastern route. They therefore decided to explore new routes via the East African ports and Galla country, but these attempts were all preempted by the Muslims. They then began to entertain the idea of traveling to Ethiopia via the Central African lakes, notably Lake Malawi. In early March 1623 the viceroy of India (F. da Gama) wrote to King Philip IV from Goa that he had heard of this lake, which was said to stretch all the way to the borders of Ethiopia. In his reply, dated Feb. 17, 1624, Philip suggested that the viceroy try to get the Jesuits interested in the project (Beccari 1912:17; Schebesta 1966:131, 475 n. 295). The then superior of the Indian Jesuit missions, Fr. André Palmeiro, who was also in charge of the East African mission field, responded by commissioning Fr. Mariana to collect the necessary information. Mariana's reply was sent directly to Fr. Palmeiro, who in his turn forwarded a copy to the superior general in Rome (Schurhammer 1920:350). The original Portuguese version of the letter remained unpublished until 1912, when it was integrally reproduced in vol. 12. of Beccari's monumental edition of early missionary documents. Until then some historians (e.g., Brucker 1878) had made use of an abbreviated Latin version, which had been included in the 1624 report of the Goanese province, composed by Fr. Sebastian Barreto (Schurhammer 1920:351 n. 1). Others made use of a somewhat garbled Italian version (*Lettere Annue* 1627), or a French rendering of that version, which appeared in 1628.

71. Reproduced in Schebesta 1966 (opp. p. 33) and Axelson 1969 (opp. p. 55).

72. Gomes (1648) 1959:200.

73. Mariana actually seems to refer to two locations, one on the southwestern lakeshore, the other between (*entre*) the lake and the Zambezi, leaving open what interpretation should be given to *entre*. Depending on the meaning attached to that word, the phrase may mean that Maravi lay somewhere midway between those two points or that it lay on the Zambezi side of the lakeshore.

74. Schoffeleers 1971; Price 1963.

75. Santos (1609) 1901:292; Schebesta 1966:129; *Lettere Annue* 1627.

76. Murray 1922:85.

CHAPTER 6: ORAL TRADITIONS AND THE RETRIEVAL OF THE DISTANT PAST

1. de Heusch 1972:15–18; 1975:363–67.

2. de Heusch 1975:365–66.

3. Dumézil 1948.

4. de Heusch 1975:363.

5. Willis 1980:32.

6. Willis 1976:2.

7. The texts specify that the rainmaker sprinkled flour on the women's bodies, which in normal circumstances women do among themselves in certain ritual contexts. The precise nature of this deviation from the norm is not altogether clear, but I suspect that, apart from the sexual connotation, it refers to a contravention of the color code, white being forbidden at rain ceremonies. The rainmaker may thus have turned himself into a rain withholder.

8. Janzen 1977:91–92.

9. Leach 1954. We know little as yet about the processes by which the Maravi states encapsulated the existing population, but the persistence of stateless pockets into the nineteenth century as documented by Gamitto (see Chapter 1) suggests the possibility of local communities oscillating like the Kachin communities between the two systems.

10. Mr. Phiri's version of the Mbona myth will be discussed in combination with Headman Mphamba's in Part 2 of this book.

11. Ntara 1973.

12. de Heusch 1982a:34–75; 1982b:331–75.

13. Wrigley 1988:372.

14. de Heusch 1972, 1975.

15. Schoffeleers 1988.

16. See Chapter 5.

17. The criteria of historicity on which I am basing my argument were first suggested by Horton (1967:67–68). They do not primarily reflect objective historicity but rather historicity as conceived by the cult community. They are three in number and refer to birth and lineage ascription, marriage and progeniture, and death and burial. A supernatural, said to have once lived a human life, is thus thought of as fully "historical" when it is known to what lineage that individual was born,

whom he or she married and the names of their offspring, and where and by whom burial took place.

18. Willis 1976.

CHAPTER 7: IDEOLOGICAL
CONFRONTATION IN ORAL TRADITION

1. Malinowski 1948.
2. Leach 1954.
3. Appadurai 1983.
4. Feierman 1974:4.
5. Mandala 1990:25–36; Lovejoy 1981.
6. Dumézil 1948; Needham 1980:63–105.
7. Tcherkézoff 1987.
8. Sumner 1906.
9. I am aware that this by no means exhausts the symbolism of the grass versus iron imagery. For one thing, the two can also be viewed in a more general sense as representing the opposition between nature and culture, but that opposition is not particularly relevant to the stage of Mang'anja history that concerns us here. Its relevance pertains rather to the early state period, when the Maravi had to legitimate themselves as purveyors of a superior culture.

MBONA BIOGRAPHIES: GENERAL INTRODUCTION

1. Chakanza 1936.
2. Rangeley 1953.

TEXT I/A

1. Central Angoniland is part of the present-day Dedza District.
2. Note the tradition of a double origin of the Mang'anja group, respectively associated with a Maravi migration under Lundu and an earlier Chipeta migration under Mbona (see Chapter 1). The principal spokesman, Ngabu Phiri, who considers himself Mbona's descendant, thereby suggests that his rights and those of the cult are older than Lundu's.
3. Murray 1922:32. The Lundu mentioned by Murray as "an unimportant village headman in the West Shire District" is a Yao chief who has no relationship with the Lundus of the Lower Shire Valley.
4. Originally, the Chiphwembwes were the counterparts of the Malemias, for whom they also deputized. After World War I, however, the Chiphwembwes managed to usurp the position of the Malemias. This was reversed once again by presidential decree in Dec. 1968 (see Chapter 3).
5. Mlungu or Mulungu is a common designation for the Mang'anja High God. For futher meaning of the term, see Text III/B, n. 3.

6. The name as presented here is composed of the locative prefix *ku*, meaning "at," and the proper name Kambiritiya or, more correctly, Kaphirintiwa.

7. Naming Mbona's father is typical of the Mbona I complex. Chingale is now the name of a chiefdom in the Zomba District. The name Chimbe or Chembe appears in Rangeley 1953, not as that of Mbona's mother but as that of one of his spirit wives.

8. It is possible that Sawawa, Samisanje, Chungu, and Tiza, mentioned here as Mbona's "real" wives, were actually spirit wives who once served at the shrine. Sawawa (Rangeley 1953:17) and Tiza (Thiza) are also mentioned as Mbona's mother. A notebook on early Mang'anja history by Mr. B. A. Phiri, Malemia village, Nsanje, which the author allowed me to cite (Jan. 4, 1980), mentions "two sons of Tiza" who quarreled with Mbona. In a subsequent interview on Jan. 6, 1980, arranged to clarify some of the problems raised by the notebook, the author specified that Thiza was the headwife of Mbona's Chipeta father, Mbona being his son by a junior wife.

9. *Mlandu* means, among other things, a lawsuit or quarrel.

10. *Msumpi* or *msumphi* is a term still in use among the central Maravi to indicate a rain priest (Bruwer 1952). The term is no longer known to the Mang'anja, which accounts for its being used here as a proper name.

11. *Mwabvi* is the Mang'anja term for poison ordeal.

12. It is interesting that Mbona (or the cult indicated by the name) should be associated with an antiordeal movement in precolonial times. The ordeal issue is also mentioned in Ntara's history of the Chewa (Ntara 1973:13), although in a different sense: Mbona is held responsible for a number of deaths caused by the ordeal.

13. Dzambawe lies to the west of the valley.

14. Mbango's village is adjacent to the shrine. It is said that it originally consisted of runaway slaves and other fugitives who upon their arrival at the shrine used to break a shaft of reed (*bango*) to indicate that they wanted to serve Mbona for the rest of their lives.

15. *Kupatikana* as a verb means "to be close together" (Scott 1892:512), which stands in contrast with the theme of fraternal hostility, which is typical of Mbona I.

16. The term *brother* should be read as "relative." The word *mbale*, which was probably used in the original text, has both meanings.

17. The statement that Tengani, though the senior chief in the southern part of the valley, was in no way related to Mbona may possibly be interpreted as another attempt to argue that the cult was originally independent of the state system.

TEXT I/B

1. The reference is to that part of eastern Zambia which borders on Malawi's Central Region.

2. Chididi lies in the Matundu Hills; Dzambawe lies on the western side of the same hills.

3. Lit.: "Agoa." This could be taken to mean that Mbona was born before the Portuguese ("Goanese") penetration of Zambesia. More likely, however, the

informant refers to the Goanese merchant, Paul Mariano Vas dos Anjos, founder of one of the famous *prazo* families of the nineteenth century (Newitt 1973:137), whose extensive land holdings lay on the other side of the Shire and whose sphere of influence covered part of the valley (see Chapter 4).

4. This is a departure from the Mbona I complex, in which the names of Mbona's parents are a fixed item (see Text I/A).

TEXT II/A

1. The date A.D. 1500 is probably borrowed from some published text.

2. The same person is known as Chirizizwa in the oral traditions of the northern Chewa, where he is mentioned as the second rather than the first of their paramounts (cf. Ntara 1973:160).

3. Undi is the dynastic title of the western Chewa paramounts (see Chapter 1). MS 2 mentions this title as belonging to a junior kinsman of Chiridzodzwe.

4. Kaphwiti is generally regarded as the founder of the earliest Mang'anja state (see Chapter 1). There still was a Kaphwiti in Livingstone's days, but the title has since become defunct. The Mlauli title, on the other hand, is still extant, but the chiefdom is now in the hands of a Kololo dynasty. Nyangu is considered to have been the ancestress of the Phiri clan. The name traditionally also indicated the position of "queen mother" at the Maravi courts.

5. The tradition about a homeland in Uganda is also found in published accounts of Chewa oral history (Ntara 1973:1). MS 2 states that the Mang'anja first lived in Burundi (cf. the "Urundi" of the present text).

6. The name Mlauli may be a derivation of the verb *-laula*, "to reveal" or "speak forth," and is translated by the main Mang'anja dictionary (Scott 1892:361) as "prophet." In the present case a more appropriate translation would have been "spirit medium."

7. Ntara (1973:4), who also mentions this early contact with the Arabs, renders the name of their leader as Hasan-bin-Ali. MS 2 states that the encounter took place at Ujiji on Lake Tanganyika. Precisely how this episode came to form part of Chewa oral traditions about their ancestors' migrations I am unable to say. It may be a fairly recent addition, although there is a possibility that the foundation of the coastal trading town of Angoche by the *wazir* of Kilwa, al-Hasan ibn-Suliman, in the late fifteenth century had its effects on early Chewa history (cf. H. Langworthy in Ntara 1973:5).

8. Lit.: "They sat down to eat the fruits of the *mtondo* tree." The *mtondo* (*Cordyla africana*) is a large shady tree, found in many village meeting places in low-lying parts of Malawi. Its fruits are edible, but they have an unpleasant smell and are only eaten by old people (Williamson 1975:80).

9. Bulrush millet (*mchewere*) is the hardiest of the cereals grown in the valley. MS 2 further dramatizes the situation by stating that the soil in that place was so sandy that not even bulrush millet would grow there.

10. I have been unable to identify this person. The original name may have been Kafara, and under Portuguese influence it has probably been corrupted to Kavalo.

11. MS 2 adds that they needed those tall trees "to build big houses." This reference to a treeless country is strikingly reminiscent of Gamitto's passage about the land of the Chipeta, which he describes as "flat, with few trees, [while] those that exist are very small" (Gamitto 1960, 1:67). It is therefore possible that the text at this point alludes to a conflict with a Chipeta group, despite the fact that the Chipeta lived rather more to the south. This might then allow us to interpret their supposed preference for big houses as an allusion to their reputation as state build-ers, large dwelling places being typical of a chief's headquarters. The phrase "big house" may also refer to a large and powerful lineage.

12. The Songwe River forms Malawi's northernmost boundary with Tanzania.

13. Changamire occupies a prominent place in Chewa oral traditions as the reputed leader of their wars against the pygmoid Twa or Batwa, who are supposed to have been in possession of the country before the Maravi.

14. The distance between the Songwe River and Mt. Zomba is over 550 kilome-ters as the crow flies, which seems rather much for a single scouting trip, but it is clearly seen as the epochal event which opened up the country for the new immigrants.

15. I have been unable to obtain further details on these two names.

16. Traditions about an original population of dwarfish people are common among the Maravi (cf. Rangeley 1963). Even nowadays it is claimed that a few Kafula or Batwa (as they are commonly named) are still living in the mountainous parts of the country, including the Lower Shire Valley. The name Mwandionerakuti ("From what distance did you notice me?") is said to derive from the question they invariably ask when meeting someone of a taller race, the correct answer being "I could see you already from afar." If one gave the correct answer, one would be left in peace, but persons not knowing it were sure to be killed. The name Aka-fupidoli also refers to their short stature.

17. Karonga, or Kalonga, is a title commonly bestowed on great chiefs (Mar-wick 1963:378) and more particularly to the Chewa paramount near Lake Malawi, who was already known to the seventeenth-century Portuguese by that name (see Chapter 5). Young (1932:90) maintains that initially it carried the meaning of "war leader," which is also what the present text suggests.

18. This is the Mang'anja spelling of Kaphirintiwa, the location of the reputed mother shrine in the Dzalanyama mountains. *Kaphiri* means "small hill." *Ntiwa* is translated by Scott (1892:471) and by the author of the present text as "a flat place." The halting of the immigrant group at or near Kaphirintiwa is a stock item in Chewa oral history (see Ntara 1973:8–10), establishing a claim to control over the shrine.

19. The Chewa system of succession and inheritance, including succession to chieftaincies and headmanships, is matrilineal, not patrilineal as the present text suggests. The author may have been influenced by the gradual shift to patrilineal-ity, which is taking place in the Lower Shire Valley under the influence of immi-grants from the south bank of the Zambezi.

20. The author does not seem to notice that, contrary to what he maintains, Chitimbe was not Chingale's cross-cousin or mother's brother's daughter, which in the conception of the Mang'anja would have resulted in an incestuous union.

Chingale and Chitimbe (Chimbe) are names borrowed from the Mbona I complex, where they figure as those of Mbona's father and mother, respectively (Text I/A, n. 7). Apparently, the author has no idea what these names stand for since they do not fulfill any function in the story. MS 2 is slightly more consistent in its effort to combine the significant names of the two complexes. There, Chingale and Chitimbe are retained as the names of Mbona's parents, while the link with the Mbona II complex is established by presenting Chingale as a son of Undi, and Chitimbe as a daughter of Kaphwiti. But even so, the principle of cross-cousin marriage is violated, since Undi and Kaphwiti are brothers.

21. Apparently, Kaphwiti had been given a chiefdom of his own. Its location is mentioned in sec. 32 of the present text as the Ntcheu District, which lies approximately ninety kilometers southeast of Kaphirintiwa. The more general opinion, however, holds that the Kaphwiti chiefdom lay somewhat more to the south, along the banks of the Wamkurumadzi River.

22. On Nyangu, see n. 4 above. Claiming descent from someone by that name used to be a device to establish a person's superior social status. Thus Shepperson and Price (1958:44) mention traditions to the effect that the mother of John Chilembwe, leader of the 1915 rising, was also called Nyangu.

23. This passage shows quite clearly the author's awareness that the Mang'anja after all are matrilineal, for he has Mbona going to live with his maternal uncle Mlauli to learn the art of rain calling and eventually to succeed him. But the confusion about the succession system remains, since in the preceding section we are told that Mlauli's office was inherited by his sons.

24. The Mang'anja chiefdoms do not have official rain callers, but they do have spirit mediums (usually women), one of whose tasks it is to indicate when a rain ceremony is due. These ceremonies are similar to those performed annually at the Mbona shrine (see Chapter 2), consisting of offerings and prayers, followed by a rain dance in which the entire congregation takes part (Rowley 1866:268–69). Yet this text as well as other versions of the Mbona story suggest that professional rain callers did exist in the past.

25. *Kandranga* daggers are used for ritual purposes only. They are approximately one foot long, and their handles and sheaths are made of two kinds of wood, respectively black and reddish in color. The blade, made of highly polished iron, is considered "white." The front side, made of the black wood, is adorned with geometric carvings, whereas the reddish back side is plain. The whole evokes the idea of a stylized human figure. The context in which this type of dagger is used further suggests that it may be interpreted as a symbolic representation of the cosmos and the seasons. The handle and the sheath may then be taken to refer to the sky and the earth, while the black and the red sides would symbolize the wet season (dark clouds) and the dry season (bush fires). The blade would be a suitable symbol for lightning, which separates the seasons — thunderstorms occurring particularly during the transitional periods — but which unite heaven and earth.

26. The name Tundu or Chitundu is a borrowing from the Mbona III complex (see chapter 6). Mphamba is the name of a headmanship which forms part of the shrine organization. Usually, only Ngabu and Makombe are named as Mbona's

sons, but Mphamba's name has been added because the author of the present text belongs to that family.

27. Although it is not explained why Mbona decided to use sorcery against his uncle, the implication clearly is that he wanted his uncle's position. MS 2 records a different tradition, according to which Mbona had accused his uncle of indecent behavior, as the latter was in the habit of surrounding himself with women and of strewing flour on their bodies when dancing. Being thus exposed by Mbona was such a humiliating experience for Mlauli that he fell ill and died. Mlauli's sickness and death in MS 2 seems to symbolize the demise of the professional rain caller's office.

28. This rain song is widely known in Malawi (see Gwengwe 1965:31).

29. Pouring flour on a person's head is done in a ritual context as a sign of joy and celebration.

30. According to MS 2, Kaphwiti becomes Mbona's main antagonist after Mlauli's death. Kaphwiti accuses Mbona of having killed his uncle by means of witchcraft and orders him to undergo the poison ordeal. When Mbona vomits, thereby proving his innocence, he is accused of secretly having taken an antidote which caused the vomiting. Mbona then realizes that the chief is out to kill him, and he takes flight.

31. The splitting up of the population into two camps is an element borrowed from the Mbona I complex (see Text I/B, sec. 5).

32. The hills referred to form an almost unbroken range along the whole of the valley's western border. They are mostly stony, uninhabited, and difficult to travel. The normal thing to do would have been for Mbona to take the road through the valley, but the implication seems to be that this would have made it easy for his pursuers to catch up with him. There is also a more symbolic side to this episode, because, being a member of the Phiri ("Hill") clan, Mbona keeps to the hills, even when trekking. The same idea is expressed in numerous oral traditions about the early migrations, where it is said that the newcomers were called Phiri because they were in the habit of traveling over hills. Finally, as will become clear further on, Mbona appears to be invulnerable when in the hills and can be killed only when he descends to the valley floor. For that reason he cannot leave the hills until he reaches Malawi Hill, at the foot of which the shrine lies.

33. According to MS 2, the pursuit was from this point onward led by Lundu.

34. Both metamorphoses evoke associations with the spirit world and may possibly be taken as presaging Mbona's impending death. Clumps of trees are reminiscent of burial groves (*msitu*), and guinea fowls (*nkhawena*), with their characteristic black and white markings, appear in certain contexts to be regarded as manifestations of the dead. They are able to develop an incredible speed afoot when pursued, which seems to fit the story quite well.

35. More usually, Mbona is said to have performed this feat only once, at a place called Dzambawe near the southernmost part of the hills range.

36. The only place where such imprints are actually shown is a rock in the Thangadzi River, a seasonal stream just north of Bangula trading center. Rangeley (1953:12) describes them as no more than ordinary weathering of the rock, except the imprint of Mbona's buttocks — two parallel grooves on the rock surface — which

appear to have come into being by Stone Age men grinding and polishing their axes. My own observations confirm this.

37. The Chimwala is a seasonal stream which passes by Mphamba village, of which the present author was the headman. This no doubt explains why he chose this particular route for Mbona to travel to the valley floor. The other texts show a preference for a route marked by one of the bigger streams in the area.

38. the Chiriwakufa ("dead Shire") is a seasonal river arm in the Dinde Marsh, opposite the shrine.

39. Etymologically, the name Ndione might be explained as a compound of the verb -*ona*, "to see," in one of its imperative forms (cf. Price 1947:97–98) and the pronoun of the first person singular, *ndi*, in its objective sense, "me." A literal translation would then be something like "look at me!" or "watch me!"

40. This is a common saying used to warn somebody not to think too easily that he can outdo an opponent. Its use at this stage, however, may have a further meaning also. One of the stock themes in the Mbona stories is that he remains invulnerable as long as he keeps to the hills. The reference to the anthill and the safety it provides may possibly be taken as an allusion to that theme.

41. Medicating oneself or having oneself medicated against spears, bullets, and the like appears to be common practice. Its being mentioned here seems in accordance with the author's portrayal of Mbona as a sorcerer. No version that we know of explains why Mbona should be invulnerable to iron weapons, but the implicit assumption always seems to be that this was a quality inherent in his person and not something effected by the use of magical substances.

42. More usually it is maintained that his assailants had to make use of a stalk or leaf of the *nansongole* grass (*Imperata cylindrica*), which grows very high and has stiff, sharply pointed leaf blades (Jackson and Wiehe 1958:46). The question why Mbona had to be killed by being cut with a blade of grass allows for a number of answers, one of them being that it may symbolize the power of the Chipeta or grasslands people (see Chapter 7).

43. The original text at this point is extremely compact, due among other things to an artful use of ideophones.

44. Once again the author has to remind his readers that one of his forefathers was a cofounder of the cult.

45. For the identification of the *mtondo* tree, see n. 8 above. The word rendered here as "sacred place" is *chitupira*, which seems an uncommon term. It occurs also in MS 2, however, which uses the term *akulu akuchitupira* (elders of the *chitupira*) when referring to the cult officers. I have also checked my translation with Mr. B. A. Phiri, the author of MS 2 (Jan. 6, 1980).

46. The indication given in this passage that a section of the invading group was responsible for the founding of the cult is fully in accordance with the Mbona II complex, one of whose functions is to legitimate positions such as Mphamba's, which seem to have their origin in the early state complex.

47. Chipironi Mountain lies in Mozambique, approximately sixty kilometers northeast of the shrine. More usually, Chitundu is said to have gone southward to the Zambezi Valley.

48. These are the titles of four of the shrine guardians.

49. To appreciate the brief description of the cult in this and the next passage, it should be contrasted with the rain ritual described earlier on (sec. 14). There, the central event was the rain dance, performed at the chief's court by a person credited with special skills. Here, the central event is an offering, made at a sacred place away from any chief's court, to the spirit of a deceased person. The contrast also extends to the atmosphere prevalent at these two events, the rain dance being characterized by a show of prowess, the offering by expressions of humbleness and guilt.

50. Beer is made from the flour of maize, kaffir corn, or bulrush millet. The brew takes six days to mature. To make the brew, malt from sprouted grain is needed. The grain is soaked for a day, the water is poured off, and the grain is put in an earthenware pot, where it remains under a cover of leaves for two or three days. Once germinated, it is dried in the sun for a while and then pounded or ground between stones (cf. Williamson 1975:261–62). It is often said that in the past, when beer was being prepared for the annual offering at the shrine, the grain needed for the malt was left in the open in large potsherds. When this had been done, it was believed that rain would fall that very night to soak the grains, thereby indicating that the ritual would be successful.

51. On the topic of pilgrimages to the shrine, see Chapter 2. Mbewe is Lundu's capital in the northern part of the valley; Chipironi is to the northeast (see n. 47); Mt. Morumbala lies to the south, close by the Shire-Zambezi confluence; and Ntcheu lies at a distance of rather more than two hundred kilometers to the north. The name Ntcheu refers here to Kaphwiti's capital, which the author associates with the Ntcheu District (see n. 21).

52. This statement was essentially correct at the time it was written. At a later stage, however, the cult lost some of its influence, due on the one hand to the rapid rise of Pentecostal churches, which have no use for it (see Chapter 4), and on the other to the closure of the Mozambique border, which has made traffic between the two countries rather hazardous.

53. On Tengani's role in the rebuilding of the shrine and his subsequent death, see Chapter 2.

TEXT II/B

1. The noun *mulungu*, here rendered as "godhead," also connotes "sky," "rain," and "thunder."

2. Undi is the name of the paramount chief of the western Chewa, who inhabit adjoining parts of Zambia and Mozambique. Part of the Shire Valley once fell under his authority (see Chapter 1).

3. The theme of tears turning into or causing rain does not occur in other Mbona traditions, but we find a parallel among the Sukuma. When the rain was too long in coming, the Sukuma king might be killed, expelled, or replaced. Alternatively, he might be beaten up to the point of tears. Tears would attract the rains (Tcherkézoff 1987:69, citing H. Cory, *The Ntemi* [London: Macmillan, 1951], 35).

4. In addition to the three crops mentioned here (in Chimang'anja, *mayere,*

chitowe, and *nzama*), the original text also mentions *nanyera,* which I am unable to identify. In published lists of plant names it appears as the Chewa term for *Brachiaria deflexa,* an annual weed belonging to the genus Graminiae, which is found at low altitudes (Jackson and Wiehe 1958:73; Binns 1972:154). It could be the name of a wild grain, but our text explicitly states that it was cultivated.

5. This interpretation of the name Mbona is the narrator's own. Scott (1892: 331, s.v. *mbona*) gives the following meanings: "a wonder," "something desirable," "an overseer," and "a witness." All these meanings convey the sense of "seeing" or "being seen" and derive from the verb *-wona,* "to see" or "to be true." The name may possibly be related also to the noun *bona,* the concluding ceremony of the mourning period, at which offerings of food and beer are made (Scott 1892:733, s.v. *true*).

6. The combination of Mbona II and Mbona III themes occasionally leads to unexpected developments in the story. Here we have a good example, for after having first been told that Mbona was still a child when he was forced to flee for his life, we now learn that he had already married two wives.

7. The wild fruits eaten by the uncles during their journey suggest drought, famine, war, or, more generally, a state of chaos.

8. For the botanical identification and symbolism of *nansongole,* see Text II/A, n. 42, and the concluding paragraph of Chapter 7. The request to be cut on the head, the place of a baby's fontanel, is a theme proper to the infancy stream, represented by Text III/B.

9. Actually, the Nyamadzere stream has its origin not at the place of the killing as our text maintains, but at a place some ten kilometers to the northeast in the Matundu Hills.

10. More commonly it is said that the pool formed itself at the very place where the killing occurred and not some distance away, as is averred here. See, for instance, Text III/A, sec. 16.

11. In this passage the medium refers to Mbona both in the first person ("I Mbona") and the third person ("That man"). This is a slip of the tongue on the narrator's part, for mediums, when in trance, use the first person only.

12. Note that Lundu, who at the beginning of the story still ranks third in the Mang'anja hierarchy, has now apparently moved to the top, for it is always the highest authority in the land who is asked to provide the spirit wife.

13. The titles Khambani and Mithanje are unknown at the shrine. At the end of this section, Khambani is changed into Kambalame ("Little Bird"), the title of the shrine's official messenger. Mbukwa is the headman of the hamlet where the shrine guardians live.

14. Ngabu is the main ritual authority and Malemia the main jural authority in the cult (see Chapter 3). Mbango is responsible for the admission or nonadmission of visitors and worshipers to the shrine grounds.

15. Since according to this text Lundu was Mbona's mother's brother and since the Mang'anja maintain that in the olden days men preferred to marry their maternal cross-cousins, the implication is that the bride given to Mbona was one of Lundu's real or classificatory daughters.

16. More usually, the person upon whose head the roof used to be constructed

was said to have been Chief Tengani, not some unknown person from Lundu's capital (see Chapters 2 and 3).

17. This text is the only one to mention that the roof of Salima's hut also had to be built upon the head of some person who would die soon afterward.

18. On the relations between Thyolo and the Khulubvi shrines, see Chapter 4. The term *college* in this case refers to a teacher training college, and the term *central school* to a full primary school comprising eight years. Such schools used to be found at central places such as mission stations, hence the name. Ordinary village schools trained their pupils from two to five years. The comparison of the shrine organization with the colonial school system is not made without reason, for especially in colonial days the term *sukulu* (school) was often also used to indicate a church or prayer house.

19. Although it is correct to say that Khulubvi stood at the apex of a complex hierarchy of shrines, it is not altogether true, as suggested here, that all those shrines were dedicated to Mbona. Virtually all were in fact dedicated to local spirits and deities.

20. Chituwi used to be one of Lundu's senior chiefs on the north bank of the Zambezi.

21. The name Lipiti may be translated as "terrific walker." It is composed of a root *-pit*, "to walk," a final *i* indicating an actor, and a prefix *li-* which is used in Chimang'anja among other things to denote something or someone awesome or dangerous, as in *lidzimu* (evil spirit).

22. It would be difficult to find a more explicit ideological statement concerning the relationship between cult and kingdom. The two are said to be one, but secular authority has precedence over ritual authority (see the first sentence of sec. 21), and the cult is presented more or less as subordinate to the king.

23. The reference is to Mbona, who is the only one allowed to use a seat, although not a wooden chair, since the latter is associated with Europeanism and is hence forbidden in the immediate neighborhood of the shrine.

24. Although it is true that the first European administrators unsuccessfully tried to collect taxes from the shrine guardians, it is not true that a compromise was reached by moving the young men from the shrine grounds to neighboring villages. Young people are simply not allowed to live there, since they are considered to be unable to observe the various taboos that the shrine guardians are supposed to keep.

TEXT III/A

1. The narrator does not specify at this stage in which part of Mozambique Mbona was born, but in sec. 15 we are told that it was in the neighborhood of the place where he was killed. The only part of Mozambique which corresponds to that description is the area across the Shire, east of the shrine. One may, however, ask oneself why this text puts so much emphasis on Mbona's provenance from Mozambique. Dr. E. C. Mandala, a native of the area, suggests that it may possibly be regarded as a subtle (or not so subtle) way of asserting Mbona's inferior

status vis-à-vis the king, since it is customary among the Mang'anja to say of one's rival or enemy that he hails from Mozambique, thereby implying that he is of slave or Chikunda ancestry (see also sec. 32 of this text, where explicit reference is made to the Mang'anja/Chikunda contrast). Dr. J. E. Chakanza, who hails from the same area, suggests that it may also be a way of recognizing Mbona's exceptional ritual power, since the inhabitants of the valley maintain that all powerful magicians come from Mozambique.

The phrase "born of a human being," which precedes the information on Mbona's birthplace and which carries the connotation of "born in the normal manner," seems designed to counteract statements about his virgin birth, which are common in folk versions of the Mbona III complex (cf. Text III/B, sec. 1). It may therefore also have the function of minimizing his status among the commoner population.

2. The reference is to the area around Lundu's headquarters, where the present text was recorded.

3. The implication of this passage is that Mbona married a woman from Lundu's own lineage, as otherwise it would be hard to explain why he had the power to give the woman away in marriage. Furthermore, since it was customary among the Mang'anja nobility to marry a cross-cousin, the woman in question would have been one of Lundu's real or classificatory daughters.

4. The marriage procedure described here is the one followed by many Mang'anja nowadays. It differs from the classic Mang'anja arrangement in that it is virilocal and the obligation of bride service is waived. It differs from Sena customary law in that no bride wealth is paid. Children issuing from this kind of arrangement remain under the tutelage of their mother's kin group.

5. The text gives us no clue about why Mbona's presence in the community had this particular effect, but it is to be noted that this passage is in the tradition of Mbona I, where Mbona is routinely portrayed as someone who causes the population to become divided against itself. It is possible that this theme from Mbona I has been retained by the royal house to convey the image of a society given to chronic internal warfare before the ascendancy of the Lundu dynasty.

6. The specification that the rain dance was to be held on a Sunday, although strictly speaking an anomaly, is not altogether without meaning, as many traditional religious ceremonies are nowadays held on Sundays and weekends, since otherwise many people would be unable to attend.

7. To "dance in mud" refers to the expectation, made explicit in virtually every account of traditional rain ceremonies, that rain should already be falling when the dance is still in progress.

8. The Chewa text has *kamwana*, which literally means "little child." Although the elders use the term as an invective (see sec. 11), it is no doubt also to be regarded as a remnant of the childhood symbolism which, as we have seen, is typical of the folk versions of the Mbona III complex.

9. The number two in this and similar cases (see Text III/B, sec. 8, n. 8) carries the notion of a totalizing duality, Mbona uniting in his person a number of opposites such as that between the dry and the wet seasons.

10. The text nowhere mentions that Mbona actually made a libation (*nsembe*) to the spirits, but the word is used here as a *pars pro toto* to indicate the entire

ceremony including the rain dance. The *nsembe* is always performed by the elders before the rain dance.

11. Usually, the basket is associated not with Mbona's wife but with his mother, whose very name, Chitundu, denotes a particular type of basket. The noun used here for "basket," however, is *nsengwa*.

12. The reference is to the axe, knife, and bow and arrows which Mang'anja men always carried when traveling any distance.

13. There appears to be some contradiction between the statement that the earth that Mbona had trodden would remain moist and the statement that not a blade of grass would sprout there. The narrator's point, however, is that Mbona's footprints remained fresh but uncovered by vegetation, so they remained visible to his pursuers.

14. For the botanical identification and symbolism of *nansongole*, see Text II/A, n. 42, and the final paragraph of Chapter 7.

15. This account differs from Text III/B, where iron and vegetal matter are applied consecutively. For a discussion, see Chapter 7.

16. The death of the assassins (or some accident befalling them) is a theme which reveals Mbona's power as a supernatural being and which normally leads the king (or whoever ordered Mbona's execution) to make amends. The present text is somewhat incongruous in that the fate of the killers does not have that effect.

17. The observation that Lundu's journey was not a flight seems somewhat contradicted by the earlier information that he wanted to escape from being held responsible for the drought which was going on at that time.

18. The "wild animals" (*zirombo*) in this case refer to the *nyau* secret societies, whose masks and zoomorphic structures are routinely called thus. The passage may therefore be taken to mean that the nascent Lundu state was threatened by the *nyau* lodges in the valley. It should also be read against the background of the numerous stories about Mbona's sacred forest, which describe the wild animals living there as entirely harmless. In accordance with this idea, the walls of Mbona's hut are made of reed and not of stout poles as are Lundu's.

19. Kabvina is the name of a dynasty which once ruled over the northwestern part of the valley. The name is now associated with a senior headmanship in that area (see also Chapter 4).

20. Selemani lies west of the Shire Valley in Mozambique. More usually, however, Kaphwiti's capital is said to have been located to the north of the valley, in Malawi. The present text also goes against established opinion by making Kaphwiti Lundu's junior and underling instead of vice versa. This is understandable, however, in view of the centuries-old rivalry between the two dynasties.

21. The narrator's intention, made explicit in the next section, is to say that Lundu ruled over the entire region between the Zambezi and the Shire highlands, including the areas on the north bank of the Zambezi which later became part of the Portuguese sphere of influence.

22. On Tengani's role in connection with the building or rebuilding, see Chapter 2, where the ritual of rebuilding the shrine is described in detail.

23. Dark blue cloth is often used to cover that part of the roof which overhangs the doorway of a shrine and is said to represent a clouded sky.

24. The phrase *mwamuna wakutha akazi* in the original Chewa text refers to a man who has already married and divorced several partners in succession and who on that count has come to be avoided by women (Dr. E. C. Mandala, private communication).

25. "Kaphirintiwa of the south" is the epithet the narrator applies to the Mbona shrine. Whether this was done intentionally or not, it is a particularly apt way to indicate that as far as the Mang'anja are concerned the Mbona shrine has come to replace the great Chewa shrine.

26. The ideophone *apo chi* in the original emphasizes availability: someone is available here and now without the king making objections (Dr. E. C. Mandala, personal communication). Compare this with Text III/B (sec. 23), where the opposite seems to hold: a king is uncertain about what to do and can get no woman for Mbona unless he captures one. It is clear that the court text makes it a point to show that the king in his role as a wife-giver to Mbona acted from a position of strength, whereas the folk version casts him in a position of weakness.

27. Salima's procession from Lundu's capital to the shrine, which is only sketchily described here, used to be a grand occasion, involving the entire population along the route (cf. Rangeley 1949–50). Accounts differ about how she used to be taken to the shrine, but there is general agreement that she was not to be seen by anybody except elderly women (see Chapter 2).

28. This is a custom mainly followed by women. It indicates solemn rejoicing and is particularly appropriate at major religious ceremonies.

29. The name Chikunda in the present context refers to all non-Mang'anja and more specifically to the immigrants from the south bank of the Zambezi who are now more commonly referred to as Sena (see Chapter 1). It is to be noted that the narrator, when speaking of the Chikunda, uses the past tense. This may possibly imply that in his view the injunction against the Chikunda has lost some of its original strictness.

30. The monkeys living in Mbona's forest are considered his "children" and "messengers." They are a standard element in descriptions of the shrine and not, as one might be inclined to think, some poetic embellishment (see Chapter 2).

31. The jars mentioned here as containing drinking water are sometimes also described as containing all manner of disease and pestilence, which the spirit wife had the power to unleash when she felt that the cult was being neglected.

32. "Soft sibilant sounds" is my attempt at rendering the onomatopoeia *sete sete*, which has the same root as the verb *-seteka*, "to lick."

33. The communications made by Mbona to the spirit wife are said to have concerned the general state of the country or impending disasters. She would relay these the following morning to the shrine officials, who were then supposed to take the necessary action (Rowley 1866:266; Chakanza 1936).

34. Why the present text describes Salima as being asleep on some occasions and not on others we are unable to say. It is possible, though, that in the former condition she is represented as an unconscious receiver of messages from the supernatural and in the latter as a person able to have direct conscious contact with the supernatural without being killed in the process.

35. Given that African pythons are great water lovers (Sweeney 1961:46–47),

there is a set of subtle contrasts at work here, for the python, which the text clearly identifies as a male animal, lives in a place (a pool to the east) which in relation to the shrine is symbolically female, while the spirit wife finds herself in the opposite situation, living at a place (the dry land to the west) which in relation to the pool is symbolically male.

36. The mysterious pieces of cloth as well as the doves are standard items in people's tales about the sacred pool. Black or dark blue cloth may be taken as referring to rain clouds (see n. 23 above). Doves are in certain contexts associated with the spirit world and as such used to play a role in funeral rites (Chafulumira 1948).

37. On the topic of forbidden fishing in the sacred pool, see Chapter 2.

38. This is so because the Lundus have an avoidance relationship with the shrine, which is usually explained as a consequence of their being wife-givers and "fathers-in-law" to Mbona.

39. Every lineage has its ritual friends (*adzukulu;* sing, *mdzukulu*) who take care of the burial ceremonies when one of its members dies. Ideally, they should belong to a different clan from the lineage they serve. Since Lundu belongs to the Phiri clan, his ritual friends should preferably be Banda clansmen.

TEXT III/B

1. Mankhokwe is here mentioned as the reputed founder of the Lundu dynasty. This reflects the claims of the Mankhokwe family to the Lundu title (see Chapter 4).

2. Kamango is the name of the drum at the Mbona shrine and, more generally, the name of the principal drum at a chief's court. Its function is to summon the population to a meeting.

3. The term *mulungu,* here translated as "God" in accordance with present-day usage, has a wide range of additional referents such as "sky," "rain," "thunder," "lightning," "spirit," "spirit world," and "spirit manifestation" (see Macdonald 1882, 1:67; Scott 1892:415).

4. In accordance with the Mang'anja system of succession and inheritance, the term *nephew* here refers only to the king's sisters' sons (real or classificatory).

5. The invectives "fool" (*chitsiru*) and "good-for-nothing" (*chopanda nchito*) refer to Mbona's unusual behavior rather than his illegitimate birth. What Mbona had done to earn such epithets is not made explicit at this point but becomes clear at a later stage, when it is said that he still used to pass the night in his mother's hut despite his age (sec. 16).

6. The role of Mbona's mother in this version of the Mbona story is reminiscent of and may indeed have partly been inspired by Roman Catholic theologizing on the role of the Virgin Mary in the life of Christ. Mary, too, is sometimes portrayed in devotional literature as having encouraged her son to undergo his passion for the sake of mankind.

7. Castor oil (*nsatsi*) plays a role in many rites of passage. It is likely, therefore, that its occurrence in this part of the story also has symbolic significance.

This is further suggested by the fact that Mbona tells his mother to keep the oil in a special medicine gourd (*nsupa*), which is used in ritual settings.

8. For a description of the *kandranga* dagger, see Text II/A, n. 25. Carrying two daggers or two spears at a time was a royal prerogative, symbolizing the concept of totalizing duality (Tcherkézoff 1987:48). See also Chapter 2, n. 12, and figure 27.

9. Among the Mang'anja, the west generally connotes maleness, while meteorologically it is associated with the short scattered rainstorms that precede the planting season. The east, on the other hand, is associated with feminine qualities and the steady rains of the wet season proper, which lasts roughly from November to March.

10. More usually, it is said that Mbona planted rice near Dzambawe, which lies at a distance of some twelve kilometers northwest of Chididi, in Mozambique (Price 1953). Chididi lies west of Nsanje township in the Matundu Hills.

11. Karonga is a Chewa term for a war leader (Text II/A, sec. 9), the title of a Chewa dynasty (see Chapter 5), and also the name of a village in the Nsanje area. Doves sometimes also figure in descriptions of the sacred pool of Ndione.

12. What is being said of the forest Nyakalambo is also (and more commonly) said of Khulubvi, the forest patch which contains the shrine (see Chapter 2).

13. This passage refers to Dzambawe, where the rice miracle took place also (see n. 10). One notices in this particular section that the narrator constantly associates the events he describes with the wrong places; the rice and the well, for instance, ought to be in the same location. This is probably due to his lack of familiarity with the topography of the Nsanje District. Nevertheless, it might be worthwhile to investigate whether or not there is some logic behind these "errors."

14. Note that in this section the name Chitundu is given three interrelated meanings. It is the proper name of Mbona's mother; it is the title of a spirit wife in Mozambique; and it is the name of the shrine where the latter is supposed to live. For a discussion of these meanings, see Chapter 5.

15. Rain callers are often said to wear their hair long and unkempt, "to make it resemble a dark cloud." Shaving it would mean chasing the clouds away, as a bald head is said to evoke the image of a brazen sky.

16. The Chipeta Tattoos are discussed in Chapters 1 and 6, where it is maintained that it is a theme proper to the Mbona I tradition. According to that tradition, these "tattoos" were carved on the rock by Mbona himself to commemorate his reputed homeland. The present version is somewhat unusual in that Mbona is only said to have passed by that rock and not to have carved anything on it.

17. The name Maere appears to be unknown at the Mbona shrine, but since the same person is mentioned further down (sec. 25) as a priestly figure, the person referred to may be Ngabu, the chief ritualist.

18. On the building of the shrine, see also Text II/A, sec. 34; Text II/B, sec. 14; and Text III/A, secs. 26–28. The statement that the roof of the shrine had to be built upon Lundu's head contradicts most traditions, which say that it had to be built upon Tengani's head. It also contradicts the avoidance relationship which exists between Lundu and Mbona as father-in-law and son-in-law, respectively, and according to which the Lundus were prohibited from visiting the shrine grounds.

The probable reason why this incongruity occurs here is discussed in the introduction to this text.

19. On the capture of a new Salima, see Chapter 2. The fact that Mbona's bride had to be an elderly woman is usually explained by saying that younger women might be given to vain talk and thus reveal what goes on during their nocturnal encounters with Mbona or that they might be seduced by young men, in which case a sacrilege would be committed. From a different angle, it is one of several ritual inversions in this text, the elderly woman serving as a symbol of fertility.

20. This passage is reminiscent of Chitundu shaving her head (sec. 18 above). Maybe Salima never dressed in white, but it is not impossible that she did so occasionally, for instance to protest against the real or supposed neglect of the cult. It is also conceivable that she dressed in white when there was too much rain, in order to make the sun appear again. There is evidence from other shrines that white cloth was being used for that purpose.

21. This passage refers to the making of malt for the annual libation at Mbona's shrine (see Text II/A, n. 50).

22. A variant text of this hymn runs as follows: "Mphambe, Mphambe, Mphambe / Kachere ndi mtunda wa mbalame / Mnjale sukwereka / M'chulu sumapita moto / Masamba u ku nsitu / Akazi sawazinga nkhata." Translation: "Lightning, lightning, lightning. / The fig tree is the home of birds. / The *mnjale* tree cannot be climbed. / Fireflames never sweep the anthill. / From the leaves of the sacred grove / Women do not fashion headpads" (Schoffeleers unpubl. 1968:225–28).

This rather enigmatic text may be explained as follows. People participating in a rain ritual — as indeed in many other rituals — have to be "cool," which means that they have to abstain from sex for at least a full day beforehand. It is this injunction to abstain from sex which appears to be conveyed by the hymn of the *mnjale* tree. The *mnjale* (*Sterculia appendiculata*) is a strikingly tall tree with a smooth whitish bark that lacks lower branches. Sexual congress is often referred to by the verb -*kwera*, "to climb," so it follows that the *mnjale* tree, which cannot be climbed, provides a suitable metaphor for sexual abstinence. The same idea seems to be conveyed by the passage on women's headpads. Used to facilitate the carrying of loads on the head, these pads are normally circular with a hole in the middle, hence their suitability as a sexual symbol. Women often fashion them in a rough-and-ready way from tufts of grass or bunches of leaves, but they are prohibited from doing so in Mbona's forest, as there is a strict rule that its plant life, like its animal life, must be left untouched.

23. This is a variant of the rain song cited in Text II/A, sec. 18.

24. Chilamwa is a shrine guardian and the master of ceremonies at the annual rain prayers.

TEXT IV

1. Chakanza 1936.
2. Rangeley 1953.
3. Rowley 1866:400–401; Wallis 1952:93–95.

4. The name Changamire (see also Text II/A, secs. 8–10) is probably a borrowing from northern Chewa oral history as recorded and published by, among other, Ntara, who specifically mentions the conflict referred to here (Ntara 1973: 16–17).

5. The noun *sing'anga*, here translated as "diviner," may also have the meaning of "healer" and "herbalist," these various functions often being exercised by one and the same person. These latter meanings, however, seem less applicable, since Mbona, here as elsewhere, is primarily described as a rain caller. The combination of this function with that of diviner or prophet is or was quite common, as suggested *inter alia* by Text II/A (secs. 2 and 14), which describes a certain Mlauli in precisely those terms. The association of Mbona's person with healing and herbalism, however, is not altogether lacking in the present text, as is evident from secs. 16 and 28.

6. In this text Lundu is apparently regarded as the paramount chief not of the entire valley but only of its northern part, while Tengani is made the chief ruler in the south. This somewhat unorthodox picture may be due to the fact that many of the author's informants were immigrants from the Nsanje District, where the Tenganis used to enjoy great renown. Since the genealogy presented here presents Tengani as Mbona's father and Lundu as his mother's brother, however, the latter would in terms of the Mang'anja kinship system still be the senior authority.

7. This is a somewhat incongruous statement, as married men among the Mang'anja usually went to live with their wife's kinfolk. It may be, though, that the author is being influenced on this point by present-day practice, which tends toward virilocality (cf. introduction to Text III/B).

8. The brackets are in the original and are meant to indicate the author's personal viewpoint. The noun *mankhwala*, here rendered as "magic," also means "medicine" in the conventional sense.

9. The theme of Mbona's being opposed by his own brother is typical of the Mbona I traditions as retained by the shrine guardians and the family of the high priest, Ngabu Phiri. Its occurrence in the chiefdom of Ngabu Banda, the geographic center of the valley, far from the shrine, suggests that the person or persons who provided the author with this particular piece of information hailed from villages close to Ngabu Phiri's.

10. By "British territory" is meant the valley proper, which until 1964 fell under the authority of the British colonial administration.

11. On Mbona's metamorphoses in the course of his flight, see also Text II/A, sec. 21, where Mbona is said to have changed himself and his followers into a clump of trees and a flock of guinea fowl. The motif of the anthill makes its appearance in that text rather more toward the end of the story, and it fulfills an altogether different function.

12. Price (1953:30) also mentions an old coal shaft in the neighborhood of Dzambawe.

13. Dzambawe is the place where, according to most traditions, Mbona took leave of his wife or his mother. Text III/B mentions that the mother afterward became a spirit wife in the Zambezi Valley. This may explain the statement, made here about Mbona's wife, that she never grows old, for since spirit wives succeed

each other under the same name, the impression is given to an outsider that the office is always occupied by one and the same person.

14. For a description of the Dzambawe site, see Price 1953.

15. Price (1953:31) confirms the existence of a variety of (wild) rice at the site, which seems to maintain itself quite successfully despite its unlikely natural environment. I have been told by Mr. Price that it is very small in quantity. Local informants told him that it existed only to succor famished travelers with a single meal, which is why it will not bear when planted in a normal subsistence garden.

16. The text is somewhat problematic at this point, since the chiefdom of Ngabu Banda, which is the one referred to here, lies to the north, not the southeast, of Dzambawe. The author was apparently misinformed about the correct location of Dzambawe, which lies approximately twelve kilometers due east of Malawi Hill.

17. For the location of the footprints, see Text II/A, n. 36, where the name of the stream concerned is more correctly rendered as Thangadzi. I have been unable to locate Chituwi, which is here mentioned as the name of a school on the Malawian side of the border, but in Text II/B (sec. 20) as that of a Mang'anja chief in Mozambique.

18. Makande is another name for the chiefdom of Ngabu Banda. I have been unable to obtain more specific information about the person referred to here as Bandawe.

19. The Nyamadzere Stream marks the northern border of the Khulubvi area (see also Text II/B, n. 9).

20. Mbona's compassion for his enemies at this stage seems somewhat contradicted by the description of the fight in the next section.

21. On Mbona's invulnerability to iron weapons, see Text II/A, n. 41. The gun is not necessarily a recent element, since firearms were already known to the Mang'anja and neighboring peoples in the second half of the sixteenth century (see Chapter 5).

22. For the botanical identification of the *nansongole* grass, see Text II/A, n. 42.

23. For the botanical identification of the *mnjale* tree, see Text III/B, n. 22.

24. It is customary among the Mang'anja to place clay pots, usually with broken bottoms, in an inverted position over the upper part of the grave. Usually they are the size of ordinary cooking pots, which are much smaller than the type referred to here.

25. Accounts differ about whether Mbona's blood changed into water (Text III/A, sec. 16) or remained unchanged, as in the present case. The more common view is that it changed into water but that it turned into blood again when a calamity occurred.

26. With regard to the beginnings of the cult, we have earlier on distinguished between accounts ascribing this to human initiative and those ascribing it to Mbona's initiative by causing a medium to become possessed (see Chapter 6 and chart 2). The present account seems to take a middle position, as Mbona reveals his wishes not directly through a medium, but indirectly by causing a drought.

27. On the use of blue cloth at the shrines, see Text III/A, n. 23.

28. *Lunguzi* or Mauritius thorn (*Esalpina decapetala*) makes an impenetrable barrier and used to be planted around homesteads and cattle kraals against wild

animals or human intruders. I have, however, seen no such hedge around the shrine.

29. Marabous (*Leptopilus crumineferus*) nest in tall trees such as the *mnjale* (see Text III/B, n. 22).

30. On the intervals between successive rebuilding ceremonies, see Chapter 2.

31. Dzimbiri village lies near the Thyolo shrine in Changata's chiefdom (see Text II/B, sec 17, and n. 18). Several women who served as spirit wives at the Thyolo shrine hailed from Dzimbiri, but it is somewhat unlikely that women from Changata's chiefdom ever served at the Nsanje shrine.

32. The incident referred to here took place not at Khulubvi, but at the Thyolo shrine, where the first Anglican missionaries to the country tried to establish themselves during 1862.

33. This injunction applies only to boys, not to girls.

34. Malemia is the chief jural authority and overseer of the cult. Important visitors and delegations from other chiefdoms customarily had to present themselves at his headquarters before being allowed to proceed to the shrine.

35. The more common information is that the participants have to wear loincloths.

36. On the death of Tengani following the rebuilding, see Chapter 2 and Text II/A, sec. 34. It is difficult to verify whether one or another Tengani ever fled in order to avoid his supposed fate.

37. On the issue of human sacrifices at the sacred pool, see Chapter 2. It is unlikely, though, that this was ever an annual event.

38. Individual chiefdoms from the entire cult region used to send delegations to Khulubvi to pray for deliverance from droughts and other general misfortunes (see Chapter 2).

39. On the injunction against fishing in the sacred pool, see Chapter 2. The enumeration of strange items dragged up by trespassing fishermen is fairly standard, but I have never investigated their possible symbolic meanings.

40. I don't know whether people actually go there to collect medicinal herbs, but it is nevertheless interesting to note that such a statement should be made in relation to the sacred pool and not the shrine. One somehow gets the impression that the shrine is strictly reserved for communal issues, whereas the pool seems to cater to individual needs as well, as illustrated by the many stories about fishing and the present reference to medicinal herbs.

41. These are the names of three small settlements on the edge of the marsh in Malemia's chiefdom, though why they should be mentioned here remains unclear.

42. The Tengani mentioned here is Molin, who was notorious for his negative attitude toward the cult (see Chapter 4).

43. On the color sequence in the Ndione pool, see n. 25 above. The implication in the present case is that the cult has to a great extent lost its power. This is particularly suggested by the alleged massive contravention of the fishing taboo which apparently goes unpunished, whereas on an earlier occasion the same action is said to have been the cause of many deaths.

44. It is doubtful whether this information about taxpaying is correct, since even in Jan. 1980 the shrine officials told us that the exemption was still maintained.

45. Mediums may hail from any village in the chiefdoms of Ngabu and Malemia,

not only from the ones mentioned here. It is to be noted, however, that Nthole's village in Malemia's chiefdom has played a prominent role in this respect, since three well-known mediums who have operated in the present century came from there. Contrary to what is stated here, these mediums do not receive their revelations in dreams; they receive and transmit them in a condition of trance possession (see Chapter 2).

46. This is essentially correct, since the medium can only move into action when he already has the weight of public opinion behind him (see Chapter 3).

47. On Mbona's nocturnal visits to Salima, see Text III/A, secs. 35–36.

48. There is a large *mtondo* tree (see Text II/A, n. 8) in the Khulubvi grove, at the base of which offerings are made following the main ceremony in Mbona's hut. It may be that the noun *nthungo* (spear) in the original text is a misspelling of *nthongo*, which means "snake" and more particularly the Shire burrowing reptile (*Typhlops tettensis*). The translation would then be "tree of the snake."

49. I have been unable to identify the first two places. Apparently the author considers these as places where important mediums used to live, but this seems unlikely in the case of Tengani, whose medium has always been of secondary importance.

50. The location of Mitseche is also unknown; Mbona's wife is now considered to be a medium in the Zambezi Valley (see n. 13 above.).

SOURCES

INTERVIEWS (in chronological order)

1. Chapirira and Kumbiwanyati, shrine guardians, at R. C. Mission, Nsanje, Aug. 24, 1964.
2. B. Nhlane, former district commissioner, Nsanje, at St. Peter's College, Oxford, May 15, 1966.
3. Headman Mbeta, Mbeta village, Malemia chiefdom, Nsanje, Oct. 7 and 19, 1966.
4. Mbukwa, Khombe, and Kambalame, shrine guardians, Mbangu village, Ngabu Phiri chiefdom, Oct. 9 and 12, 1966, and May 4, 1967.
5. Stole Chimbuto (source of Text II/B), retired primary school teacher, Ngabu Banda chiefdom, Chikwawa District, Oct. 18, 1966.
6. Chief Malemia, Nsanje District, at his headquarters, Oct. 20, 1966, Aug. 20, 1967, and Jan. 4, 1980.
7. Chambote (Josef Thom), cult medium, Thole village, Nsanje, Oct. 31, 1966, Dec. 4 and 22, 1967, Sept. 5, 1968, Dec. 24, 1971, April 1, 1972, and Sept. 18, 1972.
8. Rev. Mark Mangeya, St. Michael's Mission, Chikwawa, Dec. 29, 1966.
9. Chief Evans Makosana Lundu, Mbewe village, Chikwawa, May 2, 1967, and July 20, 1969.
10. Fryton Malemia, retired teacher and agricultural instructor, Chipolopolo village, Malemia chiefdom, Nsanje, Aug. 8, 1967.
11. Che Chapalapala (source of Text III/B), Misomali village, Chapananga chiefdom, Chikwawa, Aug. 13, 1967.
12. Che Ngwangwa (source of Text III/A), Kadzumba village, Masseah chiefdom, Chikwawa, Aug. 24, 1967.
13. Headman Chikafu Mbewe, Chikafu village, Lilongwe District, Sept. 16, 1967.
14. Cult officers, Chirenje shrine, Lilongwe District, Sept. 30, 1969.
15. Group interview, Chief Changata (M. K. Mpuka), Anthu-a-pa-mudzi (titular spirit wife, Thyolo shrine), Z. Chisinkha, and headman Mpenda, at Changata's headquarters, Thyolo District, April 13 and 14, 1971.
16. Headman Kadinga Banda (Fredson Demster), Kadinga village, Masseah chiefdom, Chikwawa, Aug. 27, 1971.
17. S. Moshtishu, Chiphwembwe village, Malemia chiefdom, Nsanje, Sept. 21, 1972.

18. Headman Mwanda, Mwanda village, Malemia chiefdom, Sept. 23, 1972.
19. Chief Ngabu Phiri, at his headquarters, Nsanje District, Sept. 24, 1972.
20. Headman Mphamba, Mphamba village, Nsanje District, Dec. 22, 1972, and Aug. 19, 1973.
21. Chief S. Tengani, at his headquarters, Nsanje District, Aug. 23, 1973.
22. Group interview, Ngabu Phiri and councillors, Aug. 16, 1973, and July 13, 1974.
23. Chief Vuntade Nyachikadza, Thuka village, Nsanje District, Aug. 20, 1973.
24. Jonas Chiriwekha and Yohane Simenti (Headman Nthole), Nthole village, Nsanje District, Aug. 25, 1973.
25. Fraser Falamenga, Mkuzaduka village, Ngabu Phiri chiefdom, Nsanje District, Aug. 30, 1973.
26. Headman Sabe Nkhuche, Nkhuche village, Malemia chiefdom, Nsanje, Sept. 21, 1973.
27. Headman E. Nsadzu, Nsadzu village, Central Region, April 10, 1974.
28. Antonio Marianno, Mopea, Zambesia, Mozambique, Oct. 28, 1976.
29. Headman Mbangu, Mbangu village, Nsanje District, April 2, 1978, and Jan. 5, 1980.
30. D. D. Forty, local leader of the African Ancestor Church, Mbeta village, Nsanje District, Dec. 31, 1978, and Jan. 6, 1979.
31. Jimu Thom, brother of the medium Josef Thom (7), at Nsanje Mission, Jan. 1, 1979.
32. B. Antonio Phiri, retired teacher, formerly of the Nsanje district council, at Chief Malemia's, Nsanje, Jan. 2, 1979, and Jan. 4 and 6, 1980.
33. Petro Thom, catechist, R. C. Mission, Tengani village, Nsanje District, Jan. 3, 1979.
34. Antonio Kamfula, catechist, R. C. Mission, Tengani village, Nsanje District, Jan. 3, 1979.
35. Group interview, P. Thom (33), A. Kamfula (34), D. D. Forty (30), Tengani village, Nsanje District, Jan. 13, 1979.
36. Group interview, B. A. Phiri (32), Chief Malemia (6), and Headman Chiphwembwe, at Malemia's headquarters, Jan. 4, 1980.
37. Mr. M. E. Rambiki (author of Text II/A), retired primary school teacher, became Headman Mphamba in 1978, Mphamba village, Nsanje District, Jan. 5, 1980.
38. Headmen Mbangu (29) and Mbukwa (4), Mbangu village, Nsanje District, Jan. 10, 1980.
39. Lusiano Rice, catechist, R. C. Mission, Nsanje, Dec. 31, 1981.
40. Group interview, Headman Chataika and sons, Chataika village, Nsanje District, Jan. 3, 1982.

ARCHIVAL MATERIALS

British Public Record Office, London
    C.O. 525/7: Case of Mr. R. R. Racey, 3d assistant, enclosure in B.C.A., no. 35, Jan. 24, 1905

Malawi National Archives, Zomba
> Department of Agriculture Monthly and Annual Reports
> Chikwawa District Monthly and Annual Reports since 1922
> Port Herald (Nsanje) District Monthly and Annual Reports since 1922
> Secretariat Files (include Monthly and Annual Reports for Lower Shire, Ruo, and West Shire districts before 1922)
> District Books: Lower Shire (4 vols.); Ruo (2 vols.); West Shire (of which Chikwawa formed part until 1922)

Society of Malawi Library, Blantyre
> Rangeley Papers: File 1/1/3, "Correspondence on Maravi History"; File 2/1/17, documents relating to the Mbona cult

PRIVATELY HELD MANUSCRIPTS

Father Darot, "Notes écrites a Nambuma en 1930," White Fathers, Lilongwe.

Father Hovington, "Notes on Chewa customs," n.d., Kachebere Seminary, Malawi.

Phiri, B. A. "Mbiri ya Amang'anja," n.d., in possession of its author, Malemia village, Nsanje District.

Rambiki, M. E. "Mbiri ya Mbona" (Text II/A), n.d., in possession of its author, Mphamba village, Nsanje District.

Tengani, S. M. "Ufumu wa Tengani," 1967, in possession of its author, Tengani village, Nsanje District.

THESES AND UNPUBLISHED PAPERS

Amanze, J. N. 1986. "The Bimbi Cult in Southern Malawi." Ph.D. diss. S.O.A.S., London.

Bhila, H. H. K. 1977. "The Kaphwiti-Lundu Complex in the Lower Shire Valley to 1800 A.D.: Myth and Reality." Paper read at the International Conference on Southern African History, Roma, Lesotho.

Mandala, E. C. 1973-74. "The Tengani Chieftaincy and Its Relations with Other Chieftaincies in Nsanje District, c. 1850-1951." Student seminar papers, History Department, University of Malawi.

Mandala, E. C. 1977. "The Kololo Interlude in Southern Malawi, 1861-1895." M.A. thesis, University of Malawi.

Phiri, K. 1975. "Chewa History in Central Malawi and the Use of Oral Tradition, 1600-1920." Ph.D. diss., University of Wisconsin-Madison.

Schoffeleers, J. M. 1968. "Social and Symbolic Aspects of Mang'anja Religion." D.Phil. diss., Oxford University.

Schoffeleers, J. M. 1977. "An Outline History of Territorial Mediumship in a Malawian District." Paper read at the International Conference on Southern African History, Roma, Lesotho.

van Breugel, J. W. M. 1976. "Traditional Chewa Religious Beliefs and Practices." Ph.D. diss., University of London.

PUBLICATIONS

Abraham, D. P. 1966. "The Roles of 'Chaminuka' and the Mhondoro Cults in Shona Political History." In *The Zambesian Past*, ed. E. Stokes and R. Brown, 28–46. Manchester: Manchester University Press.

Agnew, S., and M. Stubbs, eds. 1972. *Malawi in Maps*. London: University of London Press.

Alpers, E. A. 1967. "North of the Zambezi." In *The Middle Age of African History*, ed. R. Oliver, 78–84. London: Oxford University Press.

Alpers, E. A. 1968. "The Mutapa and Malawi Political Systems to the Time of the Ngoni Invasions." In *Aspects of Central African History*, ed. T. O. Ranger, 1–28. London: Heinemann.

Alpers, E. A. 1975. *Ivory and Slaves in East Central Africa*. London: Heinemann.

Alpers, E. A., and Ehret, C. 1975. "Eastern Africa, 1600–1790." In *The Cambridge History of Africa*, vol. 4, ed. R. Gray, 469–536. Cambridge: Cambridge University Press.

Ambali, A. 1931. *Thirty Years in Nyasaland*. London: Universities' Mission to Central Africa.

Appadurai, A. 1983. "The Past as a Scarce Resource." *Man*, n.s., 16:201–19.

Axelson, E. 1969. *Portuguese in South Africa, 1600–1700*. Johannesburg: Witwatersrand University Press.

Barreto, M. (1667) 1899. "Report upon the State and Conquest of the Rivers of Cuama." In Theal 3:463–95.

Barreto de Rezende, P. (c. 1635) 1899. "Extracts from the Book Entitled 'Of the State of India' by Captain Pedro Barreto de Rezende." In Theal 2:378–426.

Beattie, J., and J. Middleton, eds. 1969. *Spirit Mediumship and Society in Africa*. London: Routledge and Kegan Paul.

Beccari, C. 1912. *Rerum Aethiopicarum Scriptores Occidentales*, vol. 11. Rome.

Beidelman, T. O. 1970. "Myth, Legend and Oral History." *Anthropos* 65:74–97.

Beinart, W., et al. 1985. *Malawi: An Alternative Pattern of Development*. Edinburgh: Centre of African Studies.

Bennett, N. R., and M. Ylvisaker, eds. 1971. *The Central African Journal of Lovell J. Procter, 1860–1864*. Boston: African Studies Center, Boston University.

Bhebe, N. M. B. 1979. "The Ndebele and Mwari before 1893: A Religious Conquest of the Conquerors by the Vanquished." In Schoffeleers 1979a:287–96.

Bhila, H. H. K. 1982. *Trade and Politics in a Shona Kingdom: The Manyika and Their Portuguese and African Neighbours, 1575–1902*. Harlow: Longman Group Ltd.

Binns, B. 1972. *Dictionary of Plant Names in Malawi*. Zomba: Government Printer.

Blackmun, B., and J. M. Schoffeleers. 1972. "Masks of Malawi." *African Arts* 5, no. 4:36–41, 69.

Bocarro, A. (1676) 1899. "Decade Written by Antonio Bocarro, His Majesty's Chronicler for the State of India, of the Performances of the Portuguese in the East." In Theal 3:342–435.

Bourdillon, M. F. C. 1979. "The Cults of Dzivaguru and Karuva amongst the North-Eastern Shona Peoples." In Schoffeleers 1979a:235–56.

Brucker, A. 1878. "Découverte des grands lacs de l'Afrique centrale et des sources du Nil et du Zaire au seizième siècle." *Etudes* 22:775–809.

Bruwer, J. P. 1952. "Remnants of a Rain-Cult among the Achewa." *African Studies* 11, no. 4:179–82.

Buchanan, J. 1885. *The Shire Highlands as Colony and Mission.* London: Blackwood.

Central Africa: A Record of the Work of the Universities Mission. 1895. Vol. 13.

Chafulumira, W. 1948. *Mbiri ya Amang'anja.* Zomba: Nyasaland Education Department.

Chakanza, E. 1936. "Leven, dood en 'mirakelen' van Mbona." *Maria's Schepter* 2, no. 1:41–43.

Chanock, M. 1973. "Notes for an Agricultural History of Malawi." *Rural Africana* 20:27–35.

Chimombo, S. 1988. *Malawian Oral Literature.* Zomba: Centre for Social Research, University of Malawi.

Clark, J. D. 1972. "Prehistoric Origins." In Pachai, 17–27.

Cole-King, P. A. 1973. *Kukumba Mbiri mu Malawi: A Summary of Archaeological Research to March 1973.* Zomba: Government Printer.

Colman, D. R., and K. G. Garbett. 1973. *Economic and Sociological Issues in the Development of the Lower Shire Valley: The First Report of the Socio-Economic Survey of the Lower Shire Valley.* Zomba: Government of Malawi.

Colman, D. R., and K. G. Garbett. 1976. *The Labour Economy of a Peasant Community in Malawi: The Second Report of the Socio-Economic Survey of the Lower Shire Valley.* Zomba: Government of Malawi.

Coupland, R. 1928. *Kirk on the Zambesi.* Oxford: Clarendon Press.

Courtois, V. J. 1889. *Notes chronologiques sur les anciennes Missions Catholiques au Zambèze.* Lisbon.

Cunnison, I. 1951. *History on the Luapula: An Essay on the Historical Notions of a Central African Tribe.* London: Oxford University Press for the Rhodes-Livingstone Institute.

Cunnison, I. 1959. *The Luapula Peoples of Northern Rhodesia: Custom and History in Tribal Politics.* Manchester: Manchester University Press for the Rhodes-Livingstone Institute.

Cunnison, I. 1960. Preface to Gamitto.

Curtin, Ph. et al. 1978. *African History.* London: Longman.

Daneel, M. L. 1970. *The God of the Matopo Hills.* The Hague: Mouton.

de Heusch, L. 1972. *Le Roi ivre ou l'origine de l'état.* Paris: Gallimard.

de Heusch, L. 1975. "What Shall We Do with the Drunken King?" *Africa* 45, no. 4:363–72.

de Heusch, L. 1982a. *The Drunken King; or, The Origin of the State.* Translated by Roy Willis. Bloomington: Indiana University Press.

de Heusch, L. 1982b. *Rois nés d'un coeur de vache.* Paris: Gallimard.

Duly, A. W. R. 1948. "The Lower Shire District, Notes on Land Tenure and Individual Rights." *The Nyasaland Journal* 1, no. 2:11–44.

Dumézil, G. 1948. *Mitra-Varuna, Essai sur deux représentations indo-europeéenes de la souveraineté.* 2d ed. Paris: Gallimard.

Evans-Pritchard, E. E. 1956. *Nuer Religion.* London: Oxford University Press.

Faulkner, H. 1868. *Elephant Haunts.* London: Hurst and Blackett.

Feierman, S. 1974. *The Shambaa Kingdom: A History.* Madison: University of Wisconsin Press.

Foà, E. 1897. *Du Cap au Lac Nyassa.* Paris: Plon.

Foà, E. 1900. *La traversée de l'Afrique.* Paris: Plon.

Fortes, M. 1945. *The Dynamics of Clanship among the Tallensi.* London: Oxford University Press for the International African Institute.

Fortes, M. 1964. "The Political System of the Tallensi of the Northern Territories of the Gold Coast." In *African Political Systems,* ed. M. Fortes and E. E. Evans-Pritchard, 239–71. London: Oxford University Press.

Foskett, R., ed. 1965. *The Zambesi Journal and Letters of Dr. John Kirk, 1858–1863.* 2 vols. Edinburgh: Oliver and Boyd.

Gamitto, A. C. P. 1960. *King Kazembe: Diary of the Portuguese Expedition to That Potentate in the Years 1831 and 1832.* Translated by I. Cunnison. 2 vols. Lisbon: Junta de Investigações do Ultramar.

Garbett, K. 1969. "Spirit Mediums as Mediators in Korekore Society." In *Spirit Mediumship.* ed. J. Beattie and J. Middleton, 104–27. London: Routledge and Kegan Paul.

Gelfand, M. 1962. *Shona Religion.* Cape Town: Juta.

Girard, R. 1977. *Violence and the Sacred.* Baltimore: Johns Hopkins University Press.

Gluckman, M. 1964. "The Kingdom of the Zulu of South Africa." In *African Political Systems,* ed. M. Fortes and E. E. Evans-Pritchard, 35–55. London: Oxford University Press.

Gomes, A. (1648) 1959. "Viagem que fez o Padre Ant.o Gomes, da Comp.a de Jesus, ao Imperio de de [sic] Manomotapa; e assistencia que fez nas ditas terras d.e. Alg'us annos." Edited and annotated by E. A. Axelson. *Studia* 3:155–242.

Guyot, P. 1895. *Voyage au Zambèse.* Paris: Librairie Africaine et Coloniale.

Gwengwe, J. W. 1965. *Kukula ndi mwambo.* Limbe: Malawi Publications and Literature Bureau.

Hamilton, C. A. 1987. "Ideology and Oral Traditions: Listening to the Voices 'From Below.'" *History in Africa* 14:67–86.

Hamilton, R. A. 1954. "The Route of Gaspar Bocarro from Tete to Kilwa in 1616." *The Nyasaland Journal* 7, no. 2:7–14.

Hamilton, R. A. 1955. "Oral Tradition: Central Africa." In *History and Archaeology in Africa,* ed. R. A. Hamilton, 19–23. London: S.O.A.S.

Handbook of Nyasaland. 1910. 2d ed. London: Wyman and Sons.

Hanna, A. J. 1956. *The Beginnings of Nyasaland and North-Eastern Rhodesia, 1959–95.* Oxford: Clarendon Press.

Hazart, Cornelius. 1667. *Kerckelyke Historie van de Gheheele Wereldt.* Antwerp.

Heintze, B. 1970. *Besessenheits-Phänomene im Mittleren Bantu-Gebiet.* Wiesbaden: Franz Steiner Verlag.

Henige, D. 1982. *Oral Historiography.* London: Longman Group Ltd.

Hetherwick, A. 1917. "Nyanjas." In *Encyclopaedia of Religion,* ed. J. Hastings, 9:419–22.

Hodgson, A. G. O. 1933. "Note on the Achewa and Angoni of the Dowa District of the Nyasaland Protectorate." *Journal of the Royal Anthropological Institute* 63:146–52.

Horton, R. 1967. "African Traditional Thought and Western Science." *Africa* 37: 50–71, 155–87.

Horton, J. R. 1971. "Stateless Societies in the History of West Africa." In *A History of West Africa*. ed. J. F. A. Ajayi and M. Crowder, 78–119. London: Longman Group Ltd.

Isaacman, A. F. 1972. *Mozambique—The Africanization of a European Institution: The Zambezi Prazos, 1750–1902.* Madison: University of Wisconsin Press.

Isaacman, A. F. 1976. *The Tradition of Resistance in Mozambique: Anti-Colonial Activity in the Zambezi Valley, 1850–1921.* London: Heinemann.

Jackson, G. 1972. "Vegetation." In Agnew and Stubbs, 38.

Jackson, G., and P. O. Wiehe. 1958. *An Annotated Check List of Nyasaland Grasses.* Zomba: Government Printer.

Janzen, J. 1977. "The Tradition of Renewal in Kongo Religion." In *African Religions: A Symposium,* ed. N. S. Booth, 69–115. New York: Nok Publishers.

Johnston, H. H. 1897. *British Central Africa.* London: Methuen.

Junod, P. 1936. "Notes on the Ethnographical Situation in Portuguese East Africa." *Bantu Studies* 10, no. 3:293–311.

Kathamalo, B. J. 1965. "Khulubvi Thicket—Port Herald." *The Society of Malawi Journal* 18, no. 2:53–54.

Kerr, W. M. 1886. *The Far Interior.* 2 vols. London: Sampson Low.

Kopytoff, I. 1987. *The African Frontier.* Bloomington: Indiana University Press.

Krige, J. D., and E. Krige. 1943. *The Realm of a Rain-Queen.* London: Oxford University Press.

Kubik, G. 1987. *Nyau Maskenbünde im südlichen Malawi.* Vienna: Verlag der Österreichischen Akademie der Wissenschaften.

Lan, D. 1985. *Guns and Rain.* London: James Currey.

Lane-Poole, E. H. 1938. *The Native Tribes of the East Province of Northern Rhodesia: Notes on Their Migrations and History.* Livingstone: Government Printer.

Langworthy, H. W. 1971. "Chewa or Malawi Political Organisation in the Precolonial Era." In Pachai, 104–22.

Langworthy, H. W. 1972. *Zambia before 1890.* London: Longman Group Ltd.

Leach, E. 1954. *Political Systems of Highland Burma.* London: Athlone Press.

Lettere Annue d'Ethiopia, Malabar, Brasile, Goa dall'anno 1620 sin'al 1624. 1627. Rome. (French trans., 1628).

Lévi-Strauss, C. 1970. *The Raw and the Cooked.* London: Jonathan Cape.

Lienhardt, P. 1975. "The Interpretation of Rumour." In *Studies in Social Anthropology,* ed. J. H. M. Beattie and R. G. Lienhardt, 105–31. London: Oxford University Press.

Linden, I. 1972. "'Mwali' and the Luba Origin of the Chewa: Some Tentative Suggestions." *Society of Malawi Journal* 25, no. 1:11–19.

Linden, I. 1979. "Chisumphi Theology in the Religion of Central Malawi." In Schoffeleers 1979a:187–207.

Linden, I., and Linden, J. 1974. *Catholics, Peasants and Chewa Resistance in Nyasaland*. London: Heinemann.

Lindgren, N. E., and M. Schoffeleers. 1978. *Rock Art and Nyau Symbolism in Malawi*. Publication no. 18. Lilongwe: Department of Antiquities of the Government of Malawi.

Linton, R. 1943. "Nativistic Movements." *American Anthropologist* 45, no. 3:230–40.

Livingstone, D., and C. Livingstone. 1865. *Narrative of an Expedition to the Zambezi and Its Tributaries, and of the Discovery of Lakes Shirwa and Nyassa, 1858–1864*. London: John Murray.

Lobato, A. 1960. *A Expansão Portuguesa em Mocambique de 1498 a 1530; Livro 3, Aspectos e Problemas da Vida Economica de 1505 a 1530*. Lisbon: Centro de Estudios Historicos Ultramarinos.

Lovejoy, P. E., ed. 1981. *The Ideology of Slavery in Africa*. London: Sage Publications.

Lupi, E. do Couto. 1907. *Angoche-Breve memoria sobre uma das capitanais-mores de Distrito de Moçambique*. Lisbon.

Macdonald, D. 1882. *Africana; or, The Heart of Heathen Africa*. London: Simpkin Marshall and Co.

Makumbi, A. 1964. *Maliro ndi Myambo ya Acewa*. Nairobi: Longmans, Green and Co.

Malawi Government. 1964. *A Portrait of Malawi*. Zomba: Government Printer.

Malinowski, B. 1948. *Magic, Science and Religion and Other Essays*. Garden City, N.Y.: Anchor Books, Doubleday.

Mandala, E. C. 1990. *Work and Control in a Peasant Economy: A History of the Lower Tchiri Valley in Malawi, 1859–1960*. Madison: University of Wisconsin Press.

Mariana, A. 1912. "Ad Praepositum provinciae Goanae." In Beccari, 11:112–14.

Marwick, M. G. 1963. "History and Tradition in East-Central Africa through the Eyes of the Northern Rhodesian Cewa." *Journal of African History* 4:375–90.

Marwick, M. G. 1965. *Sorcery in Its Social Setting*. Manchester: Manchester University Press.

Marwick, M. G. 1968. "Notes on Some Chewa Rituals." *African Studies* 27:3–14.

Miller, J. C. 1973. "Requiem for the 'Jaga.'" *Cahiers des études africaines* 13:121–49.

Miller, J. C. 1978. "The Dynamics of Oral Tradition in Africa." In *Fonti Orali. Antropologia e Storia*, by B. Bernardi et al., 75–101. Milan: Franco Angeli.

Mitchell, J. C. 1956. *The Yao Village: A Study in the Social Structure of a Malawian Tribe*. Manchester: Manchester University Press.

Mitchell, J. C. 1961. "Chidzere's Tree: A Note on a Shona Land Shrine and Its Significance." *NADA*, no. 38.

Monclaro, F. (1569) 1899. "Relação de Viagem que fizeram os Padres da Companhia de Jesus com Francisco Barreto na Conquista de Monomotapa no Anno de 1569." In Theal 3:202–53.

Morgan, W. B. 1953. "The Lower Shire Valley of Nyasaland: A Changing System of Agriculture." *The Geographical Journal* 119:459–69.

Murdock, P. 1959. *Africa, Its Peoples and Their Culture History*. New York: McGraw-Hill.

Murray, S. S. 1922. *A Handbook of Nyasaland.* London: Crown Agents for the Colony.

Needham, R. 1980. *Reconnaissances.* Toronto: University of Toronto.

Newitt, M. D. D. 1970. "The Massingire Rising of 1884." *Journal of African History* 9, no. 1:87–105.

Newitt, M. D. D. 1973. *Portuguese Settlements on the Zambesi: Exploration, Land Tenure and Colonial Rule in East Africa.* London: Longman Group Ltd.

Newitt, M. D. D. 1982. "The Early History of the Maravi." *Journal of African History* 23:145–62.

Ntara, S. J. 1950. *Mbiri ya Achewa.* Lusaka: Publications Bureau.

Ntara, S. J. 1965. *Mbiri ya Achewa.* 2d ed. Limbe: Malawi Publications and Literature Bureau.

Ntara, S. J. 1973. *The History of the Chewa.* translated by W. S. K. Jere, with comments by H. W. Langworthy. Wiesbaden: Franz Steiner Verlag.

Nurse, G. T. 1978. "Moiety Endogamy and Anthropometrical Variation among the Maravi." *Man,* n.s., 12:397–404.

Nurse, G. T. 1988. Review of Kubik 1987. *Man,* n.s., 23, no. 2:391.

Pachai, B. ed. 1972. *The Early History of Malawi.* London: Longman Group Ltd.

Page, M. 1980. "The Great War and Chewa Society in Malawi." *Journal of Southern African Studies* 6, no. 2:171–82.

Peel, J. D. Y. 1984. "Making History: The Past in the Ijesha Present." *Man,* n.s., 19:111–32.

Phillipson, D. W. 1976. *The Prehistory of Eastern Zambia.* Nairobi: British Institute in Eastern Africa.

Phiri, K. M. 1983. "Some Changes in the Matrilineal Family System among the Chewa of Malawi since the Nineteenth Century." *Journal of African History* 24.

Pike, J. G. and G. T. Rimmington, 1965. *Malawi: A Geographical Study.* London: Oxford University Press.

Price, E. 1911. "Chididi Mission Station, Nyasaland." *The South African Pioneer* 24, no. 6.

Price, E. 1913. "Chididi Mission Station, Nyasaland." *The South African Pioneer* 26, no. 7:104–6.

Price, E. 1916. "The Defeat of Mbona the Rain Chief." *The South African Pioneer* 29, no. 7:82–83.

Price, E. 1927. "Report." *The South African Pioneer* 40, no. 8/9:103–4.

Price, T. 1947. *The Elements of Nyanja.* Blantyre, Nyasaland: Church of Scotland Mission.

Price, T. 1952. "More about the Maravi." *African Studies* 11, no. 2:75–79.

Price, T. 1953. "Mbona's Water-hole." *The Nyasaland Journal* 6, no. 1:28–33.

Price, T. 1963. "The Meaning of Mang'anja." *The Nyasaland Journal* 16, no. 1: 74–77.

Price, T. 1964. "Maravi Rain Cults." In *Religion in Africa,* 114 24. Edinburgh: Centre for African Studies.

Pringle, M. A. 1884. *Towards the Mountains of the Moon: A Journey in East Africa.* Edinburgh: William Blackwood.

Rangeley, W. H. J. 1949–50. "Nyau in Kotakota District." *The Nyasaland Journal* 2, no. 2:35–49; 3, no. 2:19–33.

Rangeley, W. H. J. 1952. "Makewana, the Mother of All People." *The Nyasaland Journal* 5, no. 2:31–50.

Rangeley, W. H. J. 1953. "Mbona — the Rain Maker." *The Nyasaland Journal* 6, no. 1:8–27.

Rangeley, W. H. J. 1954. "Bocarro's Journey." *The Nyasaland Journal* 7, no. 1:15–23.

Rangeley, W. H. J. 1959. "The Makololo of Dr. Livingstone: Origins of the Makololo, Their History up to the Coming of the British Government in Nyasaland." *The Nyasaland Journal* 12, no. 1:59–98.

Rangeley, W. H. J. 1963. "The Earliest Inhabitants of Nyasaland." *The Nyasaland Journal* 16, no. 2:35–42.

Ranger, T. O. 1963. "Revolt in Portuguese Africa: The Makombe Rising of 1917." *St. Anthony's Papers* 15.

Ranger, T. O. 1967. *Revolt in Southern Rhodesia, 1896–7.* London: Heinemann.

Ranger, T. O. 1972. "Report on the Proceedings of the Lusaka Conference on the Religious History of Central Africa." *African Religious Research* 2, no. 2: 6–34.

Ranger, T. O. 1973. "Territorial Cults in the History of Central Africa." *Journal of African History* 14, no. 4:581–97.

Ranger, T. O., and I. Kimambo, eds. 1972. *The Historical Study of African Religion.* London: Heinemann.

Ranger, T. O., and J. Weller, eds. 1975. *Themes in the Christian History of Central Africa.* London: Heinemann.

Rattray, R. S. 1907. *Some Folk-Lore Stories and Songs.* London: Society for Promoting Christian Knowledge.

Rau, W. E. 1979. "Chewa Religion and the Ngoni Conquest." In Schoffeleers 1979a: 131–46.

Rea, W. F. 1960. *Gonçulo da Silveira, Protomartyr of Southern Africa.* Salisbury: Rhodesiana Society.

Rennie, J. K. 1979. "From Zimbabwe to a Colonial Chieftaincy: Four Transformations of the Musikavanhu Territorial Cult in Rhodesia." In Schoffeleers 1979a: 257–85.

Rita-Ferreira, A. 1966. *Os Cheuas da Macanga.* Lourenço Marques: Instituto de Investigação Científica de Moçambique.

Rita-Ferreira, A. 1968. "The Nyau Brotherhood among the Mozambique Chewa." *South African Journal of Science* 64:20–24.

Roberts, A. 1976. *A History of Zambia.* London: Heinemann.

Robinson, K. R. 1970. *The Iron Age of the Southern Lake Area of Malawi.* Zomba: Department of Antiquities.

Robinson, K. R. 1973. *The Iron Age of the Upper and Lower Shire, Malawi.* Zomba: Department of Antiquities.

Rowley, H. 1866. *The Story of the Universities' Mission to Central Africa.* London: Saunders, Otley and Co.

Rowley, H. 1881. *Twenty Years in Central Africa.* London: Wells Gardner.

Santos, J. dos. (1609) 1901. *Ethiopia Oriental.* In Theal 7:1–370.

Schebesta, P. 1926. "Zur Ethnographie der Asena am Unteren Sambesi." *Bibliotheca Africana* 2:201–8, 322–34.

Schebesta, P. 1929. "Religiöse Anschauungen der Asena — *Mulungu* und seine Verehrung." *Bibliotheca Africana* 3, no. 1:1–10.

Schebesta, P. 1966. *Portugals Konquistamission in Südost-Africa. Missionsgeschichte Sambesiens und des Monomotapareiches (1560–1920)*. St. Augustin: Steyler Verlag.

Schoffeleers, J. M. 1971. "The Religious Significance of Bush Fires in Malawi." *Cahiers des religions africaines*, no. 10:278–54.

Schoffeleers, J. M. 1972. "The Meaning and Use of the Name 'Malawi' in Oral Traditions and Precolonial Documents." In Pachai, 91–103.

Schoffeleers, J. M. 1973a. "Towards the Identification of a Proto-Chewa Culture." *Journal of Social Science* (Malawi) 2:47–60.

Schoffeleers, J. M. 1973b. "Livingstone and the Mang'anja Chiefs." In *Livingstone, Man of Africa*, ed. B. Pachai, 111–30. London: Longman.

Schoffeleers, J. M. 1973c. "From Socialisation to Private Enterprise: A History of the Nomi Labour Associations in the Nsanje District of Malawi, 1892–1963." *Rural Africana* 20:11–25.

Schoffeleers, J. M. 1974. Review of Ntara 1973. *Journal of African History* 15.

Schoffeleers, J. M. 1975. "The Interaction between the Mbona Cult and Christianity." In Ranger and Weller, 14–29.

Schoffeleers, J. M. 1976. "The Nyau Societies: Our Present Understanding." *The Society of Malawi Journal* 29, no. 1:59–68.

Schoffeleers, J. M. 1977. "Cult Idioms and the Dialectics of a Region." In Werbner, 219–39.

Schoffeleers, J. M. ed. 1979a. *Guardians of the Land: Essays on Central African Territorial Cults*. Gwelo: Mambo Press for the University of Salisbury.

Schoffeleers, J. M. 1979b. Introduction to Schoffeleers 1979a:1–46.

Schoffeleers, J. M. 1979c. "The Chisumphi and Mbona Cults in Malawi: A Comparative History." In Schoffeleers 1979a:147–86.

Schoffeleers, J. M. (with R. Mwanza). 1979d. "An Organizational Model of the Mwari Shrines." In Schoffeleers 1979a:297–315.

Schoffeleers, J. M. 1980. "The Story of Mbona the Martyr." In *Man, Meaning and History: Essays in Honour of Prof. H. G. Schulte Nordholt*, ed. R. Schefold et al., 246–63. The Hague: Martinus Nijhoff.

Schoffeleers, J. M. 1985a. "Oral History and the Retrieval of the Distant Past: On the Use of Legendary Chronicles as Sources of Historical Information." In Van Binsbergen and Schoffeleers, 164–88.

Schoffeleers, J. M. (with A. Roscoe). 1985b. *Land of Fire: Oral Literature from Malawi*. Limbe: Popular Publications.

Schoffeleers, J. M. 1985c. "Economic Change and Religious Polarization in an African Rural District." In Beinart, 187–242.

Schoffeleers, J. M. 1987a. "Ideological Confrontation and the Manipulation of Oral History: A Zambesian Case." *History in Africa: A Journal of Method* 4: 257–73.

Schoffeleers, J. M. 1987b. "The Zimba and the Lundu State in the Late Sixteenth and Early Seventeenth Century." *Journal of African History* 28, no. 1:257–73.

Schoffeleers, J. M. 1988. "Myth and/or History? A Reply to Christopher Wrigley." *The Journal of African History* 30, no. 3:385–90.

Schoffeleers, J. M., and I. Linden. 1972. "The Resistance of the Nyau Cult to the Catholic Missions in Malawi." In Ranger and Kimambo, 252–73.

Schurhammer, G. 1920. "Die Entdeckung des Njassa-Sees." *Stimmen der Zeit* 99:349–56.

Scott, D. C. 1892. *A Cyclopaedic Dictionary of the Mang'anja Language*. Edinburgh: Foreign Mission Committee of the Church of Scotland.

Shepperson, G., and T. Price. 1958. *Independent African: John Chilembwe and the Origins, Setting and Significance of the Nyasaland Native Rising of 1915*. Edinburgh: University Press.

Shire Valley Agricultural Development Project (SVADP). 1975. *An Atlas of the Lower Shire Valley, Malawi*. Blantyre: Department of Surveys.

Sousa, F. de. 1881. *O Oriente Conquistado a Jesu Christo pelos Padres da Companhia de Jesus da Provincia de Goa*. 2 vols. Bombay.

Stannus, H. S. 1910. "Notes on Some Tribes of British Central Africa." *Journal of the Royal Anthropological Institute* 40:285–335.

Stuart, R. 1979. "Anglican Missionaries and a Chewa *Dini* Conversion and Rejection in Central Malawi." *Journal of Religion in Africa* 10, no. 1:46–69.

Sumner, W. G. 1906. *Folkways*. Boston: Ginn.

Sweeney, R. C. H. 1961. *Snakes of Nyasaland*. Zomba: Nyasaland Society and the Nyasaland Government.

Tabler, E. C., ed. 1963. *The Zambezi Papers of Richard Thornton*. 2 vols. London: Chatto and Windus.

Tcherkézoff, S. 1987. *Dual Classification Reconsidered: Nyamwezi Kingship and Other Examples*. New York: Cambridge University Press.

Terry, P. T. 1961. "African Agriculture in Nyasaland, 1858 to 1894." *The Nyasaland Journal* 14, no. 2:27–35.

Tew, M. 1950. *Peoples of the Lake Nyasa Region*. London: Oxford University Press for the International African Institute.

Theal, G. M., ed. 1898–1903. *Records of South-Eastern Africa*. 9 vols. London: Wm. Clowes and Sons. Rpt., Cape Town: Struik, 1964.

Topham, P. 1958. *Check List of the Forest Trees and Shrubs of the Nyasaland Protectorate*. Zomba: Government Printer.

Turner, V. W. 1974. *Dramas, Fields and Metaphors, Symbolic Action in Human Society*. Ithaca: Cornell University Press.

Vail, L., and L. White. 1980. *Capitalism and Colonialism in Mozambique: A Study of Quelimane District*. London: Heinemann.

Van Binsbergen, W., and M. Schoffeleers, eds. 1985. *Theoretical Explorations in African Religion*. London: Kegan Paul International.

Van der Merwe, N. J., and D. H. Avery. 1987. "Science and Magic in African Technology: Traditional Iron Smelting in Malawi." *Africa* 57, no. 2:143–72.

Vansina, J. 1968. "Religions et sociétés en Afrique Centrale." *Cahiers des religions africaines* 2, no. 2:95–107.

Vansina, J. 1985. *Oral Tradition as History*. London: James Currey.

Vaughan, M. 1985. "The Politics of Food Supply: Colonial Malawi in the 1940s." In *Malawi: An Alternative Pattern of Development,* ed. J. McCracken. Edinburgh: Centre for African Studies.

Wallis, J. P. R., ed. 1952. *The Zambezi Journal of James Stewart, 1862–3.* London: Chatto and Windus.

Wallis, J. P. R. 1956. *The Zambezi Expedition of David Livingstone, 1858–1863.* 2 vols. London: Chatto and Windus.

Werbner, R. P., ed. 1977. *Regional Cults.* A.S.A. Monograph no. 16. London: Academic Press.

Werner, A. 1906. *Native Tribes of British Central Africa.* London: Constable.

White, L. 1987 *Magomero: Portrait of an African Village.* London: Cambridge University Press.

Williamson, J. 1975. *Useful Plants of Malawi.* Zomba: University of Malawi.

Willis, R. 1976. *On Historical Reconstruction from Oral-Traditional Sources: A Structuralist Approach.* Twelfth Melville J. Herskovits Memorial Lecture. Evanston, Ill.: Northwestern University Program of African Studies.

Willis, R. 1980. "The Literalist Fallacy and the Problem of Oral Tradition." *Social Analysis* 4:28–37.

Willis, R. 1981. *A State in the Making: Myth, History, and Social Transformation on Pre-Colonial Ufipa.* Bloomington: Indiana University Press.

Winterbottom, J. M. 1950. "Outline Histories of Two Northern Rhodesian Tribes." *Human Problems in British Central Africa* 9:14–25.

Wishlade, R. L. 1965. *Sectarianism in Southern Nyasaland.* London: Oxford University Press.

Wrigley, C., 1988. "The River-God and the Historians: Myth in the Shire Valley and Elsewhere." *Journal of African History* 29:367–83.

Yoshida, K. 1991. *Masks and Transformation among the Chewa of Eastern Zambia.* Osaka: Senri Ethnological Studies.

Yoshida, K. Forthcoming. "Nyau, the Masked Association of the Cewa."

Young, E. D. 1868. *The Search after Livingstone.* London: Letts.

Young, T. C. 1932. *Notes on the History of the Tumbuka-Kamanga Peoples in the Northern Province of Nyasaland.* London: Religious Tracts Society.

INDEX